Developing Skills
with
Information Technology

WILEY SERIES

NEW TECHNOLOGIES AND WORK

Series Editor: **Bernhard Wilpert** Technische Universität Berlin

NEW TECHNOLOGY AND HUMAN ERROR

Edited by Jens Rasmussen, Keith Duncan and Jacques Leplat

THE MEANING OF WORK AND TECHNOLOGICAL OPTIONS

Edited by Véronique de Keyser, Thoralf Qvale, Bernhard Wilpert
and S. Antonio Ruiz Quintanilla

DEVELOPING SKILLS WITH INFORMATION TECHNOLOGY

Edited by Lisanne Bainbridge and S. Antonio Ruiz Quintanilla

Further titles in preparation

Developing Skills
with
Information Technology

Edited
by

Lisanne Bainbridge and **S. Antonio Ruiz Quintanilla**

JOHN WILEY & SONS

Chichester · New York · Brisbane · Toronto · Singapore

Copyright © 1989 by John Wiley & Sons Ltd.
    Baffins Lane, Chichester
    West Sussex PO19 1UD, England

Other Wiley Editorial Offices

John Wiley & Sons, Inc., 605 Third Avenue,
New York, NY 10158-0012, USA

Jacaranda Wiley Ltd, G.P.O. Box 859, Brisbane,
Queensland 4001, Australia

John Wiley & Sons (Canada) Ltd, 22 Worcester Road,
Rexdale, Ontario M9W 1L1, Canada

John Wiley & Sons (SEA) Pte Ltd, 37 Jalan Pemimpin 05-04,
Block B, Union Industrial Building, Singapore 2057

Library of Congress Cataloging-in-Publication Data:
Developing skills with information technology / edited by Lisanne
    Bainbridge and S. Antonio Ruiz Quintanilla.
        p.   cm.—(New technologies and work)
    Bibliography: p.
    Includes indexes.
    ISBN 0 471 92396 6
        1. Technology—Study and teaching.   2. Information technology.
    3. Employees, Training of.   I. Bainbridge, L. D.   II. Ruiz
    Quintanilla, S. Antonio.   III. Series.
    T49.5.D48   1989
    658.3'124—dc20
                                                    89-14652
                                                    CIP

British Library Cataloguing in Publication Data:
Developing skills with information technology.
    —(New technologies and work).
    1. Industrial training. Curriculum subjects.
    Computer systems
    I. Bainbridge, Lisanne   II. Ruiz
    Quintanilla, S. Antonio   III. Series
    004
    ISBN 0 471 92396 6

Typeset by Acorn Bookwork, Salisbury, Wiltshire
Printed and bound in Great Britain by Biddles Ltd, Guildford, Surrey

Contents

Section 3: Training as Part of the Total Job Support System

Section 4: Training Tools

List of Contributors

Alexandra Altmann

Department of Psychology, University of Munich, Leopoldstr. 13, D-8000, Munich 40, FRG.

Lisanne Bainbridge

Department of Psychology, University College, London, WC1E 6BT, UK.

Sue Baker

Address at time of writing paper: OECD Halden Reactor Project, Halden, Norway.
Present address: RAF Institute of Aviation Medicine, Farnborough, UK.

Ken Eason

HUSAT Research Centre, Department of Human Sciences and Department of Computer Studies, Loughborough University of Technology, Loughborough, Leicestershire, LE11 3TU, UK.

Michael Frese

Department of Psychology, University of Munich, Leopoldstr. 13, D-8000, Munich 40, FRG.

C. J. Hinde

Department of Human Sciences and Department of Computer Studies, Loughborough University of Technology, Loughborough, Leicestershire, LE11 3TU, UK.

Jacques Leplat

Laboratoire de Psychologie du Travail de l'Ecole Pratique des Hautes Etudes, Groupement Scientifique du CNRS, 41 rue Gay-Lussac, 75005 Paris, France.

Edward Marshall

Address at time of writing paper: OECD Halden Reactor Project, Halden, Norway.

Present address: Central Electricity Research
Laboratories, Leatherhead, UK.

J. L. Mercy

Department of Work Psychology, University of
Liège, FAPSE B32, B-4000 Liège, Belgium.

Martin Mulder

Department of Education, University of
Twente, PO Box 217, 7500 AE Enschede, The
Netherlands.

Wim J. Nijhof

Department of Education, University of
Twente, PO Box 217, 7500 AE Enschede, The
Netherlands.

Leena Norros

Electrical Engineering Laboratory, Technical
Research Centre, Espoo, Finland.

Henning Salling Olesen

Department of Educational Research, Roskilde University Centre, Denmark.

Svend Erik Olsen

Psychological Department, Defence Centre for
Leadership, Christianshavns Voldgade 8, 1424
Copenhagen K, Denmark.

Jens Rasmussen

Risø National Laboratory, Roskilde, Denmark.

S. Antonio Ruiz
Quintanilla

Institute of Psychology, Berlin University of
Technology, FRG.

Andrew Shepherd

Department of Human Sciences and Depart-
ment of Computer Studies, Loughborough
University of Technology, Loughborough,
Leicestershire, LE11 3TU, UK.

Advisory Board

John Child *Aston University, Aston Triangle, Birmingham B4 7ET, UK.*

Pieter J. D. Drenth *Institute of Psychology, Free University Amsterdam, De Boelelaan 1081, NL-1011 Amsterdam, Netherlands.*

Frank A. Heller *Tavistock Institute of Human Relations, Centre of Decision Making Studies, Belsize Lane, London NW3 5BA, UK.*

Thomas A. Kochan *Sloan School of Management, Massachusetts Institute of Technology, Cambridge, Massachusetts 02139, USA.*

Jacques Leplat *Ecole Pratique des Hautes Etudes, Lab. de Psychologie du Travail, 41, rue Gay-Lussac, F-75005 Paris, France.*

Maurice de Montmollin *Groupe Communication et Travail, Université Paris-Nord, F-93430 Villetaneuse, France.*

Koji Okubayashi *School of Business Administration, Kobe University, Rokko, Kobe, Japan.*

Jens Rasmussen *Risø National Laboratory, PO Box 49, DK-4000 Roskilde, Denmark.*

Thoralf Qvale *Work Research Institutes, PO Box 8171, N-0034 Oslo 1, Norway.*

Wolfgang H. Staehle *Freie Universität Berlin, FB Wirtschaftswissenschaft Fachrichtung Organisation und Personalwissenschaft, Garystr. 21, 1000 Berlin 33, FRG.*

To the memory of Dr Gisela Forchner

Foreword

This volume is part of a publication series emerging from an international interdisciplinary study group on 'New Technologies and Work (NeTWork)'. NeTWork is sponsored jointly by the Werner-Reimers-Foundation (Bad Homburg, Federal Republic of Germany) and the Maison des Sciences de l'Homme (Paris). The NeTWork study group[1] has set itself the task to scrutinize the most important problem domains posed by the introduction and spread of new technologies in work settings. This problem focus requires interdisciplinary cooperation. The usual mode of operating is to identify an important problem area within the NeTWork scope, to attempt to prestructure it and, then, to invite original contributions from European researchers or research teams actively involved in relevant analytic or developmental work. A specific workshop serves to cross-fertilize the different approaches and to help to integrate more fully the individual contributions. Two volumes of the NeTWork activities have so far appeared in the Wiley Series 'New Technologies and Work'.[2]

Further volumes on 'New Technology and Distributed Decision Making' (eds. J. Rasmussen, J. Leplat and B. Brehmer) and 'New Technology and Manufacturing Management' (eds. M. Warner, W. Wobbe and P. Brodner) are being prepared for publication in this Wiley Series. The present volume deals with some of the most urgent and challenging requirements and opportunities of new information technologies: the need to improve the competence and skills for their effective use on the one hand and their instrumental use in improving such competences on the other. Given the scope of this perspective, the book should interest readers from academic disciplines as well as educational practitioners.

Bernhard Wilpert

[1]Members (1989) are: Professor Dr L. Bainbridge, UK; Dr A. Borseix, France; Professor Dr P. Drenth, Netherlands; Professor Dr K. Duncan, UK; Dr J. Evans, UK; Professor Dr V. de Keyser, Belgium; Professor Dr U. Kleinbeck, FRG; Professor Dr J. Leplat, France; Professor Dr M. de Montmollin, France; Professor Dr O. Pastré, France; Professor Dr F. Rapp, FRG; Professor Dr J. Rasmussen, Denmark; Professor Dr J.-D. Reynaud, France; Professor Dr R. Roe, Netherlands; Dr S. A. Ruiz Quintanilla, FRG; Professor Dr T. Qvale, Norway; Professor Dr B. Wilpert, FRG.

[2]J. Rasmussen, K. Duncan and J. Leplat (eds.): *New Technology and Human Error*, 1987. V. de Keyser, T. Qvale, B. Wilpert and S. A. Ruiz Quintanilla (eds.): *The Meaning of Work and Technological Options*, 1988.

Introduction

Information technology (IT) has had two types of impact on training. It provides new tools for training and more control over the training process. These are topics that are widely discussed. However, most IT equipment also requires new types of skill from its users. Training for these new types of work raises new questions which will be discussed in this book.

This book has been developed from the New Technology and Work (NeTWork) activities of the European Network of Work and Organisational Psychologists (ENOP). Invited papers were thoroughly discussed at a workshop of all the contributors that took place with the support of the Werner-Reimers Foundation and the Maison des Sciences de l'Homme (Paris), in Bad Homburg, Germany, during 9–11 April 1987. Most of the chapters in this book have been written or rewritten since the workshop, as a result of the discussions.

It has been very interesting to find that people from different European countries, who had not met before, are raising the same questions about the nature of training. The common themes and concerns in this European perspective may not be unique to training for IT but they are emphasized by the flexibility which much IT equipment provides. The themes are:

1. The changing nature of work requires training in the skills of using flexible equipment with many potential functions. IT equipment emphasizes the need for cognitive skills rather than perceptual–motor skills (the traditional domain of training). In particular, people need help with finding out how to use the equipment. This involves problem-solving and planning. We need to understand the nature of these complex cognitive functions in order to devise appropriate training.
2. Training is one of several ways of improving system performance. Other aspects are interface design, job-aid support, person–machine function allocation and job design. Design decisions about any one of these aspects can affect design decisions about all the others, so training provision can no longer be thought of in isolation from other aspects of system design.

In this Introduction, we will indicate the main points made in this book, first about changes in the nature of work and then about the background concepts and practice of training. We will refer in general to the main sections of the book, which are on:

1. The nature and development of expertise.
2. Training needs analysis and methods.
3. Training as part of the total job support system.
4. Training tools.

For guidance on specific chapters that discuss particular points, see the separate Introductions to the four sections.

CHANGES IN THE NATURE OF WORK

The flexibility of IT equipment, the many functions which can be carried out with it, means that users do not just need to know standard operating procedures. The users of IT equipment may need to work out for themselves what to do to meet their particular needs, on the basis of understanding how the equipment works.

Understanding how the equipment works is difficult, both because it is flexible and also because its workings are invisible. They are not only unobservable (one may not be able to see inside a car engine, but one can understand a diagram of what is going on inside it) but the actual underlying events are logical and microscopic, so they have to be described at a more general level and translated into physical analogies which may be more or less misleading. There is also no close relation between action and effect. When one throws away a real file, one can see and feel it happening. Typing in a command and the filename does not have the same sort of impact.

Planning how to use unfamiliar equipment involves thinking for oneself, problem-solving, one of the most difficult and least understood of cognitive skills. Knowledge about the equipment, what it does and what to do to it to get certain effects, must be organized within a framework of understanding the task goals and the methods available for meeting them. These skills of knowledge, understanding and problem-solving are not ones that are conveyed by conventional training methods.

The changes in approach needed for analysing, specifying and training these new types of skill are discussed in Sections 1 and 2. Sections 3 and 4 also raise wider perspectives. The chapters in Section 3 (and some in Section 4) point out that information technology does not just change what is done at individual workplaces. It changes the whole way in which an organization meets its needs. Therefore training for individual tasks must only be part of a whole process of organizational redesign. One can also consider issues wider than the particular organization. If one takes a person-centred rather than a technology or organization-centred view, then one can ask questions about the nature of society. If a person acquires new skills, what does this imply about their work values and motives, their self-esteem, their opportunities, their place in society and indeed the nature of groups in society? These points are important ones, but they are only briefly discussed in Section 3 of this book. Most of them are discussed in another volume of this series (de Keyser *et al.*, 1988).

CHANGES IN TRAINING

The context of training

1. Skills and their acquisition. The nature of expertise and its development need to be considered, because classic training methods are primarily concerned with the development of perceptual–motor skills, while IT-based tasks require cognitive skills. Therefore we need to understand their nature before considering training schemes to develop and optimize them. This is the topic of main concern in Section 1.
2. System optimization. Training is not the only way of improving system performance. It may be more effective to improve task performance by changing the interface, to provide point-of-need support, to change the allocation of function between person and machine or between people in the organization, or to remove blockages in the flow of information or materials between people in the organization. Therefore task analysis extends into system analysis, to recognizing a wider range of potential blocks to good performance.
3. Attitudes. Another possible block to performance is less easily perceived, because it is less concrete. This is attitudes towards the new equipment People may expect too much or be suspicious, hostile and uncooperative. One feature of introducing new technology into an organization may be the training which is oriented, not towards specific job skills, but towards helping people to understand the potential and limits of the new equipment and the reasons for changes in the organization. This is discussed in Section 3 and also in Norros (Chapter 17).

Training practice

1. Training need analysis. With the change in type of skill which may be needed for IT equipment, there is also a need for different methods of analysing and specifying what a training scheme should be trying to achieve. In particular, task analysis for cognitive skill needs to be concerned with the goals–methods structure of the task and with the knowledge of the equipment that the person needs. These issues are discussed in

Section 2. Although we are beginning to understand the nature of these skills, there is still a large amount of research to be done to identify taxonomies of cognitive skills and how to identify the level of performance needed in particular tasks.

2. Methods of training. The classic training methods were developed to teach perceptual–motor skills by repetition. They can be extended to the training of cognitive activities in which there is a standard procedure. However, the training of people to think things out for themselves requires new methods, with opportunities for the trainee to explore and discuss and to view an error as an opportunity for learning about the limits to one's knowledge and strategies, rather than as something to be punished. These issues are discussed in Sections 2 and 4.

3. Training equipment. Information technology also changes the way in which training is done by providing flexible tools for presenting the learning experience and for measuring performance. Section 4 discusses the use of simulators and 'intelligent' tutoring devices. However, in common with the rest of the book, these chapters do not discuss the equipment from the technical point of view but from the perspective of the task that they pose to the trainee, what relation this has to the 'real' task, and in what ways the tutoring experiences can optimize the progress of learning.

The chapters contain some interesting and thought-provoking case studies. Grouped by the type of work involved, these are:
Office applications:
Eason (Section 3), Frese and Altmann (Section 1), Mercy (Section 3), Nijhof and Mulder (Section 2), Shepherd (Section 2).

Production control:
Olesen (Section 3).

Process operation:
Baker and Marshall (Section 4), Marshall and Baker (Section 3), Norros (Section 4).

Flexible manufacturing systems:
Nijhof and Mulder (Section 2), Norros (Section 4).

The chapters in this book do not give a complete coverage of all training problems. A conspicuous gap is that there is little discussion of transfer of training. As much IT equipment needs flexibility on the part of the user, the teaching of skills which enable people to move from one job to another or from one type of equipment to another becomes of major importance.

Unfortunately this is not fully explored here. However, what we do have are some fascinating and substantial discussions of other major issues that are raised by training for information technology.

REFERENCE

de Keyser, V., Qvale, T., Wilpert, B., and Ruiz Quintanilla, S. A. (eds.) (1988) *The Meaning of Work and Technological Options*. Chichester: John Wiley and Sons.

THE EDITORS
L. Bainbridge
S. A. Ruiz Quintanilla

Section 1

The Nature and Development of Expertise

Outline of Section

It is appropriate to begin a book on training in relation to new technology by considering the nature of skill/expertise. Information technology makes demands on the user which change the emphasis in our concept of skill, from a hierarchy of automated units of behaviour to flexible behaviour adaptive to changing goals. This change in focus also underlies the changes that are needed in our approach to training. Although this section does not contain much practical guidance on training methods, except in the chapter by Frese and Altmann (Chapter 3), the concepts discussed are fundamental to the new approaches to training which are discussed in the rest of the book.

The chapters in this section are complementary; no one is a complete account. This is not surprising in such a complex domain. Two of the chapters, by Olsen and Rasmussen (Chapter 1) and by Leplat (Chapter 2), are general discussions. The other two chapters, by Frese and Altmann (Chapter 3) and by Bainbridge (Chapter 4), are more specifically focused on the nature of errors and on the mechanisms underlying skill. This introduction can only be a very inadequate guide to the topics that are discussed, and in no way represents the wise, wide-ranging interest of the points made.

The main topics discussed fall into four general categories:

— the nature of skill,
— changes in the processes underlying behaviour during the development of expertise,
— the place of errors in this development,
— the effects of skill, its advantages and disadvantages.

THE NATURE OF 'SKILL'

I have used the word 'skill' here for two reasons. Each chapter in this section uses a different terminology, and I have attempted to align them in Table 1. In general, Olsen and Rasmussen use the word 'skill' to refer to a particular type of cognitive processing mechanism, while the other authors use the

Table 1: Suggested parallels between the terms used in the four chapters in section 1

Olsen and Rasmussen	Frese and Altmann	Shiffrin and Schnieder (Leplat)	Bainbridge
Skill-based	Sensorimotor Flexible action pattern	Automatic	Habit Perceptual–motor skill
Rule-based (learned S–R relations) Rule-based (procedure)			
Knowledge-based	Intellectual	Controlled	Familiar cognitive skills
Knowledge-based	Abstract Metacognition	Controlled	Problem-solving

word in the more general sense familiar to psychologists, to describe efficient and effective behaviour of any type. Olsen and Rasmussen use the word 'expertise' for this. For training purposes, the notion of 'expertise' is defined relative to the level of performance required in a particular task, rather than to particular underlying mechanisms, and the chapters in this section are concerned with the mechanisms underlying behaviour, rather than with particular levels of performance.

Norros, in Chapter 17 of this volume, also discusses the nature of skill. In this section, most of the discussion is general, but Frese and Altmann and Bainbridge give detailed examples.

Leplat's chapter is a useful review of current psychological ideas about the nature of skill and the mechanisms underlying its development, advantages and disadvantages. He defines skill as having the following characteristics: skilled behaviour is learned, coordinated, goal-oriented, adaptive, with increased speed, consistency and availability, and decreased workload.

All of these chapters distinguish between the cognitive processes or knowledge of how to do the task and the knowledge of the environment that these processes refer to. Olsen and Rasmussen and Leplat both refer to Anderson's distinction between declarative and procedural knowledge, though Olsen and Rasmussen point out some limitations to this approach. Olsen and Rasmussen, Frese and Altmann, and Bainbridge all give frameworks for different types of cognitive process (see Table 1). That of Olsen and Rasmussen is Rasmussen's widely referenced skill/rule/knowledge-based structure; Bainbridge's structure is more related to the concepts used by cognitive psychologists and ergonomists; and Frese and Altmann relate their structure to the mechanisms of error and the implications for the treatment of errors in training programmes. Although these different processing mechanisms are sometimes referred to as 'levels' of behaviour, there was much emphasis in the workshop discussions that we are concerned with several subsystems of behaviour which are used in parallel with different emphasis in different tasks, rather than considering any one as 'higher' than any other.

All of the chapters emphasize the nature of skill as goal-directed behaviour. While early training methods often gave little emphasis to the goal-directed nature of behaviour, this was often implicit in the training. With the flexible adaptive use of multifunctional equipment, which is emphasized by information technology, goal-oriented training and a goal-oriented understanding of skill are essential.

The general and familiar notion of skill is that it develops by automating small units of behaviour, which allows them to be done without conscious attention, so freeing the attention for integrating larger units of behaviour, and so on. Leplat reviews this approach, while Bainbridge questions the extent to which it is valid to think of this progression as a hierarchy.

All of the chapters consider the development of the knowledge to which cognitive processes refer as an important feature of cognitive skill, though there is less discussion of the possible types or organization of this knowledge than there is of the cognitive mechanisms that refer to it. Olsen and Rasmussen and Bainbridge mention the way in which different types of thinking use different types of knowledge base. Olsen and Rasmussen emphasize the importance of changing representations of the problem space in the development of ability to solve problems. Bainbridge emphasizes the importance of rapid access to knowledge as an aspect of cognitive skill.

CHANGES DURING THE ACQUISITION OF SKILL

Having discussed the nature of skill in terms of the differences between a novice and an expert, all of the chapters then discuss, in more or less detail, the changes in cognitive processes which underly these differences and the route by which people come to use different cognitive mechanisms in doing a task. Norros, in Chapter 17, also discusses the nature of the learning process.

Although there is some discussion of the skill development as a progress through a series of 'levels' of processing, Olsen and Rasmussen explicitly criticize a model that describes skill acquisition in a sequence of stages and emphasize that skill development is not unidimensional but involves simultaneous changes of several types, in 'aggregation' (equivalent to automatization), in the ways information is interpreted (with good examples) and in the nature of knowledge.

Leplat gives more detail about the available theories for two of these changes, the increasing automatization of behaviour and its restructuring, and describes Anderson's theory in which, with experience, declarative knowledge is progressively transformed into procedural knowledge.

Frese and Altmann and Bainbridge (and Norros) give a more active account of the changes in behaviour. They include not only learning processes, which take place automatically as a result of repetition, but also consider the learner as someone who actively considers feedback from the task in revising working strategies. Bainbridge gives an explicit example of the different cognitive mechanisms used by a novice and an experienced person, with a simple model of the process by which someone decides that it is necessary to devise a different working method. However, the processes by which this revision is made are not discussed. Frese and Altmann give more information on this by discussing the way in which mistakes can give information about how to change the way in which the task is done.

THE USE OF ERRORS IN DEVELOPING SKILL

Frese and Altmann focus on the place of errors in learning. There are two aspects to their discussion. With Olsen and Rasmussen (and Leplat in Chapter 15 of this volume), they discuss errors as clues to underlying cognitive mechanisms, and offer a taxonomy of the nature and origin of errors.

The main part of their discussion is concerned with the usefulness of errors as an essential part of training for complex tasks. This is another example of the way in which training attitudes have had to change, as the conventional attitude is that errors should be avoided in training programmes. Olsen and Rasmussen point out that errors indicate the limits to acceptable behaviour. Bainbridge's discussion of errors is implicit, differences between the actual effect of an action and what was intended motivate the revision of strategies. Frese and Altmann discuss this in more detail. They point out that errors are useful in learning because they indicate that automatization of behaviour has gone too far, as well as that a revised method may be necessary. Leplat (Chapter 15) also discusses the use of knowledge of results in training. Frese and Altmann have an extended discussion of the explicit use of errors in a training programme, which will be returned to in Section 2. In summary, they point out that because error causes are multiple, it is necessary to design training courses to guide the interpretation of errors, to ensure that errors are motivating and interesting rather than stressful and to train people explicitly in error management, so that they can deal with changed situations.

THE EFFECTS OF SKILL

The effects of skill that are discussed here fall into four categories:

— the effects of prior knowledge,
— the effects on workload,
— the disadvantages of skill,
— the possibility of learning to learn.

Prior knowledge

No person coming to a task for the first time is a novice in all ways. The prior knowledge and skills that a novice brings to a task have a major influence on how easily a task can be learned. Bainbridge and Leplat mention this briefly (Bainbridge gives an example of the use of prior knowledge), while Olsen and Rasmussen give a fuller discussion. Eason also discusses this issue in Chapter 12 of this volume.

This prior knowledge can lead to interference or facilitation in learning the new task. Olsen and Rasmussen give some good examples of the effect of interference. Both Leplat and Bainbridge mention the specific example of interference when working instructions are not compatible with the prior knowledge and assumptions of a new user. This whole issue is part of the general problem of transfer of training, which is mentioned by Leplat, and is discussed more fully in the chapters in Section 4.

Workload and skill

Although Bainbridge's chapter includes 'workload' in the title, the discussion of workload is restricted to its place in the particular model that is being described. The importance of skill in the reduction of stress and the choice between alternative methods of doing a task according to the amount of workload they involve are emphasized. Leplat, however, has the fullest review of theories of workload in relation to cognitive skill, discussing the notion of multiple resources and the skill of dealing with many simultaneous responsibilities, and raises many questions about the nature of skill to which we do not yet have adequate answers.

Disadvantages of skill

One aspect of skill is that a skilled person in a stable environment knows beforehand the result of doing any particular action, so does not need to check it. This is an advantage leading to lower workload or increased efficiency, as discussed by Bainbridge. However, as Leplat points out, this also has disadvantages.

1. When the task can be done in the same way every time, without thinking, this over-learning or habit leads to rigidity of execution and to inflexible behaviour that cannot be adapted to the details of a new context if one does arise.
2. Assumptions about the context also lead to premature release of behaviour which may be inappropriate.
3. A person may apply a subclass of well-known methods to a task that actually requires development of a new method.
4. If it is not regularly referred to, the data base about the task, which is used in working out new strategies, becomes impoverished and less easily available.

In essence, the more frequently repeated the behaviour, the less adaptive it becomes and the less likely someone may be to devise new working methods. Eason and Mercy, in Chapters 12 and 13 of this volume, discuss the effects of this on the difficulties of introducing new technology into existing workplaces. Leplat makes some recommendations for training to avoid this, which we will return to in Section 2.

'Learning to learn'

Olsen and Rasmussen, Frese and Altmann and Bainbridge all comment on the importance of learning to learn. Olsen and Rasmussen (and Norros in Chapter 17) point out that an expert can be capable of reflecting on their own behaviour, of 'meta-cognition' (Norros uses this as a training method). Bainbridge mentions learning general problem-solving methods and frames for organizing knowledge of the environment as a type of skill that could be developed for dealing with unusual situations, though this suggestion is not developed in detail. Frese and Altmann discuss this within the context of users learning to interpret errors, to obtain information on how to devise more successful working methods.

In general, these four chapters give an interesting indication of the changes in the concept of skill that are taking place in response to the need to account for the more complex types of behaviour demanded of the users of information technology based equipment. The next section discusses, among other material, the implications of these ideas for the development of training schemes.

1. The Reflective Expert and the Prenovice: Notes on Skill-, Rule- and Knowledge-based Performance in the Setting of Instruction and Training

Svend Erik Olsen and Jens Rasmussen

ABSTRACT

Characterizations of novice and expert performance in terms of explicit, conscious rule-following versus automatic, intuitive skill-based performance are too narrow and misleading. Both novice and expert performance include skill-, rule- and knowledge-based performance, and the development from novice to expert should be modelled as different contents in and integrations of the skill-, rule- and knowledge levels. This point of view has important consequences for instruction and training which are emphasized through the terms 'prenovice' and 'reflective expert' pointing to the multifaceted content of both novice and expert performance.

INTRODUCTION

The distinction between expert and novice performance is of relevance whenever learning processes are in focus. The popularity of the terms 'expert' and 'novice' has increased rapidly in recent years. In the first edition of Anderson's *Cognitive Psychology and Its Implications* from 1980 the subject did not occur. However, in the 1984 edition the subject appears in the index and a whole chapter is devoted to it. In the same period a large and increasing number of studies have appeared in the journals (see, for example, Larkin *et al.*, 1980; Chi, Feltovich and Glaser, 1981; Schoenfeld and Herrmann, 1982; Kolodner, 1983; Murphy and Wright, 1984; and Adelson, 1984).

Why is it that the terms 'expert' and 'novice' have become so popular in recent years? One explanation is that rapid technological change leads to a continuous introduction of new tools for work in many domains and, consequently, a need for effective training methods. Another explanation is the opportunity offered by advanced information technology to match the system interfaces to the different requirements posed by expert and novice users.

Developing Skills with Information Technology
Edited by Lisanne Bainbridge and S. Antonio Ruiz Quintanilla
© 1989 John Wiley & Sons Ltd

In addition, the trend towards large-scale systems with their special requirements for reliable human performance also during infrequent disturbances has caused a concern with performance of users and operators both during situations when they can perform as 'experts' and in unfamiliar situations when they are to be considered as 'novices'. Requirements for training and other support for these situations are different and, therefore, it has become necessary to acquire knowledge of the characteristics of expert and novice performance in order to provide some support during instruction, training and later performance.

Furthermore, expert performance has become increasingly interesting because of the attempts to model such performance in expert systems and similar kinds of knowledge-based systems in the area of 'artificial intelligence'. Both the knowledge elicitation from the experts and the user interface of the expert system may require knowledge about the expert's expertise.

The terms 'novice' and 'expert' do not denote discontinuous and separated entities. What we have is a continuum on which novice and expert performance are the endpoints. Performance is always to be judged as more or less novice-like or more or less expert-like depending on the dynamically varying match between task requirements and human resources. The distinction expert–novice is not related to individuals in isolation but rather to the situation-dependent human–task interaction.

For practical reasons, then, as well as for theoretical reasons it is important to analyse and study what novices and experts do and what the transition from novice to expert consists of. In the following we will discuss some suggestions made by Dreyfus and Dreyfus (1980, 1986) and we will put forward some proposals of our own while we relate novice and expert performance to the skill, rule and knowledge model of human performance (Rasmussen, 1986c; Goodstein, Andersen and Olsen, 1988). By focusing on the novice and the expert we hope to be able to clarify some important aspects of the starting point and the goal of instruction and training.

THE NOVICE AND THE EXPERT

Dreyfus and Dreyfus (1986) suggest that it is important to distinguish five steps on the dimension from novice to expert. Their aim is to show that expertise cannot be reduced to a kind of rule-following conscious rationality.

They start out by emphasizing the honourable distinction between 'know-how' and 'know-that'. They notice that very often those things a person can do perfectly well, such as riding a bicycle or carry on a conversation, are not accessible to the person in the form of facts and rules. Even though the person has 'know-how', he or she does not have the kind of knowledge that is implied by 'know-that'.

'Knowing-that' implies verbalizability and rule-guidedness according to Dreyfus and Dreyfus. They argue that experts are not rule-guided and often cannot verbalize what they are doing. 'If you are a carpenter, you know how to use tools in a way that escapes verbalization' (p. 17).

Skill acquisition is seen by Dreyfus and Dreyfus as a process that goes from rule-guided 'know-that' to experience-based 'know-how'. They claim that at least five stages of skill acquisition can be distinguished. These stages are referred to as: novice, advanced beginner, competent performer, proficient performer and expert.

It is not our intention to go into a discussion about stages or levels in acquisition or performance. In most cases, stages or levels are best considered as practical distinctions which present idealized pictures of more continuous realities. Our aim here is rather to question the starting and especially the ending point in the suggested stage model. However, our discussion about the starting and ending points will nevertheless lead us to reject the stage-sequence model.

According to Dreyfus and Dreyfus the novice stage is characterized by a verbalizable or explicit fact-, feature- and rule-learning which is relatively detached from the overall situation. Elements and rules at this stage are labelled by Dreyfus and Dreyfus as 'context-free' which means that the elements and rules are applied rather rigidly without considering the immediate demands of the situation.

Dreyfus and Dreyfus mention briefly that what they discuss is the acquisition of a new skill 'through instruction'. Although this is indeed relevant, it should be emphasized that the above characteristic is only a tiny part of the whole picture.

The context-free and explicit fact-, feature- and rule-learning abilities presuppose that the learner is already highly skilled in several areas, for example in the areas of motor and language skills. In order to enter the novice stage and understand instructions the person in question must have some degree of expertise in some areas.

These considerations emphasize the fact that the expert–novice distinction is not related to individuals but to the situation-dependent match to task requirements. Therefore we are forced to realize what we already know, namely that the acquisition of skills does not always require instruction.

Skill acquisition assisted by instruction is important, but it is not the only way to proceed. Animals and small children learn complex cognitive and behavioural performance without any instruction (if this is not to be called 'acquisition of skills' then at least we are entitled to ask for a delimiting and non-circular definition of 'skill'). Neither animals nor small children have to enter the 'novice' stage in order to acquire 'expertise' (again it is possible to construct definitions that avoid the problem—and again it is easy to end with circular and non-informative definitions).

The implications are that the status and description of the novice stage can be seriously questioned. First of all the novice stage—as defined above—cannot in general be the first stage in all learning processes, because (some of) these processes can go on without the context-free and explicit fact- feature- and rule-learning. Second, even in the novice stage itself, the learner has already acquired knowledge in certain other areas. And Third, it is an open question as to whether the novice stage can be exhaustively characterized by the context-free fact-, feature- and rule-learning. It can be expected that, in conjunction with the more explicit processes, it will be possible to find learning processes of the non-context-free and less explicit nature.

To conclude the discussion of the novice stage in skill acquisition we want to emphasize that it will be important to take the above-mentioned precautions into consideration. These precautions are what we call attention to when we introduce the notion of 'prenovice'.

Concerning expert performance, Dreyfus and Dreyfus argue that it is reached through a series of stages and that it is characterized by quite the opposite of the novice stage: expert performance is 'ongoing' and 'non-reflective'. Experts do not make decisions in an analytical way. They have know-how which is non-verbalizable and they are not detached as novices often are. Furthermore, experts are highly involved. They are performing in a context-dependent manner based on 'experience-based holistic recognition of similarity' which allows 'deep situational understanding' (p. 32). Dreyfus and Dreyfus give the following example:

> The expert driver not only knows by feel and familiarity when an action such as slowing is required, but generally knows how to perform the act without evaluating and comparing alternatives (p. 32).

Dreyfus and Dreyfus are motivated by a desire to show that 'logic machines' (computers) in their computations cannot be likened with human experts. We do not want to argue against Dreyfus and Dreyfus on that point, but we find the description of expert performance somewhat problematic.

Is it really sufficient to describe expertise as automatic skill performance? The skill-based performance surely is a very important part of the performance of an expert, but it does not exhaustively characterize expertise.

In the ordinary language of everyday life the term 'expert' is not restricted to non-verbalizing skill-performers. In everyday language an 'expert' is (very often) also a person who is able to advise and instruct those who need it.

From this observation there is only a small step to the conclusion that the expert stage in Dreyfus and Dreyfus' descriptions is not the last stage at all or better it is not a sufficient description of all the different elements of expertise. Maybe we ought to include other types of expertise in order to differentiate those experts who are able to reason about and evaluate novice and expert performance in their field. We suggest the term 'reflective expert' for this kind of expert.

Actually Dreyfus and Dreyfus themselves come very close to such a conclusion. They make a distinction between the conscious use of calculative rationality of the novice or other lower-level performers and the deliberative rationality of those who perform at higher stages. This kind of deliberative rationality does not according to Dreyfus and Dreyfus focus on context-free elements but on whole intuitions which are tested and improved. However, Dreyfus and Dreyfus do not try to integrate these considerations into their stage-model.

Dreyfus and Dreyfus also present examples of experts who are able to analyse and evaluate the performance of novices, of themselves or of other experts. This ability implies that experts may have competences besides their ongoing, non-reflective and automatic skill-based performance. Again Dreyfus and Dreyfus do not seem to see any implications for expertise in these examples.

Our conclusion must be that expertise is not just a matter of simple skill acquisition. Expert performance is in most cases very diverse and complex. If we want to capture at least some of the complexities of expertise, we have to work with a model that allows us to see the complexities.

We have suggested that the notions of 'prenovice' and 'reflective expert' ought to be included in the description of the development of expertise. By doing this we have actually seriously questioned the whole idea of constructing a sequence of stages which should capture the process of development from novice to expert. Rather we will suggest that the development should be modelled as different contents in and integrations of the skill-, rule- and knowledge-levels.

SKILLS, RULES AND KNOWLEDGE (SRK)

When we distinguish categories of human behaviour according to basically different ways of representing the properties of a deterministic environment as a basis for control of actions, three typical levels of performance emerge: skill-, rule- and knowledge-based performance. These levels and a simplified illustration of their interrelation are shown in Figure 1.

Skill-based behaviour represents sensorimotor performance during acts or activities that, eventually after a statement of an intention, take place without conscious control as smooth, automated and highly integrated patterns of behaviour. In most skilled sensorimotor tasks, the body acts as a multivariable, continuous control system, synchronizing movements with the behaviour of the environment. This performance is based on feedforward control and depends upon a very flexible and efficient dynamic world model. In some cases, performance is one continuous, integrated dynamic whole, such as bicycle riding or musical performance. In these cases the higher-level control may take the form of conscious anticipation of upcoming demands in general terms, resulting in an updating of the state of the dynamic world model and thereby in the appropriate 'modulation' of the skilled response.

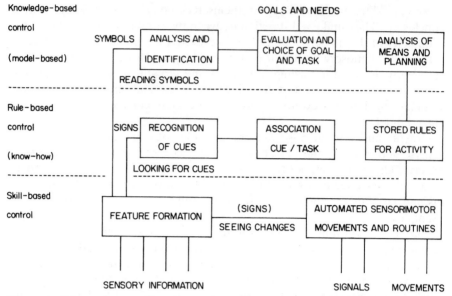

Figure 1. Schematic map illustrating different levels in cognitive control of human behaviour. The basic level represents the highly skilled sensorimotor performance controlled by automated patterns of movements. Sequences of such subroutines will be controlled by stored rules, activated by signs. Problem-solving in unfamiliar tasks will be based on conceptual models at the knowledge-based level which serve to generate the necessary rules *ad hoc*. The figure illustrates the flow of information, not the control of this flow. The figure is not meant to show humans as passive and subjects to information 'input'. On the contrary, they actively seek information, guided by their expectations which, in turn, are controlled by an internal, dynamic 'world model'

In general, human activities can be considered as a sequence of such skilled acts or activities composed for the actual occasion. The flexibility of skilled performance is due to the ability to compose the sets suited for specific purposes from a large repertoire of automated subroutines. The individual routines are activated and chained by perceived patterns that are acting as signs; the person is not consciously choosing among alternatives.

At the next level of rule-based behaviour the composition of a sequence of subroutines in a familiar work situation is typically consciously controlled by a stored rule or procedure that may have been derived empirically during previous occasions, communicated from other persons' know-how as an instruction or a cookbook recipe, or it may be prepared on occasion by conscious problem solving and planning.

The point here is that performance is goal-oriented, but structured by 'feedforward control' through a stored rule. In other words, the person is aware that alternative actions are possible and has to make a choice. The choice is based on 'signs' in the environment which have been found to be correlated to one of the alternative actions. Very often, the goal is not even explicitly formulated, but is found implicitly in the situation releasing the stored rules. The control is teleologic in the sense that the rule or control is selected from previous successful experiences. The control evolves by 'survival of the fittest' rule.

In general, skill-based performance rolls along without conscious attention, and the actor will be unable to describe the information used to act. The higher-level rule-based coordination in general is based on explicit know-how, and the rules used can often be reported by the person, although the cues releasing a rule may not be explicitly known.

During unfamiliar situations for which no know-how or rules for control are available from previous encounters, the control must move to a higher conceptual level, in which performance is goal-controlled and knowledge-based. (Knowledge is here taken in a rather restricted sense as possession of a conceptual, structural model or, in AI terminology, of deep knowledge. The level, therefore, might also be called 'mental model-based'.) In this situation, the goal is explicitly formulated, based on an analysis of the environment and the overall aims of the person. Then a useful plan is developed by selection. Different plans are considered and their effect tested against the goal, physically by trial and error or conceptually by means of 'thought experiments'. At this level of functional reasoning, the internal structure of the system is explicitly represented by a 'mental model' that may take several different forms.

A very important aspect of the cognitive control to be captured by models of human behaviour is the dynamic interaction between the activities at the three levels.

The time dimension of cognitive control will be different for the three levels. One of the basic features of the hierarchical organization of cognitive control is that interaction at the sensorimotor skill level is based on real-time, multivariable and synchronous coordination of physical movements with a dynamical environment. Quantitative, time–space signals are continuously controlling movements, and patterns are interpreted as signs serving to adjust the world model and maintain synchronism with the environment. The dynamic control of the patterns depends on high-capacity signal processing in a feedforward mode governed by the internal world model. During run-off of such routines, conscious attention is free to cope with other matters on a time-sharing basis.

At the rule-based level, the conscious attention may run ahead of the skilled performance, preparing rules for coming requirements. It may be necessary to memorize rules, to rehearse their application and to update more generic rules with the details of the present environment. Stored rules will frequently be formulated at a generalized function level, and thus need to be implemented in the present physical context. In other cases, rules are not ready in explicit formulation, and previously successful coping with a similar situation will have to be memorized to establish transfer.

In general, control at the rule-based level requires conscious preparation of the sequence ahead of the timing of the skilled activity. Otherwise, a break in the smooth performance will take place. The conscious mind only very infrequently is operating in synchronism with the interaction with the environment. Attention will wander ahead to identify the need for rules and backwards to recollect the rules of past encounters. If none is available, switch over to deduction of rules by means of 'a mental model' is required which, in general, will require even more foresight if a break in performance is to be avoided.

In ordinary circumstances humans are always conscious of something in themselves or in the environment, and they are very seldom in a state where they are behaviourally doing nothing. Furthermore, in most cases they possess rules which can be put to work rather easily. Activity at one level does not exclude parallel or integrated activity at the other levels. Therefore we have to realize that the overall activity of a given person at a given moment consists of and is embedded in components related to both skills, rules and knowledge.

SKILLS, RULES AND KNOWLEDGE IN LEARNING A SKILL

It is clear from the discussion in the previous section that the three levels of control are intimately interacting. In order to evaluate the degree to which the underlying models are separate concepts or just different aspects of the same internal representation, it may be useful to discuss how they relate to learning a skill.

Distinctions between different categories of human behaviour similar to the SRK levels have previously been proposed in relation to learning a skill. Fitts and Posner (1962) distinguish between three phases: the early or cognitive phase, the intermediate or associative phase, and the final or autonomous phase. If we consider that in real life a person will meet situations with a varying degree of training when performing a task depending on variations and disturbances, the correspondence with the three levels in the present context is clear.

In the three-level model, the final stage in adaptation to a task environment is, in instructional contexts, often the skill-based level. However, in other contexts neither the rule- nor the knowledge-based levels are relevant, and in these cases there are no reasons to consider the skill-based level to be the 'final' one, as it is the only one. Learning can take place directly at the skilled level by imitation and trial and error, as, for instance, learning to play an instrument by ear or children learning to talk, walk, etc.

In other cases, control at the rule-based behavioural level will be efficient during development of the automated skill. The rules may be obtained from an instructor or a textbook, as is typically the case when learning to drive a car, to operate tools and technical devices supplied with an instruction manual or to manage social interactions from 'rules of good manners'. Finally, persons with a basic knowledge of the structure and functioning will be able to generate for themselves a set of rules to control activities related to various purposes during early phases of learning. This involves what Anderson (1983) calls 'compiling declarative knowledge'.

Human errors have important functions in this learning process. Fine-tuning of manual skills depends upon a continuous updating of the sensori-motor schemata to the time–space features of the task environment. If the optimization criteria are speed and smoothness, the limits of acceptable adaptation can only be found by the one-in-a-while experience gained when crossing the precision tolerance limits, that is by the experience of errors or near-errors. Also at the more consciously controlled rule-following level, development of know-how and rules of thumb depend upon opportunities for experiments to find shortcuts and identify convenient and reliable signs which make it possible to recognize recurrent conditions without analytical diagnosis.

In problem solving, testing hypotheses is important. It is typically expected that, for instance, process operators check their diagnostic hypothesis conceptually—by thought experiments—before actions on the plant. This, however, appears to be an unrealistic assumption, since it may be tempting to test a hypothesis on the system itself in order to avoid the strain from reasoning in a complex causal network.

An important point is that is is not the behavioural patterns of the higher levels that are becoming automated skills. Automated time–space behavioural patterns are developing while they are controlled and supervised by the higher-level activities—which will eventually deteriorate—and their basis in knowledge and rules may deteriorate. In fact, the period when this is happening may lead to errors due to interference between a not fully developed sensorimotor skill and a gradually deteriorated rule system. This kind of interference is known also to highly skilled musicians when they occasionally start to analyse their performance during fast passages. It seems plausible also that this effect can play a role for pilots of about 100 hours' flying experience, which is known to be an error-prone period among pilots.

Anderson (1983) also discusses the interaction between declarative knowledge and procedural knowledge. He describes the development of procedural knowledge during learning as a 'compilation'. Generally, compilation refers to a transformation of knowledge from one form of representation to another. According to the SRK framework, however, procedural knowledge derived by compilation of declarative mental models is a possible, but not an inevitable, first phase of rule-based behaviour. In later phases procedural knowledge is typically not derived from the basic, 'deep' knowledge, but has an empirical, heuristic basis, and compilation is not a suitable metaphor.

Following the lines of reasoning suggested above, the transfer of control to new mental representations is a very complex process involving change along several different orthogonal dimensions. First, when trained responses evolve, the structure of the underlying representation shifts from a set of separate component models towards a more holistic representation. This is discussed by Bartlett (1943) in relation to pilot fatigue, and Moray (in 1987) analyses how such model aggregation can lead process operators into trouble during plant disturbances, because the process is irreversible, that is the regeneration of a structured model needed for causal reasoning in unfamiliar situations is not possible from the aggregated model.

The learning model implied in the SRK framework indicates that skill acquisition involves more than an aggregation of mental models. Typically, control by a structural, declarative model will be replaced by empirical, procedural knowledge concurrent with a shift from a symbolic to a stereotype sign interpretation of observations. This means that training involves at least three concurrent and structurally independent shifts, in terms of aggregation, of declarative–procedural knowledge and of interpretation of information.

THE PRENOVICE AND THE NOVICE IN AN INSTRUCTIONAL CONTEXT

The novice brings into the instructional setting a whole repertoire of dispositions and capacities concerning skill-, rule- and knowledge-based activities. Even if the object of the instructional process is entirely new to the novice subject, he or she must, of course, rely on previously acquired skills, rules and knowledge during the learning process. Although this fact is generally agreed upon, it is so important that it cannot be overemphasized.

On the front page of the textbook *Educational Psychology* Ausubel has put the following motto: 'The most important single factor influencing learning is what the learner already knows. Ascertain this and teach him accordingly' (Ausubel, Nowak and Hanesian, 1978). These preinstructional or prenovice dispositions and capacities are important first because they are the basis on which the new dispositions and capacities will be built and second because they may have long-lasting and even distorting effects on both the instructional process and the postinstructional activity. The preinstructional dispositions and capacities can be more or less intimately related to the domain which the instruction is directed at. The most intimately domain-related dispositions and capacities are the most interesting in this context.

Corresponding to the fact that expertise is a situation-related rather than a person-related concept, previously learned skill-based activity can interfere with new learning processes or with newly learned skills, and under special circumstances seemingly forgotten skills can suddenly come alive again (see, for example, Welford, 1968). In the study of memory, interference has for a long time been an important topic both as a phenomenon and as an explanatory construct (see, for example, Baddeley, 1976). Also in other areas of cognitive research, interference of or use of previously acquired knowledge and beliefs has a very central place. We will only present a few examples to make the point clear.

Caramazza, McCloskey and Green (1981) investigated how students solve simple problems about the trajectories of falling objects. Most of the students revealed misconceptions about motion. The students had abstracted from their ordinary experience general principles concerning the motion of objects, but these principles were often not in agreement with fundamental physical laws—they were reminiscent of 'pre-Galilean models of motion'. This was the case not only for students who had no formal instruction in physics but also for students who had received some formal instruction at high school or college level. Only a third of the formally instructed students were able to solve the simple problems correctly.

Caramazza, McCloskey and Green conclude that it is important to provide more detailed descriptions of people's belief about moving objects and to explore the origin of these beliefs and the ways in which they are altered during instruction. In general we will emphasize that mental models of a system which most often is complex and multifaceted (Rasmussen, 1986c), must be central focusing points both in the instructional and the post-instructional setting.

Clement (1982) has found that students have stable misconceptions about the relationship between force and acceleration, summarized in the equation $F = ma$. Clement gives the following account:

> An understanding of $F = ma$ is made difficult because it conflicts with the beginner's intuitive preconceptions about motion. In the real world, where friction is present, one must push on an object to keep it moving. Since friction is often not recognised as a force by the beginner, the student may believe that continuing motion implies the presence of a continuing force in the same direction, as a necessary cause of the motion (p. 66).

The misconception shows up, according to Clement, also in problem situations where one would not expect it—and an 'alarmingly' high number of students with formal instruction in physics could not solve some basic problems correctly. Clement continues:

> This was in spite of the fact that none of the problems require advanced mathematical skills. What they do require is an adequate knowledge of the basic qualitative model for how forces affect motion.

Beside the misconception concerning friction White (1983) has found that the erroneous answers of the students concerning force and motion problems may also stem from partially understood classroom examples and from misplaced transfer of properties of scalar arithmetic to problems requiring vector arithmetic. White concludes (p. 41) that the students employ knowledge which seem relevant to the solution of these problems, 'but which often have properties that conflict with the implications of Newton's law of motion' (p. 69).

In the domain of human–computer interaction Bonar and Soloway (1985) have found that previous knowledge is a major source of misconceptions in novice programmers. Their idea is that many programming mistakes are due to an inappropriate use of preprogramming knowledge of step-by-step procedural specifications in natural language. In other words, performance related to situations in which people are experts interferes during 'novice' situations.

The preinstructional knowledge about the given domain does not necessarily produce misconceptions that will act as barriers in the instructional processes. The preinstructional knowledge will in many cases be indispensable and can indeed enhance the instructional processes. DiSessa (1983) has termed the basic preconceptions 'phenomenological primitives' or 'p-prims', and they are considered to be relatively minimal abstractions of simple common phenomena. These p-prims can support or block the instructional processes. DiSessa suggests that:

> . . . it is important to know about a naive person's repertoire of p-prims and how easily their priorities can be folded when considering how one should explain advanced notions in such a way as to be understandable at the student's level, but just as important, in such a way as to develop naturally into expert understanding (p. 33).

It is, then, of central importance for the effectiveness of the instructional processes that the preinstructional knowledge of the prenovice be taken into account. This point is of even greater importance when the instructed persons are to become operators of complex systems where faulty reasoning can have dangerous consequences.

In conclusion, we can state that effective and deep instructional processes have to start with investigations of the repertoire of skill-, rule- and knowledge-based activities of the prenovice. The results of these investigations must be used as indicators of both the activities that have to be changed or suppressed and the activities that can be used as a more permanent basis for the instructional process.

SOME IMPORTANT CHARACTERISTICS OF EXPERTISE

In complex task situations no person can be expected to have a high degree of expertise in every aspect of the task. This means that the actual performance of an expert in a complex situation generally will be the result of a mixture of several activities which may be characterized as more or less expert-like.

Furthermore, an expert may have more or less expertise in performance at a skill-based, rule-based or knowledge-based level, or in selecting an adequate level of performance. In this way we get a very complicated picture of expertise.

As a general characteristic of expertise we can state that an expert is someone who has acquired a set of dispositions and capacities for optimal skill-, rule- and knowledge-based performance in a certain task domain. A task analysis is necessary in order to explicate the skill-, rule- and knowledge-based capacities which are required in a given task. Therefore the more specific characteristics of expertise will vary from task to task.

This definition makes it less attractive to use the label 'expert' about animals, small children and technical systems which may perform highly skilled activities, but which are not able to give advice at the rule-based level or to generate responses at the knowledge-based level. The definition also makes it important to differentiate between the expertise of the highly skilled performer, who has developed relatively less capacity for performance at the rule- and knowledge-based levels, and the reflective expert, who has to be able also to perform at the rule- and knowledge-based levels. In the end it may even turn out that the skill-based performance of a person who is also capable (to some extent at least) of rule- and knowledge-based performance in the task domain is different from the skill-based performance of an agent or system which does not possess capabilities for the rule- or knowledge-based performance in the domain.

What counts as optimal performance will vary from one domain to another and from task to task. However, optimal performance at a given level of cognitive control may nevertheless have different general features than optimal performance at another level. For example, at the skill-based level optimal performance may be characterized as fast, effortless and fluent routines, but knowledge-based optimal performance may rather be characterized as flexible, relevance-testing and goal-seeking.

Experts have often been shown to be better at perceiving the characteristics of a problem than novices. The classical investigations by de Groot (1965) and the replications by Chase and Simon (1973) showed that Master chess players were able to perceive and remember a midgame chess board position after just a short glance. Novices in chess playing did not have this ability. On the other hand, Voss, Tyler and Yengo (1985) have shown that experts in a social science domain will use more time than novices in developing an initial representation of a given problem.

These results are not contradictory—in part they can be accounted for by referring to differences in the task domain, but more importantly they can be accounted for within the skill, rules and knowledge framework. From the previous characterization we would expect that experts would be able to perform at different levels. Quickly perceiving the characteristics of a problem is a skill-based ability. Analytical development of an adequate initial problem representation is a knowledge- and rule-based performance. Performance at the different levels can go on simultaneously and can take care of different aspects of a given task. Of course, a given task may also call for performance at a specific level—in isolation or in sequence with other performances. The important point is that optimal handling of a given task often requires performances at different levels—experts realize this and act accordingly.

Hammond *et al.* have recently (1987) investigated the efficacy of intuitive and analytical cognition in expert judgement. They developed indices for measuring the location of a series of information display conditions on a continuum ranging from intuition-inducing to analysis-inducing. Furthermore, they measured the degree of intuitive and analytical cognition of expert highway engineers who participated in the investigation. They found that the information display conditions indeed tended to induce the expected intuitive or analytical cognition in the experts. They also found that the judgemental accuracy was related to a correspondence between the task conditions and the type of cognition: highest accuracy was reached if the expert used intuitive cognition in the intuition-inducing task conditions and analytical cognition in the analysis-inducing task conditions. They also found that the intuitive cognition frequently outperformed the analytical cognition.

As intuitive cognition largely belongs to the category of skill-based performance and analytical cognition to the knowledge- and rule-based performance, Hammond *et al.*'s investigation indicates that expertise is not restricted to a single level of performance. The actual choice of level of performance is guided by characteristics of the task. Our early investigations of electronic troubleshooting (Rasmussen and Jensen, 1973, 1974) pointed in the same direction: although the repair men in the study had some preferred search procedures mostly related to skill-based performance, they were able to change their procedures and did so if the subjective formulation of task and performance criteria required it.

Referring to investigations on social science experts Voss *et al.* (1984) suggest that the experts have more strategies available for using knowledge than novices, and they reason that the experts' flexibility stems from encounters with many different kinds of problems in their domain.

Hammond *et al.* explicate the practical implications of their investigation with three principles:

1. Designers should attend to the correspondence between task and cognition in order to increase their awareness and anticipate the kind of cognition which is likely to occur.
2. When the display features of the task cannot be changed, the designer should analyse and locate the task with respect to the kind of cognition it is likely to induce in order to choose the most adequate kind of cognition.

3. When the kind of cognition used on a task cannot be changed, the designer should try to make the task display features that correspond to the anticipated kind of cognition.

Attention to the correspondence between task and cognition is indeed important. In cognitive task analysis (Rasmussen, 1986a, 1986c) the cognitive components of a given task are emphasized in order to improve the design of the system with which the human operator has to interact. The analysis of skill-, rule- and knowledge-based activity—including the intuitive and analytical cognitive activity—is just one of several analyses that is to be carried out if a more thorough cognitive task analysis has to be achieved. Another important subject of analysis is the problem space within which the problem-solver has to operate (Rasmussen, 1986b, 1986c).

The problem space in technical domains is primarily constituted by means–end and part–whole relations. Several other relationships and other aspects are also relevant—for example causal relations, generic relations and value aspects as well (Rasmussen, 1986b). These other relations can be conceived of as thought-guiding subprinciples which act under the framework establishing superprinciples of the means–end and part–whole relations. Since the mental construction of the problem space requires a certain amount of skills, rules and knowledge, the novice and the expert will come to and perform in a problem-solving situation with different problem spaces.

It has been consistently found that while novices are easily caught by the superficial features of the problem-solving situation, the experts are able to employ more abstract, theoretical principles. Chi, Feltovich and Glaser (1981) found that

> ...the experts initially abstract physics principles to approach and solve a problem representation, whereas novices base their representation and approaches on the problem's literal features (p. 121).

Schoenfeld and Herrmann (1982) examined students' problem perception in mathematics before and after an intensive course in mathematical problem-solving. The students were asked to categorize mathematical problems on the basis of similarity. Before the course the students categorized on the basis of superficial features in the problem statements. After the course they categorized—like experts—on the basis of features related to principles or methods relevant for the solution of the problems. Schoenfeld and Herrmann conclude that criteria for problem perception change when knowledge is acquired.

In terms of the problem space it is important to notice that the use of abstract or theoretical principles found in the expert's performance can be located at the level of abstract functions on the means–end dimension (Rasmussen, 1986c). To perform at this level in a knowledge-rich domain will indeed require training and experience; therefore experts and novices will differ greatly here. However, we expect that experts and novices will differ in their performance at any other level in the problem space as well.

Evidence and indications concerning these suggestions exist already. For example, Simon and Simon (1978) found that experts in physics tend to use a 'working-forward' strategy while novices tend to use a 'working-backward' strategy. Lesgold (1984) emphasizes that a working-forward strategy requires (1) an elaborated problem representation which allows inferences leading to the solution and (2) knowledge which makes it possible to choose the most promising partial solutions. In short, the expert's working-forward strategy includes much goal-related knowledge. The working-backward strategy of the novices requires less goal-related knowledge.

In terms of the levels and dimensions of the problem space, this means that experts not only have more knowledge pertaining to the level of abstract functions but they also have more knowledge pertaining to the level of functional goals. In general we expect to find that experts and novices differ in their conceptions of the physical components at the lowest level of the means–end dimension and in their goal conceptions at the highest level. In addition, they will also differ in the way that they decompose and aggregate on the part–whole dimension.

Another interesting difference between experts and novices has been noted by Murphy and Wright (1984) who found that category distinctiveness decreased with expertise. The categories of novices seem to be rather sharply differentiated while the categories of experts seem to be less sharply differentiated in the sense that they contain many shared features. This finding does not necessarily contradict the general feeling that the concepts and categories of novices are more vague and loose than those of experts. The more sharp differentiation may come about partly as a result of less knowledge and partly because novices actively try to counteract the vagueness and looseness of their concepts and categories. Inside a given domain the categories and concepts of an expert are both more richly connected and less vague.

Murphy and Medin (1985) emphasize the importance of a theoretical framework for a person's category structure and use. Obviously, the theories of novices and experts in a given domain will differ, not only in content but also in explicitness. According to Vygotsky (1962), the fundamental difference between everyday life 'spontaneous' concepts and theory-embedded 'scientific' concepts taught in school settings is the 'absence of a system' of the former. The latter type of concepts are located in a system and are more easily accessible for conscious activity. The more expertise a person has in a domain which includes conceptual, theoretical frameworks, the more the person will be able to exhibit reflective expert performance.

Our conclusion must be that the performance of a person in a given task domain is multifaceted. Expert performance is only an aspect of the total performance picture—and what counts as expert performance depends upon the task. There is no reason to delimit the label 'expertise' to the automated, skill-based performance. This conclusion gives rise to the following principle for educational practice: when the goals of instruction and training are to be formulated, it is important to analyse and explicate not only the degree of expertise but also the kind of expertise that is required and has to be achieved in a given task performance.

CHARACTERISTICS OF TASKS IN HIGH-TECH SYSTEMS

In traditional manual tasks and crafts involved in traditional work environments, for example in mechanical production, there is a very intimate relationship between the three levels of cognitive control. The shift of control among the levels during training is a very organic process. This is because the task primarily involves manipulation or shaping of visible physical objects. This is not the case in many modern, high-tech systems such as chemical process systems, nor in systems based on very complex thermodynamical processes such as power plants, nor in information systems, for example for control of financial transactions. Work conditions in such centralized and automated systems have some very characteristic features which will influence the requirements for interface design and operator training:

1. Operators are required to control an invisible process.
2. There is no simple mapping between the visible 'control surface' and the internal process.
3. There is no close relation between the manual skill and the actual work content.
4. There can be a high cost for errors.
5. There can be a time delay between acts and their effects on the internal process, making error recovery difficult.
6. Concern is focused on the ability to cope with complex rare events.
7. There are occasions when adequate competency will not be maintained during normal routine activities.

In order to illustrate the problems encountered in many advanced systems, supervisory control in complex industrial process systems will be discussed in some detail. In many existing automated systems, the prime task of the operating staff has been to take over the control of plant operation and production during failure of automatic controllers. This was caused by the low reliability of equipment based on vacuum-tube technology. During recent years, this situation has changed considerably. The reliability of control systems based on integrated semiconductor technology has been dramatically improved, and the complexity of the automatic control algorithms for advanced systems has been correspondingly increased. The general trend towards large-scale systems, not only for industrial production units but also for consumer goods distribution systems, information systems and systems for financial operations, has caused a large potential for loss and damage in the case of technical faults in equipment and of human errors made during operation and maintenance. It is, therefore, no longer acceptable that single component failures or human errors can release a chain of events leading to accidents and losses, and a design philosophy of 'defence in depth' has evolved. This philosophy implies that systems have several lines of defence such as protective functions, barriers against fault propagation, etc., which can serve to terminate accidental chains of events before serious damage occurs. Such stand-by equipment and automatic protective functions are intended to bring the process system to an alternative, safe state of operation.

Consequently, the task of the operating staff will not be to take over manual control of the normal production. Instead, the task will be to monitor the performance of the automatic take-over by stand-by equipment and the function of the protective measures. This task, in fact, is not related to manual control of normal system operation. Instead, the operating staff will have to consider whether the automatic protective functions are adequately designed for the particular disturbance which may not have been explicitly considered by the initial system designer. If this is not the case, the staff is supposed to manually reconfigure the system so as to bring the available equipment and functions into the most appropriate use, and to control the resulting, improvised configuration. The task, in this way, is to complete the task of the initial designer, involving planning of system configuration and of operating procedures for situations not included in the design. Consequently, manual operation of the normally functioning system will not adequately maintain and support the skills and knowledge for this task during rare circumstances.

The resulting situation has been characterized by plant operators as being continued boredom, punctuated by rare moments of sheer terror. To change this situation, it will be necessary not only to discuss training but more generally to ask: Who are the operators of future advanced systems? The task of future operators will require a new kind of training; their entire job content has to be reconsidered in order to maintain the competence needed during emergencies and to make work meaningful. This also implies that the organization of the operating staff must be reconsidered.

Typically, training of system operators and users is discussed and planned in isolation when systems have already been designed and built. This is most unfortunate. In a period of rapid technological change it is necessary to consider the design of user interfaces, planning of the organization of the operating staff, design of the job content of its members and, finally, the required training as integrated parts of an integrated system design. This can be very difficult because the time required to accept changes will be very different for the various institutions and organizations involved, such as equipment manufacturers, design teams, operating companies and workers' unions. These issues related to institutional policies will not be considered in the following sections.

WHAT TO TEACH FOR HIGH-TECH SYSTEMS?

The state of training initially given to operators for activities at the skill- and rule-based levels will be modified and updated during the normal task performance, as already mentioned in the previous sections, gradually turning a novice into an expert operator. The initial training at these levels of cognitive control is not different from the training developed for systems of more moderate size and complexity, except that special training simulators may be used to avoid the initial training on the operating plants. This kind of training will not be discussed in more detail here. Instead, focus will be on two training problems which are considered to be particularly important for future large-scale, complex systems. One aspect is related to the problem of avoiding degeneration of critical procedures with special safety constraints. The other aspect is training for knowledge-based disturbance control.

Teaching the bases of critical work procedures

An important consequence of the 'defence-in-depth' design philosophy, which is typically applied for modern, centralized systems, is that the system very often will not respond actively to single faults. Consequently, violation of safety preconditions during work on the system probably will not result in immediate functional response, and latent effects of erroneous acts can therefore be left in the system. When such errors are allowed to be present in a system over a longer period of time, the probability of coincidence of the multiple faults necessary for release of an accident is drastically increased.

The problem of violation of the preconditions for safe operation is increased by the fact that both individuals and organizations are continuously striving to optimize performance in terms of functionality, effort and economic pay-off. At the individual level, development of skill and know-how depends on experiments and opportunity for changes in work procedures. At the organizational level, survival in a competitive environment presupposes optimization of operation, rationalization of work procedures and modification of production processes and equipment. This optimization will be guided by more or less directly observable evidence.

In contrast, the limits of acceptable optimization, as they are defined by the preconditions for safe operation, are not directly visible when a system is based on the defence-in-depth principle. Correspondingly, analyses of industrial accidents typically indicate that pressure from functional or economic adaptation leads to a gradual erosion of the individual redundant safety preconditions until the time comes when violation of just one more precondition or a single component fault will release an accident. In a previous section it was argued that functional optimization of work procedures is an important prerequisite for development of expertise and know-how. Consequently, insistence that operators should learn and maintain without change the prescribed work instructions appears to be an unrealistic position. Instead, work conditions and training should be designed to support error detection and recovery.

A problem is caused, however, by the delay of the effect of control actions. Typically, operating procedures include a long sequence of simple actions, and error detection depending on the ultimate effect of the procedure will frequently be too late to be reversible. Effective error recovery, instead, will require that the operator be intimately familiar with the purposes and the intentions of the designer for the individual parts of a procedure, and that he or she be able to understand and monitor the functional response of the system all along the procedure execution. This implies a knowledge-based monitoring and analysis even during familiar, rule-based activity.

What kind of knowledge is necessary for this functional monitoring? What constitutes functional understanding? Physical systems are responding to changes and to human acts according to basic laws of nature. Their response can be explained or predicted by means of functional reasoning, serving to track a causal sequence of events through the system. However, system complexity frequently makes this approach impossible during real-life decision-making. Many technical systems such as control systems and information-processing systems are very complex and have no simple relationship between their basic physical processes and their function in the information domain. Therefore, predictions regarding their behaviour are more readily made when considering the intentions of the designer together with the present operating conditions. It is possible to understand the function of an automatic system from its purpose and general function irrespective of its physical implementation. Frequently, operators can be seen in verbal protocols to develop an explanation of system behaviour from a top-down 'redesign' of a reasonable functional structure from its supposed purpose, rather than to collect information on its actual, physical structure, that is understanding is based on reasoning top-down through ends–means relations with little or no consideration of the internal causal structures or functions. This is similar to judging the behaviour of people from their motives and present capabilities.

In consequence, the knowledge needed by system operators to avoid degeneration of the safety-related features of certain work procedures will include a general functional understanding of the technology applied for the system, together with an intimate familiarity with the intentions and reasons for the design of the system and the control procedures. In the design of procedures and control rooms much effort is spent on factual information and measured plant status data. It appears that more concern should be directed towards supplying the operators, by training and decision aids, with information on the reasons and intentions underlying system and procedure design.

At present, data bases for industrial control rooms and training courses for operators include only little information about the complex relationship between overall purposes and goals and the intentions behind the design at the lower levels of functions and equipment. This is so partly because such information is difficult to formalize, but also because it is only implicitly present in the form of company policies, design practices and system designers' subjective preferences, which do not find their way into drawings and technical manuals. When operators are provided with this kind of information, they will be able to develop the competence required by 'reflective experts' at the knowledge-based level even further.

Knowledge-based disturbance control

Planning of action at the knowledge-based level in its pure and systematic form is characteristic of work such as research and engineering design. Such activity is based on search and inference in a problem space of conceptual, frequently causal or means–end relations representing the functional properties of the work domain. These activities are typically supported by formal calculation or simulation tools. In modern complex systems, operators have to cope with disturbances and faults by reconfiguration of the components of the system, frequently while it is still operating, in order to protect plant and/ or production. If the particular situation has not been foreseen by the designer and the operating staff properly instructed, the task is, in fact, a supplement or continuation of a design task which could not be completed by the designers themselves. Consequently, it will require the same kind of knowledge-based behaviour as the design itself and unfortunately under much more difficult circumstances.

The basic problem in this situation is that, for modern, reliable systems, situations calling for actual knowledge-based reasoning will be infrequent and, therefore, the knowledge required to cope with them will degenerate during the adaptation to the work requirements, as discussed above. Another argument against the requirement that plant operators should be able to reason at abstract functional levels has been that this way of reasoning is unnatural for operators who normally think in terms of physical components and their behaviour. During major disturbances, operators are supposed to take over control. However, the task will not be to take over the usual automatic control. The plant will typically require the operating staff to redesign the plant configuration and operating procedures to meet the abnormal condition. For this task they have to understand the basic process. A keeping-the-man-in-the-loop philosophy will not solve the problem of the rare events, since normal operation will not support the required knowledge. For large-scale, high-risk installations, therefore, other solutions are necessary. It will be necessary to supply, at the surface of the system, an adequate representation of the internal process of the system, to arrange an education of operators reflecting the new requirements and to change the organization of work in order to provide operators with tasks between disturbances that will maintain their basic knowledge and supply the proper intuition at the conceptual level. This, however, does not necessarily imply that system operators should be taught the same theoretical knowledge that is found in engineering curricula. Engineering is a profession of design, of matching new equipment and its functions to new demands and purposes. Paradoxically, this is not what is generally taught in engineering schools. Instead, students are given tools and methods for analysis and optimization of systems that are already existing. 'Design' will be learned for a particular application domain after graduation, that is, 'on the job'.

On the other hand, if operators are supposed to identify the actual state of affairs in a complex system, for example based on thermodynamical processes, and they have to reconfigure the system and to control it during unfamiliar circumstances, they should necessarily be familiar with the processes and functions of the system. This familiarity should not only include the properties of components at the concrete level but also the abstract processes at a higher system related level. Large accidents normally involve disturbances of large energy processes depending on complex relationships (represented by water–steam phase diagrams, for instance), and operators have to understand such relationships and be able to select the means for control 'on-line' if they are supposed to improvise during emergencies. The problem appears to be that future operators will be required to have the same understanding of the fundamental processes of an industrial system as an engineer, but not the tools and methods for using that knowledge which are typically included in engineering curricula. The tools and methods would be rather those acquired from practical experience with system design and experimental work on such systems.

This background can be supplemented by formal training in accident management. A critical task is the diagnostic identification of the system state. Analyses of diagnostic performance in actual tasks have shown that several different strategies are useful for the task, depending on the performance criteria adopted to resolve resource–demand conflicts in the actual work situation (Rasmussen, 1986c). Experimental work (Rouse, 1982) has shown that diagnostic abilities can be improved by training based on flexible use of several basic strategies derived from generalized results of field studies. The flexibility of optimal knowledge-based performance depends upon the availability of alternative strategies and knowledge-based representations and upon development of subjective performance criteria which can guide the choice of strategy and representation (Rasmussen, 1984; Olsen and Andersen, 1986). Adequate instruction and training at the knowledge-based level have to provide the operator with alternatives and criteria for choice among them—and thereby foster a reflective expert.

CONCLUSION

Categorization of system users and operators in terms of novices and experts and description of the development of effective performance in terms of phases can be an appropriate description in case of rather stable work environments for which expertise can be characterized as the ultimate stage of skill acquisition. It is not, however, an adequate description of the development of the expertise required from actors and decision-makers in modern high-tech systems. In this case, expertise also includes the ability to 'know when you are no longer an expert', that is to be able to perceive when skill and intuition is no longer valid, and to shift to analytical reasoning and planning. Real expertise depends on flexibility in the use of several modes of cognitive control.

One important conclusion which can be suggested from this discussion is that future, centralized systems which offer potential for large-scale losses and damage in the case of failure and disturbances will require very special qualifications of the users and operators. The qualifications required by system designers and users with respect to the functional characteristics of the work content will be very similar. System designers must be very familiar with the future operational conditions of systems because decision support aids will normally be included in advanced interfaces. On the other hand, users and operators will have to be familiar with the intentions and reasons behind system design to be able to avoid degeneration of critical work procedures and to generate new procedures during unusual conditions. The discussion has been illustrated by requirements of modern industrial process systems, but it is important to stress that similar requirements will be posed also by systems in other domains. To take an example, the recent plunge of the Wall Street stock market has been attributed to uncritical use of automated market transactions—apparently more knowledge by system users about the design basis and intentions would have been an advantage (Waldrop, 1987).

In general, the understanding of the interaction between expert and novice performance in advanced systems is crucial for design of training schemes and it will be important to consider system design, organization of user and operating staff, and teaching/training facilities in one integrated approach.

REFERENCES

Adelson, B. (1984) When novices surpass experts: the difficulty of a task may increase with expertise. *Journal of Experimental Psychology: Learning, Memory, and Cognition*, **10**, 483–95.

Anderson, J. R. (1980) *Cognitive Psychology and Its Implications* (2nd revised ed. 1984). New York: Freeman and Company.

Anderson, J. R. (1983) *The Architecture of Cognition*. Cambridge, Mass.: Harvard University Press.

Ausubel, D. P., Novak, J. D., and Hanesian, H. (1978) *Educational Psychology*, New York: Holt, Rinehart and Winston.

Baddeley, A. D. (1976) *The Psychology of Memory*. New York: Harper and Row.

Bartlett, F. C. (1943) Fatigue following highly skilled work. *Proceedings of Royal Society of London*, **131**, 247–57.

Bonar, J., and Soloway, E. (1985). Preprogramming knowledge: a major source of misconceptions in novice programmers. *Human–Computer Interaction*, **1**, 133–61.

Caramazza, A., McCloskey, M., and Green, B. (1981) Naive beliefs in 'sophisticated' subjects: misconceptions about trajectories of objects. *Cognition*, **9**, 117–23.

Chase, W. G., and Simon, H. A. (1973) Perception in chess. *Cognitive Psychology*, **4**, 55–81.

Chi, M. T. H., Feltovich, P. J., and Glaser, R. (1981) Categorization and representation of physics problems by experts and novices. *Cognitive Science*, **5**, 121–52.

Clement, J. (1982) Students' preconceptions in introductory mechanics. *American Journal of Physics*, **50**, 66–71.

de Groot, A. D. (1965) *Thought and Choice in Chess*. The Hague: Mouton.

diSessa, A. A. (1983) Phenomenology and the evolution of intuition. In D. Gentner and A. L. Stevens (eds.), *Mental Models*. Hillsdale, N. J.: Lawrence Erlbaum.

Dreyfus, S. E., and Dreyfus, H. L. (1980) *A Five-Stage Model of the Mental Activities Involved in Directed Skill Acquisition*. Operations Research Center, ORC-80-2. Berkeley: University of California.

Dreyfus, S. E., and Dreyfus, H. L. (1986) *Mind Over Machine*. Oxford: Basil Blackwell.

Fitts, P. M., and Posner, M. I. (1962) *Human Performance*. Monterey, Calif.: Brooks/ Cole Publishing Co.

Goodstein, L. P., Andersen, H. B., and Olsen, S. E. (eds.) (1988) *Tasks, Errors and Mental Models*. London: Taylor and Francis.

Hammond, K. R., Hamm, R. M., Grassia, J., and Pearson, T. (1987) Direct comparison of the efficacy of intuitive and analytical cognition in expert judgement. *IEEE Trans. Systems, Man, and Cybernetics*, **SMC-17**, 753–70.

Kolodner, J. L. (1983) Towards an understanding of the role of experience in the evolution from novice to expert. *International Journal of Man–Machine Studies*, **19**, 497–518.

Larkin, J. L., McDermott, J., Simon, D. P., and Simon, H. A. (1980) Expert and novice performance in solving physics problems. *Science*, **208**, 1335–42.

Lesgold, A. M. (1984) Acquiring expertise. In J. R. Anderson and S. M. Kosslyn (eds.), *Tutorials in Learning and Memory*. New York: Freeman.

Moray, N. (1987) Intelligent aids, mental models, and the theory of machine. *International Journal of Man–Machine Systems* (in press).

Murphy, G. L., and D. L. Medin (1985) The role of theories in conceptual coherence. *Psychological Review*, **92**, 289–316.

Murphy, G. L., and Wright, J. C. (1984) Changes in conceptual structure with expertise: differences between real-world experts and novices. *Journal of Experimental Psychology: Learning, Memory, and Cognition*, **10**, 144–55.

Olsen, S. E., and Andersen, H. B. (1986) On the use of metacognition in problem solving and in interpretation of protocols. In H.-P. Willumeit (ed.), *Human Decision Making and Manual Control*. Amsterdam: Elsevier Science Publishers.

Rasmussen, J. R. (1984) Strategies for state identification and diagnosis in supervisory control tasks, and design of computer-based support systems. *Advances in Man–Machine Systems Research*, **1**, 139–93.

Rasmussen, J. (1986a) A framework for cognitive task analysis in systems design. In E. Hollnagel, G. Mancini and D. Woods (eds.), *Intelligent Decision Support in Process Environments*, Heidelberg: Springer Verlag.

Rasmussen, J. (1986b) A cognitive engineering approach to the modelling of decision making and its organization in process control, emergency management, CAD/CAM, office systems, library systems. Risø-M-2589, 105 pp. Also in W. B. Rouse (ed.), *Advances in Man–Machine System Research*, Vol. 4, JAI Press (1988).

Rasmussen, J. (1986c) *Information Processing and Human–Machine Interaction: an Approach to Cognitive Engineering*. North Holland, 1986.

Rasmussen, J. R., and Jensen, A. (1973) A study of mental procedures in electronic trouble shooting. DAEC Research Establishment Risø, Risø-M-1582.

Rasmussen, J. R., and Jensen, A. (1974) Mental procedures in real-life tasks: a case study of electronic trouble shooting. *Ergonomics*, **17**, 293–307.

Rouse, W. B. (1982) A mixed-fidelity approach to technical training. *Journal of Educational Technology Systems*, **11**(2), 103–15.

Schoenfeld, A. H., and Herrmann, D. J. (1982) Problem perception and knowledge structure in expert and novice mathematical problem solvers. *Journal of Experimental Psychology: Learning, Memory, and Cognition*, **8**, 484–94.

Simon, D. P., and Simon, H. A. (1978) Individual differences in solving physics problems. In R. Siegler (ed.), *Children's Thinking: What Develops?* Hillsdale, N.J.: Lawrence Erlbaum.

Voss, J. F., Tyler, S. W., and Yengo, L. A. (1985) Individual differences in the solving of social science problems. In R. F. Dillon and R. R. Schmeck (eds.), *Individual Differences in Cognition*. New York: Academic Press.

Voss, J. F., Greene, T. R., Post, T. A., and Penner, B. C. (1984) Problem solving skill in the social sciences. In G. H. Bower (ed.), *The Psychology of Learning and Motivation*, Vol. 18. New York: Academic Press.

Vygotsky, L. S. (1962) *Thought and Language*. Cambridge, Mass.: MIT Press.

Waldrop, M. M. (1987) Computers amplify Black Monday. *Science*, **238**, 602–4.

Welford, A. T. (1968) *Fundamentals of Skill*. London: Methuen.

White, B. Y. (1983) Sources of difficulty in understanding Newtonian dynamics. *Cognitive Science*, **7**, 41–65.

2. Cognitive Skills at Work

Jacques Leplat

SUMMARY

Working situations make a particularly approppriate field for the study of cognitive skills. The nature and properties of these skills will be outlined. Some research perspectives within which the mechanisms of skill acquisition have been studied will be indicated; they also allow us to understand the phenomena of skill degradation. The final part considers the problem of complex skills, their constitution and what principles can help us to analyse them.

INTRODUCTION

It is not surprising that one turns to working situations when one studies cognitive skills, if one considers that their acquisition requires long experience. At the beginning of an article on this topic, Anderson (1982) writes that it requires 'at least 100 hours of learning and practice to acquire any significant cognitive skill to a reasonable degree of proficiency'. For instance, after 100 hours a student learning to program a computer has achieved only a very modest facility in the skill (p. 369). In working situations, one appropriately finds skills that result from practice over periods of various lengths, often periods considerably longer than those one can find in the longest laboratory experiments. Competitive sports and games offer the same types of examples. One can also note that the first reported systematic study on 'the acquisition of speed skill', frequently cited since, is of practical work in cigar manufacture, in which Crossman (1959) gives the times for a short cycle of activity and up to 40 000 repetitions: execution time is still continuing to reduce at the end of this period. Specialists in work organization who are concerned with predicting this decrease in manufacturing time have studied this phenomenon and proposed models of it (Eugene, 1961).

Developing Skills with Information Technology
Edited by Lisanne Bainbridge and S. Antonio Ruiz Quintanilla
© 1989 John Wiley & Sons Ltd

The space available for this paper means that we can discuss only some of the many aspects of the general theme of this chapter. We will start with problems of definition and then underline some characteristics of cognitive skill. We then look at the important features of the acquisition and degradation of cognitive skills. Finally, we will discuss the problem of analysis and identification of skills.

SOME PROBLEMS OF DEFINITION

The notion of 'skill' has a long history in psychology in English-speaking countries. One cannot mention it without referring to Barlett (for example, 1943), who has demonstrated the interest in it during the 1940s, and then to Welford who began to analyse its nature. The classic texts by these authors and several others can be found in the collection edited by Legge (1970).

We can take as our point of departure this very general definition: a skill is the possibility acquired by an individual of executing a class of tasks at a raised level of efficiency. Landa (1983) defines skill as the ability to 'apply' knowledge, which manifests itself in special 'actions' on knowledge and/or its objects. The distinction between knowledge and skill is similar to Gagne's distinction between 'verbal information and intellectual skill' and to Merril's distinction between the 'remember' level and the 'use' level (Reigeluth, 1983). The first research on skill had been concerned with the sensorimotor domain, and the expression 'sensorimotor skill' had become so common that they seemed indissociable. However, as early as 1958, Welford had noted that 'all activity which expresses a skill is mental in the sense that it demands knowledge and judgement, and all skills imply some manifest activity of co-ordination, by the hands, the organs of speech or other effectors' (p. 22). Welford also defined the distinctive features of skill:

> In manual skills, the manifest actions clearly make up an essential part of the activity: in mental skills (we now say 'cognitive') the manifest activity plays a more incidental role, often serving to give expression to a skill of which it makes an essential part. The manifest actions can thus vary within very wide limits without destroying the nature of the underlying skill (p. 22).

The last remark suggests that the passage from an observable activity to the underlying skill is never simple and itself constitutes a problem. It underlines the hypothetical nature of skill: one does not observe a skill, only its manifestations. This is even more true for cognitive skills.

The concept of skill is close to some neighbouring and more or less synonymous concepts, of capacity, competence and expertise (de Montmollin, 1986). It is rare for an author to appeal to one of these concepts without evoking at least one of the others. These concepts have made another concept fall into disuse which is one of their forebears, that of habit, which earlier authors (Ravaisson, 1838; Guillaume, 1947) defined as a 'manner of being which is acquired'. We would now call by the name 'acquisition of skill' the chief content of the excellent book by Guillaume on the 'formation of habits'.

The notion of expertise is often put forward to indicate complex cognitive skills. Its use has been extended by the development of expert systems, in which it is often essential to know the relationship with human expertise.

The links between skill and automatic behaviour are of another type. 'Automatism' refers to a mode of cognitive function that is distinct from the 'controlled' mode. Skill is defined as the capacity to execute a class of tasks, and it can include the two modes of functioning in varying proportions at successive moments of its acquisition. One can say that skill is built up thanks to the automatization of components of the activity. This point of view is defended by Shiffrin and Dumais (1981) who write:

> Automated processing will develop as skill acquisition proceeds . . . . We think automatization is a major component of the acquisition of skill in both the cognitive and motor domains . . . . Separating skilled performance into automatic and controlled components is surely a difficult and delicate matter (p. 139).

The links between skill and automatism (and also the differentiation of types of automatism) is an object of study in the sensorimotor domain. Pailhous (1987) who talks of cognitive modulation of sensorimotor activity writes 'while it is true that man has the possibility of directing cognitively his sensory-motor activities, very often he is content to influence the automatic synergies without modifying their fundamental properties (structural invariants)' (p. 3). It is still necessary to examine the extent to which cognitive automatisms and sensorimotor automatisms can be aligned and exploited as analogies.

Characteristic features of skill

We will outline the chief features of skill, of which some will be discussed in more detail below.

Skills are 'learned'

They are acquired by practice and their processes of acquisition should be analysed to understand their nature. Writings on cognitive skill insistently underline the role of practice. Newell and Rosenbloom (1981) begin the first chapter of a book on cognitive skill by declaring that 'almost always, practice brings improvement and more practice brings more improvement' and they remark that even laboratory experiments involve a certain amount of practice and must take account of the effect of practice. The same writers note that the first edition of Woodworth's book includes a chapter titled 'practice and skill' in which it is said that 'there is no essential difference between practice and learning except that the practice experiment takes longer' (p. 156). If practice or prolonged training arouse great interest in cognitive psychology, this is because it appears that acquisition continues even after numerous repetitions of the same task. This is true not only for sensorimotor activities but also for predominantly cognitive activities, which makes these authors speak of a ubiquitous law of practice.

Skills consist of 'coordinated units' with the aim of attaining a goal

The hierarchical character of skills has often been underlined: 'skills are building bricks which are put together to generate more complex skills' (Singleton, 1978, p. 10). Bruner (1970) has often insisted on the 'modular' character of skills. Fischer (1980), in giving to the concept of skill a sense related to that of schema, has proposed a theory of cognitive development called 'skill theory' in which he defined 'the control and construction of hierarchies of skills'.

The hierarchical character of skills does not imply that the constituent units are unchanged when they are integrated into a skill of a higher order. When skill has been acquired at a higher level, it is usually difficult to extract the initial constituents to make them the elements of another skill. These initial constituents have been transformed by their integration and have to some extent lost their individuality.

Skills are 'goal-directed'

They are organized with a view to an end and are therefore intimately linked to the notion of a procedure. Skills can also be defined as what is often called *savoir-faire*, that is to say using knowledge with the aim of realizing a goal or, which is equivalent, the execution of a task.

Skills must rightly be considered relative to a task: one is 'skilled at . . .' or for something, and all skills are also defined by the class of tasks that they make it possible to accomplish. In his theory, Fischer (1980) frequently emphasizes this point. The literature in industrial psychology is rich in descriptions of skills as a function of the task: skills of diagnosis, of fault detection, of control of such and such a process, etc. . . .

Skills are 'adaptive'

This adaptive character of sensorimotor skills has often been noted. For example, Saltzman and Scott Kelso (1987) consider it one of the essential features of skill in this domain: 'the fact that skilled movements show a flexibility specific to the task, in the realisation of the goals of the task' (p. 85). If there is a disturbance during execution, these authors note, and on condition that it is not too large, that subjects can compensate for it by organizing their behaviour in such a way that the goal continues to be attained. In more cognitive domains, this adaptive character often appears in descriptions of expertise. Expert subjects know how to deal with situations which they have not previously encountered, they know how to use their knowledge in an original way and they also know how to find alternative activities which allow them to attain the goal originally set when the habitual methods are not available. In this sense, skill is not defined solely by the operations used, but also by the class of tasks that makes it possible to deal with and that is not always easy to define.

Effects of practice and properties of skill

To define the effects of practice is also to identify the properties of skill and to define the criteria by which one can recognize the transformations that they introduce into activity.

Increase in speed of execution

From the detailed examination of the effects of prolonged practice (several hundred or even thousands of trials) on twelve tasks of very diverse types, Newell and Rosenbloom (1981) conclude that:

1. The execution time T of a trial n is a strong function of the number N of trials:

$$T = T(0) + BN^{-\alpha}$$

which is often written in a logarithmic form because the relation then becomes linear:

$$\log[T - T(0)] = \log B - \alpha \log N$$

$T(0)$ is the asymptotic execution time; $T(0) + B$ the time of execution of the first trial. Alpha represents the rate of learning and the slope of the line on a log–log graph. 'The value of alpha is almost always in the interval (0–1)' (Anderson, 1981, p. 398) in the known studies.
2. 'The same law is general for all types of mental behaviour . . .' (p. 34).

Speed has always been considered as a special mark of skill. In the industrial context of repetitive tasks, speed has always been spoken of as skill.

Improvement in stability

This stability is a consequence of the preceding 'law of practice' which shows that the effect of training becomes weaker and weaker with practice, that is to say the rate of training becomes more and more reduced with practice, the variations in absolute time become smaller and smaller. This stability which accrues to execution time is true for a range of tasks when the activity is exercised under the usual conditions. The appearance of some excessive variability is therefore a sign that the external or internal (to the subject) conditions have changed. Abruzzi (1952) has proposed statistical procedures derived from those used in quality control to identify these differences and has interpreted them for industrial tasks.

Improvement of availability

When a skill is acquired the corresponding activity can be brought into use more rapidly. Everything happens as if the essential aspects of the procedure have been thoroughly interiorized, the conditions of execution are well known and quickly identified, and the actions to be done are determined without hesitation.

Reduction in costs

Ravaisson was already noting in 1838 that 'by repeated or prolonged exercise, we learn to allocate the quantity of effort and choose the point of application for it which conforms to the end that we wish to attain: and at the same time the consciousness of effort disappears' (p. 35). In industrial psychology, the notion of mental load is often evoked to characterize activities with a strong cognitive component. In cognitive psychology, too, one speaks of cognitive cost, of mental effort, of human resources (Navon and Gopher, 1980; Wickens, 1984). It is useful to introduce here the notion of efficiency and to distinguish it from that of efficacy. An activity will be said to be more efficient if it makes it possible to attain with less cost the same level of efficacy. Skill can be interpreted as both efficacy and improved efficiency.

Evaluating this cost remains a complex problem which has been approached by diverse methods (psychophysiological indicators, double task methods, subjective load, etc). It seems that acquired skill reduces the cost, in identical execution conditions. We will have to examine further the mechanisms of this reduction, which appear notably in the possibility of greater and greater freedom to execute a second task and in increasing resistance to stress.

Negative effects

The preceding criteria, which are not exhaustive, consist in general of qualities that have been researched: equally they are the signs of efficacy of skills obtained by practice. However, these qualities have a reverse which can lead to perverse effects, particularly when the task which the operator must deal with is outside the domain of tasks for which the skill has been acquired. Therefore, if conditions change during the course of execution, the speed of execution can make it difficult to stop at the due time. The price paid for stability can be a certain rigidity in the mode of execution. The improved availability of actions can, on its part, lead to the premature release of actions on the basis of minimal evidence, without relation to modified conditions which required another type of response. Reason (1987) has well described the negative effects of this availability on reasoning according to rules:

> The most likely effect of the availability heuristic in rule matching is to bias the problem solver in favour of rules that spring quickly to mind, even though they may not always be relevant or applicable. In short, there will be a 'first come, best preferred' bias at work (p. 75).

The resulting reduced cost of skills can itself lead to inconvenience; subjects who are less mobilized become more sensitive to distractions (Berlyne, 1960) and their reduced vigilance renders them less apt to respond correctly and with an acceptable level of delay to unanticipated urgent situations.

One can recognize in some of these negative effects the sources of a type of error designated by Norman (1981) and by Reason and Mycielska (1982) by the name of 'slip'. These are the errors that arise when the operators choose a correct goal for their action, but do not take into account the conditions for realization of this goal—which are not the usual conditions: they envisage the correct goal, but do not do what is necessary to attain it. A typical category of these slips is 'capture errors' which arise from the fact that a habitual activity is substituted for a new activity that has some relationship to it (finding oneself on the way to one's office when one ought to be going to an appointment somewhere else). Many categories of slips described by Norman (1981) make good illustrations of these negative effects of skill.

ACQUISITION AND DEGRADATION OF SKILLS

The role of repetition is important in the acquisition of skill, but Guillaume (1947) was already pointing out the 'equivocal nature' of this notion of repetition. 'There is a contradiction between the idea of "repetition", in the rigorous sense of repetition of the same act, and the idea of "acquisition" of a new mode of action. If one always repeats the "same" act, there is no possibility of change; one would learn nothing new' (pp. 18, 19). In fact, what remains identical is the task to be done, while the activity initiated to do it can vary considerably. It is therefore essential to indicate the relatipns between these transformations in the activity and the properties described in the previous pages. This is the purpose of the present section.

The mechanisms for acquisition of skills

The study of these mechanisms has always been an important theme in psychology (cf., for example, Bilodeau, 1966). It has been approached from various levels and within various theoretical frameworks, but in the early period dealt mainly with perceptual-motor skills. These studies show that skills build up progressively and that the characteristics of skills vary during this progression, as witnessed by the correlation between a criterion for execution of the task studied and the criteria for execution of other tasks representative of other skills. Studying 'the differential effects of training and their implications', Perruchet (1985) puts forward as a general phenomenon the fact that 'the correlations between two tasks can, depending on the particular case, decrease or increase in a progressive and systematic fashion during the repetitive execution of one of them' (p. 136). While noting the interest of correlational methods as 'tools for developing our knowledge of the transformations which intervene in the course of some given training' (p. 142), he also notes that the existence of varying activities 'leads to ambiguities in the interpretation of the data which are difficult to remove' (*op. cit.*) and he concludes that 'taking account of these difficulties, all inferences made from correlational data and formulated in terms of processes can only make a hypothesis generating step, guided by theoretical developments in general psychology' (*op. cit.*).

It is to these developments that recent experimental studies of the acquisition of cognitive skills, which aim to define the cognitive functions needed to account for the evolution of observable performance during training, are linked. We will only note some essential features here. The studies by Anderson (1982, 1983) and his group are among the most systematic and the most ambitious: they belong within the perspective of studies on information processing, and are supported by many experiments. They also have the merit of trying to show the relation to older studies, and to propose an interpretative framework with the potential of accounting for a large number of studies. The cognitive system is seen by Anderson as a set of production rules (of the type 'if . . . then . . .') which utilize the facts contained in a declarative data base. The process of acquisition consists of two essential stages: 'a "declarative stage" in which facts about the skill domain are interpreted, and a "procedural stage" in which the domain knowledge is directly embodied in procedures for performing the skill' (Anderson, 1982, p. 369).

1. *The declarative phase.* During the 'declarative phase' the knowledge is translated into rules which make it possible to control the first attempts and the task to be done. This phase is usually obligatory because the instructions rarely prescribe a procedure compatible with the actual skill of the subject. 'One of the reasons why instruction is often so inadequate is that the teacher likewise has a poor conception of the flow of control in the student' (p. 380). Anderson describes the mechanism of this 'interpretation' by which initial knowledge passes into rules of execution.

   The gradual process of transition from the declarative phase to the procedural phase is called the 'compilation' of knowledge. Anderson distinguishes two important subprocesses in this compilation:

   (a) The first, called 'composition', consists of condensing the rules and the stages.

   For example, if the pressure passes the tolerance limit, then the process enters a critical zone which is not dealt with by the automatic devices. If one enters such a zone, then take over manual control.

   With practice, these two rules are composed into one: if the pressure passes the tolerance limit, then take over manual control.

   This process is not without similarities to that of 'chunking'.

   (b) The second process is called 'proceduralization' and consists of specifying the instructions. For example, the last rule above becomes, in a particular context: if the pressure passes 4 bars, press the button 'manual'.

   'An important consequence of proceduralisation is that it reduces the load on working memory, in that the long-term information need no longer be held in working memory' (p. 383). Anderson also shows how a too-rapid compilation phase can lead to errors which are no longer perceived by the subject ('slip' errors; Norman 1981).

2. *The procedural phase.* When the production rules have been transformed by the process of compilation, other types of progress can follow. We know that with experience methods of execution change; the rules can be used differently. Exploration of the task space can be made in a more organized and more selective way, leading to more rapid success. Three mechanisms are invoked for this process of adjustment (tuning) of the skill: 'A generalisation process by which production rules become broader in their range of applicability, a discrimination process by which the rules become narrower and a strengthening process by which better rules are strengthened and poorer rules become weaker' (p. 390). The author shows that the mechanisms in these different phases can be formalized in a model that leads to the law of practice which he has shown applies to a wide range of skills (cf. above).

This presentation of the two phases in terms of knowledge must not lead us to forget that the evolution thus described is correlated with an interiorization of the procedures. It is by this progressive interiorization that the evolution becomes possible. Inversely, the conversion of procedural knowledge into 'effective procedures' is not direct, and can pose difficulties, as shown by the execution of instructions: 'these difficulties also illustrate the necessity of making use of knowledge which is not explicit in the instructions, in order to work according to them' (George, 1983, ch. IV).

Another line of research concerned with skill acquisition is that opened and developed by Shiffrin, Schneider and their group. Their initial work (1977) showed the existence of two types of information processing: 'automatic processing' and 'controlled processing'. We will limit ourselves here to mentioning the essential features of these two modes of processing, of which the importance varies during the acquisition of a skill. We will borrow a summary from the authors (Shiffrin and Schneider, 1984):

> ... Automatic processing is generally a fast parallel, fairly effortless process, that is not limited by short-term memory capacity, is not under direct subject control, and performs well-developed skilled behaviours. It typically develops when subjects process in a consistent fashion over many trials, and it is difficult to suppress, modify or ignore once learned. 'Controlled processing' is often slow, generally serial, effortful, capacity limited, subject regulated, and is used to deal with novel or inconsistent information. It is needed in situations where the responses required to stimuli vary from one trial or situation to the next, and is easily modified, suppressed or ignored, at the desire of the subject (p. 269).

These authors add (which is particularly important for understanding the nature of complex skills) that 'finally, all tasks are carried out by complex mixtures of controlled and automatic processes, used in combination' (p. 269). Shiffrin and Dumais (1981) were already insisting on this idea that 'many processes will have pronounced automatic components along with some controlled components' (p. 117) and they cite in particular the case of processes initiated by controlled processing which are then followed through automatically. One can go home to fetch a forgotten object and then start a series of automatic processes (go up the stairs, unlock the door, etc.), but as the authors remark, it is frequently difficult to distinguish the two types of processing within a given action. The authors who enumerate these and other characteristics often emphasize that they are to be taken as tendencies and that research needs to be done to make them more precise.

The two strains of research which have just been mentioned also propose several mechanisms with the potential of accounting for the acquisition of skill, and it is not always easy to distinguish their respective effects, as has been shown by a recent controversy between Schneider and Shiffrin (1985) and Cheng (1985). The latter, criticizing the conclusions that the former draw from their experiments, declares that 'the improvement in performance can be explained in other ways. In particular it can be due to a restructuring of the task components so that they are co-ordinated, integrated or reorganised into new perceptual, cognitive and motor units' (p. 414). The outcome of this controversy, which must remain unresolved here, is that the process of acquisition involves several mechanisms which are not mutually exclusive and which it is difficult to isolate. It is therefore dangerous to try to attribute all the stated effects to one of them. 'Automaticity and restructuring are not mutually exclusive (processes can conceivably be both restructured and automatized)' (Cheng, 1985, p. 415). If experiments show that the hypothesis of categorization (or of restructuring) is correct, they also show that 'it and several related hypotheses are insufficient to explain a number of key findings' (Schneider and Shiffrin, 1985, p. 424).

Summary on the nature of skill

In the light of the preceding theoretical papers, which bear on simple and well-controlled tasks, one can try better to define the nature of the cognitive skills corresponding to the more complex tasks met in work. One can first note that skill has its degrees, corresponding to the stages of acquisition, and that this acquisition continues over very long periods. The changes that underpin this acquisition are at several levels, as Shiffrin and Dumais (1981) point out. They can concern knowledge of the data base: this can be enriched and restructured. Changes also take place in controlled processing, and Anderson's theory gives us several mechanisms which intervene here: composition, proceduralization, development of strategies or heuristics for elaborating paths in the problem space more efficiently. Finally, important changes can be imputed to the automatization of certain parts of the activity. This automatization reduces the workload—or if one prefers, the cognitive cost—releases processing capacity and can allow acquisition of other parts of the activity. 'We think automatization is a major component of skill acquisition in both the cognitive and motor domains, and suggest that this factor be given prominent attention in research in this domain' (Shiffrin and Dumais, 1981, p. 138).

The skill acquired in a complex task is thus an organization in which several mechanisms intervene, of which analysis attempts to sort out their role and interactions. One can consider that automatization allows the field of control to expand, and that inversely this expansion facilitates automatization. The characteristics of the external environment, in particular its stability, also constitute without doubt a major element in the organization of skill at different moments.

The degradation of skill

One characteristic of numerous skills acquired in working conditions is that they can be exercised over a very long time in relatively stable conditions. Inconveniences can result from this, which are linked both to what are properly called degradations in skills in the sense that these become less apt for responding to some of the task demands and also to the obstacle that this skill can become in the acquisition of other skills.

Narrowing of the field of a skill

When the class of tasks to be dealt with is restricted, the subject can become extremely facile at executing the current tasks, but remains less able to deal with unusual tasks. This leads the subject to extend inappropriately to all tasks the class of skill acquired for one subclass. One has here a characteristic of the routine (in the classic sense of the word) and a trait frequently shown by older people (Welford, 1964; Belbin and Belbin, 1969), which consists of applying known procedures to a new task which actually requires an original precedure.

This narrowing of the field of skill can be thought of as the counterpart of the mechanisms necessary to its development. This, which has frequently been described under the title of the loss of the cognitive motivation for a skill (the subject no longer knows how to justify the method), could result from the loss of the declarative representation which has been made unnecessary by proceduralization (Anderson, 1981, p. 383). For example, the subject has good procedures for dealing with classic breakdowns, but has forgotten the properties of the equipment that would allow them to deal with other faults.

This will frequently be the case when the skill becomes enclosed, that is to say, when it is not a means to acquiring skills at a higher level. In these conditions the skill becomes automatic; it tends to become rigid and to lose its adaptive character. This can also lead to disturbing effects such as the accidental release of automatic action in circumstances in which it is not relevant, on the simple appearance of a signal that has a family resemblance to the usual signal (Teiger, 1980).

Teiger *et al.* (1977) have given some typical examples of this 'persistence of automatisations acquired during the task' in telephone exchange operators.

> Certain situations of everyday life, as far as these have some similarity with the working situation, automatically release the stereotyped behaviour imposed by the professional activity. . . . It is for this reason that the operators often surprise themselves by replying 'hello' instead of 'what' in the most varied situations, at meals, or in the grocers or the hairdressers . . . (pp. 65–6).

Another example is: '. . . the most often is the sound made before the doors close on the Metro, which leads some operators to the response acquired to the sound announcing a call: "Good morning, can I help you?", which never fails to surprise the other travellers' (p. 66). The authors note that 'these events are more frequent the more distant the last rest period' (p. 67).

It is to avoid this narrowing and these negative consequences in situations in which safety is important that operators who usually work repeatedly on the same tasks are periodically retrained to deal with incidents in a simulator. By this means one attempts to keep readily accessible the declarative knowledge or the safety procedures which lead them to treat correctly and quickly the exceptional incidents that can occur in their work.

Reduction in the possibilities for acquisition

This form of degradation is linked to the preceding one: subjects who have acquired and for a long time used one skill for a class of tasks are more likely to assimilate a new task to this known class and apply the corresponding procedure to it, than to search for a new, more adequate procedure. Belbin and Belbin (1969), as the outcome of research on ageing workers, note that 'long continuous experience in a limited field can lead to a rigidity of spirit which makes it difficult to eliminate not only habits but also the attitudes which have been acquired during the previous work' (p. 69).

From no longer having recourse to the declarative data base from which the long-practised skills have been elaborated, this becomes less accessible and impoverished: it is thus more and more difficult and costly to refer to it to enlarge the field of a skill or to acquire a new one.

'Overlearning' acquired in a limited and unique domain thus becomes a handicap in the acquisition of new learning. A sociologist has rightly remarked that: 'The non use of cognitive structures by a manual worker is as mutilating as expenditure of excessive energy' (Mothe, 1976, p. 27). To combat this rigidity of skill, which imposes a brake on the acquisition of new skills, it is therefore important to avoid the overspecialization of operators and to place them in varied conditions which lead them to use their knowledge in an extended and diverse field and to build up an enlarged and more adaptive skill.

THE ANALYSIS OF COMPLEX COGNITIVE SKILLS

We will define as complex those skills that require prolonged training and preparatory skills already acquired: working situations offer many examples. The analysis of skills for more specifically cognitive tasks has been the object of numerous studies, of which many have been brought together by Singleton (1978, 1979). These analyses, which arise from diverse theoretical frameworks, have made use of equally diverse methods: observation in the work-place, interview, questionnaire, simulation, experimentation, etc.

The practical interest of such analyses has often been the driving force for their development: in effect they are the necessary preliminary for the design of training and ergonomics actions. The studies in English-speaking countries grouped under the title of 'skill analysis' correspond in general to those that have been classified in France under the name of 'psychological analysis of work': they are all concerned with analysing the activities used to respond to task demands in work situations (Leplat and Cuny, 1984). In the last few years, with the development of expert systems and to contribute to their design, analyses of more specifically cognitive tasks have developed, under the name of knowledge elicitation (Leplat, 1985). These analyses are usually the responsibility of specialist 'cognitive scientists' who have often been inspired by the methods of task analysis.

In this final section we will examine how complex skills are developed and how this development can be guided. We will indicate some frameworks proposed for this analysis and finally we will consider the relations between cognitive skill and some notions that may facilitate this analysis.

The development of complex skills

We have already noted the hierarchical character of skills, and Bruner (1970) among others has often insisted on this character in his studies of sensori-motor skills: one must also say this about cognitive skills. He underlined the modular character of skill and described the elaboration of skill as the incorporation of previously acquired units into a larger unit which itself ultimately becomes an elementary unit of a superior unit.

This incorporation requires that the elementary unit has become a skill. 'I believe that it is a question of attentional capacity' (p. 71) he writes, by which he means to say that it is when the cognitive load represented by a unit becomes sufficiently small that this higher-order integration of skill can be made. 'Once the attention is freed, then a new pattern emerges' (p. 71). The skilled components are 'controlled and evaluated as a function of their adjustment to the goal of a skill of a higher order. Thus, an action on a larger scale, with a more extended goal, takes over control of the actions constitut-ing the new module' (p. 66).

Leontiev (1972) has described this same process as 'the metamorphosis of actions, by knowing their transformation into operations' (p. 95). By 'actions' he means 'a process subordinated to the result which must be attained, that is to say a process subordinate to a conscious goal' (p. 118). An 'operation' consists of the content of an action without identifying it with a goal. 'One and the same action can be realised by means of different operations' (p. 295), operations that can eventually be entrusted to an automatic mechanism. The process of transformation from action to operation illuminates the elaboration of skill. 'Every operation results from a transformation of an action, coming from its incorporation in another action and it's following automatisation' (Leontiev, 1975, p. 119). We can give here the example of car driving suggested by Leontiev (1975), which clearly illustrates this transformation:

> At first, each operation—for example using the clutch—is formed as an action precisely subordinate to this goal and having its conscious "orienting foundation" (Galperine). Later, this action becomes part of another action with a complex operational form—for example the action of changing gear in the car. From now on, the action of using the clutch becomes one of the means of executing the action of changing gear, an operation which realises that aim, and it ceases to be carried out like a process oriented towards a more local goal. Its goal is no longer distinct. . . . the action of using the clutch seems to be no longer completely conscious. He (the driver) does other things: he starts the motor, goes up hills, . . . stops the car, etc. (p. 119).

It is within the framework of this theory that Galperine (1966) and his school have described 'training by stages in the actions and concepts' and defined the laws of this formation. A large place has been given to the notion of a ramifying system of representations of an action and of its conditions of execution (see also Leplat and Pailhous, 1976; Savoyant, 1978).

Rasmussen (1986) has proposed a scheme of analysis allowing one to determine the modes of level of control involved in the exercise of a skill (in the sense that we have given to this word, and not in that which he himself adopts for 'skill'). This schema defines a certain number of stages in the treatment of information: activation, observation, identification, interpretation, evaluation, definition of the task, definition of the procedure, execution. In knowledge-based behaviour, the situation must be interpreted, the goal evaluated, and this often demands that all the stages are exercised. In rule-based activity, it is only necessary to identify the situation; the execution follows directly from this identification ('if this state, then that action'). In automated behaviour, the simple observation releases the response for execution. Each of these levels of control is associated with types of error, which inversely can aid in identifying the levels. To mention only some brief examples, errors in the goal generally reflect a fault in control at the first (knowledge-based) level, errors of omission of a condition to functioning at the second level and 'slip' errors to functioning at the third level (Reason, 1987).

The hierarchical conception of skills proposed by Gagne (1970) rests on a different principle, on knowing that there are hierarchical relations between eight types of learning used in the acquisition of skills: learning of the signals, the stimulus–response relations, sequences, verbal associations, discriminations, concepts, rules and problem-solving. Learning of one type demands that learning of another type has previously been realized (pp. 65 nn). For example, learning a rule requires prior learning of the concepts that it uses. There is therefore a 'learning hierarchy' which one must try to define when one must teach a task. 'A learning hierarchy identifies a set of intellectual skills that are ordered in a manner indicating the substantial amounts of positive transfer from those skills of lower position to connected ones of higher position' (p. 329). In such a hierarchy, 'the basic functional unit consists of a "pair" of intellectual skills, one subordinate to the other'. The subordinate skill constitutes the prerequisite of the other, and its learning improves that transfer. Gagne has given examples of the hierarchical structure of skill in several domains and has tested their validity. This notion of hierarchization as applied to training has been the object of criticism. The progressive integration of subordinate units is not always so simple. Lewis and Pask (1965) have emphasized that training of superordinate elements must begin before training at a high level of the subordinate units. Bisseret and Enard (1970) on their part show that the subject must be able to access the different levels of the hierarchy very easily. They propose that at different moments in the acquisition of a complex skill (air-traffic control) these interactions between levels may be facilitated. Their method was appropriately called 'training by constant interaction of programmed units'.

Here is an example give by these authors (Bisseret and Enard, 1970):

> The process of 'editing flight strips' has as an associated process 'the detection and resolution of conflicts [between aircraft]'. In the programme dedicated to training for 'editing flight strips', one finds tasks/responses which include the detection and resolution of conflicts although the student has not yet learned about them: the student will therefore have to be entirely guided in order to do them, the proper 'editing' tasks being themselves less and less guided (p. 643).

In this way, the subject is also motivated by the meaning that they can give to learning the elementary units.

A hierarchical conception of skill in terms of level of abstraction, presented by Rasmussen (1986), is particularly relevant to the study of activity in the control of industrial processes. It is founded on the idea that the functional properties of a system can be represented by the subject at different levels which can be ordered on a scale from abstract to concrete, with steps such as 'functional goal' (example: objective of the system), 'physical functions' (example: electrical, mechanical, physical processes within the components of the system) and 'physical form' (example: physical appearance, location). 'A change of level of abstraction implies, for the representation, a change in the concepts and the structure as well as a change in the information appropriate to characterise the functional or operational state at various levels' (p. 121). Thus Rasmussen remarks that the questions which one asks about a task and its environment depend on the level of abstraction at which the mental representation is situated. He notes that models at a low level of abstraction, corresponding to physical realization, can be used for several goals, while the inverse is also true: a goal defined at a higher level of abstraction can be met by several types of physical realization.

Cognitive skill (in a sense which is not that which Rasmussen gives to the word 'skill'—which corresponds more to automatization) consists of the possibility of being capable of controlling one's activity at several levels. When the tasks have little variety, they end by being dealt with at a very concrete level; physical characteristics suffice to initiate and control the activity. When the task is very varied and presents some new characteristics each time, it must be dealt with at a more abstract level, by recourse to symbolic representations: Rasmussen (1986) talks here of analogical reasoning. To each level of abstraction correspond types of model and of processing. Therefore, changing the model can be very efficacious in a problem situation because processing at another level could be easier, the processing rules simpler or better known, or the results from previous instances could be available. A particular example of this strategy is problem-solving by analogy, which depends on the fact that different physical systems can have the same representations at higher levels of abstraction. 'Higher level models for one physical configuration may therefore be reinterpreted to solve problems related to a different, unfamiliar configuration' (p. 123).

Analysis of complex cognitive skills

If this analysis remains necessary in many cases, this is primarily because skill acquired during practice departs considerably from the contents of the instructions first given during training or in written documents. The maintenance technician or the process controller, for example, and many others come to execute tasks for which they have worked out the procedures, or sometimes adapted, detailed or enlarged the procedures learned. English-speaking sociologists (Jones and Wood, 1984; Wood, 1986) have proposed the notion of 'tacit skill' to designate this part of skill which has not been taught, which is not explicit in the documentation and which ignores the definition of the task (Leplat, 1986, 1988). This tacit skill is that which may be acquired as a result of practice, often of long duration (the 'adaptation time'). Teachers and instructors were advised very early, and more recently the designers of job aids or expert systems have been, that it is important to make this tacit skill explicit to be able to exploit it in the improvement of training or in the design of expert systems. In the latter case, one sometimes uses the term 'knowledge elicitation' to designate this skill analysis (Leplat, 1985). 'Skill analysis' has been the object of many studies in English-speaking countries, of which Singleton (1978, 1979) has given examples and collected together several case studies. In France, this analysis is better known under the name of work analysis (psychologically understood) (Ombredane and Faverge, 1955; Leplat and Cuny, 1984; de Montmollin, 1986). The analysis of skills such as those at work is primarily interested in predominantly motor activities, and there is a long history of this type of analysis, a story that does not depend solely on psychologists. One can illustrate this in particular by the methods of time-and-motion study (Barnes, 1949).

The multiplication of tasks which make a greater call on cognitive skills has given rise to new difficulties for analysts, because cognitive activity is not directly observable, but must be inferred from indicators taken from the activity. An increasing interest in the development of methods of analysis has been born from this difficulty, and the efforts undertaken to surmount it have greatly profited from theoretical perspectives which have been enriched in parallel. Numerous texts have presented a synthesis of these methods (for example Singleton, 1978; Fleishman and Quaintance, 1984; Leplat and Cuny, 1984). We will restrict ourselves here to recalling some important characteristics of this analysis of complex cognitive skills.

Collection of observable data

It is necessary to start from observable data, from which inferences can be made about the characteristics of cognitive skills. These data fall into two general categories. The first consists of data and indicators arising from spontaneous activity, that is to say from the activity exercised in its usual conditions (of tools used, controls manipulated, orders, data, recordings of the behaviour of the subject or the system that they control). The second category consists of data collected from specially 'provoked' activity, of which the most typical is the collection of verbal protocols (Leplat and Hoc, 1981; Ericsson and Simon, 1984).

The fundamental methodological problem is to link the observable data to the mechanisms that produced them. The hypotheses suggested by one type of indicator may be verified by others, to acquire increasing credibility.

Individual differences

By controlling the characteristics of the subjects, one could aid in the elaboration and testing of hypotheses on the nature of skill. One could use for this end: the prior training and experience of the subjects, the instructions that one gives them before the task, their state of fatigue (Bartlett, 1943), the time within the diurnal rhythm (Gadbois and Queinnec, 1984), personality traits (Huteau, 1987). One preferred variation difference is linked to practice of the task to be studied itself: this leads to comparison of the activities of subjects at different levels of acquisition, which is freqeuently reduced to comparing beginners with experienced subjects. This comparative method could give useful indications about the constitution of the modules or units making up the skill at different stages.

Variations in the task

To generate and test hypotheses on cognitive skill one could therefore define the class of tasks which the subject must execute, which one could designate as the domain of his or her skill. With this aim, one would systematically modify the reference task with the goal of testing the effect of these modifications. One could also (which is ultimately only a variation of the preceding case) make the task be carried out in a wider or narrower range of conditions. Thus, in a study of the activity of an air-traffic controller (Leplat and Bisseret, 1965), we gave to the subjects a test set of flight situations, with the aim of testing hypotheses about the procedures that they used. If the supposed procedure was the actual one, then the time to resolve conflicts (which the controller had to detect) would be ordered in a certain manner: it was therefore a question of testing whether the actual results corresponded with this order.

The components of skill

The analysis of complex skills is often oriented towards the identification of the units composing this skill. This is particularly the case when the analyst is interested in using these results as the basis for training. In this case, the model of skill can become the basis for the model of training, and the value of this model is tested by the success of the latter. The algorithm–heuristic theory of Landa illustrates this step in several of its aspects. To 'construct and test models of unobservable cognitive processes' Landa (1983) first poses the problem of how to decompose the complex cognitive processes into relatively elementary operations. He says that an operation is elementary for an operator if it can be executed by him in a uniform, normalized, regular manner (p. 173). From this point of view, 'a block of operations constituting an entity may be viewed as an elementary operation' (op. cit.). The ensemble of operations used to resolve a problem constitutes a process which may be algorithmic or heuristic depending on whether it can or cannot, in given conditions, resolve all the problems of a given class (p. 175). An analysis of the processes that represent the skill can be made by identifying the rules for sequencing of operations. These rules define the conditions of use for an operation ('if' such a condition, 'then' such an operation).

Some of these notions can be found in the framework for analysis proposed by Hoc (1977, 1978, 1987). He distinguishes the notion of representation—that is the declarative knowlege about facts or states—from that of processes —operations that are executed on these facts or states and arise from procedural knowledge. These representations and processes are organized into systems (systèmes de répresentation et de traitment, SRT). These systems can be hierarchical in several ways, notably in terms of fineness, the units of representation and processing being more or less detailed. Skill is frequently characterized by the acquired possibility of passing easily from one SRT to another and/or by the possibility of passing from one level of the hierarchy to another (particularly in the planning of actions).

The possibilities for transfer of skill

When the domain of the task is fixed, one may be able to define the skill very precisely, or at least to verify its existence and its level, for example by criteria for success. Another problem will be to determine what is the skill that the subject has acquired by practising the task. This skill always goes beyond the domain of the task that the subject has learned to execute. The subject who has learned to fault-find on equipment 'A' will be able to fault-find equipment 'A' of other types. They will also have learned some competence which will allow them to learn more easily to fault-find on other equipment. The study of transfer from one class of tasks to another constitutes another route for analysing skills. From the teaching point of view, it can lead to determining the skills which one must have previously acquired to be able to acquire a new one: one often speaks of prior requirements to designate these skills.

Certain acquisitions can therefore have a value as exemplars, and serve as a pivot for an ensemble of acquisitions. This problem is often evoked by training specialists, but is difficult to study systematically. One could link this to the more systematically studied problem of reasoning by analogy: as we saw above, the transposition of a problem into another system of representation which is more familiar to the subject than that in which it has been presented, can improve the skill of solving the problem, and at the same time permits us to understand better the nature of this skill.

Examples of analysis

The complexity of working situations means that it is difficult to isolate the cognitive aspects of effective activity of the sensorimotor type. If one recalls that cognitive activities can only be inferred from the observable data, one will understand that the analysis of cognitive skills is closely linked to that of skills in general and to the analysis of work. Textbooks of industrial psychology and of ergonomics give examples of skills analyses and references to the original studies. In Singleton (1978) there are reports of studies by their authors on the train driver, the pilot, the air-traffic controller, the process controller, the architect and the information systems designer. Studies by Sperandio (1981, 1984, 1987) give detailed examples of the skills of air-traffic controllers and the skills of different tasks involved with computers. We have, with Cuny (Leplat and Cuny, 1984), thrown some light on the skills used in process control and the tasks involved in automation. One can also find good examples of the analysis of cognitive skills related to the use of computer displays in Norman and Draper (1986), in Hoc (1987) and in Karnas (1987). The skills of conception, understanding and use of technical drawings are the object of a group of studies collected by Rabardel and Weill-Fassina (1987). An excellent article by Peruch *et al.* (1986) also describes an analysis of the skills used in visual control of the route in marine navigation. The analysis of errors in relation to cognitive skills has been tackled and exemplified by the studies of Rasmussen (1986) and Rasmussen and Vicente (1988).

It is not possible to enumerate completely the examples of skill analysis in working situations. They use a great variety of methods which cannot be discussed here, and this variety is linked to the nature of skill, to the objectives of the analysis and to the constraints within which it is made (de Montmollin, 1986).

These examples also show that the analysis of complex cognitive skills can be pursued at very diverse levels: from the general architecture of the skill of dealing with a very large task to the fine study of skill in executing a very elementary subtask. This variety is also found in the numerous and varied definitions of the term skill: diagnostic skill (in very diverse types of work . . .), skill at detecting a signal or a critical configuration, pilot skill, data-processing skill, etc. A reading of Singleton (1978) would easily allow one to extend this list. When skills become more complex and their study changes in scale, the problems take on new dimensions which have been noted particularly by Bainbridge (1981) for process control and by Marshall, Duncan and Baker (1981) for fault diagnosis in the control of a chemical plant. We can only discuss one of the features that emerges from these studies, the importance of planning or the elaboration and use of plans. Hoc (1987), who has particularly studied this aspect of complex skills, defines a plan as 'a schematic and (or) hierarchical representation capable of "guiding" the activity of the subject' (p. 69). Planning therefore appears to be a process essential to complex cognitive skills and its analysis constitutes an important phase of their study, as is witnessed by the studies mentioned above. Planning is closely linked to the time dimension and is found as a subpart of studies more directly focused on the temporal organization of skills, for which Teiger (1987) has proposed an analysis and given some good examples.

Skill and efficiency

We have already noted the efficient character of skill, that is the possibility that it gives to the subject of attaining the same goal at lower cost. This notion of the cost of a skill has received the attention of industrial psychologists who, in reusing a common expression, frequently speak of workload (Welford, 1977; Sperandio, 1984). This notion comes from the established fact that if one increases task demands, a stage can arrive at which the task is no longer executable without error. When the demands are small, one can also carry out a second task, which is no longer possible at a certain level if one does not wish to commit errors in the primary task. From this comes the idea of a level of load that cannot be passed. One therefore speaks of the limited capacity of the channel for information processing (Welford, 1977) which gives the idea of measuring the workload (or cost or processing resources used) by the fraction of the capacity (or of the total allowable load) mobilized by the task to be evaluated.

From this we have

$$m[C(T)] = m[C(e)] + m[C(r)]$$

where

$m[C(T)]$ measures the total capacity
$m[C(e)]$ measures the capacity mobilized by the task to be evaluated
$m[C(r)]$ measures the residual capacity

The load represented by the task to be evaluated can be estimated by the fraction $f(e)$ of the capacity mobilized by this task:

$$f(e) = \frac{m[C(T)] - m[C(r)]}{m[C(T)]}$$

In the classic experiments, a task is chosen for which the efficacy can be easily measured to evaluate $C(r)$. Then priority is given to $C(T)$ and the task to be evaluated. These experiments show that in effect the load represented by a task diminishes with the acquisition of skill.

The theory of a unique and undifferentiated capacity has been put in doubt by some paradoxical results which can be characterized by the following experimental paradigm. Given two tasks $t(1)$ and $t(2)$ for which one wants to compare the load, first with an added task $t(3)$ and then with a very different task $t(4)$. With the task $t(3)$, the load of $t(1)$ (evaluated, for example, by the method above) appears greater than that of $t(2)$, while with task $t(4)$ one concludes the inverse. In other words, according to the nature of the added task, either one or the other of the tasks to be compared can appear to cause the greater load.

This type of result has led Norman and Bobrow (1975) and Navon and Gopher (1979) to suppose that there is not one undifferentiated reservoir of processing resources, but several reservoirs which correspond to resources of different types. The demands of one task fall on a certain pattern of resources, which can vary from one task to another, and finally depend on the mode of execution and the level of training of the subject.

With this new perspective, it becomes possible to differentiate the notion of load and in conjunction to analyse the nature of skill. Wickens (1984) has opened several paths in this direction. He proposes defining resources on three dichotomous dimensions: the processing stage (receptor–central–effector); the modality of coding (visual–auditory); the processing code (spatial–verbal). One task interferes more with another when it calls on the same types of resource. It is not possible to discuss this model here, and Wickens himself has outlined its limits, but we will take from it the possibility that it gives for analysing the type and quantity of resources used by a skill.

In effect, by making the subject carry out at the same time a task that uses the skill to be studied and a task that calls on a pattern of resources which has been previously determined, one might evaluate the resources used by the skill. Vankerschaver (1982) has given a good example of this type of use in the analysis of a sporting skill and Wickens *et al.* (1986) for aircraft piloting.

Double task situations are similar to those called time-sharing, which are actually very frequent in work. Examination of this latter situation has the effect that the notion of skill appears from another direction. One must ask if the demands of the double task situation can be considered as the sum of the demands of the simple tasks. It is apparent that the response to this question is negative, and so one must ask about the nature of this skill of dealing with two tasks conjointly ('time-sharing skill') (for a detailed discussion see Wickens, 1984, ch. 7 appropriately entitled 'Attention, time-sharing and workload'). Does this skill consist of passing rapidly from one task to another or of treating the data in parallel (Damos and Wickens, 1980), or, again, is the processing oriented towards the task in hand or towards interruptions (Miyata and Norman, 1986)? One can also ask whether this skill has a general character. On this last point Ackermann, Schneider and Wickens (1984), at the end of a review of the questions on this subject, note that methodological weaknesses prevent clear conclusions.

When the tasks are complex, the measurement of load and of resources can be made in various ways: by double tasks, by subjective evaluation and in certain cases by physiological or performance measures (Welford, 1977; Leplat and Cuny, 1984).

Skills and techniques

Analysing skill from the perspective of training makes a good introduction to examining the links between skill and technique (Leplat and Pailhous, 1981). 'Technique' is defined as using means (cognitive, material) with the aim of attaining an objective determined by an external demand. The concept of technique is of the same type as that of procedure. Extensive interiorization of a technique results in a skill. Inversely, exteriorization of a skill does not inevitably constitute a technique. For this to be the case, it is necessary that the exteriorization (in the form of written instructions, for example) is a social experience capable of being transmitted. A heuristic for fault diagnosis developed by a technician only becomes a technique if it is exteriorizable in a form that makes it communicable to others. If a technique has been based on the development of a skill, its characteristics can give us information about the nature of skill acquisition. For example, according to whether the technique for fault detection is a 'checklist', requiring only the identification of control points, or whether it rests on knowledge of the function of the device, which is the justification for the recommended procedure, one can assume that the nature of the skill will be different. In the first case skill will be limited to a very circumscribed task appearing in a standard form; in the second, it will have an adaptive character and be capable of handling a more or less broad class of tasks.

However, we know that skill acquired by practice extends in general beyond that which results from interiorization of a technique. A taught technique is integrated with other knowledge, and exercised in conditions that are complex but always very stable. This 'learning by action', well described by George (1983), enlarges the domain of skill. Thus one looks for ways of eliciting this knowledge which enriches the technique, in order to design help systems (sometimes called intelligent decision aids) or expert systems. The differences between exteriorized skill and the basic technique can reveal both the cognitive mechanisms which control the execution of the task and also the limits or inadequacies of the techniques (cf. above on the notion of tacit skill). This passage from skill to technique is characteristic of certain stages of artificial intelligence.

CONCLUSION

It will be apparent from this chapter that the notion of skill is far from being clear and that it covers diverse contents depending on the theoretical framework within which it is used and the situations to which it refers. It is not the only notion in psychology to suffer from these handicaps: one could also mention notions such as intelligence or attention. These notions which use a common language cover phenomena that have sufficient interrelation to be united in the same concept, but reveal all their diversity when they are subjected to a detailed analysis. It is no doubt not an accident that these notions persist despite the most acid criticisms!

An essential feature of skill is its 'goal-directedness': one is skilled at . . . . But at what and how? We have given some elements of a reply to these questions, which still remain open to a considerable extent. We have seen the relations between skill and the concepts of procedure and technique. In the same sense that one speaks of artificial intelligence, one can also speak of artificial skill, given the development of decision–aid systems and expert systems. The design of the latter leads one to ask about the nature of skill, and has already contributed to making progress in our knowledge.

Skill develops with the 'automatization' of relations, which we have tried to clarify but which are not simple. A complex skill cannot be built up without automatic components which liberate cognitive functioning from a certain number of constraints. How is this passage to automatization made, how is the automatization articulated with the skill in which it is inserted, what is its degree of autonomy, how is the area of automatization defined, can one define the area of automatization, of skill? Therefore there are many very important questions to which we have tried to bring some elements of a reply, but for which fully satisfactory replies remain to be discovered.

Can what we learn from laboratory experiments, from simple tasks with elementary mechanisms of automatization and skill, be transposed to complex skills? Do the automated units at different levels have identical properties? In giving importance to the results of these studies we have given a partially positive reply to this question, and we have justified it—notably by recourse to the notions of efficiency and of processing resources. One must not forget, however, and it is necessary to insist on this, that the increasing complexity of skills brings up new problems, linked to the organization of component skills at different times during their acquisition. How the subjects organize this acquisition and how one can help them to do it constitute new questions which lead into the field of activity planning, which will become an important chapter in cognitive psychology when more interest is given to complex tasks.

The reference made in this chapter to 'work' has many consequences. It underlines first that one will have to deal with complex skills, for which the acquisition often takes a considerable time. It also reminds one not to make too artificial a distinction between cognitive skill and simple skill, to avoid reintroducing the opposition between physical work and mental work. This is why we 'ave frequently omitted the qualificative 'cognition', because all skill is in some of its aspects more or less cognitive.

The reference to work also leads to the point that the skills to be studied are already *in situ*; the analyst does not often have the possibility of controlling their conditions of acquisition in a satisfactory manner. From this follows the importance of 'analysis' in the study of these working skills. Particular insistence has been laid on this phase, on the methods and the knowledge that it can lead to. When psychologists can neither create nor entirely control their object of study, some new problems appear, to which we have indicated some of the possible responses. It also remains to be examined how a better understanding of cognitive skills could contribute to the design of working situations, notably in training and ergonomics, but this contribution will often appear clearly enough. The 'deconstruction' of skills by analysis is essential in all cases to guide the acquisition of these skills and to give the subjects cognitive control over their actions.

REFERENCES

Abruzzi, A. (1952) *Work Measurement*. New York: Columbia University Press.

Ackermann, P., Schneider, W., and Wickens, C. D. (1984) Deciding the existence of the time-sharing ability: a combined methodological and theoretical approach. *Human Factors*, **26**, 71–82

Anderson, J. R. (ed.) (1981) *Cognitive Skills and Their Acquisition*, Hillsdale, N.J.: Erlbaum.

Anderson, J. R. (1982) Acquisition of cognitive skill. *Psychological Review*, **89**, 369–406.

Anderson, J. R. (1983) *The Architecture of Cognition*, Cambridge, Mass.: Harvard University Press.

Bainbridge, L. (1981) Le contrôle de processus. *Bulletin de Psychologie*, **XXXIV**, 352, 813–832.

Barnes, R. M. (1949) *Etude des Mouvements et des Temps*, Paris: Les Editions d'Organisation.

Bartlett, F. C. (1970) Fatigue following highly skilled work. In D. Legge (ed.), *Skills*. Harmondsworth: Penguin Books, pp. 297–310.

Belbin, E., and Belbin, R. M. (1969) Selecting and training adults for new work. In A. T. Welford (ed.), *Decision Making and Age*. Bale: S. Karger, pp. 66–81.

Berlyne, D. E. (1960) *Conflict Arousal and Curiosity*, New York: McGraw-Hill.

Bilodeau, E. A. (1966) *Acquisition of Skill*. New York: Academic Press.

Bisseret, A., and Enard, C. (1970) Le problème de la structuration de l'apprentissage d'un travail complexe. *Bulletin de Psychologie*, **XXIII**, 632–48.

Bruner, J. J. (1970) The growth and structure of skill. In K. J. Connolly (ed.), *Mechanisms of Motor Skill Development*. London: Academic Press, pp. 63–91.

Cheng, P. W. (1985) Restructuring versus automaticity: alternative accounts of skill acquisitions. *Psychological Review*, **12**, 414–23.

Crossman, E. (1959) A theory of the acquisition of speed skill. *Ergonomics*, **2**, 153–66.

Damos, D., and Wickens, C. D. (1980) The acquisition and transfer of time-sharing skills. *Acta Psychologica*, **6**, 569–77.

de Montmollin, M. (1986) *L'Intelligence de la tache*, 2nd ed. Berne: Peter Lang.

Ericsson, K. A., and Simon, H. A. (1984) *Verbal Reports as Data*. Cambridge, Mass.: The MIT Press.

Eugene, J. (1961) Etablissement d'une méthode synthétique d'évaluation de la décroissance de temps unitaire de fabrication dans l'industrie aéronautique. *Bulletin du CERP*, **10**, 157–92.

Fischer, K. W. (1980) A theory of cognitive development. The control and construction of hierarchies of skills. *Psychological Review*, **87**, 477–531.

Fleishman, E. A., and Quaintance, M. K. (1984) *Taxonomies of Human Performance: The Description of Human Tasks*. New York: Academic Press.

Gadbois, C., and Queinnec, Y. (1984) Travail de nuits, rythmes circadiens et régulations des activités. *Le Travail Humain*, **47**, 195–225.

Gagne, R. A. (1970) *The Conditions of Learning*, 2nd ed. London: Holt, Rinehart and Winston.

Galperine, P. (1966) Essai sur la formation par étapes des actions et des concepts. In *Recherches Psychologiques en URSS*. Moscow: Editions due Progrés, pp. 114–42.

George, C. (1983) *Apprendre par l'Action*. Paris: Presses Universitaires de France.

Guillaume, P. (1947) *La Formation des Habitudes*. Paris: Presses Universitaires de France.

Hoc, J. M. (1977) Méthode d'analyse psychologique d'un travail de programmation. *Le Travail Humain*, **40**, 15–28.

Hoc, J. M. (1978) Etude de la formation d'une méthode de programmation informatique. *Le Travail Humain*, **41**, 111–26.

Hoc, J. M. (1987) *Psychologie Cognitive de la Planification*. Grenoble: Presses Universitaires de Grenoble.

Huteau, M. (1987) *Style Cognitif et Personnalité*. Lille: Presses Universitaires de Lille.

Jones, B., and Wood, S. (1984) Qualification, division du travail et nouvelles technologies. *Sociologie de Travail*, **16**, 407–21.

Karnas, G. (1987). L'analyse du travail. In C. Levy-Leboyer and J. C. Sperandio (eds.), *Traité de Psychologie du Travail*. Paris: Presses Universitaires de France, pp. 609–26.

Landa, L. N. (1983) The algo-heuristic theory of instruction. In C. M. Reigeluth (ed.), *Instructional Design Theories and Models*. Hillsdale, N.J.: Lawrence Erlbaum, pp. 55–73.

Legge, D. (1970) *Skills*. Harmondsworth: Penguin Books.

Leontiev, A. (1972) *Le Développement du Psychisme*, Paris: Editions Sociales.

Leontiev, A. (1975) *Activité, Conscience, Personnalité*. Moscow: Editions du Progrés.

Leplat, J. (1985) *Erreur Humaine, Fiabilité Humaine dans le Travail*. Paris: Colin.

Leplat, J. (1986) The elicitation of expert knowledge. In E. Hollnagel, G. Mancini and D. D. Woods (eds.), *Intelligent Decision Support in Process Environments*. Berlin: Springer Verlag, pp. 107–22.

Leplat, J. (1988) Skills and tacit skills: a psychological perspective. *International Journal of Applied Psychology* (in press).

Leplat, J., and Bisseret, A. (1965) Analyse de processus et traitement de l'information chez le controleur de la navigation aérienne. *Bulletin du CERP*, **XIV**, 297–304.

Leplat, J., and Cuny, X. (1984) *Introduction à la Psychologie du Travail*, 2nd ed. Paris: Presses Universitaires de France.

Leplat, J., and Hoc, J. M. (1981) Subsequent verbalization in the study of cognitive processes. *Ergonomics*, **24**, 743–55.

Leplat, J., and Pailhous, J. (1976) Conditions cognitives de l'exercice et de l'acquisition des habiletés sensori-motrices. *Bulletin de Psychologie*, **XXIX**, 205–11.

Leplat, J., and Pailhous, J. (1981) L'acquisition des habiletés manuelles: la place des techniques. *Le Travail Humain*, **44**, 275–82.

Lewis, B. N., and Pask, G. (1965) The theory and practice of adaptative teaching systems. In R. Glaser (ed.), *Teaching Machines and Programmed Learning*. National Education Association, USA, pp. 213–66.

Marshall, E. C., Duncan, K. D., and Baker, S. M. (1981) The role of withheld information in the training of process plant fault diagnosis: *Ergonomics*, **24**, 711–24.

Miyata, Y., and Norman, D. A. (1986) Psychological issues on support of multiple activities. In D. A. Norman and S. V. Draper (eds.), *User Centred System Design*. Hillsdale, N.J.: Lawrence Erlbaum, pp. 265–84.

Mothe, D. (1976) *Autogestion et Conditions de Travail*. Paris: CERF.

Navon, D. and Gopher, D. (1979) On the economy of the human-processing system. *Psychological Review*, **86**, 214–55.

Navon, D., and Gopher, D. (1980) Task difficulty resources and dual-task performance. In R. S. Nickerson (ed.), *Attention and Performance*, Vol. VIII. Hillsdale, N.J.: Lawrence Erlbaum, pp. 300–15.

Newell, A., and Rosenbloom, P. S. (1981) Mechanisms of skills acquisition and the law of practice. In J. R. Anderson (ed.), *Cognitive Skills and Their Acquisition.* Hillsdale, N.J.: Lawrence Erlbaum, pp. 1–56.

Norman, D. A. (1981) Categorization of action slips. *Psychological Review*, **88**, 1–51.

Norman, D. A, and Bobrow, D. J. (1975) On data-limited and resource-limited processes. *Cognitive Psychology*, **7**, 44–64.

Norman, D. A., and Draper, S. W. (1986) *User Centered System Design.* Hillsdale, N.J.: Lawrence Erlbaum.

Ombredane, A., and Faverge, J. M. (1955) *L'Analyse du Travail.* Paris: Presses Universitaires de France.

Pailhous, J. (1987) Modulation cognitives des activités sensori-motrices. In *Les Apprentissages: Perspectives Actuelles.* Paris: Colloque de la Société Française de Psychologie.

Perruch, P., Pailhous, J. and Deutsch, C. (1986) How do we locate ourselves on a map: a method for analysing self-location processes. *Acta Psychologica*, **61**, 71–88.

Perruchet, P. (1985) Les effets différentiels de l'entrainement et leurs implications. *Le Travail Humain*, **48**, 129–45.

Rabardel. P., and Weill-Fassina, A. (1987) *Le Dessin Technique.* Paris: Hermes.

Rasmussen, J. (1986) *On Information Processing and Human–Machine Interaction. An Approach to Cognitive Engineering.* New York: North-Holland.

Rasmussen, J., and Vicente, K. (1988) Coping with human errors through system design. *International Journal of Man–Machine Studies* (in press).

Ravaisson, J. (1838) *De l'Habitude*, Paris; revised edition 1984, *Corpus des Oeuvres de Philosophie en Lanque Française.* Paris: Fayard.

Reason, J. (1987) Generic error-modelling system (GEMS): a cognitive framework for locating common human error forms. In J. Rasmussen, K. Duncan and J. Leplat (eds.), *New Technology and Human Error.* Chichester: John Wiley and Sons.

Reason, J., and Mycielska, K. (1982) *Absent-minded? The Psychology of Mental Lapses and Every Day Errors.* Englewood Cliffs, N.J.: Prentice Hall.

Reigeluth, L. M. (1983) *Instructional Design Theories and Models.* Hillsdale, N.J.: Lawrence Erlbaum.

Saltzman, E., and Scott Kelso, J. A. (1987) Skilled actions—a task dynamic approach. *Psychological Review*, **94**, 84–106.

Savoyant, A. (1978). Eléments d'un cadre d'analyse de l'activité: quelques conceptions essentielles de la psychologie soviétique. *Cahiers de Psychologie*, **22**, 17–28.

Shiffrin, R. M., and Dumais, J. T. (1981) The development of automatism. In J. R. Anderson (ed.), *Cognitive Skills and their Acquisition.* Hillsdale, N.J.: Lawrence Erlbaum, pp. 111–39.

Shiffrin, R. M., and Schneider, W. (1977) Controls and automatic human information processing II. Perceptual learning automatic attending and a general theory. *Psychological Review*, **84**, 187–90.

Shiffrin, R. M., and Schneider, W. (1984) Automatic and controlled processing revisited. *Psychological Review*, **91**, 269–76.

Schneider, W., and Shiffrin, R. M. (1977) Control and automatic human information processing I. Detection search and attention. *Psychological Review*, **84**, 1–66.

Schneider, W., and Shiffrin, R. M. (1985) Categorization (restructuring) and automatization: two separable factors. *Psychological Review*, **92**, 424–8.

Singleton, W. T. (1978) *The Study of Real Skills*, Vol. I, The Analysis of Practical Skills. Lancaster: MTP Press.

Singleton, W. T. (1979) *The Study of Real Skills*, Vol. II, *Compliance and Excellence.* Lancaster: MTP Press.

Sperandio, J. C. (1981) *La Psychologie en Ergonomie*. Paris: Presses Universitaires de France.

Sperandio, J. C. (1984) *L'Ergonomie du Travail Mental*. Paris: Masson.

Sperandio, J. C. (1987) Les aspects cognitifs du travail. In C. Levy-Leboyer and J. C. Sperandio (eds.), *Traité de Psychologie de Travail*. Paris: Presses Universitaires de France.

Teiger, C. (1980) Les empreintes du travail. In *Societé Française de Psychologie* (ed.), *Equilibre et Fatique par le Travail*. Paris: Entreprise Moderne d'Edition.

Teiger, C. (1987) L'organisation temporelle des activités. In C. Levy-Leboyer and J. C. Sperandio (eds,), *Traité de Psychologie du Travail*. Paris: Presses Universitaires de France, pp. 659–82.

Teiger, C., Laville, A., Dessors, D., and Gadbois, C. (1977) *Renseignements Téléphonique avec Lecture de Micro-fiches sous Contrainte Temporelle*. Report No. 53 of the Laboratoire de Physiologie du Travail et d'Ergonomie, CNAM, Paris.

Vankerschaver, J. (1982) *Capacités de traitement des Informations dans une Habileté Sensori-motrice*. Doctoral thesis of the III cycle, University of Aix-Marseille.

Welford, A. T. (1958) On the nature of skill. In D. Legge (ed.), *Skills*. Harmondsworth: Penguin Books, pp. 21–32.

Welford, A. T. (1964). *Vieillissement et Aptitudes Humaines*. Paris: Presses Universitaires de France.

Welford, A. T. (1977) La charge mentale de travail comme fonction des exigences de la capacité de la stratégie et de l'habileté. *Le Travail Humain*, **40**, 283–304.

Wickens, C. D. (1984) *Engineering Psychology and Human Performance*. Columbus: Merril Publishing.

Wickens, C. D., Hyman, F., Dellineer, J., Taylor, H., and Meador, M. (1986) The Sternberg memory search task as an index of pilot work load. *Ergonomics*, **29**, 1371–84.

Wood, S. (1986) From Braverman to Cyberman workshop. In *Information Technology, Competence and Employment*, Workshop Bad-Hambourg, Roneod document.

3. The Treatment of Errors in Learning and Training

Michael Frese and Alexandra Altmann

ABSTRACT

Since empirical research on errors in human–computer interaction is still in its beginnings, a theoretically derived taxonomy of errors is suggested in this paper. This taxonomy is based on action theory, differentiating levels of regulation and steps in the action process. Furthermore, slips and mistakes are to be distinguished. It is useful to analyse errors with the help of this taxonomy, for example whether errors stem from problems in the knowledge base for regulation, from goal and plan development and decisions, from lack of monitoring, or difficulties of perceiving or interpreting feedback. This is shown when qualitatively analysing different errors over the course of training and between different software systems (one on direct manipulation and one more traditional). We suggest that strategies of error management should be incorporated into the training process. Error management implies that one has to learn where errors will appear and how to deal with them effectively.

INTRODUCTION

We would like to discuss some functions of errors in learning and how one should deal with them in training computer-related skills. Essentially these are theoretical arguments but we also refer to one study of learning two different word-processing systems in which we recorded errors made by the trainees. This qualitative study serves mainly illustrative purposes. Our general notion is that the emphasis should be on error management. This means that training should teach the trainees to be able to deal with errors rather than to try to avoid errors. This should be so because people at work will invariably commit errors because not all the necessary features can be taught in training and new tasks and new software features appear. More-

Developing Skills with Information Technology
Edited by Lisanne Bainbridge and S. Antonio Ruiz Quintanilla
© 1989 John Wiley & Sons Ltd

over, most software systems are not completely without problems, which may contribute to errors. If users have learned to manage errors effectively this will help them to be able to explore the system and to use errors as an inspiration to learn rather than to feel stressed. Before we can develop the notion of error management in training, it is necessary to introduce some general ideas on errors, including a taxonomy of errors.

ON THEORY

There are essentially two general lines of argument with regard to errors in training. One position argues that errors should be avoided as much as possible. This view has been particularly popular in two different scientific traditions, in behaviourism and in one particular brand of humanism. Alternatively, errors should be included into the learning process because they can also have a positive function. This position is more akin to cognitivistic concepts and to action theory.

What are the arguments for each position? The behavioristic tradition (particularly Skinner, 1953) argues that a person learns best through positive reinforcement. Errors are conceptualized to be punishment. Punishment does not lead to positive learning. Punishment just leads to a temporary suppression of a certain behaviour; it leads to emotional arousal and it does not tell the learner what he or she should really do (just doing nothing helps to avoid punishment as well) (Skinner, 1953). This line of argument led, of course, to the now famous programmed learning machines (Skinner, 1968).

There is a brand of humanism that proposes a similar way of thinking (although it uses a different nomenclature). Here errors are conceptualized to frustrate the student. Frustration leads to anxieties. Hence, the minimization of errors leads to a reduction of frustration and reduces the anxieties associated with learning.

Finally, behaviouristic quarters (less so Skinner than Hull and Guthrie) have argued that when an error is committed, one cannot help but learn something wrong. For example, every movement made leads to learning this movement. Therefore, this movement is repeated under certain circumstances even if the movement is known to be incorrect. Therefore, if one learns the correct movement immediately there are no competing response tendencies.

In contrast to this, cognitivistic and action theories argue that errors help under certain circumstances to actually increase the knowledge (mental model) about a system (for example Semmer and Pfäfflin, 1978). Thus, training should not attempt to restrict the chances to make errors but should incorporate 'typical' errors, train for them and use them to understand what one is doing. This latter position is, of course, related to some forms of exploratory learning (Bruner, 1960), since exploratory learning also uses learning from mistakes.

The above-mentioned differences in general educational approaches also exist in the literature on training human–computer interaction skills. In one reseach project, the system did not allow the trainees to make any errors at all (Carroll and Carrithers, 1984; Carroll and Kay, 1985). In sharp contrast, another study used error training (Greif, 1986). Both reported good results with their respective methods.

It is one of the tasks of this article to reconcile these different findings and different approaches to errors in the training process; to do this, we first want to develop a concept of errors and then discuss a theoretically derived taxonomy of errors.

The concept of errors

Errors produce the non-attainment of a goal. Not every non-attainment of the goal is an error, however. Only when actions have been performed that were potentially avoidable and that violated some rule can one speak of errors (Wingert, 1985). Every error violates some kind of goal (or supergoal) of the individual. As Norman (1984) pointed out, there are two types of errors: slips which result from wrong plans but right intentions and mistakes in which the intentions were wrong but the plan conformed to the intention. If a person deletes a file accidentally by hitting the wrong keys, it is a slip. If a person intends to delete a file, but recognizes later on that it is actually needed again, a mistake has been made. Note that even in the case of mistakes, the error is related to some higher-order goal. This higher-order goal may be, for example, not to waste time and energy (for example by having to write something twice).

This differentiation is not without problems. As the above examples show, behavioural data alone never tell us whether it was a slip or a mistake (in both cases the behaviour was the same—erasing the file). Even when we know the intention, however, it is not quite clear what a certain behaviour signifies. One could argue that the person who made the mistake actually made a slip in goal-setting (the wrong goal of erasing the file was set, even though it was still needed). In spite of these conceptual problems, the differentiation between slips and mistakes is phenomenologically useful (and particularly useful in the field of training). When a slip is pointed out, the person will most likely say, 'Oh yes, of course, it was an error.' If a mistake is pointed out, however, the person will want to be convinced because it is not obvious to the person that in fact a mistake has been made (because the fact of still needing access to the erased file is not in that person's working memory).

Mistakes usually signify some lack of knowledge or something missing in working memory. An additional characteristic of mistakes is that the boundary lines between mistakes and inefficient behaviours (Semmer and Frese, 1985) are blurred. People are, in general, oriented to behaving efficiently (Schönpflug, 1985). When a person makes a large detour, it will usually be called a mistake because the 'wrong' route was taken at some intersection. Was it a mistake or simply inefficient behaviour? It is hard to decide and we have to live with this conceptual fuzziness. If the person has the (super-)goal of not wanting to waste energy, making a detour was a mistake. If no such goal exists, it was inefficient behaviour. The judgement of whether a certain behaviour is inefficient can be done without having to refer to the person's goals. On the other hand, whether or not something is an error can only be judged by knowing the person's goals. Practically, the differentiation is not quite so important, since one of the tasks of training is to teach the trainee to make few 'detours' and hence few mistakes.

A taxonomy of errors

In Figure 1, we suggest a taxonomy of errors adapted from Frese and Peters (1988) which results from an action theory perspective (cf. Frese and Sabini, 1985; Norman, 1986). The steps of the action process consist of the development of goals and decisions between them, the development of plans and decisions, the execution of the plan and its monitoring, perception of feedback and interpretation of feedback. Influencing all of these steps is the knowledge base for regulation, an equivalent to the concept of an internal model. The knowledge base provides the material from which to develop goals and plans and to interpret feedback.

Similarly to Hacker (1973) and Rasmussen (1985), we distinguish four levels of regulation (after Semmer and Frese, 1985). These levels of the postulated hierarchy (or better heterarchy) can be distinguished by their generality (higher levels) and specificity (lower levels) and by whether they involve conscious thought. Actions regulated by higher levels require conscious attention; those regulated by lower levels are relatively automatic, with higher levels used only for occasional monitoring.

Sensorimotor level

This is the lowest level of regulation in which stereotypical and automatic movement sequences are organized without conscious attention. These highly automatic actions can be consciously regulated only within narrow limits because processing of feedback is done on the lower levels as well. Thus, substantial modifications are not possible at this level. Conscious regulation cannot modify such action programs; at most it can stop performance.

Steps in the action process

Levels of regulation	Goals/goal decisions	Plans/plan decisions	Monitoring execution of action	Perception and interpretation of feedback
Level of abstract thinking	N	N	■	N
Intellectual level of regulation	N	N	N / E	N
Level of flexible action patterns	N	N / E	E	N / E
Sensorimotor level of regulation	■	E	E	E

Knowledge base for regulation

Figure 1. A preliminary theoretically derived taxonomy of action errors. The knowledge base for regulation has an impact on all the steps in the action process; however, it has more influence on the upper levels of regulations. Black cells do not exist. N = novice; E = expert

Thus, action programs on the sensorimotor level may assert themselves—contrary to insight—because they have been well routinized. This is one reason for occasional slips, for example when a person wants to go shopping and drives a part of the way along a familar route that goes to the shop and to home. After a while the person finds himself at home without having done any shopping.

Level of flexible action patterns

At this level general action patterns are regulated that are relatively constant in their structure but whose parameters can be changed flexibly. Using block commands may be an example.

Intellectual level

At this level, complex analyses of situations and of problems are regulated. Learning a word-processing system is done at first on this level.

Level of abstract thinking

This is the highest level. General and abstract thought processes are regulated here; logical inconsistencies are tested and abstract heuristics are generated here. These heuristics may take the form of action styles, that is general and abstract heuristics that help in developing plans and goals and the use of feedback. The use of these heuristics may become automatized as well (Frese, Stewart and Hannover, 1987).

On the vertical side of Figure 1, the levels of regulation are described; on the horizontal side the steps in the action process are shown. The knowledge base for regulation has an influence on all of these steps of the action process.

Knowledge base for regulation

The knowledge base is the material from which a person can develop goals and plans, compare the action with a set of parameters and perceive and interpret feedback. Errors may appear here because of objective information deficits or wrongly conceived information and because of inadequate mental models or metaphors (including not knowing the boundary conditions of these metaphors).

Goal development and goal decisions

Errors may appear as inadequate development of goals, wrong decisions between goals or wrong derivation of subgoals. An example for an inadequate goal is an unrealistic goal and an example related to wrong decisions between goals may be unresolved goal conflicts.

Plan development and plan decisions

There is a large overlap between this step and goal development decisions. Errors can occur because of inadequate plans, wrong decisions between plans or derivation of inadequate subplans. Thus, errors can be due to inadequate or unrealistic methods and means. One error condition is due to inflexible use of plans or to giving up the plans before one can be really sure that they have not worked (Volpert, 1974).

Monitoring of execution of action

Sometimes it is possible to detect that one is about to make an error before one actually commits it. Monitoring helps here to reduce the error rate. The less one monitors one's actions, the more easily errors can occur.

Perception and interpretation of feedback

Here there are three conditions that lead to errors: not noticing feedback signals, wrong perception or wrong identification of feedback, and wrong interpretation of feedback signals.

Novices make mistakes more often and their mistakes are regulated in the upper part of Figure 1 (and have been labelled 'N'). Experts make more slips/errors because they are more often related to an automatic plan (or interpretation) of taking over an action; therefore experts show a preponderance of lower-level errors (they are presented as 'E' in Figure 1).

QUALITATIVE OBSERVATION OF ERRORS IN THE LEARNING PROCESS

This taxonomy is useful when looking empirically at errors in the learning process. The course of errors in the learning process and the different kinds of errors as a result of different systems could be observed during a long-term study (7 × 2 hours) of 24 students learning two different text-processing systems: the WordStar with its command language and the MacWrite (using the Macintosh) with its icons, its desk top metaphor and the use of a mouse (Altmann, 1987; Schulte-Göcking, 1987). The subjects had no experience with a computer. The training simulated the learning situation of a person who had just bought a computer and had to learn with the help of a manual; additionally the trainees used material and worked on problems that had been especially designed for this study. The experimenters observed the subjects at all times, intervening only after they had been asked for help and after the subjects tried out a first attempt to solve the problems themselves. Records on all errors were kept. We were especially interested in whether the errors followed a specific course over time.

Errors in the course of learning

The level of regulation as in Figure 1 is changed by learning. The novice regulates most actions on a higher level; after some practice the regulation is delegated to lower levels. This implies that the novice is most likely to make errors of the mistake kind. These mistakes may be due to knowing too little about the system, to using wrong or inadequate mental models or metaphors, to developing unrealistic goals and plans, to not knowing the right feedback signals and to misinterpreting the signals given. However, there is also room for slips that appear because attention is not given to the action at hand. Inattention leads then to leaving out, repeating or misordering crucial steps in an action sequence (Norman, 1981). The problem of inattention to important system parameters is crucial in the beginning of the training process, because there is constant information overload, since all of the information has to be consciously stored in working memory and little information is chunked.

The chances to make slips are greater for experts, however, because skilled behaviours contain many automatized components. Thus, they tend to regulate many actions on lower levels. Therefore, the lower levels may become activated without conscious control, leading to actions that were not intended—the most famous source of this kind of slip being the capture error (Norman, 1981).

Indeed, in the first sessions of the learning process, the subjects in our study had problems on all levels of regulation and with all steps of the action process. There was a high prevalence of mistakes, most of them due to the lack of basic understanding of word processing with a computer.

More concretely, special features of both systems like RETURN and BLANKs produced difficulties for the novices since they used a typewriter metaphor and, therefore, had problems understanding the special implications of these features in word processing. For example, they often used the RETURN key or the space bar instead of using the cursor keys, thus 'tearing apart' the text. Apparently, the knowledge base for regulation had not included a clear differentiation between cursor movement and editing functions.

After making errors such as the one above, the subjects had difficulties recovering from the error situation. Since they did not know that simply using delete commands would fix the text, the real trouble began now. The subjects were not able to interpret the outcome of their actions properly and, therefore, could not find the right problem-solving strategies. They only saw the text as 'torn apart' and were now searching for a command to 'combine', 'move' or 'format' texts. Since they did not know that RETURNs and BLANKs are represented and treated as characters in a word-processing system they could not find the solution. Moreover, these characters were invisible and, therefore, the subjects thought (and argued) that 'one cannot delete "nothing"'.

There is a difference between passively acquired knowledge and knowledge that is actively used. Purely 'telling' somebody the right answer did not help the subjects to actually use this information. Although they were told the abstract notion on how BLANKs and RETURNs are represented in a word-processing system and how to treat them, the subjects had to get to know the boundaries of their metaphor by actually making many mistakes before they could realize the uniqueness of these features in word-processing programs. Thus, it is sometimes necessary to make the errors actively before learning takes place.

The typewriter analogy did not only lead to errors on the intellectual level of regulation but also on the sensorimotor level. Thus, skilful typists had some particular problems in using automatized movements like pressing the RETURN key at the end of each line. Working with a word-processing system one has to use a RETURN key only at the end of each paragraph. Otherwise it is impossible to reformat the text at a later time. Again, there is a discrepancy between knowing something and being able to use the information. After a skill has been automatized, like pressing the RETURN key after each line, the reintellectualization process is difficult. Thus, this error was repeated over and over although the subjects knew that it was wrong. The habit first had to be broken to be able to establish new strategies of action.

Besides error prevention, error diagnosis (feedback perception and interpretation) is a special problem for the novice. For example, the CTRL key was sometimes not simultaneously pressed with the letter key so that the system did not interpret this as a command but as a letter. Thus a letter appeared on the screen that was not noticed by the subjects because they expected something 'big' to happen. Therefore, they thought that they had to find another command instead of the correct one just used.

Another typical problem in error diagnosis appears when the CTRL key is accidentally pressed instead of the shift key, thus giving a command instead of a capital letter. This error is also made by many experts, but in contrast to the novices they can rectify this relatively quickly. The novices became quite helpless because of the unexpected consequences of this slip (for example the appearance of the help menu or the next page on the screen). Since they could not interpret the feedback correctly, they were unable to find a solution to the situation.

In summary, in the first sessions of the learning process errors were made on all levels of regulation but the most prominent errors were made on the intellectual level of regulation, for example in the inadequate interpretation of feedback. Furthermore, an inadequate knowledge base was an important cause of errors.

. However, as soon as the basic difficulties were solved, other kinds of errors dominated in later sessions. Even though comprehension errors were constantly made since the trainees learned something new in each session, slips and memory lapses became more important. Thus, the ratio of slips to mistakes changed, with slips and lapses becoming more frequent. These lower-level slips presented themselves as lapses in WordStar and as motoric coordination slips in MacWrite.

In WordStar, commands were forgotten or mixed up more frequently. For example, many errors using the command language system consisted of mixing up similar commands (like CTRL-KD with CTRL-KP or .op with .pa). Such lapses are the result of the abstact and confusing command names and an additional interference stemming from learning many new and different names. The reader may note that this area is not represented in the theoretical taxonomy of errors given in Figure 1. The study showed us that the important area of memory lapses should be incorporated.

When using the direct manipulation system, an example of those errors, which are often caused by the lower levels of regulation of Figure 1, is as follows: some subjects pulled down the menu but clicked at the wrong place because they were already thinking of the next step. Apparently, the subjects now felt more sure of their use of the commands, thus putting less attention on these matters and using the level of flexible action patterns. On the other hand, their level of expertise was not high enough, so that a higher degree of conscious attention would have been warranted. Thus, errors of the following type appeared: the subjects actually knew the correct procedure but made errors that they could recover from relatively quickly.

Moreover, in later sessions, the differences between the two systems led to different types of errors. Therefore, we will treat these differences in the next section.

Errors and different styles of human–computer interaction: direct manipulation versus traditional system

As mentioned earlier, two word-processing systems with different styles of human–computer interaction were learned in the experiment. WordStar is operated by a complex command language and offers additional menus as memory aids. This is called a traditional system. MacWrite is icon-oriented and presents a 'model world' with diverse objects that can be directly manipulated with the help of a mouse. The model world consists of a desk top metaphor with files, rulers or a waste paper basket. These two different interaction styles produced different kinds of errors in later sessions starting with about the fourth session.

In WordStar the menus are not self-explanatory and many subjects had difficulties using them. For example, it often happened that a person got into a submenu (for example CTRL-K) to search for a specific command (for example CTRL-KD). As soon as the correct command was found CTRL-KD was repeated without realizing he or she was in the submenu and, therefore, had to give only the second part of the command (for example D). The system, however, interpreted the input of CTRL-KD in the K submenu as CTRL-KK and, therefore, inserted a print control character for 'end of block' into the text. Most often, the person did not notice this, which could cause great confusion later on. For example, the person might want to mark the beginning of a block further down in the text and would then receive an error message on the fact that the block marker 'end of block' was set before the one 'beginning of block'. This could not be interpreted since at this time the causal relationship of this error message to the prior action was no longer obvious to the learner.

Thus, the subjects did not grasp the hierarchical structure of the WordStar menu system—a problem of the intellectual level of regulation of the action plans. Moreover, the feedback on the errors was not clear and could not be easily interpreted. The result: error management was usually difficult. This led in turn to an overly cautious and non-exploratory strategy when using WordStar because errors were seen as a constant 'bother' rather than as an impetus to learn.

In contrast to WordStar, MacWrite did not present any major problems for using the menus or remembering the commands. Here the menus were very simple and clearly arranged and could be popped up quickly and without complication using the mouse. The errors using the MacWrite system were of a different nature and came about because of difficulties of the model world symbols and metaphors. There were three special problems:

1. Some procedures were too easy. For instance, some people had problems in activating a 'window'. In order to do this, one must simply point at the specific window and press the mouse key. The subjects expected a more complicated procedure. When they did not find any solution in spite of an intensive search, they resigned and asked the experimenter for help. Conclusion: the right procedure was *too* simple in comparison to their expectations.

2. Metaphors were taken too literally. For example, an object to be worked with must be marked at first by 'pointing *at* it'. Initially many people took this 'pointing *at*' too literally and moved the cursor that had the form of an arrow next to the object. Thus, they made the arrow point *at* the object instead of directly moving the arrow *onto* the object, which is the proper way of doing it.

3. Metaphors were designed inconsistently. For example, the function of the rulers in MacWrite is to set tabs, margins and spacing. This is not consistent with the actual function that rulers would have on a real-life desk, such as measuring something or drawing a line with them. Moreover, it is possible to make them invisible by using the command 'hide rulers'. This inconsistency of the design of the ruler symbols was the source of many errors. For example, the commands 'show rulers' and 'add rulers' were constantly mixed up, or the symbols on the ruler (for example for tabs) were falsely interpreted (for example as the bell ringing at the end of the line).

There is a clear difference in the number of errors of the WordStar group to the MacWrite group. More errors were made in the WordStar group because the subjects had forgotten commands or procedures and could not understand them from looking at the menus. Unfortunately we were not able to count the exact numbers of errors made with both systems, but our qualitative analysis tells us that approximately twice as many errors were made using WordStar.

When comparing the quality of the errors made with WordStar or with MacWrite it becomes obvious that they have completely different consequences. Errors using MacWrite very rarely caused a perplexing chaos as they did for WordStar. Because of this, MacWrite errors had few demotivating and frustrating effects. MacWrite supported error management much better.

THE FUNCTION OF ERRORS IN THE LEARNING PROCESS AND THE NOTION OF ERROR MANAGEMENT IN TRAINING

Our discussion so far suggests some hypotheses about the function and problems of errors in the learning process. Errors can have potentially positive as well as negative functions in the training process. This also gives us a clue as to what error management should mean. Error management strategies should be taught in training so as to enhance the positive functions of errors and minimize the negative functions.

The positive functions of errors in the training process

The positive function of errors conforms to the adage that one learns from errors. In one study a training group that received a sequential training (the subjects learned each command sequentially without any higher-order explanation) in which no errors were possible, performed worse than another group that allowed and encouraged the subjects to make errors (Frese et al., in preparation). Errors provide feedback to the person. However, feedback is only useful when the trainee is able to perceive and interpret the feedback (an error message like 'error 024' will not do) and to leave the 'error situation' after having committed the error. Sometimes trainees get hopelessly lost when they find themselves in a situation that they did not want to be in and that they do not know how to change. Depending upon the level of regulation, there are different functions of errors. On the level of abstract thinking, errors help the individual to learn which metacognitions work and which ones do not. When the trainee learns that every 'typo' has quite negative effects when giving commands to a computer system, he or she will use the metacognition of meticulous typing (including checking before one 'sends off' the command with the return key). Similarly, when the person has learned strategies and heuristics to deal with errors effectively, the metacognition of using errors as challenges rather than as stressors will prevail. On the intellectual level of regulation, the boundary conditions of metaphors (cf. Carroll and Thomas, 1982) are discovered. For example, if the trainee thinks of the system in terms of a typewriter model, the boundary lines for this thinking become clear when he or she makes the error to write over a blank in the insert mode and finds out that this is not possible.

Errors usually lead to a reintellectualization of action patterns that used to be regulated on lower levels. When one employs a plan as usual (without thinking about it) and it suddenly does not work any more or produces error messages, one is forced to think about the action again. Therefore, errors (at least those with clear feedback) have the function of stopping premature automatization of a skill. Mistakes signify that the implications of a command may not have been completely understood yet and that one has to rethink and possibly retrain again. One prerequisite is, of course, that the training is done under realistic conditions where those errors that are prone to appear when performing real-life tasks will appear as well. There are many reports in the literature on sensorimotor learning (cf., for example, Volpert, 1981) showing that non-realistic feedback appearing concurrently with an action is worse than none because realistic errors can not be made under these conditions.

There is one more (positive) function of errors that is often overlooked: errors may spur creative solutions and new exploratory strategies. If the trainee does not know the difference between the 'insert mode' and the 'overwrite mode' and makes a mistake because of this, this might lead him or her to explore these different modes. Similarly, all the possible uses of an UNDO button (or back-up files) may be explored after one has made a mistake. Often, an accidental use of a command may produce an interest to find out how this command can be used and what its functions are.

This positive function can also be substantiated in our study on the learning process. When a menu was accidentally popped up using the MacWrite system this often led to an interest to explore the commands of this menu. This was so because the menus were presented very clearly and it was very easy to undo accidental errors. It often happened that a person said: 'Oh, what's this? I'd like to try it out!' The menus were therefore adequately used as a tool that stimulated exploration. Error management was supported by the system.

Additionally, subjects who made certain errors of basic understanding (that is those concerning RETURNs and BLANKs) earlier in the learning process were able to rectify them and to proceed without any further impediments. In each case, the other subjects would encounter this particular problem later on anyhow, but by this time they were already working on more complex problem situations, so that it was much more difficult for them to understand the actual error causes and to manage these errors effectively.

The negative function of errors in the training process

Given this set of advantages just discussed, one wonders why errors have a 'bad name' in the training literature. The main reason why they do is that they are upsetting. Errors provide feedback but feedback does not only have an informational side (what is not known yet?) but also a motivational component. Errors may, therefore, also demotivate the trainee (this is, of course, the important issue in Skinner's thinking). Depending upon their interpretation of the error feedback, the trainees may think that they are, for example, not smart enough to do it right. Errors—particularly mistakes but also slips with grave consequences (for example inadvertently deleting an important file)—are noticed and diagnosed on a conscious level. In such a case an attributional process sets in and the errors are interpreted according to who or what is at fault. Thus, negative attributions may develop; for example 'I am not able to learn to use such a complicated machine because I am too dumb' (Peterson and Seligman, 1984). However even when in a psychological sense benign attributions follow an error, one may lose fun and motivation in dealing with a system. A person may then 'leave the field' and stop working with this system.

In one of our studies (Frese *et al.*, in preparation), in which one part of the training consisted of error training, we presented subjects with heuristics that implied that it was positive to commit an error. Our qualitative observations were here that the negative attributions of errors persisted in the beginning and were slowly replaced by a much more active attitude towards making an error. Errors were then seen as chances to learn rather than as stressors.

Nevertheless, besides reducing motivation, errors may produce stress and anxiety. This has several implications for the learning process. First, stress can be conceptualized to be another—emotional—task the person has to cope with. This means, that several tasks have to be dealt with at once. Since the trainee is overloaded with information anyhow that has to be processed on a conscious level, the working memory becomes even more overloaded. Therefore, new errors (both slips and mistakes) can occur. The implication is that error management (which leads to acquiring a more positive attitude towards errors in the learning process) may actually lead to a reduction of errors.

People also have the tendency to revert back to overlearned responses when they are under stress (Semmer and Pfäfflin, 1978). This means that responses that are already regulated on a lower level will be preferred under stress conditions: since much of adult training is really *re*training, reintellectualization of formerly automatized responses and a conscious regulation of them is required. Since errors produce stress, this process of reintellectualization becomes disrupted and lower-level regulation is preferred. Again new errors (particularly slips) may result.

One important disruptive consequence of errors is related to system feedback. Does the feedback give information to the trainee and reduce its potentially demotivating function? Feedback is informative when the trainee learns to answer these four questions: (1) What specific error did I make? (help in feedback interpretation); (2) How did I get into this? (the knowledge base for regulation is improved); (3) What do I have to do so that I will not make this error again? (plans, goals and monitoring are implicated here); (4) What do I have to do to get out of the error state? (coping with an error situation—again referring to goals and plans).

The last point is actually the most important. Much of the aversiveness of errors in the human–computer field stems from the fact that errors (slips and mistakes) produce states that are difficult to leave. The novice will sometimes be forced to use a cold restart of the machine, with the effect that much or all of what was produced up to this point is lost. This problem became evident when observing the learning of WordStar. Incomprehensible error consequences often made the subjects very fearful of using the menus. This in turn reduced exploration and prevented a correction of inefficient methods.

Therefore, the training programme has to concentrate on this issue (but not only the training programme—also the error messages of the system and particularly the manual; cf. Wendel and Frese, 1987). Training has to ensure that one learns strategies to get out of the error state.

In summary, there are potentially negative effects of making errors—they may demotivate and increase stress and anxiety and lead to 'points of no return'. These effects will dampen exploratory strategies leading to anxious sticking to one particular method that may not be efficient and useful. To reduce these negative effects and to maximize the positive ones, it is necessary to explicitly integrate the problem of errors into the training process and to develop strategies of error management.

The notion of error management: integrating errors into the training process

When describing the notion of error management, one can again refer to the steps in the action process and to the knowledge base for regulation in Figure 1.

Knowledge base for regulation

In order to undertake effective error management, the person has to know potential error sources (of the program) and error tendencies (of him- or herself). Thus, knowledge of error 'spots' of the software system and a certain amount of realistic self-perception of one's error tendencies are important. When these exist, one can develop better hypotheses once the error has been committed and better ideas of when and where to be careful because error-free performance is important.

Goal development and goal decision

Whether or not an error is seen as a challenge or as a stressor depends on user's goals. Similarly, attributions are different depending upon the goals. If the goal in training is not to be error-free, but actually to get to know potential problem areas of the program and one's own proclivities for errors, in other words if committing errors is seen as part of what one should do in the training process, then committing an error is not reducing motivation to work with the system but rather enhancing it. For something to be frustrating, it has to be seen as negative—as something to be avoided. If the production of errors is seen as something positive (note: in the training process) then errors are not frustrating any more. Furthermore, if the goal consists of making errors, there will be no negative attributions in the Peterson and Seligman (1984) sense, which only appear after negative events. When it is the goal to make errors in the training process, the necessary knowledge can be developed to reduce the amount of errors in actual work situations, to get out of error situations and to be less anxious when trying out new things and committing errors again.

Plan development and decisions

Two aspects are important here: developing strategies to learn from errors and strategies to get out of error states. Strategies to learn from errors include, for example, learning how to interpret error messages, to look things up in the manual and to actively recapitulate what one has learned from an error.

One problem for novices is often that one error is followed by the next one and that they get deeper and deeper into an error state. Therefore, strategies to get out of the error states have to be learned. These may include, for example, ways of jumping from one menu to the other, of being able to use the escape and UNDO keys or of knowing how to do a warm restart. At a more metacognitive level (level of abstract thinking) it implies that one learns not to give up too easily and to try various and diverse ways of dealing with error states.

Perception and interpretation of feedback

Error diagnosis is often difficult (or made difficult by a particular software). It is not always obvious what the error was, what the system feedback means and where the error stems from. Therefore, the trainees have to be taught how to diagnose their errors. This implies two aspects. The first is to learn how to construct one's own feedback since not all errors produce obvious error messages. For example, SPSS version 9 has led to many errors in the treatment of missing values, because the COMPUTE command needed an additional ASSIGN MISSING command to treat missing data correctly. However, there was no error message when the ASSIGN MISSING command was missing. Therefore, error diagnosis implies here that the trainee had to learn to look for these mistakes by watching the number of cases in the output closely. Thus, an explicit strategy of error diagnosis has to be taught.

Second, where does the error stem from? This is also not always obvious. Sometimes it was not the last command that really led to the error but one occurring a few commands before (for example when using the overwrite mode and then trying to use the backward delete in the MS-WORD word-processing system). The problem here is that people tend to cling to their first hypothesis even if many reasons speak against this. This has been variously described as the problem of mental set (Luchins and Luchins, 1959, Levine, 1971) or as cognitive hysteresis (Norman, 1984). Therefore, trainees have to be taught to develop a set of heterogeneous hypotheses about error causes, to explore these alternatives and to be more skeptical about their first set of hypotheses.

To include these aspects of error management in the training process implies the following:

1. In general, the training should teach and support an active and exploratory approach. This implies, for example, that the trainees should be encouraged to develop their own hypotheses and their own mental model of the system, to use 'risky' strategies, to look into aspects of the system not yet known, to experiment when they are not quite sure, etc. (cf. Carroll and Mack, 1985; Frese et al., in press). Only within such a training strategy does it make sense to develop error management strategies. When the training is structured according to programmed learning principles, when the trainee has to follow the instructions passively or when only one 'correct' answer is allowed, error management strategies cannot be taught.
2. An error training should be integrated into training programmes (cf., for example, Greif, 1986). In each case this implies that the trainee has to make some kind of mistake and then learn to get out of the error state. In our own trainings and experiments (for example Frese et al., in preparation) we have variously tried the following strategies: (a) The trainees were asked to make as many different mistakes as they could think of. (b) The trainees had to follow through mistakes that were often made by other trainees. (c) One trainee had to learn how to get out of the errors of a second trainee. (d) Error states were reproduced on the screen or on

photographs and the trainees were asked to tell us how the error had come about and how to get out of the problem again. (e) Potential errors and strategies to get out of these resulting error states were explicitly described in a manual. (f) The trainees had to solve problems that were much too difficult; they were bound to make errors. When an error appeared, they were asked to try to get out of the error state.

In this type of error training, it is useful to ask two people to work together because then the experience is less frustrating. The error training has several functions. First, the trainee becomes familiar with the system. This enlarges the mental model and gives boundary lines for metaphors. Second, the trainee becomes accustomed to the use of exploratory strategies. Since errors and their negative functions are the main reason for giving up to explore, an error training may be a counter-strategy against this tendency. Third, errors are seen as more natural after such an error training and, therefore, produce less anxiety and stress. The trainee simply gets used to making mistakes and, therefore, the errors lose some of their threatening characteristics. Fourth, error training helps the trainee to learn strategies for getting out of difficult situations that resulted from the errors. Since it is one of the most disturbing aspects of the training process for beginners—that they do not know what to do any more—error training will counter despair and tendencies to leave the field (that is stop working with this programme). It is important, of course, that strategies to deal with errors have to be explicitly taught. At the moment we know rather little about which strategies have to be taught and which ones are effective. Furthermore, we do not know which strategies are typically used by good and not-so-good trainees and users. Research is needed here.

3. Most people (particularly adults) come into training with the concept that it is bad to commit errors. Therefore, every error is seen as a sign of weakness, of misunderstanding, of non-intelligence, etc. To counteract this strategy, it pays to present explicit heuristics (Skell, 1972). These heuristics should, for example, say: it is good to make mistakes; look at the screen to find out what happened when an error was made; you can learn from errors. With the help of these heuristics, the goal changes from not-wanting-to-make-any-error to let-me-see-what-I-can-learn-from-this-error.

4. Training should progress in a specific pattern over time, some things needing to be taught in the beginning and some at the end. We can, again, refer to Figure 1. In the beginning, the trainee has to work on the higher levels of regulation for each and every command. This implies that the trainee is overwhelmed with information and the limits of central processing capacity are often reached. Giving error training at this time only increases this information overload. Therefore, it would be useless to do error training at the beginning of the learning process. As a matter of fact,

some rather surprising research results (Carroll and Carrithers, 1984; Carroll and Kay, 1985) pointing to the positive function of giving the trainee little feedback on errors may be due to this overload at the beginning of training. During such a training, the trainee has to concentrate only on the necessary keys, new commands, etc., and does not have to deal with self-produced problems. However, not giving any error training at all may lead to other problems, discussed above. Therefore, we suggest that error training should be done in the middle of the training. This reduces the overload for the novice in the beginning but gives the trainee a chance to use the experiences made in this section of the training later.

CONCLUSION

We still know very little about the 'typical' errors that trainees make. From informal observation, we know that most beginners use a typewriter analogy when learning word processing. This leads, for example, to difficulties in learning how to delete a blank space or a new line command. The type of error is probably related to prior knowledge of computers, to the metaphors used and to prior knowledge of the tasks that have to be done with the system. However, all in all, we know very little in this area.[1]

It is useful to analyse errors with the help of the theoretically derived taxonomy. However, it is not always easy to put empirical examples of errors into the cells of Figure 1 since it is hard to decide what causes an incorrect action. Errors have to be seen in relation to the goals and ideas of the person and these cannot be observed directly. For example, the MacWrite commands 'scroll down' and 'scroll up' were very often mixed up. There are two symbols: an arrow pointing upwards and an arrow pointing downwards. Normally such errors (mixing up commands) would be described in the cell 'level of flexible action patterns/plan decisions'. By chance one of our subjects explained the underlying cause of her error. Instead of clicking on the downwards pointing arrow to scroll up the text she clicked on the upwards pointing arrow. She described her reason for doing this: 'Oh, I must have been thinking of using a typewriter because if I wanted to see the text below I had to pull the sheet of paper up making an upward hand movement. This is why I always click the upwards pointing arrow.' This would actually mean that this error should have been classified as belonging to 'knowledge base for regulation' since it was caused by a 'wrong' mental model.

---

[1]Therefore, we are currently involved in a large empirical research project to answer what type of errors are typical of novices, intermediates and experts and how error treatment can be improved in software design, in software quality control and in training (Project FAUST, cf. the Acknowledgements).

Empirically it proves helpful to regard the errors with the help of the two dimensions in Figure 1. One could, for example, observe a trend over time to move from the intellectual and sensorimotor level to the level of flexible action patterns. This is so because new material is first learned on the intellectual level and with practice regulated one level further down. At the same time, old inadequate behaviour patterns that are still regulated on the sensorimotor level are reintellectualized and therefore moved upwards and then with practice moved again downwards in the hierarchy of the levels of regulation. A second trend over the period of the training can be seen in the move from goal decisions and feedback interpretation to plan decisions. Goals do not have to be developed and decided upon each time after one has become a more skilful user of a system and feedback interpretation is easier because there is a better mental model. However, plan decisions are becoming more complicated because the skilful user has many more alternatives at his or her disposal.

One can also differentiate between the two computer systems. For example, errors on the sensorimotor level have more negative consequences when using WordStar than when working with MacWrite because MacWrite is better in the support of error management. Interestingly, most errors using the MacWrite system could be categorized to be due to the knowledge base for regulation because some metaphors were unclear or inconsistent (e.g. the ruler). WordStar errors most often related to problems in goal decisions and feedback perception or interpretation because of the complexity and intransparency of the menu system and the abstract naming of the commands.

Thus, the taxonomy of slips and mistakes can serve to present a theoretically derived order to the confusing heterogeneity of errors. Additionally, the taxonomy has some practical relevance. If it can be shown that, for example, WordStar leads to feedback interpretation problems, one can treat the problem specifically. Either one can improve the system and present more obvious system reactions on the screen, or one can introduce a specific lesson during training with the goal of making the trainee monitor the screen carefully. It would also be valuable to the trainer to know the potential errors and their causes to be able to anticipate these and to take them into specific consideration during training (compare our remarks on error training).

In our view, errors may have positive and negative functions in the learning process. In a way, our argument is that both Skinner and the cognitive theorists are right, the Skinnerians with their view that errors lead to little motivation and the cognitive and action theorists with their emphasis on what can be learned from errors. In contrast to Skinner, however, we argue for the chance to make errors (although it might be better to reduce the chances in the very beginning of the training process and with very anxious trainees). Moreover, we think that error management is one important goal of training. Since the trainee has to be able to use newly developed skills in real-life tasks and since the trainee is bound to make some errors, he or she has to learn how to expect these errors and how to cope with them effectively. The concept of error management helps to develop the prerequisites for dealing with errors and to develop ways of incorporating the teaching of error management strategies into the training process.

ACKNOWLEDGEMENTS

This article was produced as part of a research project financed by a grant to the first author from the Humanization of Work Fund of the Ministry of Science and Technology of the Federal Republic of Germany (01 HK 806 7): Project FAUST (Fehler Analyse zur Untersuchung von Software und Training). Other researchers in this project were: F. Brodbeck, H. Peters, J. Prümper and D. Zapf. We would like to thank L. Kershaw and D. Zapf for critical comments on a draft of this article.

REFERENCES

Altmann, A. (1987) Direkte Manipulation: Empirische Befunde zum Einfluß der Benutzeroberfläche auf die Erlernbarkeit von Textsystemen. *Zeitschrift für Arbeits- und Organisations-Psychologie*, **31**, 108–14.
Bruner, J. S. (1960) *The Process of Education*. Cambridge, Mass.: Harvard University Press.
Carroll, J. M., and Carrithers, C. (1984) Training wheels in a user interface. *Communications of the ACM*, **27**, 800–6.
Carroll, J. M., and Kay, D. S. (1985) Prompting, feedback and error correction in the design of a scenario machine. *Proceedings of the CHI'85 Conference on Human Factors in Computing Systems*, San Francisco, pp. 149–54.
Carroll, J. M., and Mack, R. L. (1985) Metaphor, computing systems, and active learning. *International Journal of Man–Machine Studies*, **22**, 39–57.
Carroll, J. M., and Thomas, J. C. (1982) Metaphor and the cognitive representation of computing systems. *IEEE Transactions on Systems, Man, and Cybernetics*, **12**, 107–16.
Frese, M., and Peters, H. (1988) Fehlerbehandlung in der Software-Ergonomie: Theoretische und praktische Überlegungen. *Zeitschrift für Arbeitswissenschaft*, **42**, 9–17.
Frese, M., and Sabini, J. (eds.) (1985) *Goal Directed Behavior: The Concept of Action in Psychology*. Hillsdale, N.J.: Lawrence Erlbaum.
Frese, M., Stewart, J., and Hannover, B. (1987) Goal-orientation and planfulness: action styles as personality concepts. *Journal of Personality and Social Psychology*, **52**, 1182–94.
Frese, M., Albrecht, K., Altmann, A., Lang, J., Papstein, P. V., Peyerl, R., Prümper, J., Schulte-Göcking, H., Wankmüller, I., and Wendel, R. (in press) The effects of an active development of the mental model in the training process: experimental results on a word processing system. *Behaviour and Information Technology*.
Frese, M., Brodbeck, F., Heinbokel, T., Mooser, C., Schleiffenbaum, E., and

Thoeman, P. (in preparation) Errors in training computer skills: Experimental results on the positive function of errors.

Greif, S. (1986) Job design and computer training. *Bulletin of the British Psychological Society*, **39**, 166–9.

Hacker, W. (1973) *Allgemeine Arbeits- und Ingenieurpsychologie*. Berlin: VEB Deutscher Verlag der Wissenschaften.

Levine, M. (1971) Hypothesis theory and nonlearning despite ideal S-R-reinforcement contingencies. *Psychological Review*, **78**, 130–40.

Luchins, A. S., and Luchins, E. H. (1959) *Rigidity of Behavior*. Eugene: University of Oregon.

Norman, D. A. (1981) Categorization of action slips. *Psychological Review*, **88**, 1–15.

Norman, D. A. (1984) *Working Papers on Errors and Error Detection*. San Diego, Calif.: University of California.

Norman, D. A. (1986) Cognitive engineering. In D. A. Norman and S. W. Draper (eds.), *User Centered System Design*. Hillsdale, N.J.: Lawrence Erlbaum.

Peterson, C., and Seligman, M. E. P. (1984) Causal explanations as a risk factor for depression: theory and evidence. *Psychological Review*, **91**, 347–74.

Rasmussen, J. (1985) *Risk and Information Processing*. Denmark: Riso National Laboratory.

Schönpflug, W. (1985) Goal directed behavior as a source of stress: psychological origins and consequences of inefficiency. In M. Frese and J. Sabini (eds.), *Goal Directed Behavior: The Concept of Action in Psychology*. Hillsdale, N.J.: Lawrence Erlbaum, pp. 172–88.

Schulte-Göcking, H. (1987) Die Erfassung von unterschiedlichen Lernstilen. Unpublished thesis, Department of Psychology, University of Munich.

Semmer, N., and Frese, M. (1985) Action theory in clinical psychology. In M. Frese and J. Sabini (eds.), *Goal Directed Behavior: The Concept of Action in Psychology*. Hillsdale, N.J.: Lawrence Erlbaum.

Semmer, N., and Pfäfflin, M. (1978) *Interaktionstraining. Ein handlungs-theoretischer Ansatz zum Training sozialer Fertigkeiten*. Weinheim: Basel.

Skell, W. (1972) Analyse von Denkleistungen bei der Planung und praktischen Durchführung von Produktionsarbeiten in der Berufsausbildung. In W. Skell (ed.), *Psychologische Analysen von Denkleistungen in der Produktion*. Berlin: VEB Deutscher Verlag der Wissenschaften, pp. 13–100.

Skinner, B. F. (1953) *Science and Human Behavior*. New York: Free Press.

Skinner, B. F. (1968) *The Technology of Teaching*. New York: Meredith Corporation.

Volpert, W. (1974) *Handlungsstukturanalyse*. Köln: Pahl-Rugenstein.

Volpert, W. (1981) *Sensumotorisches Lernen: Zur Theorie des Trainings in Industrie und Sport*, Vol. 3. Frankfurt/M.: Fachbuchhandlung für Psychologie.

Wendel. R., and Frese, M. (1987) Developing exploratory strategies in training: the general approach and a specific example for manual use. in H.-J. Bullinger and B. Shacker (eds.), *Human–Computer Interaction—INTERACT '87*. North-Holland, Elsevier, pp. 943–8.

Wingert, B. (1985) *Workshop Mensch–Maschine-Kommunikation '85*. Arbeitsgruppe: Entstehung und Behandlung von Fehlern.

4. Development of Skill, Reduction of Workload

Lisanne Bainbridge

SUMMARY

This chapter describes some examples of cognitive activity. It suggests three underlying organizing structures—for knowledge of the environment, one's own activity and working memory—three types of skill—which use different underlying mechanisms and are automated in different ways—and a mechanism for the flexibility of cognitive skill.

INTRODUCTION

Equipment based on information technology often provides flexible facilities which can be used for many purposes. This flexibility puts the emphasis on the users' cognitive skills. Classical training methods teach standard prespecified sequences of behaviour, but these can now be programmed, so what the user is asked to do involves problem-solving and understanding. To help people acquire these sorts of skills we need a change of emphasis in our understanding of skill, putting the focus on adaptability and cognitive aspects rather than simply on 'automatic' behaviour.

The simplest general definition of 'skill' is that it is the efficient use of appropriate behaviour which develops with experience. A skilled person does a task effectively and with minimum effort. In this way, the notion of workload is intrinsically linked with that of skill. Beyond this simple definition, we will see that the notion of skill is very complex.

The aim of this chapter is to provide a simple framework for understanding the nature of cognitive skill and flexible behaviour. We will start by describing some simple examples of cognitive activity, as they illustrate some of the constituents of cognitive skill and its development. We will then consider a simple schema for the relation between different types of skill, and will

Developing Skills with Information Technology
Edited by Lisanne Bainbridge and S. Antonio Ruiz Quintanilla
© 1989 John Wiley & Sons Ltd

discuss a possible basis for the flexibility of skill. We will mention how workload changes with the development of skill, and also the control of, or response to, workload as an aspect of skill. The practical implications for training will be outlined in another chapter (Chapter 8 of this volume).

EXAMPLES OF COGNITIVE ACTIVITY

To illustrate cognitive behaviour, we will look at two examples, one simple and one more complex, of what is involved in following written instructions. This sort of example has been chosen because it is often assumed that following instructions is a 'mindless' activity in which behaviour is fully prespecified, while actually it can involve problem-solving. These examples will illustrate cognitive mechanisms in operation in a simple situation and illustrate the development of cognitive skill.

Following simple written instructions

Although an instruction may look like a fully specified account of what should be done, for a novice it is often a statement of a goal to be achieved, rather than a command whose meaning is obvious.

Suppose someone has bought a new hi-fi. The instruction book contains the message: 'Turn antistatic knob to obtain the best sound quality.' How does someone go about following this instruction? As they have never used this equipment before, they have to find the required control and devise a method for changing its position. They then have to try this plan out, listen to whether it has the expected effect, and if not think of something else to do. A schema for this is shown in Figure 1. The main sequence of activity is shown down the left: the main goals are met by doing subsidiary activities which, in the diagram, are linked to them by stepped arrows. The knowledge bases referred to during this thinking are in boxes on the right.

To describe this processing in more detail, the person has to work out and then use a plan of action. First there is a need to interpret the sentence, by referring to knowledge bases about the likely meanings of the words. A user with appropriate prior knowledge can then make some best guesses about three things: that the object of interest has a certain shape and label and will be in a particular area, that a particular hand posture and movement will be needed and that the changes of sound quality will be of a certain type.

The user makes a plan of action based on these best guesses, and tries it out. The first problem might be that the user cannot find a knob labelled 'antistatic', so might look for knobs with labels with related meanings, or for non-knobs with this label. If the control turns out not be a knob at all they will have to change the type of movement planned. If the sound does not apparently change in quality when this control is turned, then they also need to try something else or go back to the instruction book. Once they have found a plan that has the expected sort of effect, they can go on using it until they find an optimum sound. Plans that at first have the effect of reducing the distance to the goal, but finally do not actually get to it, are the ones that are the most difficult to relinquish or revise.

In this simple sort of situation someone learns very quickly what to do, as well as specific knowledge about the components of the device and how to act towards it to get particular effects. Thus the cognitive processes needed after

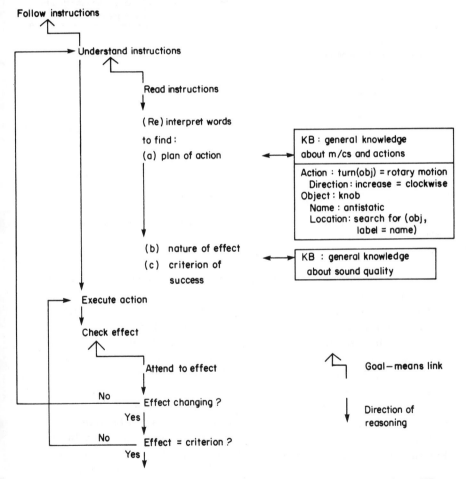

Figure 1. Sequence of activity in following an instruction for the first time. KB = knowledge base, m/c = machine

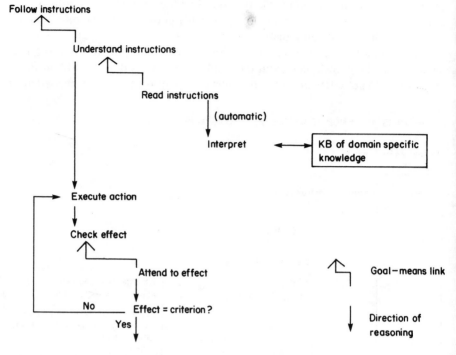

Figure 2. Activity in following an operating instruction when the user has some knowledge about the device

experience are simpler, as suggested in Figure 2. Finally, the actions will be done from memory, perhaps without much conscious attention.

What general points can be extracted from this about the nature and development of skill? Even a very simple activity can involve problem-solving during the first attempts. The 'simplicity' of an activity lies not necessarily in how simple it is at first but in how simple and undemanding the cognitive processes involved can become after a little experience.

After practice, the user no longer needs to devise a plan of action, or to test and revise it. Figure 3 shows a schema for revising working methods on the basis of experience. After practice, the person knows which methods have which effects, so chooses an appropriate action first time; only the part of Figure 3 above the broken line may be needed. That is, once the person has situation-specific knowledge, they can do the task in a different way, different cognitive processes can be used and the goal reached more quickly and more accurately. For both reasons, the person has less workload.

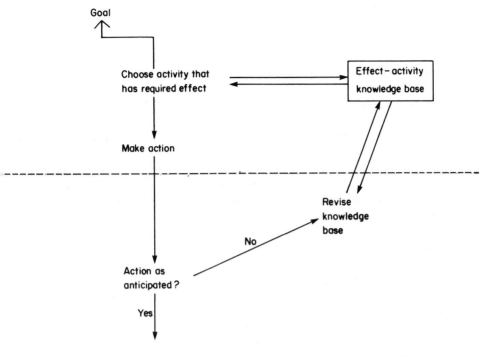

Figure 3. Developing skill by acquiring relevant knowledge. Once the effect of an action is known it is possible (in a stable environment) to choose an effective action without revising either the execution of the action or the action's knowledge base

An ergonomist has three approaches to optimizing this transformation of task thinking from complex to simple, by the design of interface, operating manuals and training schemes.

1. A basic ergonomic principle is that information should be compatible with the task, as well as easy to see. In this case instructions and interface have to be compatible (for example 'knobs' are knobs), so that the prior assumptions that people bring to interpreting the instructions do not have to be revised.
2. The instructions need to be both goal-centred and laid out in such a way that it is easy to pick out the key notions and the sequence of activity.
3. Task analysis for training should identify (see also Section 2 of this volume) what the user needs in a knowledge base (what repertoire of actions and what information about machine properties) without which it will be difficult to develop device-specific skills. It is these prior knowledge bases which college-based training schemes attempt to identify and

develop (for example see Nijhof and Mulder, Chapter 6 of this volume, and Diaper and Johnson, 1989).

Parallels with perceptual–motor skill

At the most general level, the development of cognitive and perceptual–motor skills can be very similar.

The classic example of perceptual–motor skill is given by Miller, Galanter and Pribram (1960, Figs. 2–5). Movements change from being monitored visually to being monitored kinaesthetically; that is there is a change in the 'resources' used as skill develops. The subunits of behaviour also build up into a nested hierarchy (though this notion is inadequate for representing adaptable skills, as we will see later).

Figure 4 shows what can happen (unconsciously) during the development of control skill. At first the person does not know the best time lag and control gain to use in choosing a control action. However, after experience, the effects of actions may be known so well that the first action chosen is effective, so it is no longer necessary to revise the way actions are chosen. Simultaneously this means, in a stable environment at least, that there is no need to check the result of the action, because an action has been chosen that is known to have the required result. The workload is therefore reduced in two ways (Bainbridge, 1978). Figure 4 is similar in principle to Figure 3.

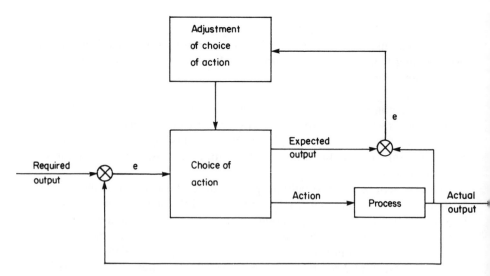

Figure 4. Developing control skill. e = error (from Bainbridge, 1978)

Following a more complex instruction

We will add to the concepts that we need to account for cognitive skill by considering a more complex example of following instructions.

Suppose an operator following a fault management procedure in a nuclear power plant reads the instruction: 'Close initial steam valve (RAXXS003) of SG in question'. What do they need to do to respond adequately to this instruction? (SG = steam generator?).

Norros and Sammatti (1986) have shown that operators need to use intelligence when following the procedures for operating a complex plant. They cannot simply follow instructions but have to think for themselves. For example, the valve might be stuck open or there might be two faults and the procedure for the other fault might say that this valve should be kept open. In either case, the action specified by the procedure is not available, so the operator must think of an alternative way of achieving the aim which would have been achieved by closing the valve.

Figure 5 is a simplified representation of the processes involved. This is a complex diagram, but it has the same general layout as Figure 1. The main sequence of activity is shown down the left; the knowledge bases referred to are described in large boxes down the right. The small squares make an additional feature explicit, the working memory used. There are several general features of this representation.

The top left of Figure 5 indicates the goal of the activity. In this case it is to get the plant into a safe stable state. In many industrial processes the written procedures do not say what the purpose of an activity is, so it can be difficult for the operator to work out whether the procedural step is appropriate in a particular incident.

The general framework for following a step in a procedure is shown down the left of Figure 5. The sequence is:

1. Devise plan, that is (sequence of) action(s) to be made.
2. Check whether action:
   is available?
   will have the required effect?
   (Operators do check the applicability of procedures in this way; see Pew, Miller and Feeher, 1981, on the Prairie Island incident.)
3. If the action is not appropriate, find another action that will have the required effect.
4. Execute the action(s).
5. Monitor its effect. (Even highly experienced operators must monitor in a fault situation, because the behaviour of the process cannot necessarily be predicted from how it has responded to this sort of action in the past.)
6. Assess whether the goal has been met and revise the plan if not.

CLOSE INITIAL STEAM VALVE RAXXSOO3 OF SG IN QUESTION

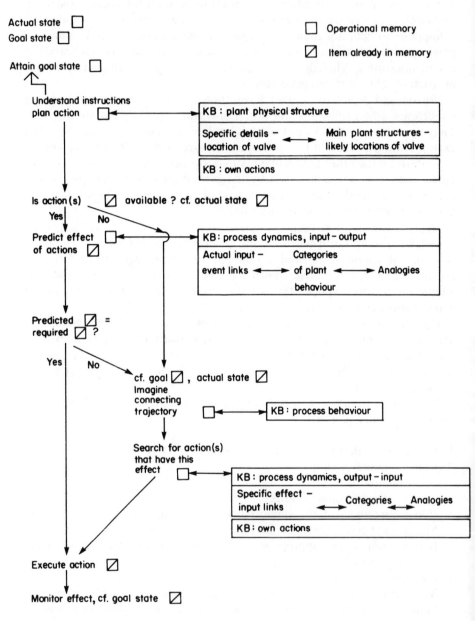

Figure 5. The cognitive activity and knowledge bases used in following part of an industrial process operating procedure

We will now describe these activities in more detail:

1. The first step is to understand the instruction and make a plan (as in Figure 1). The plan is built up from information in two knowledge bases. One is a knowledge base (KB) about the physical structure of the plant, including the positions of valves, either the actual location of this valve on the plant (or of its associated control on the interface) or general knowledge about likely locations of the valve (control). The other KB is the operators' knowledge of their own actions, how to reach and move the valve, or the social or communication skills involved in asking the shop-floor operator to do so.

   The plan of action built up may itself consist of a hierarchy of subframeworks, each of which is a set of subgoals which are themselves met by subsidiary methods. For example, the framework of hand movements, at the lowest level in an action to change a control position, could be aim, acquire, move, release, and each of these could involve subsidiary perceptual–motor skills.

   The plan will be built up, not necessarily in the sequence in which it is executed, in working memory. Working memory contains not only information about the actual state of the external world but also information about future activities which are being considered (Bainbridge, 1974a, 1975).

2. The second step is to check the appropriateness of the action planned. One aspect of this is to check whether the action is available. This would probably be done while the plan is being developed, if working memory contains information about the recent status of the valve.

   The second aspect is to predict the effect of the action. This effect could be modelled in working memory (in the strict sense of the term 'mental modelling' as originally used by Craik, 1948). The effect would be predicted by referring to knowledge about process behaviour, in particular how it responds (output) to specific control actions (input). The prediction could be made on the basis of specific knowledge about this particular valve, or general knowledge about the effects of valves, or from analogies with other devices that affect flow, such as taps.

   The predicted effect is then assessed against the required state.

3. If the action is not available or not suitable, the operator needs to think of another one. They could imagine (in working memory again) the trajectory of process states needed to reach the required state and then search for an action that has this effect. This search would use a knowledge base of information about process dynamics which is organized in the following direction: required process state to action that causes it. Note that this cannot be done simply by working backwards through the cause to effect, or input to output, knowledge base used in step 2, as human knowledge bases are not automatically reversible.

Note that the whole framework in Figure 5 includes two inverse types of activity. One is to take a given action and predict and assess its effects (steps 1 and 2). The other is to formulate a goal state and devise a plan for reaching it (step 3). The latter would classically be called problem-solving, but actually does not always involve the development of new working methods. We will discuss this further in the next section where problem-solving skills are discussed.

A SIMPLE SCHEMA FOR TYPES OF SKILL

We will now generalize the mechanisms, which we suggested in these two examples, to give a simple schema or model for the processes and knowledge underlying skill.

The aim of modelling is to provide a framework for thinking about a particular category of problems. The simple schema discussed in this section (see Figure 6) provides a structure for understanding the relation between different types of skill. As we will see in the next section, several important types of cognitive skill are not represented in this schema, and we need to know some operating details about parts of the schema before we can draw inferences about its practical implications, for example for training.

We will outline the main structures in this schema before discussing the types of skill it summarizes.

The main structures in the schema

The schema includes:

1. Knowledge of one's own activities, and a general problem-solving framework.
2. Knowledge of the structure and behaviour of the environment.
3. Working memory.

These have all been used in the 'following instructions' examples. We need to make some more general points about each of these before discussing types of skill.

Frameworks of activity, 'levels' of specificity

We have suggested that there is a standard pattern of activity in following operating procedures (as in Figure 5 or Figure 10), a 'frame', 'script' or 'strategy' for this general category of task. We will use the word 'framework' as the notion used here behaves both like a series of instructions and like a simultaneous pattern.

Such a framework for a cognitive activity could be at any one of (at least) three 'levels' of cognitive skill difficulty (using 'skill' in the sense of being able to draw on existing frameworks for activity, which make it easier to respond to given task requirements). Note that these three 'levels' are not distinct categories but points along a continuum. The three are:

1. Familiar specific situations. The framework is a standard method for dealing with a frequently recurring specific situation which is sufficiently stable for the same method to be used each time, though it may vary in

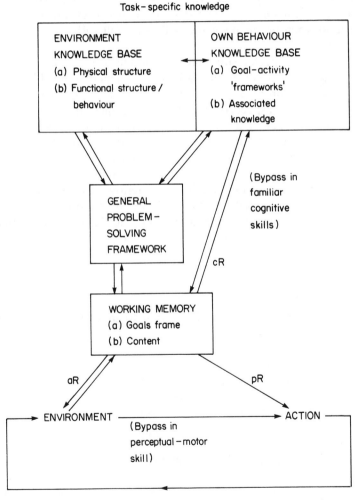

Figure 6. A schema for the main mechanisms underlying skill (see text)

detail, for example choosing the furnace to alter when allocating electric power between steel-melting furnaces (Bainbridge, 1974a, fig. 2).

2. Familiar general tasks. The framework for a familiar general category of task, such as following a procedure, can be applied to unfamiliar specific situations in this category. This general framework can be skilled, because the operator can have frequently practised the general category of task. Figures 5 and 10 show a general framework for understanding, assessing and revising instructions.

3. Unfamiliar tasks. More unfamiliar tasks can be dealt with by more general problem-solving and planning skills. An example is the emergency management planning described by Samurcay and Rogalski (1988). The general problem-solving framework will be discussed further in the next subsection when problem-solving skills are dealt with.

In a well-known specific situation three frameworks for activity could be available: a method specific to this task, a general method for this category of task or a general problem-solving method. How is the working method chosen? Two general aspects of the way in which these three are invoked are usually proposed. The first is that any situation is dealt with by passing through the three 'levels' (for example Rouse, 1983), a task-specific method is only used if a situation-specific method is not available and a general method is only used if a task-specific method is not available. The second general assumption is that, once someone has an extensive vocabulary of situation-specific or task-specific methods, then they are likely to try to apply one of these rather than to use the general method, and this can lead to restricted reactions to problem situations (for example see Leplat, Chapter 2 of this volume).

Types of knowledge of the environment

The cognitive activities in Figure 5 referred to several types of knowledge base:

1. Plant/environment knowledge:
    that is its physical structure,
        functional structural and constraints on operation,
            in the directions input to output,
                output to input.
2. Operator knowledge:
    subframeworks for achieving subgoals.

Each of these types of knowledge was referred to by a different part of the activity represented in Figure 5.

Developing a cognitive skill does not only consist of developing methods for doing tasks and of acquiring the necessary reference information. It also involves developing appropriate structures and categories for the knowledge and developing rapid access from a framework of activity to the part of the data base that it refers to.

It is useful to make another distinction between two types of background information/reference data:

— standard data about what may occur in a task situation, for example the possible states a steel furnace can be in,
— knowledge of the structure and behaviour of the task environment, on the basis of which one can understand events, explain the reasons for one's behaviour or think out new working methods.

If the task situation is very stable, this latter general knowledge about the properties of the environment, which may formerly have been used in developing the working method, may no longer be actively required for generating new behaviour methods, although it may still be accessible for giving explanations. If the environment is so stable that new methods do not need to be developed, then this information may become progressively less accessible (see Leplat, Chapter 2 of this volume).

Knowledge bases which describe the properties of the environment will not be discussed further in this chapter. For more information see Bainbridge (1988).

Working memory

The final important mechanism suggested in the diagram is working memory. The contents of this working memory are not, as in laboratory studies of working memory, an exact replica of external data. Instead this is a working space in which data structures are built up and then provide a context for choosing appropriate behaviour (Bainbridge, 1974a, 1975; Johnson-Laird, 1983). In complex industrial tasks the working memory contains information which is the result of thinking about the task: about required, actual and future plant states, with associated plans of action and their evaluation.

Probably the concept of working memory that best fits the data on complex behaviour is to consider it as a 'blackboard' (Rumelhart, 1977), in the sense that the information is available in parallel and built up and assessed in parallel, rather than in a sequence of separate steps as implied by Figure 5. However, note that it is a 'structured' blackboard, structured by the framework of the task; that is the 'framework' for the sequence of activity subgoals can also be the structure underlying the contents of working memory (Bainbridge, 1975).

Types of skill

It is usual to talk about 'skill' as more 'automated' behaviour (Leplat, Chapter 2 of this volume). However, it can be confusing if one does not distinguish between the different ways in which behaviour can become more automatic, which are classically called:

— perceptual–motor skill,
— cognitive skill,
— problem-solving skill.

These different types of skill can be characterized as using different subsets of the mechanisms in the schema in Figure 6. The schema emphasizes both the notion of skill as a change in type of processing and the centrality of working memory in the organization of behaviour. In summary, the three types of skill are:

1. Perceptual–motor skill. A skilled person can react appropriately to the environment without using conscious attention, that is this type of skill bypasses working memory.
2. Familiar cognitive skill. In familiar situations for which methods and knowledge are already available, a skilled person can do the task without first having to work out a method for doing it, that is this type of skill bypasses the need for problem-solving.
   Most cognitive behaviour is concerned with building up working memory, i.e. with actively searching for the information needed to meet goals rather with than passive reaction to inputs. A framework for activity may involve directing attention to the environment (aR), and accessing or processing knowledge (cR), as well as acting on the environment (pR).
3. Problem-solving skill. When someone does need to devise a new method, or acquire or reconfigure knowledge, these processes too can be skilled in the sense that they can draw on existing frameworks and environmental knowledge, and become easier and more effective after practice.

These three general types of behaviour are not necessarily easy to distinguish in practice. Cognitive behaviour is dynamic. In any task, any one of its substeps might be done in any of these ways. The three mechanisms could be active in different concentrations depending on the familiarity and stability of the environment. This flexibility will be discussed further in the next section. Despite this interdependence, the three categories will be discussed in more detail separately.

Perceptual–motor skill

Within the context of this book, we are concerned with the perceptual–motor skills which are involved in primarily cognitive tasks, such as interpreting and using a complex interface, rather than with the full range of perceptual–motor skills in tasks which involve:

— skills of physical coordination which seem to be impossible to describe in words, such as swimming, bike riding or flying a helicopter,
— exertion of physical effort, in which good ergonomic design and skill development have the effect of minimizing and optimizing the application of human muscular effort.

When using a complex conventional interface, an operator with the relevant perceptual–motor skills can automatically look to the required display, interpret the meaning of a display, move to the required control, etc., without conscious attention to this subtask. This is the domain of much of classical interface ergonomics, in which one of the primary principles is to maximize the possibility of using an interface without conscious attention. For example, if the values of a process variable is presented on an analogue instrument, deviations from target can be detected by automatic pattern recognition. If the same value is presented as a digital number, finding the deviation from target involves a sequence such as:

1. Locate and read the actual value.
2. Locate and read or remember the target value.
3. Do the calculation to compare (1, 2).
4. Do the calculation to compare (3) with the tolerance limit.

That is, to interpret a digital display requires a framework of activity and considerable use of working memory, which may well disrupt the thinking about the primary task. Therefore an analogue display is preferred.

Figure 7 suggests the three main routes by which we can respond to the environment in ways that bypass working memory/conscious attention. This bypass is sometimes called 'implicit' processing. In more classic psychological language, Figure 7 shows three types of 'attention mechanism'. The first has a genetic basis. The others depend on learning; they can only be done automatically after considerable practice.

1. Orienting response. This is the override mechanism which is built into the nervous system, by which particularly strong (salient) signals attract attention whatever the current task activity. This is an important danger

RESPONSES TO ENVIRONMENT
that bypass working memory

'BUILT IN'

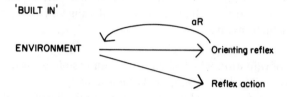

SKILLED:

1. As part of goal-directed search for information

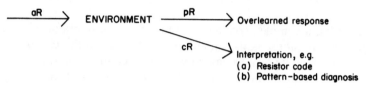

2. Serendipity (notice item relevant to currently not active goal)

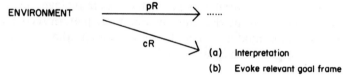

(aR : attention response ; pR : physical response ; cR : cognitive response)

Figure 7. Ways of responding to the environment which bypass working memory

response, which is taken advantage of in the design of alarm and attention-getting displays.

2. Active search. People involved in goal-directed activity usually actively search for the information they need, rather than passively reacting to information as it arrives. Initiating this search for the required information (by directing attention in the environment, aR, or by accessing stored knowledge, cR) may be an activity/subgoal within a framework for achieving a higher goal, or it may be in a framework for dividing attention between time-sharing tasks.

The reaction to the information attended to may be automatic, using:

(a) A highly practised physical response (pR). This can lead into an 'automatic' sequence of behaviour, if the result of the response is a signal from the environment which also has an automatic overlearned response, and so on.

(b) An automatic cognitive response (cR). The meaning of the signal is automatically brought into working memory without having to consider or search for it, for example in pattern-based fault diagnosis (Shepherd *et al.*, 1977).

3. Serendipity ('making happy discoveries by accident'). This is the type of behaviour in which someone notices and responds to something in the environment that is relevant to a goal which may be at the back of their mind but is not currently active. For example, when someone notices information that explains a previous event which they have not had time to think about or when they do something on the way from one part of the main task to another (for example Beishon, 1969). (This is the type of shopping supermarkets are designed to encourage.) The automatic cognitive response in this case may be to bring the relevant framework for goal-related activity into working memory.

'Serendipity' typically happens when a person is somewhat disengaged from their main goal, either because they are searching for information or because they are between activities in the main sequence, for example walking from one place to another.

Which way someone chooses, of the two ways of responding to the environment which involve learning (active search or serendipity), might depend on personality type or on the task situation (for example work or leisure) as well as on opportunity.

Familiar cognitive skills

The second main group of skills involves evoking frameworks of cognitive activity which have been practised frequently so there is no need to work out what to do. A skilled person has a library of task-related frameworks, whose availability depends on their frequency of use. Only a subset of the mechanisms in Figure 6 are used, as shown in Figure 8. While classic interface ergonomics aims to bypass working memory, cognitive ergonomics aims to bypass problem-solving.

Problem-solving skills

Table 1 gives a preliminary classification of types of cognitive skill according to the relevant knowledge bases that are available. Problem-solving is required when either activity frameworks or reference knowledge are not available.

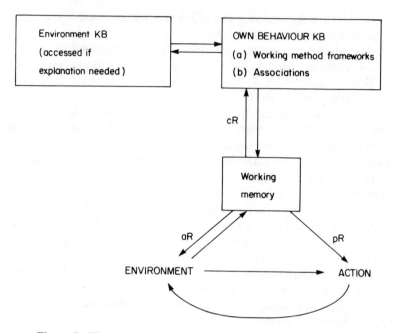

Figure 8. The mechanisms involved in familiar cognitive tasks

Problem-solving can, of course, itself be skilled, if general working methods and ways of structuring information are already available and practised. The classification in Table 1 will need to be extended. There are several important types of cognitive process that are not represented here or in the general schema in Figure 6. Some of these will be mentioned briefly in the next section.

The main dimensions of Table 1 are concerned with whether activity frameworks are or are not already available, and whether knowledge about the properties of the environment is or is not available. This defines four main types of task-processing:

1. Goal–activity frameworks +
   Environment knowledge +

This is the category for the familiar cognitive skills dealt with in the previous section. In the table these are distinguished from scheduling/ planning (in the simple sense) tasks. In those, an overall method for deciding on a sequence of events is available but a new sequence has to be devised each time (for example Shackel and Klein, 1976). This distinction has been made because, in tasks such as steel-furnace control (Bainbridge,

Table 1: Types of more complex cognitive behaviour, classified according to: (a) knowledge available, (b) use of working memory

	Domain specific reference knowledge available		Use of WM
	+	−	
Goal–action frameworks available +	Familiar cognitive skills Planning scheduling	'Professional' skills	Understand state of environment
−	New frameworks in familiar domain; framework skills	New framework developing skills; information structuring skills	'Mentally modelling' hypothetical states of environment

1974a), the structure built up in working memory is concerned with the actual state of the environment while, in scheduling, the structure in working memory is a model of alternative proposed states of the environment. (Most complex tasks build up both 'real' and hypothetical structures in different proportions.) The standard ergonomics method for minimising working memory load in scheduling tasks is to provide an 'external memory' aid for trying out the scheduling alternatives, e.g. Shackel and Klein op cit.

2. Goal–activity frameworks +
   Environmental knowledge frames +, content −

In this case, task-specific activity frameworks are available, but situation-specific reference information is not. This could describe tasks that involve a general area of professional expertise, such as accountancy, in which someone knows what to do and what information they need to know and how to find it. This is work in which the general methods include frames for information search and structuring, which build up a situation-specific data base for decision-making. Other examples are maintenance technicians (Rasmussen and Jensen, 1974) or operators using complex procedures as in Figure 5.

3. Goal–activity frameworks −
   Environmental knowledge −

This is what is considered as the true problem-solving situation, in which neither methods nor domain-specific information is available.. An example would be learning computer programming for the first time (Hoc, 1987). Norros (Chapter 17 of this volume) describes learning to use unfamiliar complex equipment as 'research'.

The problem-solving task situation is particularly difficult because the person has not only to devise working methods and to acquire the task-relevant data but also to devise task-appropriate structures for it, for example: How do different parts of the equipment fit together, physically or functionally? What are the task-related ways of categorizing the information? All the structures must be built up at the same time, often starting from scratch. When a casual user approaches most IT equipment for the first time, they are faced with an unknown machine and poorly indexed reference literature. The instruction books typically do not directly answer the questions: How do I find out how the machine works? How do I find out how to do task x? The user is not sure where to start or where a given piece of information fits in, and may be using inappropriate analogies to understand the equipment (Eason, Chapter 12 of this volume; Hoc, 1987).

A general problem-solving framework for devising a new working method could consist of the steps shown in Figure 9. (The figure does not include the processes involved in organizing knowledge structures in a task-efficient way.) In this general problem-solving framework, note that:

(a) There may be few constraints on the sequence in which these steps are done.

(b) The steps may be done in parallel rather than in series.

(c) Any step 'later' in the list may require that a step 'earler' in the list is revised (for example Hayes-Roth and Hayes-Roth, 1979).

(d) Each step could be done by any type of skill.

(e) If either automatic perceptual–motor skill or a more specific cognitive framework is evoked at or within any step, this may bypass the need for some of the other steps.

It is interesting to consider the possibility of training to develop general, rather than task-specific, cognitive skills, for example by practising developing plans (in the complex sense of devising new working methods) or acquiring and structuring information for new tasks.

4. Goal–activity frameworks −
Environment knowledge +

This is the situation in which domain knowledge is available, but not frameworks for appropriate activity, for example when working in a familiar domain with a new goal. An example would be dealing with a fault situation in an industrial process, when the usual method of stabilizing the plant is not available so the operator has to think of a new plant configuration. Reference information is available, and low-level goal–activity frame-

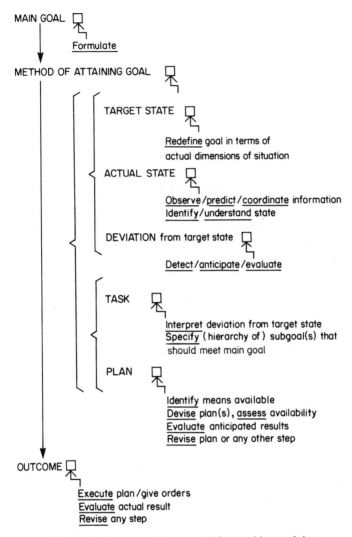

MAIN GOAL

Formulate

METHOD OF ATTAINING GOAL

TARGET STATE

Redefine goal in terms of
actual dimensions of situation

ACTUAL STATE

Observe/predict/coordinate information
Identify/understand state

DEVIATION from target state

Detect/anticipate/evaluate

TASK

Interpret deviation from target state
Specify (hierarchy of) subgoal(s) that
should meet main goal

PLAN

Identify means available
Devise plan(s), assess availability
Evaluate anticipated results
Revise plan or any other step

OUTCOME

Execute plan/give orders
Evaluate actual result
Revise any step

Figure 9. A general framework for problem-solving

works, but they need to be combined in a new task-specific strategy at a higher level.

It seems that this type of task may be difficult because the availability of domain-specific information is only apparent. Actually a new goal may require recognizing new features of the domain and restructuring existing knowledge. This type of activity therefore does also involve information acquisition and structuring skills, and its seems that existing knowledge bases which have been used frequently become rather inflexible in structure. Restructuring seems to be more difficult, the more familar (and therefore automatically accessed) the domain specific information. One therefore needs practice in using old knowledge in new ways.

FLEXIBILITY OF SKILL

There are two ways in which we will expand this discussion of skill: by mentioning types of skill that are not represented in the simple schema in Figure 6 and by discussing in more detail the nature of behaviour flexibility.

Types of skill not represented in the schema

There are at least three important aspects of cognitive processes in working situations, for which there is no mechanism in the schema in Figure 6. These are areas that are in need of major research effort, as we understand little about them. Without them, this and any other schema is inadequate.

1. Prototype reasoning. People actually typically reason, not by thinking through a general causal chain but by thinking of an example situation or a past specific situation, and using that as a basis for considering action in the present context (for example Shepherd, Chapter 10 of this volume; Bainbridge, 1981; Rumelhart and Norman, 1981).
2. Time-sharing tasks. Most real-life working situations involve dividing attention between multiple responsibilities (for example Beishon, 1969; Page, Heyden and Liere, 1983). How do people decide how to divide their time between several tasks? What makes this more or less difficult? Leplat (Chapter 2 of this volume) summarizes some of the points that have been made about this aspect of skill.
3. Unspecified goals. The representation of skill in this chapter is entirely goal-oriented, but how might one account for behaviour in which there is a general goal, such as 'safety', but the dimensions and criteria defining an actual goal state cannot clearly be specified beforehand (Bainbridge, 1981; Norman, 1986; Samurcay and Rogalski, 1988)? When can the goal state be recognized once it has been achieved, but not clearly defined beforehand?

Despite their importance, we will not discuss these aspects of cognitive behaviour. We have also not discussed the more predominantly perceptual–motor skill aspects of the lower traingle in the schema in Figure 6, nor the cognitive mechanisms underlying optimum mappings between different cognitive representations (for example Barnard, 1987).

The final taxonomy of types of cognitive process should have implications not only for training. It should also be linked to recommendations for interface and job aid design, to knowledge elicitation techniques (Bainbridge, 1986) and to implications for error mechanisms and their prevention.

A mechanism for flexible skill

A major (although it may superficially appear small) change in emphasis in the basic concept of skill is needed to deal with training and other support for IT tasks.

It has frequently been held, at least since Bryan and Harter (1899), that skill develops by automating subunits of behaviour. When these subunits no longer require attention, then this attention can be used for integrating groups of smaller units into larger units. By learning the arbitrary associations between a concatenation of lower-level items, the higher-level unit itself becomes automatic, and so on. This leads to two notions, that skill has an underlying hierarchical tree structure, in which both control and conscious attention are at the highest level, and that the purpose of task analysis for training is to identify this prespecifiable hierarchy.

This account does not contain sufficiently rich concepts to deal with IT tasks. In particular, IT equipment usually offers flexible functions which can be used for many purposes, so it is not possible to give a prespecified account of the behaviour needed to use it. Training schemes and instruction manuals frequently concentrate on individual functions, demonstrating that a given action will have a particular effect. Trainees and manual users then find it difficult to use the equipment, because they have been given information which is both inadequate and the inverse of what they need. The account of the equipment that they should be given needs to be goal-directed at at least two levels. (This is an oversimplification; for more discussion of task analysis see Section 2 of this volume.) The users need help with how the functions available can lead to their own goals, which is not necessarily obvious (Norman calls this a 'gulf', 1986). At the lower level, they need the information in the following form: given that you want to achieve this function, this is what to do. This is the opposite to the order in which the information is frequently presented, and human reasoning chains are not automatically reversible.

These difficulties with a simple model of skill imply that we need a model of skill in which the link between a goal and the means of achieving it is a key feature. As an example, Figure 10 represents the main behaviour in Figure 5 in a way that focuses on the goals–means relations. We can suggest that the key features of a more flexible account of skill are all aspects of this goal–means link.

The 'means' as a 'Gestalt' of subgoals

A method of achieving a goal can itself be a set of subgoals, which in turn refer to further subgoals, until they reach the subcerebral level. However, the set of subgoals that achieves a higher goal is not necessarily an arbitrary concatenation of items, but a group of items that together 'make sense' in

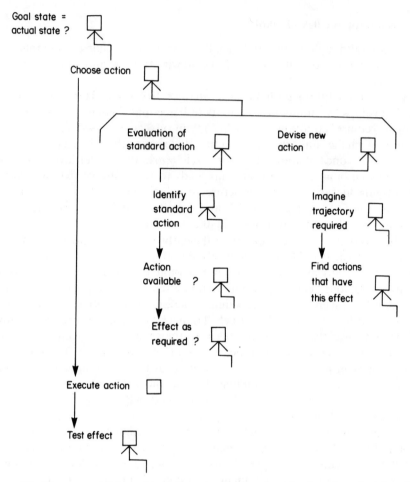

Figure 10. The general 'hierarchical' framework of goals and subgoals underlying the behaviour described in Figure 5

some overall way. They provide an organizing structure for the activity, a sort of 'information processing Gestalt' in which the whole is greater than the sum of the parts.

Although there are higher and lower levels of this structure of subgoals, the structure of 'levels' can be more flexible than a hierarchical tree. Goals can be met by various means, and means can be used for reaching various goals. So the behaviour organization may be a heterarchy or network, rather than a hierarchy with unique links. This specific 'level' of a particular unit of behaviour cannot be identified without reference to its use in a particular task situation (Bainbridge, 1975).

The skill of behaviour choice

Choosing behaviour appropriate to a given task context may become automatic in very stable tasks (Leplat, chapter 2 of this volume). However, behaviour choice is usually flexible, adapted to the particular task context. To simplify, we can suggest that there are four aspects of the skill in making this choice:

1. Alternative 'means'. Alternative frameworks of activity that can meet the goal.
2. Knowledge about the properties of each method. From experience, a person can learn the general properties of each of these frameworks for activity, for example (a) the processing resources it needs, (b) the outcome of the activity. This could be either in general terms such as the level of accuracy achieved and the time taken, or, in highly practised and particu-

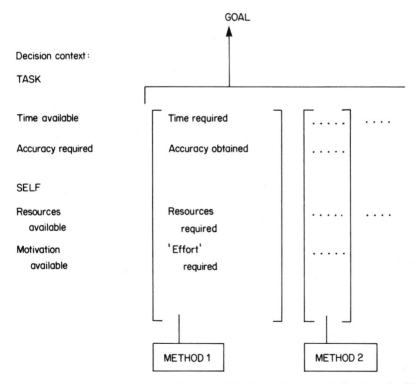

Figure 11. Choice between alternative methods of reaching a goal. Each method has stored with it information about its general properties and requirements, which is used in choosing the most appropriate method at a particular time (from Bainbridge, 1975)

larly in perceptual–motor skills, the exact output which will be obtained for a given input, on the basis of which the person could work open-loop, without checking for feedback. Each method will have this information stored with it, as in Figure 11 (Bainbridge, 1975).

Even general problem-solving methods could have general information associated with them, such as the likelihood of success. This could, for example, make this 'goal choice between means' point the location of the mechanism for 'success' and 'failure' personality types. Several aspects of 'cognitive style', such as working for speed or accuracy, might be located in the choice at this point.

3. Skilled choice between methods. The ability to make a rapid optimum choice between alternative methods, by comparing the known properties of a method with the requirements of the task context, seems to be a skill that can be learned. Sperandio (1972) presents data which suggest that choosing the strategy as a function of task demands, to control the level of workload subjectively experienced, may be done more effectively by more experienced people. There may be two aspects of this skill: comparing the learned properties of a method with the requirements of the task context and also configuring one's information processing resources to match those required by the activity, according to the level of effort the person is willing to commit to it (Hockey, 1984, 1986).

4. Flexibility in the use of type of skill. There could be flexibility at this goal–means choice point, not only through choosing between available task-specific alternatives but also because it is possible to access other frameworks, for example searching for methods that are not usually used in this context but that have some of the appropriate properties, or accessing general problem-solving methods when no suitable specific frameworks for activity are available. Familiarity with finding and using 'unusual' methods can be an important aspect of problem-solving skill.

Access to general problem-solving methods could happen at any point in a framework of subgoals and at any level in the task organization, if a usual method either has not been developed or is not available in this specific context. Inversely, when using a general problem-solving framework, as in Figure 9, it may not be necessary to devise a method for any step for which a method is already available. Therefore real behaviour can be a complex mixture of new and existing working methods, according to the details of a particular situation. During the development of skill, problem-solving attention may be predominantly given to increasingly 'higher' levels of behaviour organization as skill develops. Actually it may be given to any level below this (see Leplat, Chapter 2 of this volume). Once the skill is acquired, conscious or 'controlled' attention could be allocated to any level of task organization at which there is a problem, while other levels are simultaneously being dealt with 'automatically'. (This condition exists unless the task context for this unit of behaviour is so stable that all task decisions are made in the same way each time, when internal flexibility is lost. See Leplat, Chapter 2 of this volume, for some implications of this for training.)

5. Planning a sequence of activity, allocating attention between different tasks. This could also make use of the general information about working methods that are stored with them, as indicated in Figure 11.

ADDITIONAL IMPLICATIONS FOR WORKLOAD

The relation between increasing automatization of skill and reducing workload is well known (Leplat, Chapter 2 of this volume; Bainbridge, 1978). However, this relation is by no means simple. This chapter suggests some extensions of this idea.

The three general categories of skill have been distinguished because the mechanism of reduction in workload takes a different form in each. Increasing perceptual–motor skill leads to lower working memory/attentional/ monitoring load. Increasing cognitive skill means that frameworks for activity are already developed, with appropriate frames for, and content of, the information they need to refer to, so there is lower problem-solving load. Problem-solving skills may develop when people have experienced with, and learn the properties of, the general problem-solving methods, which reduces workload by increasing effectiveness and confidence. We might argue that processing capacity is limited and single-channel during problem-solving, in contrast with other types of skill in which impressive amounts of parallel processing can be done, because all the cognitive processing mechanisms are held available during problem-solving in case they are needed.

Although it may be possible in simple laboratory tasks to investigate the relation between a task and the load that it imposes on processing resources, in any real task the flexible way in which working methods are chosen in relation to the particular task context means that there can be moment-to-moment changes in the processing resources used, and short-term changes in the effort needed.

If there are alternative methods which are equally effective in meeting the task goals but which require different amounts of cognitive processing and use different resources, then one would not expect to find a monotonic relation between the task demands achieved and either a general measure of the workload needed to meet them or a specific measure of the use of a particular 'cognitive processing resource' (see Leplat, Chapter 5 of this volume; Sperandio, 1972; Bainbridge, 1974b). Therefore, as with other aspects of ergonomic design, it is much easier for an ergonomist to predict ordinal changes in workload ('if' this task feature changes in this way 'then' workload will increase/decrease) than to make specific numerical workload predictions about the outcome of the interactions of all these many factors.

CONCLUSION

Although many topics have been touched on in this chapter, the main focus has been to outline the general mechanisms underlying skill. After outlining two examples of cognitive behaviour, we suggested that five basic mechanisms are involved:

1. A knowledge base of information about the environment, which is referred to when thinking out what to do to achieve particular goals. For someone who is skilled, the information is organized in task-relevant groupings, and easily accessed.
2. A knowledge base of standard 'frameworks' for activity. Within these the goal–method link is an important decision point. A skilled person is flexible in their working method, and chooses methods that are appropriate at a particular time, by comparing information about the properties of each method with the context.
3. Working memory, in which information about the working context and the results of task decisions, is built up into a structure given by the current framework for activity.
4. A general problem-solving framework, which makes use of information in any knowledge base and is evoked when an appropriate existing method is not available. In familiar cognitive skills, this is not necessary.
5. 'Automatic' responses to the environment. These perceptual–motor skills do not use working memory in thinking about the task.

Classic ergonomic methods are concerned with optimizing perceptual–motor skills by making the choice of response 'obvious' (and by reducing physical workloads). Classic training methods are appropriate for structuring the extended practice needed to develop these skills.

Cognitive ergonomics and training are concerned with minimizing the amount of 'problem-solving' that a new user needs to do before they can develop a standard way of doing a task.

Most of the chapters in this book are concerned with the flexible problem-solving behaviour required from the users of much IT equipment. Training for these tasks needs to develop the knowledge bases of relevant information, by giving practice in using them in typical task situations. The many training methods for this which have been mentioned throughout this book are summarized by Bainbridge in Chapter 8 of Section 2.

ACKNOWLEDGEMENT

Many of the ideas presented in this chapter were developed during a two-month visit to the Laboratoire de Psychologie du Travail de l'Ecole Pratique des Hautes Etudes, Paris, supported by the French Ministere de l'Education Nationale. The author would like to thank Professor J. Leplat and his colleagues for their hospitality and for many interesting seminars and discussions. The author would also like to thank Antonio Ruiz Quintanilla and Andrew Shepherd for their constructive comments on an earlier manuscript.

REFERENCES

Bainbridge, L. (1974a) Analysis of verbal protocols from a process control task. In E. Edwards and F. P. Lees (eds.), *The Human Operator in Process Control*. London: Taylor and Francis, pp. 146–58.

Bainbridge, L. (1974b) Problems in the assessment of mental load. *Le Travail Humain*, **37**, 279–302.

Bainbridge, L. (1975) The representation of working storage, and its use in the organisation of behaviour. In W. T. Singleton and P. Spurgeon (eds.), *Measurement of Human Resources*. London: Taylor and Francis, pp. 165–83.

Bainbridge, L. (1978) Forgotten alternatives in skill and workload. *Ergonomics*, **21**, 169–85.

Bainbridge, L. (1981) Mathematical equations or processing routines? In J. Rasmussen and W. B. Rouse (eds.), *Human Detection and Diagnosis of System Failures*. New York: Plenum Press, pp. 259–86.

Bainbridge, L. (1986) Asking questions and accessing knowledge. *Future Computing Systems*, **1**, 143–9.

Bainbridge, L. (1988) Types of representation. In L. P. Goodstein, H. B. Anderson and S. E. Olsen (eds.), *Mental Models, Tasks and Errors*. London: Taylor and Francis, pp. 70–91.

Barnard, P. (1987) Cognitive resources and the learning of human–computer dialogues. In J. M. Carroll (ed.), *Interfacing Thought: Cognitive Aspects of Human–Computer Interaction*. Cambridge, Mass.: MIT Press.

Beishon, R. J. (1969) An analysis and simulation of an operator's behaviour in controlling continuous baking ovens. Reprinted in E. Edwards and F. P. Lees (eds.), *The Human Operator in Process Control*. London: Taylor and Francis, pp. 79–90.

Bryan, W. L., and Harter, N. (1899) Studies on the telegraphic language. The acquisition of a hierarchy of habits. *Psychological Review, 6*, 345–75.

Craik, K. J. W. (1948) *The Nature of Explanation*. Cambridge: Cambridge University Press, 123 pp.

Diaper, D., and Johnson, P. (1989) Task analysis for knowledge descriptions: theory and application in training. In J. Long and A. Whitefield (eds.), *Cognitive Ergonomics and Human–Computer Interaction*. Cambridge: Cambridge University Press.

Hayes-Roth, B., and Hayes-Roth, F. (1979) A cognitive model of planning. *Cognitive Science, 3*, 275–310.

Hoc, J-M. (1987) *Psychologie Cognitive de la Planification*. Grenoble: Presses Universitaires de Grenoble, 197 pp.

Hockey, G. R. J. (1984) Varieties of attentional state: the effects of environment. In R. Parasuraman and D. R. Davies (eds.), *Varieties of Attention*. London: Academic Press, pp. 449–83.

Hockey, G. R. J. (1986) A state control theory of adaptation and individual differences in stress management. In G. R. J. Hockey, A. W. K. Gaillard and M. G. H. Coles (eds.), *Energetics and Human Information Processing*. Dordrecht: Martinus Nijhof, pp. 284–98.

Johnson-Laird, P. N. (1983) *Mental Models*. Cambridge: Cambridge University Press, 513 pp.

Miller, G. A., Galanter, E., and Pribram, K. H. (1960) *Plans and the Structure of Behaviour*. New York: Holt, Rinehart and Winston, 226 pp.

Norman, D. A. (1986) Cognitive engineering. In D. A. Norman and S. W. Draper (eds.), *User Centred System Design*. Hillsdale, N.J.: Erlbaum, pp. 31–61.

Norros, L., and Sammatti, P. (1986) Nuclear power plant operators errors during simulator training. Research Report 446, Technical Research Centre of Finland, Espoo, Finland.

Page, S. J., Heyden, W., and Liere, B. (1983) Verhalten des Kernkraftverk-Wartenpersonals. Phase I : Pilotuntersuchung. Institut fur Unfallforschung, Technischer Uberwachungs-Verein, Koln.

Pew, R. W., Miller, D. C., and Feeher, C. E. (1981) Evaluation of proposed control room improvements through analysis of critical operator decisions. Research Project 891, NP-1982, Electric Power Research Institute, Palo Alto, Calif.

Rasmussen, J., and Jensen, Aa. (1974) Mental procedures in real life tasks: a case study of electronic trouble shooting. *Ergonomics*, **17**, 293–307.

Rouse, W. B. (1983) Models of human problem solving: detection, diagnosis, and compensation for system failure. *Automatica*, **19**, 613–25.

Rumelhart, D. E. (1977) Towards an interactive model of reading. In S. Dornic (ed.), *Attention and Performance* Vol. VI. Hillsdale, N.J.: Lawrence Erlbaum, pp. 573–603.

Rumelhart, D. E., and Norman, D. A. (1981) Analogical processes in learning. In J. R. Anderson (ed.), *Cognitive Skills and Their Acquisition*. Hillsdale, N.J.: Lawrence Erlbaum, pp. 335–59.

Samurcay, R., and Rogalski, J. (1988) Analysis of operator's cognitive activities in learning and using a method for decision making in public safety. In J. Patrick and K. D. Duncan (eds.), *Training, Human Decision Making and Control*. Amsterdam: North-Holland, pp. 133–52.

Shackel, B., and Klein, L. (1976) ESSO London airport refuelling control centre redesign—an ergonomics case study. *Applied Ergonomics*, **7**, 37–45.

Shepherd, A., Marshall, E. C., Turner, A., and Duncan, K. D. (1977) Control panel diagnosis: a comparison of three training methods. *Ergonomics*, **20**, 347–61.

Sperandio, J. C. (1972) Charge de travail et regulation des processus operatoires. *Le Travail Humain*, **35**, 85–98.

Section 2

Training Needs Analysis and Methods

Outline of Section

The chapters in this section focus on the way in which training needs have changed, and what to do about it. Although equipment based on information technology does not raise unique training problems, it does emphasize the need for different approaches to training. Nijhof and Mulder (Chapter 6) and Shepherd (Chapter 9) describe case studies which illustrate the sorts of skills that are now needed in the work force. People need to be helped to use equipment which can best be used only if the operator has some understanding of how it works. Previous approaches to training specified a set working sequence, and the main aim of training was to develop the trainee's ability and speed in this prespecified task. Now that working flexibility is required, this raises the need for new methods for specifying training objectives, for describing what needs to be done and for training.

There are two main categories of training, according to the objectives involved. One is task-oriented: the training of on-the-job skills using particular equipment. This sort of training can be quite specialized and specific, rather than oriented to the general principles of the work or the equipment. The other is vocationally oriented: for example at a technical college before starting a first job.

Obviously the skills taught at a training college need to be more general, so they help people to adapt to a wide variety of working situations and equipment. This raises questions about how to identify what are the 'basic' skills and concepts involved in using IT equipment. One can also ask, with the frequent changes in equipment and jobs that are now expected of the workforce, whether it is irresponsible of companies to give employees training that is specifically focused only on particular equipment. Not only could this make it more difficult for the employee to change to another job in another company but it could also make the employee less able to change to other equipment and other jobs within the same company.

Nijhof and Mulder are particulary concerned with training objectives in vocational education. They present the results of an interesting study on training needs for both office technology and flexible-manufacturing systems. Their analysis shows that understanding and applying knowledge about the task and the equipment are just as important as skills of execution (which classic training methods concentrated on) and that more flexibility is required of employees. This justifies the repeated emphasis in this book on the need for these skills of understanding. Like Norros (Chapter 17 of this volume) they found that higher levels of skill and wider knowledge are needed in flexible-manufacturing systems, including the need for knowledge about business administration and production cost-benefits.

All the chapters in this section are concerned with developing flexible/ problem-solving types of skills. However, there is one major gap in the book. Few of the chapters come from an educational rather than a specific industrial perspective. The main aim of vocational training is to convey transferable skills, and these are little discussed in this book.

Although there is some discussion of transfer of training in Marshall and Baker (Chapter 11 of this volume), there is no analysis of the central skills and concepts needed by a workforce that is sufficiently flexible to transfer at least between different types of equipment and preferably also between different types of work. This should need the minimum of new learning, and the minimum un-learning of previous skills which interfere with what is needed in the new situation. (There is discussion of this interference in the chapters in Section 1, particularly those by Olsen and Rasmussen and Leplat). Inversely, how can one test that the general skills taught do actually transfer to real specific working situations? What additional training is needed on the job, and how can one identify that this has been minimized? Of course, these issues also depend on standardization of equipment, but the nature of 'general' skills and knowledge is something that needs more research.

The rest of this note introduces the main points made in the chapters in this section, in two main groups: on identifying and defining training needs and on training methods. As we will see (in common with Section 3 of this book), to concentrate on training needs is too narrow a focus in trying to improve the performance of people using new equipment in new tasks.

TRAINING NEEDS ANALYSIS

There are two stages in defining training and skill needs: obtaining information about the work to be done and then expressing this information within a task description that has implications for training.

Sources of information

There are two sources of information about what is involved in doing a particular task, the workforce itself and various other people who have expertise in either the relevant industry or in training for that industry.

Information from the workforce

The problems of getting information from the workforce are mainly discussed in chapters in other sections of this book. Leplat (Chapter 2) discusses the limitations and difficulties of eliciting information from skilled people doing existing jobs. The main problem with using the existing workforce when designing IT jobs that use new equipment is that these people may not have the appropriate expertise to make the best contribution. Mercy (Chapter 13) and Norros (Chapter 17) outline the advantages and difficulties of involving the workforce in the development of new working methods.

Both Shepherd (Chapter 9) and Norros (Chapter 17) point out the difficulties that arise because people bring the wrong 'mental model' of the new equipment, either in learning how to use it or in discussing how it could be used. People may use a misleading analogy for equipment, such as thinking of a word processor as a typewriter. They may think that the changes are only in technology, and not think of wider changes in the organization as a whole. Conversely, if they are overawed by the new technology, they may assume that it is the best solution to all problems, rather than being aware of its limitations and able to see that other approaches may give a better solution.

Information from experts

The experts consulted about what to include in a training programme may be either experts about the job or experts on training.

Nijhof and Mulder (Chapter 6) used both in their study of vocational training objectives. They discuss the advantages and problems of using a 'curriculum conference' method for eliciting and combining the information from a mixed group of experts, with details of the results obtained from a study using this method.

Shepherd and Hinde (Chapter 7) are concerned with the problems of devising an 'expert system' to do training needs analysis. They make an interesting analysis of what a training expert does. They point out that while most task analysis techniques are formal algorithms for describing a task, in fact training experts tend to use these only for unfamiliar tasks. With familiar tasks, training experts use heuristics. They are familiar with the characteristics of particular tasks and working contexts, and use these general 'prototypes' as reference points for analysing related tasks. The authors discuss the problems of using an expert system for this type of analysis.

Other factors in defining training needs

While we have some understanding of how to analyse task procedures, we have much less understanding of how to analyse and specify the general skills involved in particular work. This sort of analysis should be basic to training which can transfer to other situations. This is another major area of development in training in the new technological context which has not been adequately explored in this book.

Even within the 'task analysis' area there are different approaches to defining what the task involves. Leplat (Chapter 5) analyses the difference between the task 'prescribed' to meet an organization's needs and the 'effective' task, the many ways in which a person might meet this official prescription. Often the official task description is incomplete, so it is necessary to study how people actually do the job. This raises problems of knowledge and skill elicitation.

It is also important to consider the wider context of training, which has two aspects:

1. Skills other than those in using equipment. Introducing new technology into the workplace tends to focus the attention on this technology and to assume that all the training problems are concerned with using the new equipment. In fact, as Shepherd illustrates with a case study, and Nijhof and Mulder also mention, the task as a whole changes with the introduction of new tools, and training in new social or communication skills may have more effect on task achievement than training in how to operate the new equipment.
2. Other aspects that affect performance efficiency. Shepherd and Hinde discuss the problems of identifying the context which 'enables' the work to be carried out effectively. Training is not necessarily the best solution to production difficulties. There are two types of wider issues to consider, to ensure that training is designed within the context of an effective whole:
   (a) Performance may be improved by changes in other aspects of the work, for instances the interface or the allocation of functions between person and machine. These issues are discussed in Section 3 of this book.
   (b) Performance may be limited by factors in the organizational context, for example failures in the flow of information or materials between parts of the organization. It may be more effective to remove these limitations than to concentrate on training to improve the workrate at a particular workplace.

Training methods

Training methods are not reviewed in this introduction because the chapter by Bainbridge (Chapter 8) surveys all the training methods that are mentioned throughout the book. As elsewhere in the book, this chapter emphasizes the change in training methods needed to develop a more flexible way of working, and argues that training for understanding and problem-solving requires the use of learning experiences that develop these skills, rather than the classic training emphasis on repetition in order to automate given behaviour. The chapter also suggests that the need for these more flexible cognitive processes affects training decisions about the place of errors in training and about the fidelity of training equipment.

5. Relations Between Task and Activity in Training

Jacques Leplat

SUMMARY

Training generally has a normative aspect to it in that the trainer attempts to provide the trainee with the capacity to execute a task or a class of tasks, that is the capacity to perform those actions necessary for a satisfactory fulfilment of the task demands. The trainee does not immediately acquire this capacity and the actions performed do not completely satisfy the demands. This relation between activity and task, that evolves during learning, is a very complex one. Hackman (1969) provided an analysis that remains up to date and relevant today. Work psychology has provided its own useful reflection on this theme and this short chapter will remind us of some of the most salient points that help solve some of the psychological problems related to training.

FIRST IMPORTANT DISTINCTION: PRESCRIBED TASK AND EFFECTIVE TASK

The task can be defined as a goal to be reached in given conditions. I have shown with Hoc (Leplat and Hoc, 1983) that these conditions can be expressed in various ways: stages to go through, possible operations, procedures to follow.

The *prescribed task* is defined by the person who controls its execution. In most cases, it is defined by the organization that the work situation is a part of. In the case of training it is the instructor who provides the definition, having often received it from the training programme he or she has followed. The task can be prescribed to a more or less detailed degree: from the simple definition of the goal to a full definition of the execution procedure. The degree of explicitness provided depends on the task designer's idea of the competence of the subject who the task is addressed to and on the type of

Developing Skills with Information Technology
Edited by Lisanne Bainbridge and S. Antonio Ruiz Quintanilla
© 1989 Jacques Leplat
Published by John Wiley & Sons Ltd

training that will be given. A vaguely prescribed task requires more elaboration by the subject, and this can only be rapidly carried out if he or she is already well trained. Otherwise adequate training must be allowed for in order to provide the necessary level.

The prescribed task can be considered as the model that the prescriber develops of the activity of the subject who is going to perform the task. This more or less detailed model may be represented in written instructions or taught orally. The prescribed task is in principle objectively identifiable.

The response to this task is an *activity* which can be more or less successful and more or less satisfy the prescribed demands. This activity has two sides to it. First, it is observable in that it can be recorded and described and one can collect traces of it (through the transformed product for example). The activity also has a hidden side that corresponds to the internal mechanisms that govern its operation. These cognitive mechanisms are not observable and can only be induced from the previous observations.

Associated with this activity is a task where the goals and conditions actually taken into consideration by the subject are represented. As already indicated above, this task does not always correspond to the prescribed task and it is important to distinguish the two. We shall call this task the 'effective task' and we shall speak of two types of task. The effective task is a hypothetical notion inferred from activity. To help us make such an inference we can use our knowledge of the prescribed task and our psychological knowledge of the subject's mode of functioning. This effective task corresponds to a model of the activity elaborated by the psychologist or the analyst. As noted by Hackman (1969), the two types of task—prescribed and effective—are still tasks and therefore can be described and differentiated on the same dimensions (p. 102) (differentiated since they generally do not coincide).

Hackman (1969) has provided a good analysis of the sources of difference between the prescribed and effective tasks, and he speaks of the effective task as the redefined task. Hackman mentions four factors likely to affect the redefinition process:

> a. The degree to which the performer *understands* the task (and if he misunderstands, in what ways); b. The degree to which he accepts the task and is willing to cooperate with its demands; c. The idiosyncratic needs and values which the performer brings to the task situation, and d. The impact of his previous experience with similar tasks (p. 119).

In the other direction one can use these comments to elaborate a certain number of recommendations for training, in order that the prescribed task is internalized with the least distortion possible.

The same kind of analysis of differences between the prescribed and effective task can be used for training. It occurs when the trainer identifies the trainee's errors and seeks their origin. These analyses lead to an examination of how the trainee forms the goals to be attained and how he or she internalizes the task demands (Leplat, 1981; Leplat and Cuny, 1984; Pailhous, 1987).

TERMINOLOGICAL VARIATIONS RELATED TO TRAINING

As often occurs in everyday language, the terms task and activity are polysemous. In particular, within the domain of training, there exists another meaning for task analysis. Resnick (1976) means 'by task analysis the study of complex performances so as to reveal the psychological processes involved. These analyses translate "subject matter" descriptions into psychological descriptions of behavior' (p. 51). In our own terminology we would say that what Resnick is describing as task analysis is the passage from the prescribed task to the activity of the individual carrying it out—thus the passage from the prescribed to the effective task. This is more clearly seen with the distinction the author introduces between rational and empirical task analysis: 'Rational analyses are descriptions of "idealized" performances—that is, performances that succeed in responding to task demands (. . .) not necessarily in the ways in which humans actually perform the task' (p. 64). Empirical task analyses are based on interpretation of the data (errors, latencies, self-reports, eye or hand movements, etc.) from human performance of the task; the aim of such analyses is to develop a description (model) of processes that would account for those data.

The rational task analysis corresponds to a description of the prescribed task, to a model of this task. Within the training context the notion of prescribed task often corresponds simply to a statement of the goal (the problem posed). The rational task corresponds to a more or less detailed description of the procedure in terms of operations that the trainee is supposedly capable of performing but is not informed about. It consists of the description of the prescribed task which is not completely communicated to the subject. If this was not the case, in terms corresponding to the subject's competence, it would allow the immediate execution of the task, and in this case the activity would be pure *execution*. In the first case the activity involves *elaboration* since the subject must discover a procedure of execution that leads to attaining the assigned goals. The empirical task corresponds to the effective task and its analysis is obviously an analysis of the activity for which the effective task is a model. The distinction between task and activity should allow us to remove a number of sources of ambiguity caused by using the notion of task too loosely.

THE TRAINEE'S REPRESENTATIONS OF THE TASK

When studying training it could be useful to know something about the representations of the prescribed and effective tasks that the trainee has developed. These representations must be distinguished from the effective task which is a representation elaborated by the psychologist on the basis of the subject's activity. Indeed, the subject does not necessarily have a clear and precise representation of his or her activity.

The trainee's representation of the prescribed task

We shall attempt to obtain this by asking the following type of question: What is the task you have to do? What is expected from you? The divergences between the representation of the prescribed task and the prescribed task itself will reveal to what extent this task has been badly presented or badly understood by the subject.

The subject's representation of the task he or she is going to perform

This may be obtained with questions such as: What do you aim to do? What task have you given yourself? Any divergence from the previous representation will indicate that the subject has not accepted all the conditions of the task ascribed to him or her; the subject may modify it, often voluntarily, in order to adapt it to his or her possibilities or to the constraints of the group. Studies of workload and its effects on adopted strategies (Leplat, 1975; Sperandio, 1980, 1984) are a good illustration of these divergences.

Any divergence of the results from the prescribed goal constitutes an error for the expert. Any divergence of the results from the goal set by the subject constitutes an error for the subject. What has just been said above shows that these errors do not necessarily coincide.

The difference between the goal set by the subject and the prescribed goal produces planning errors, referred to as mistakes (Reason, 1987), in that the subject actually attains the goal he or she is trying to reach. When the set goal is not attained, the types of error produced are referred to as slips.

The subject's representation of activity after its execution

This would correspond to the question: What have you done? or What task have you performed? The task defined in this way constitutes the model for the subject of the activity that has been performed, to be distinguished from the effective task, the model of the task elaborated by the analyst. Any divergence between these two representations can indicate that the subject does not know how to make the activity explicit or is not totally conscious of it.

Among this set of notions that are usefully distinguished, some are observable 'objects' and others are representations. The first observable object is composed of the modes of expression of the prescribed task. Indeed, this task takes the form of written documents: instructions, work orders. The second observable object is the observable side of the activity. The second type of notion is the representations concerned with these objects. They are unobservable and can only be induced on the basis of different traces. The subject's representations are principally induced from their verbalizations: here we encounter the well-known methodological problems associated with the relationship between verbalizations and what they are supposed to account for (Ericsson and Simon, 1984; Leplat and Hoc, 1983). In particular, the type of question asked by the analyst and the underlying models will play an important role in this externalization. The psychologist's representation of the activity which provides the definition of the effective task is not free of problems either, and it is important to keep in mind the modelistic nature of the notion of effective task. McGrath and Altmann (1966, p. 65, quoted by Hackman, 1969) were correct in noting that 'task is an artificial construct' (p. 100), task meaning effective task here. It is the activity that is observable and not the effective task that is inferred from this activity and constitutes its model.

CONCLUSION

This short chapter has attempted to show the importance of keeping distinctions clear in order to correctly formulate problems related to training. In particular, the notion of task must be carefully defined. The prescribed task, when completely explicit, constitutes the rational task. The trainer has to judge how explicitly the task is to be presented to the trainee, as a function of the trainee's competence. If the level of explicitness corrsponds to the trainee's competence the activity will be purely a question of execution: the subject can directly perform the task on the basis of the instructions. If the level of explicitness is insufficient than the activity will involve elaboration: the subject will have to devise a means or procedure for executing the task. The choice of how the prescribed task is to be defined is a very important aspect of training and should be clearly motivated.

Finally, the study of the subject's representations of the prescribed task and the various phases of the activity, as well as the interpretation of any divergence between these representations, is an important source of information for understanding the underlying mechanisms of the training process. A good knowledge of the prescribed task is very useful in activity analysis. 'It may provide the starting point for empirical data collection, leading to an iterative process in which successively closer matches to human performance models are made' (Resnick, 1976, p. 65). These models concern the activity corresponding to the 'effective task'. This dialectic between prescribed and effective tasks is one of the essential characteristics of the study of work as well as training. It is through the precision of these theoretical and methodological aspects that progress may be made in these two domains.

REFERENCES

Ericsson, K. A., and Simon, H. A. (1984) *Verbal Reports as Data*. Cambridge, Mass.: The MIT Press.

Hackman, J. R. (1969) Toward understanding the role of tasks in behavioral research. *Acta Psychologica*, **31**, 97–128.

Leplat, J. (1975) La charge de travail dans la regulation de l'activite: quelques applications pour les operateurs vieillissants. In A. Laville, C. Teiger and A. Wisner (eds.), *Age et Contraintes de Travail*. Paris, NEB, pp. 209–24.

Leplat, J. (1981) Task analysis and activity analysis in saturation of field diagnosis. In J. Rasmussen and W. B. Rouse (eds.), *Human Detection and Diagnosis of System Failure*. New York: Plenum Press NATO Conference Series, pp. 287–300.

Leplat, J., and Cuny, X. (1984) *Introduction a l'Analyse du Travail*, 2nd ed. Paris: PUF.

Leplat, J., and Hoc, J. M. (1983) Tache et activité dans l'analyse psychologique des situations. *Cahiers de Psychologie Cognitive*, **3**(1), 49–64.

Pailhous, J. (1987) L'organisation des conduites et des donnees. In J. Piaget, P. Mounoud and J. P. Bronckart (eds.), *Psychologie*. Paris: Gallimard, pp. 903–31.

Reason, J. (1987) Generic error-modelling system (GEMS) cognitive framework for locating common human error forms. In J. Rasmussen *et al.* (eds.), *New Technology and Human Error*. Chichester: John Wiley and Sons, pp. 63–86.

Resnick, L. R. (1976) Task analysis in instructional design: some cases from mathematics. In D. Klahr (ed.), *Cognition and Instruction*. Hillsdale, N.J.: Lawrence Erlbaum, pp. 51–80.

Sperandio, J. C. (1980) *La Psychologie en Ergonomie*, Paris: Collègè le Psychologue, PUF.

Sperandio, J. C. (1984) *L'Ergonomie du Travail Mental*. Paris: Masson, 130 pp.

6. Performance Requirements Analysis and Determination

Wim J. Nijhof and Martin Mulder

SUMMARY

In this chapter the authors describe a new method: the curriculum conference in order to fill the gap between job analysis techniques and curriculum design, and development techniques. The conference has been used in two cases, respectively in office automation and in mechanical engineering, in order to find generic objectives (cognitive, skills and attitudes). The conference proved to be an adequate procedure, although some practical and methodological issues remain to be solved. For vocational education lists with generic training, objectives are generated and validated with reference to new information technologies.

CONTEXT

In 1984 the Dutch government began a programme to stimulate and implement new technologies in general and vocational education. This programme, known as INSP, was a rather new innovation because it is the first time the Department of Education and Sciences (DES) has decided to coordinate departments of government in this field of education. Likewise, administrators have never tried to organize a centralized system of innovation in this field. The INSP organization is divided into five clusters:

(a) coordination of infrastructures;
(b) development of educational software and prototypes for primary, secondary, vocational education including adult education;
(c) in-service training;
(d) schooling and preservice training of teachers;
(e) educational research and evaluation on NIT.

Developing Skills with Information Technology
Edited by Lisanne Bainbridge and S. Antonio Ruiz Quintanilla
© 1989 John Wiley & Sons Ltd

Each cluster has a project manager who builds a coordinating team together with a top coordinator.

It is quite clear that this organizational structure was set up to follow a top-down strategy in order to reach the best results in The Netherlands, especially in general education and particularly in primary and secondary education.

The developments in information technology and computer sciences confront business and industry and vocational education with new training demands and needs, linked to hardware and software. Organizations from business and industry and especially from technical schools tried, by means of lobby activities and politicians with a vested interest, to obtain sufficient training apparatus and training programmes. The Dutch Department of Education's policy included the introduction of some regional centres with a central and coordinating function for schools and factories. So far, however, the policy in The Netherlands has been very decentralized in the sense that every school has training facilities.

Every school expected to be given additional facilities as a consequence of the new demands and training needs arising from the developments in computer technology. However, the economic situation and cut-backs during the 1980s have left the Dutch government with insufficient funds to fulfil the needs of every school. Thinking over this problem the Department of Education and Sciences (DES) tried to discover if a policy could be formulated in the direction of general or generic training goals for all vocational schools in The Netherlands. Moreover, the concept of regional training centres could have a special function for all technical schools in training students in specific competencies (in-service training).

The Dutch educational system is highly categorized and selective in nature. Vocational education is split into three levels, a lower, a medium and a higher level. Each level has been further divided into tracks (technical, agriculture, commerce, health and so on). In the framework of this chapter we talk about the medium level of technical education and the lower level of administrative economics education.

These, then, are some components of the Dutch context to give a good understanding of what will follow.

INTRODUCTION AND OUTLINE OF THE ARTICLE

In this contribution we will report some of the results of a research project on the determination and justification of performance requirements for new employees (starters) and the determination of new information technology applications. This project, called BAVBO project, was awarded a grant by the Foundation of Educational Research in the Netherlands (SVO) and was carried out from December 1984 to January 1986. The whole project design and the results are documented in Nijhof and Mulder (1986), Nijhof, Mulder and Remmers (1986) and Nijhof, Remmers and Mulder (1986).

First the problem and research questions are described. In short, the problem is how to analyse and determine performance requirements and how to formulate generic training objectives in the field of office automation (OA) and flexible production automation (FPA). Second, the research and development design will be described. In the BAVBO project the curriculum conference (Frey, 1982) is used as a possible solution to the problem. The curriculum conference is a problem-solving method by groups in which results of research (literature, future developments, survey results and other data) are validated and transformed into a list of possible performance requirements. By means of rating and ranking, the scores are finally used to formulate generic training objectives, and the results and conclusions are described. We have separated the results and conclusions about the performance requirements in OA and FPA because the two domains are different. The evaluation of the curriculum conferences and the comparison between the training objectives in the two domains will be presented.

Finally, we will discuss some of the problems related to the curriculum conference (CC) as a tool for transforming and translating data into generic training objectives and designs for instruction.

DESCRIPTION OF THE PROBLEM AND RESEARCH QUESTIONS

Definitions and focus

New information technology (NIT) applications in business and industry raise new training needs in vocational-oriented curricula. By training needs, we mean discrepancies between the actual and desired situation (Kaufman and English, 1979; Stufflebeam et al., 1985). By curriculum, we mean a document or plan in which instructional processes are planned (Johnson, 1967; Nijhof, 1983). NIT applications denote hardware and software which is available for OA and FPA. Other NIT applications were not investigated. These applications, however, are very diverse and performance requirements in the world of work are very differentiated. We perceive performance requirements as statements about the necessary knowledge and skills for carrying out certain tasks in working situations.

The client system of vocational education is so heterogeneous and so many stakeholders are involved in the decision-making process about new training objectives that the problem arises of how to analyse and determine performance requirements and how to formulate generic training objectives. When found and formulated these can be used as a starting point for further curriculum development.

Thus the focus of our research was mainly the 'what' of training NIT rather than the 'how'. By generic training objectives, we mean the broad knowledge and skill expected of school-leavers who possess the qualifying certificate from a vocational training institution. These skills are, of course, transferable to related job situations and are essential to the performance of many tasks (Smith, 1973, 1974; Mertens, 1974; Lipsmeier, 1982; Laur-Ernst, 1983; Nijhof and Mulder, 1986).

One of the considerations we have to take into account when discussing and determining performance requirements is the optimum configuration for instruction of NIT. We have distinguished four classes of instrumentation related to instruction or training: the traditional technology (that is formal teaching related to conventional apparatus), simulation apparatus, instruction and production apparatus. A combination of instrumentation possibilities gives a certain configuration for instruction.

Searching for solutions

The problem of performance requirements, analysis and determination, and formulating generic training objectives has two sides: first the problem of analysis of job information and second the problem of defining training objectives. The perennial problem, however, is to combine both sources of information in a process of transformation (see Figure 1).

There have been numerous attempts to solve the problem of job analysis, depending on the function this analysis has to fulfil (Teryek, 1979; Peterson and Bownas, 1982; Dedering and Schimming, 1984; Finch and Crunkilton, 1984; Carlisle, 1986; Nijhof, 1986). We assume that most of the job analysis techniques are known, so we will not elaborate further on this. The question is which technique or combination of techniques will lead to precise performance requirements and could be helpful in translating them into generic training objectives. Suffice it to say that in our opinion most of these techniques are not operational enough, nor adequate to solve this problem.

One of the best-known techniques designated for the design of new training programmes using specific task or job analyses is DACUM (Develop A CUrriculuM) (Norton, 1985). This technique uses a workshop of professionals in order to produce a so-called DACUM chart, a map with a systematic description of jobs in terms of duties and tasks. No indications are

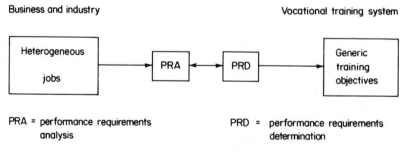

Figure 1. Both sides of the problem

given to determine the performance requirements or to formulate generic training objectives. This job will be left to a curriculum development team. The techniques for determination or justifying performance requirements for educational purposes are to be found in curriculum design and development literature. Although there are many models (Andrews and Goodson, 1980), research synthesis indicates that very little progress has been made on performance requirements analyses related to this determination (Goldstein, 1980). Furthermore, recent strategies for curriculum design and development contain few procedural specifications for the process of determining generic training objectives (Oliva, 1982; Dick and Carey, 1985; Robinson, Ross and White, 1985). The missing link between the two domains of techniques is the structural relation between job (analysis) and educational and instructional requirements. Peterson and Bownas (1982) have tried to develop a matrix of performance requirements in which two categories of taxonomies, task taxonomies and educational taxonomies, are related to each other, but the practical implications and applications of this matrix are not yet clear.

Our aim must therefore be to try and develop a technique or procedure in order to fill this gap. To solve this problem the following research questions are formulated:

1. How can new performance requirements on new information technology applications be analysed within the heterogeneous world of work?
2. How can the decision-making process be structured in such a way that generic training objectives are determined?

ASSUMPTIONS, DESIGN AND EFFECTS

To enable us to cope with our research questions we designed a research and development project called 'Generic knowledge, skills, and attitudes on computer applications in office automation and flexible production systems'. The project consisted of four main stages:

Stage 1. Initial performance requirements analysis.
Stage 2. Curriculum conference.
Stage 3. Formation of training objectives.
Stage 4. Evaluation.

Our main consideration was how to solve the problem of the structural relation between job analysis and determining performance requirements. We believed this link could be found by using a problem-solving method by groups in which representatives of business and industry, on the one hand, and those from the vocational training system, on the other, would solve this problem by deliberation on the basis of data and by means of procedural specifications.

The curriculum conference (CC) is such a technique, developed by Karl Frey (1982). This technique is based on rationality, expertise from the educational field (curriculum expertise) and competence in deliberation. Solutions have to be found by consensus. Although Frey has used this technique mainly in projects oriented to general education, some experiences have been induced from vocational education. A curriculum conference is a strongly prestructured group deliberation situation of 1 to 3 days in which a maximum of 20 representatives of several social institutions (relevant to a particular subject) validate the results of a performance requirements analysis and specify the content (knowledge and skills) of a curriculum that has to be developed. The major task of the group is to reach consensus on its conclusions on the basis of (empirical) research findings, group scores and knowledge, skill and attitudinal statements. During the CC, chaired by the project manager of the research project, subject specialists are available to clarify problems that inhibit the decision-making process.

The theoretical background of the CC has been extensively described in Frey (1982), Hameyer, Frey and Haft (1983) and Nijhof and Mulder (1986).

Stage 1. Initial performance requirements analysis (PRA)

In this stage the target group for training is identified (namely 187 schools for lower administrative vocational education and 62 schools for medium technical vocational education). For these groups PRA was carried out by several techniques. We distinguished the following methods:

— interviews with subject matter specialists;
— questionnaires from expert performers (vocation-, job or task profile holders);
— questionnaires from representatives of personnel officers, training, research and development departments in business and industry;
— observations on the job, walk-and-talk techniques;
— surveys on task profiles with school-leavers;
— structured interviews with teachers, trainers;
— structured interviews with researchers;
— document analysis (curricula, instructional materials);
— literature on future developments on, and actual use of, NIT.

This whole range of data-gathering techniques has been used in order to make an aggregated description of the current state of NIT in schools and in factories and offices (Spenner, 1985).

Because performance requirements are analysed in a heterogeneous world of work, it is necessary to detect those variables that are responsible for most of the variance in performance requirements. The variables we distinguished are: company size, type of economic activity, rate of technological innovation and vocational group of the respondent. The results of this stage were aggregated in three chapters of a research report with information about: (a) school-leavers/starters; (b) business and industry; (c) the vocational training system (split up into office administration and technical education).

As a result of a content analysis of the research findings a list of possible knowledge, skill and attitude aspects was compiled. This information was the input for stage 2.

Stage 2. The curriculum conference

Two curriculum conferences were organized, one for office automation and one for mechanical engineering (technical education). Representatives from both the educational system and from business and industry were selected to analyse the results of the information document and to rate the performance requirements on a scale with two dimensions: the level of performance (behaviour) and the level of relevance.

During the preparation of the CC the following steps were taken:

— formulating the goal of the CC;
— inviting the participants;
— producing the information document;
— producing the working document;
— practical preparation;
— planning the conference program (logistics);
— making guidelines for the participants.

The participants of the CC prepared for the sessions by reading the information document of 50 pages and by filling in a working document.

The working document contains: (a) forms to write down conclusions about the chapters of the information document from stage 1; (b) a questionnaire about the personal expectations of the CC and the assessment of the information document; and (c) the knowledge, skill and attitude score forms. The scores were formatted with a taxonomy developed by Olbrich and Pfeiffer (1980).

The taxonomy of Olbrich and Pfeiffer contains two dimensions. The first describes the job aspects: the kind of work, the sequence of tasks, the frame factors of work, conditions for cooperation and responsibility related to levels of mastery. The second dimension describes mainly the cognitive and affective aspects: the kind of learning behaviour, the organization of the learning process, the use of media, the use of subject matter and, lastly, the motivational aspects of learning. All of those are related to levels of mastery.

We used the second dimension because the job aspects have been covered by stage 1. In the cognitive dimension four levels of mastery of educational aims are defined: knowing, understanding, application and evaluation. There is a clear analogy with the well-known Bloom taxonomy (Bloom, 1956; Romiszowski, 1981)

The conference itself consisted of four stages: (a) introduction; (b) analysis of the information document; (c) deliberation and decision-making about the knowledge, skills and attitudes necessary; consensus ought to be reached; (d) evaluation of the CC.

Stage 3. Formulation of training objectives

Given the fact that the CC is a very intensive procedure for participants and the chairman, the research team must, after the conference, put the finishing touch on formulating the (training) objectives in operational terms. As a consequence of the deliberations, several arguments and statements are made about the context and the implications of the knowledge, skills and attitudes related to automation and NIT. It is therefore essential that a precise job should be done. Although it would be worthwhile to assess the final result from the participants, this did not take place because the refinement of the formulation of objectives did not change the substance, and also because of a lack of time and money.

Stage 4. Evaluation of the curriculum conference as a tool

One of the goals of the whole project was to evaluate the effectiveness and efficiency of the CC. Because of the use of the CC in two domains, we can speak of two different projects within the main route we described earlier. It becomes possible to formulate conclusions by comparing the two conferences. The design of the evaluation is depicted in Figure 2.

This design is based on the principle that in conventional research (surveys) respondents will rate statements offered by a research team. On the basis of cluster or discriminant analysis the interpretation can lead to dominant profiles of statements referring to cognitive, psychomotor and attitudinal skills. However, we know that the validity and reliability of such procedures might be low, especially when the non-response is very high or when the sample is biased (Bilderbeek and Smits, 1985)

Consensus in a CC might be a better measure. However, even here some methodological issues arise. The group is rather small and perhaps not representative of the population of expert workers in education and industrial training. On the other hand, deliberation can lead to a valid and reliable analysis of concepts and statements. Whatever route we take we may establish agreement. Finally we can discuss the question of whether group behaviour will model the behaviour of every member of the group. Dominant roles, charisma, the place and the status of members in the group can mould the

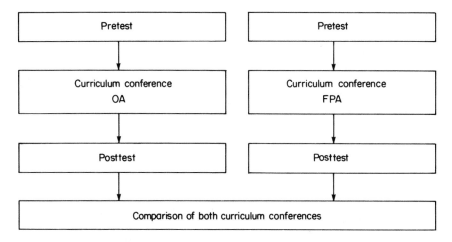

Figure 2. Design of the evaluation of the curriculum conference

deliberation process in an unwanted and unforeseeable direction. To allow some control of this process we can measure intervening variables like feelings in the group, group cohesion, satisfaction and commitment with the ultimate results.

In order to gather relevant data we used an analogy of the one-group pretest–posttest design (Campbell and Stanley, 1971). The pretest consisted of an individual questionnaire with three categories of questions: (a) personal data; (b) motives and expectancies; (c) assessment of the information document.

The posttest consisted of individual questionnaires with questions on the following topics: (a) the effectiveness of the information document; (b) information during the CC; (c) experiences related to expectancies and motives; (d) personal experiences during the CC; (e) judgement of the procedure as a whole.

The whole process of the two conferences has been registered on video-tapes. These have been used for further analysis (communication structure, arguments analysis, deliberation and rationality). Some results of this analysis were added to the final report, while others are integrated in a comprehensive review article on the use of curriculum conferences (Mulder, Nijhof and Remmers, 1987), on the basis of several studies within our Department of Education, Division of Curriculum Technology, University of Twente.

RESULTS

In this section we will describe the results on the performance-requirements analysis of OA and FPA, the curriculum conferences and the determination of generic training objectives.

Performance requirements in office automation (OA)

The major characteristic of OA in business and industry is that it has structural consequences for the information flow in the organization. More complete data are available, which can be reached more quickly. These data can be used at policy level for management decisions. Office automation has radical consequences for lower administrative jobs because many of the tasks are taken over by automated systems.

The following performance requirements are stated by respondents from 25 firms:

— knowledge of hard- and software;
— an understanding of the place of the tasks in the working unit or department of a company;
— an understanding of the data source, data destination and the consequences of error;
— numeric and alphanumeric keyboard skills;
— perseverance;
— precision, coping with stress;
— interactive skills.

We have seen that the work of administrative personnel becomes more service and client oriented, which is easier with automated office systems. This process has the following consequences for performance requirements and therefore for the formulation of training objectives:

— basic language skills;
— commerical understanding;
— knowledge of the importance of information and information processing;
— client-oriented actions.

In small- or medium-sized companies, the performance requirements cover a broader range and are of a higher level compared with the larger companies, because of the more integrated functions in one job. Performance requirements stated by representatives of vocational education are:

— understanding of computer systems;
— knowledge of the English jargon;
— knowledge of some software packages (like text processing, financial programs, coding and decoding, sorting programs, file management, invoice program, spreadsheets, data communication);
— skills on text processing;
— keyboard handling;

— starting the system;
— data entry and data modification;
— working with menus;
— capable of reading instructions (manuals);
— working with integrated software packages;
— handling of output, listing;
— storage of data carriers.

Research on school leavers has pointed out that 16 per cent of the certificated students have found a job within 0 to 12 months after leaving school. Only 4 per cent of the population, however, worked with computers in 1985. Therefore it seems to be more appropriate to identify the performance requirements that are relevant for *further* training in administration because of the expected growth of automation in The Netherlands (Mulder and van Lent, 1988).

Performance requirements in flexible production automation (FPA)

The main characteristic of FPA is that rather independent working places and machinery will be integrated into group technology, controlled by some closely cooperating workers. Controlling the complex total of production methods requires knowledge of the relations between the various machines and machine parts and of the technological meaning of the sequence of production phases. We observed a much closer link between work preparation and production in the companies than we expected from our knowledge of the literature or from interviews with experts. This implies a much greater knowledge and (meta-)skill level for trainees and school-leavers than was expected. This is particularly true of a more general knowledge about planning, management of organizations and connections between parts of the organization, which is crucial when working with automated systems. Representatives of 20 companies have stated the following performance requirements:

— general knowledge of informatics (computer science);
— digital control technique;
— electronics;
— computer-aided design (CAD);
— robotics and process controlling;
— practical skills in traditional mechanical engineering, like milling, turning, lathing, installing;
— knowlege of tools and materials on computer numeric controlled (CNC) machines;
— subject matter (disciplines) like mathematics, stereometry and geometry will again become important;

— much emphasis is also laid upon administration;
— planning and management, work preparation and cost-effectiveness analysis competencies are considered to be extremely important.

Representatives from vocational education have stated the following requirements:

— theoretical knowledge of computer science;
— knowing how to handle CNC machines (programming, service, safety aspects, etc.);
— mastery of digital control techniques;
— elementary knowledge of electronics;
— computer aided design (CAD), as an essential tool and technique;
— electrotechnical engineering as a practical tool;
— business administration, management and organizational knowledge are important;
— robotics is not a major issue; attention has to be paid to developments in this field;
— process control is an important object, theoretical as well as practical;
— attitudinal components like quality control, responsibility towards apparatus, being systematic and having skills to communicate with people in the plant.

Comparison between office automation and flexible production automation

If we compare the results of the foregoing analysis we see that the performance requirements in OA stated by the representatives of the companies are more global than those in FPA. Within both domains the representatives of vocational education overestimate the rate of technological innovation in offices and factories and therefore the necessary performance requirements. All participants in both domains state that there is no structural communication between vocational education and companies in order to update the common knowledge, which has a negative effect on the revision of curricula for NIT.

NIT tends to upgrade the level of competency needed for work with FPA, including a higher degree of mental preplanning of the production process. Computer applications in office automation, however, seem to demand higher performance requirements in front office jobs and lower ones in back office jobs. For all the applications of NIT we see that knowledge of the non-automated working process remains very important. The attitudinal component of the generic cognitive training objectives are very much emphasized although these requirements have not yet been differentiated.

Two other aspects arise from the evaluation of the results. Representatives from business and industry have more problems in explicitly and specifically formulating the necessary performance requirements. Their statements are rather global, whereas participants from the vocational system are used to formulating and specifying competencies. This might seem a trivial conclusion, and indeed it is, but it means that a mix of information sources for this group to analyse performance requirements might be very helpful and instructive. A second point concerns the preferable kind of instruction mode. Companies do not prefer computer simulation as an instruction tool, or instructional production machines, as the *only* preparation for work with very expensive computer numerically controlled (CNC) machines. They favour modest use of this new equipment, as well as conventional techniques of training.

The curriculum conference: processes and products

The CC as an approach to determining the design of a curriculum including instructional or training objectives has been effective but only partly efficient because of difficulties with the rating of statements at the preparation stage of the participants. The content dimension as used in the Olbrich and Pfeiffer taxonomy proved to be multi-interpretable and the scoring of the behavioural component was not clear. During the sessions these problems could be corrected, but it caused a partial loss of the data of the pretest.

The taxonomy for the analysis and rating of performance requirements ought to facilitate and structure the decision-making process. In practice, however, the use of taxonomies requires some kind of training. We tried to offer a 'simple' part out of the taxonomy of Olbrich and Pfeiffer, because validation processes must not be blocked by complex instruments. Certain well-defined clusters of generic knowledge, skills and attitudes on NIT applications related to OA and FPA systems have been formulated and justified and will presumably be translated into curricula. Corporations and non-profit organizations can provide additional specific competence-based training (on the job).

The generic training objectives

List of generic training objectives were compiled as a result of the curriculum conferences. This, however, proved to be no simple process of bargaining or deliberation, because the relationships between relevance and transferability of both lateral and vertical objectives within jobs had to be conjectured. The process of deliberation was sometimes tough and intensive, but open and constructive, and led to 51 objectives for OA and 68 for FPA. These objectives were grouped into main clusters, most of them induced from the prestudies and the school curricula (see Table 1).

Table 1: Clusters of generic training objectives for office and flexible production automation

Office automation		Flexible production automation	
1. Automation in working organizations	(12)	1. Basic informatics	(5)
2. Computer use and		2. Business administration	(9)
administration	(16)	3. Controlling technique	(12)
3. Data entry and control	(8)	4. CAD systems	(9)
4. Data processing	(8)	5. Electronics	(1)
5. Text processing	(7)	6. Electronic technology	(5)
		7. Measuring and regulation technology	(4)
		8. CNC technology	(8)
		9. Process technology	(2)
		10. Robotics	(13)
Total	(51)		(68)

(. .) = number of generic training objectives per cluster

A simple view of this table shows two dominant categories in OA related to NIT in organizations and administration, whereas the spread over categories in FPA is broader. For this the two dominant categories are use and knowledge of robots and control techniques. Table 1 gives a general overview of the number of objectives related to main categories. To give some insight into the nature of the generic training objectives we take four objectives from the FPA cluster 'measuring and regulation technology':

1. The student is capable to handle knowledge on cybernetics.
2. The student is capable to handle knowledge on automatization related to pneumatic analogical apparatus.
3. The student knows how to use electronic digital apparatus related to automatization of regulation systems.
4. The student knows how to use electronic analogous apparatus related to automatization of regulation systems.
He knows how to handle mathematical equations and tools in order to solve problems of this kind. He is capable to enact on the basis of detailed plans and prescriptions. (Nijhof and Mulder, 1986, p. 236).

Table 2 is more important for our purposes, however. The groups were required to make judgements of relevance on the cognitive (K) and skills (S) aspects, each of them consisting of four levels. The cognitive aspect contains: knowing (K1), understanding (K2), application (K3), and evaluation (K4). The skills aspect contains: observing (S1), handling (S2), executing (S3), mastery (S4).
After a general plenum discussion the participants decided to exclude levels

Table 2: Indication of the relevance and level of generic training objectives in office and flexible production automation

Office automation							Flexible production automation						
Cluster	K1	K2	K3	S1	S2	S3	Cluster	K1	K2	K3	S1	S2	S3
1		×		Not relevant			1			*			*
2		*			*		2		*		×		
3		*			*		3		×			×	
4		×		*			4		*				×
5		*			*		5	×			×		
							6	×			×		
							7		×		*		
							8		*				*
							9		*			*	
							10	×					×

Cluster 1 to *n*, see Table 1.
K1 = knowing   S1 = observing   × = important
K2 = understanding   S2 = handling   * = absolutely necessary
K3 = application   S3 = executing

K4 and S4. No school-leaver or new employee can be expected to show complete mastery of a job; moreover, generic skills must give him or her the opportunity to learn and train in the future (on the job–off the job) in order to reach full competence and qualifications.

Table 2 presents the dominant scores on the knowledge and skill aspects in each cluster, showing relative importance and level of mastery. In this table, the mean of the unanimous subgroup scores are indicated. For a good understanding of the measure it is necessary to give some background information. During the curriculum conference the group as a whole is striving to reach consensus. It proved not be be realistic and feasible to discuss all the possible performance requirements in one group, so we decided to cover the whole by splitting up the group in five subgroups of four persons. Every group would take half of the main categories in such a way that the whole task was covered. Each group should argue the various aspects and reach consensus by rating and ranking. The mean score of all subgroup scores was taken as the criterion for decision-making.

As we can see from this table the conference members decided also to exclude the K1 and S1 objectives. The rationale is that knowing and observing are prerequisites for the other levels, but can be seen as basics, not as generic objectives with transferability. So the main categories are understanding (K2), application (K3), handling (S2), and executing (S3). Further, there is a strong correspondence between the cognitive and skills level. This means that understanding and handling, on the one hand, and application and executing, on the other, have common grounds and a related psychological basis. Most of the objectives selected in OA are absolutely necessary, whereas in FPA the number of important objectives ($\times$) ($n = 11$) dominates the absolutely necessary ones (*) ($n = 9$).

It is remarkable to see that all the clusters are relevant or absolutely necessary, except cluster 1 for OA in the skills domain. The reason for cluster 1 is that a new employee should know how important automation is for the organization, but he or she need not be capable of handling or executing the implementation of automatization.

The conferences formulated clear but rather global statements with regard to attitudinal aspects. As a consequence of NIT and automation, OA and FPA employers expect much more flexibility from employees. This is because (meta-)cognitive skills like systematic thinking and planning, analytical reasoning, problem-solving attitudes, adaptiveness and an innovative attitude are essential to their function. As a consequence of these aspects we found that communication skills and taking initiatives are very important, as are those competencies of employees that concern possible risks in an organization, such as responsibility, cost-effectiveness, attitude and being accurate and precise. The reason for this is clearly because every fault or mistake can have tremendous consequences, especially in firms where precious apparatus is used and the production has been completely automated (Nijhof and Mulder, 1986, pp. 252 and 272).

Conclusions on results

Returning to research questions about the way in which performance requirements in NIT applications can be analysed within the heterogeneous world of work and how the decision-making process can be structured in such a way that generic training objectives are determined, we draw the following final conclusions.

First of all we want to avoid the mistake that there should be a one-to-one relationship between performance requirements and the curriculum content of vocational training objectives. Second, the vocational training system should not be technologically determined by business and industry. Many variables that are responsible for variance in the curriculum-development process should be taken into account during the process of performance-requirements analysis and determination. Various sources of information ought to be used.

Our conclusion is that the curriculum conference is a worthwhile instrument for filling the gap between performance-requirements analysis and the determination of instructional objectives. The structure of the curriculum conference itself and the guidelines for executing the conference and its preparation proved to be successful in two cases, office automation and flexible production automation.

The conference is a generic method, a problem-solving method by groups, and its strength is based on a combination of expertise, rationality, cooperation and intelligence, which will lead to valid and reliable outcomes.

In our case we tried to find generic training objectives for two vocational domains closely connected to NIT. Although we did succeed, some practical and methodological issues have not yet been completely solved and need further discussion.

DISCUSSION

In this chapter the curriculum conference method as a tool was the central element in the process of generating and justifying instructional objectives for vocational training in new information technologies. We opted for this method because of our earlier experiences of it in the printing industry, and other experiences we had in combination with the National Institute for Curriculum Development in The Netherlands (SLO). Moreover, the conference is based on explicit assumptions on rationality and consensus-building from the argumentation theory of the Erlanger Schule (Frey, 1982; Hameyer, Frey and Haft, 1983; Nijhof, 1985) and on the generic guiding model from Frey and from Aregger (1973).

The conference is of practical use in the sense that the procedural specifications are clear, and are very open to the user. We, for instance, decided to use the taxonomy of Olbrich and Pfeiffer (1980) in order to arrange and rearrange the complexity of information and possible instructional objectives.

The conference model is quite suitable for research and evaluation purposes. Different studies are still in progress, comparing the processes and effects of the DACUM method and the curriculum conference (Hesse and Nijhof, 1988).

In this section we first discuss some problems related to the curriculum conference as a method, and second we will discuss the question of the implications of the generic skills for training and transfer.

The curriculum conference as method: some problems

The *selection of participants* is a crucial part of the CC. The question is who is the right person to participate in the decision-making process. There is no single and simple answer to this question. We distinguish fifteen personal and group criteria. The personal criteria are: knowledge of the target group, of the subject, and of job practice, communication skills, and positive attitude to education and training. Group criteria are: company size, sector of economic activity, rate of technological innovation, functional area, region, subjects and relation to curriculum development. A question related to the problem of selection criteria is whether one should select persons on these criteria and, if so, how? In many cases there is no possibility of selecting participants for a CC, because of practical constraints or ethical objections. Some people from small industries cannot be spared from their organization, not even for one day. Sometimes the processes of production are confidential, so people are not free to speak openly.

Even so, the group composition will influence the results. For purposes of research, to control the process variables, the selection of participants has to be carried out by means of well-defined criteria. Selection on the basis of an ideal group profile might be a solution.

The *information document* is a crucial source in the CC. Although these materials were available ten days or more before the CC, a certain number of participants did not read them or refused to fill in the working document. The consequence is a (partial) loss of data and a (partial) loss of reliability of the analysis and determination process due to the differences in preparation level. Part of the problem was that participants did not understand the taxonomy to be used in order to rate the cognitive and skill aspects of the job. This problem might be avoided by taking more time for instruction, reading and scoring. Frey prefers conferences that take longer than we were able to do—five days for a whole curriculum design. We used two days for justifying the instructional objectives and for arranging them in main clusters or disciplines.

A third problem has to do with the *reliability and validity* of the scoring procedure we used. Is it really true that differences between individuals can be eliminated by a rather short deliberation process? We have seen large shifts of individual scores towards group scores. Do these shifts hold after a period of time, or do they stand only during the conference days? If not, the curriculum conference has led to generic training objectives that are not very solid. A follow-up project (Van den Berg and Nijhof, 1987) checked whether the formulated generic training objectives hold for constructing instructional materials for mechanical engineering. For office automation the National Institute for Curriculum Development (SLO) used the objectives for constructing curriculum materials.

The participants believe the whole project has delivered many generic training objectives. These objectives can be added to the curriculum, or they can replace others. As far as the attitudinal aspects are concerned, we found many statements referring to general cognitive qualities and competencies. These are not new but underline the necessity to strengthen these competencies to such a degree that the generic training objectives are more or less bound to specific matter at higher levels than before.

A serious problem arises. Do we need an additional curriculum approach or do we need an integrated one? The second might prove promising. The whole content and structure of the existing curricula together with the frame factors have not been part of the BAVBO project. For an implementation of these objectives in schools and training centres, curriculum teams have to be built with specific knowledge of the frame factors of mechanical engineering and with knowledge of the total structure of the curriculum.

Implications for transfer and training

In this last subsection we will discuss some implications of generic training objectives for instruction and for transferability.

Let us remind the reader of the fact that the focus of research was to generate generic skills and objectives related to new information technologies. Thus the main focus of the project was curricular in nature, that is to say, the 'what' question had to be answered. The question is, however, whether we can justify objectives that cannot be implemented in instruction or do not have the expected transferability. The quality of transfer was the most crucial point in the definition of generic skills. We have seen that the participants of the conferences decided to exclude two levels of objectives, the simple level of knowing (cognitive aspect) and observing (skills aspect) and the level of evaluation (cognitive aspect) and mastery (skill aspect). The question is whether or not the two other levels in the taxonomy of Olbrich and Pfeiffer have transfer abilities in principle. This depends on the definition of transfer, of course. 'In general terms, the word *transfer* refers to the influence of learning in one situation or context upon subsequent learning in another situation or context. Thus we would be concerned with transfer when we studied . . . the effect of learning in school on performance outside school or, more generally, the effect of past learning on present learning' (Ausubel and Robinson, 1969, p. 136). According to the theory of transfer Ausubel and Robinson distinguish three forms of transfer: lateral, sequential and vertical. Lateral and sequential transfer are essentially horizontal in that the learner stays within the same behavioural category in making a transfer (p. 138). Vertical transfer, however, facilitates learning from one behavioural level to a higher behavioural level, for instance comprehension can lead to problem-solving. If we stay within the taxonomy of Olbrich and Pfeiffer we know that the generic objectives have been formulated at the level of understanding (comprehension) and application, for the cognitive aspect. The skills aspects were handling and executing. From the connotations and descriptions of Olbrich and Pfeiffer we know that at these levels *rule learning* will take place and generalizations will be fostered by using similar situations, cases and circumstances. Also, in principle, all objectives must have transferability when the participants and the research staff have checked and formulated them according to this principle.

However, the kind of transfer might differentiate between lateral, sequential and vertical transfer. In office automation, for instance, within the domain of text processing, we must ask whether training with 'word perfect' will lead to lateral tansfer to other text-processing packages or whether knowledge of the basic principles of mathematics and electronics will lead to problem-solving in programming CNC machines (vertical transfer).

How the training should be carried out for generic objectives is an interesting question because different options are available. In our questionnaires and interviews we asked the companies and schools to indicate what kind of instruction (on-the-job–off-the-job–in-service training) would be the best at what stage of experience. We received no clear answer. The use of modern equipment, teaching machines, simulation apparatus, CNC machines are encouraged in mechanical engineering, but in a very wise arrangement. In office automation the biggest need is for text-processing machines. Classrooms in office automation courses look like real offices, so the experience in working with modern machinery stimulates the transfer from school to work.

The in-service training of teachers in new training techniques like simulation and CNC apparatus takes place within the framework of the national project on information technology (INSP). This special project is called NABONT and its purpose is to have personnel trained to an advanced level in schools and regional centres, in order to foster the transfer of knowledge between school and work and between teacher and student. Experimental studies will have to prove which kind of instruction will have better transfer effects (better retention of older learning, better results on standard tests, significantly better problem-solving behaviour and so on). However, first of all we need instructional plans and curricula based on generic objectives. Once these have been supplied the proof will follow.

ACKNOWLEDGEMENTS

We gratefully acknowledge the help of Mrs Anne Simpson for editing the text. This article is based on a study funded by the National Institute for Educational Research in The Netherlands (SVO) in The Hague.

REFERENCES

Andrews, D. H., and Goodson, L. A. (1980) A comparative analysis of models of instructional design. *Journal of Instructional Development*, **3**(4), 2–16.
Aregger, K. (1973) Interaktion im Lehrerzentrierten Curriculumprozess. In *Analysen und Perspectiven über die Freiburger Lehrplanreform*. Basel: EBAC-PS-projekt.
Ausubel, D. P., and Robinson, F. G. (1969) School learning. *An Introduction to Educational Psychology*. London: Holt, Rinehart and Winston.
Bilderbeek, R. H., and Smits, R. E. H. M. (1985) Methoden en Technieken van toekomstonderzoek en de aansluiting onderwijs—arbeid; op zoek naar mogelijkheden. In *Beleidsstudies en Informatie*. Apeldoorn: TNO.

Bloom, B. S. (1956) *Taxonomy of educational objectives*. Handbook I: *Cognitive Domain*. New York: Longmans Green.

Campbell, D. T., and Stanley, J. C. (1971) Experimental and quasi-experimental designs for research on teaching. In N. L. Gage (ed.), *Handbook of Research on Teaching*. Chicago: Rand McNally and Company, pp. 171–247.

Carlisle, K. E. (1986) *Analyzing Jobs and Tasks*. Englewood Cliffs, N.J.: Educational Technology Publications.

Dedering, H., and Schimming, P. (1984) *Qualifikationsforschung und arbeitsorientierte Bildung*. Opladen: Westdeutscher Verlag.

Dick, W., and Carey, L. (1985) *The Systematic Design of Instruction*. Glenview, Illinois/London: Scott, Foreman and Company.

Finch, C. R. and Crunkilton, J. R. (1984) *Curriculum Development in Vocational and Technical Education: Planning, Content and Implementation*. New York: Allyn and Bacon.

Frey, K. (1982) *Curriculum Conference: an Approach for Curriculum Development in Groups*. Kiel: Institute for Science Education.

Goldstein, I. R. (1980) Training in work organizations. In M. R. Rosenweig and L. W. Porter (eds.), *Annual Review of Psychology*, Vol. 31. Palo Alto, pp. 229–72.

Hameyer, U., Frey, K., and Haft, H. (eds.) (1983) *Handbuch der Curriculumforschung*. Weinheim/Basel: Beltz Verlag.

Hesse, C. G., and Nijhof, W. J. (1988). *Dacum in de Boekenbranche. Beroepsprofielen van uitgevers en boekhandelaren in relatie tot moderne technologieën*. Enschede/Amsterdam.

Johnson, M. (1967) Definitions and models in curriculum theory. *Educational Theory*, 17(2), 127–39.

Kaufman, R., and English, F. W. (1979) *Needs Assessment. Concept and Application*. Englewood Cliffs, N.J.: Educational Technology Publication.

Laur-Ernst, U. (1983) Zur Vermittlung berufsübergreifender Qualifikationen. Oder: Warum und wie lernt man abstraktes Denken? *Berufsbildung in Wissenschaft und Praxis*, 12(6), December, 187–90.

Lipsmeier, A. (1982) Die didaktische Struktur des beruflichen Bildungswesens. In *Enzyklopädie Erziehungswissenschaft*, Vol. 9, Section II. Jugendbildung zwischen Schule und Beruf. Teil 1: Handbuch. Stuttgart: Klett-Cotha, pp. 227–50.

Mertens, D. (1974) Schlüsselqualifikationen. Thesen zur Schulung für eine moderne Gesellschaft. *Mitteilungen aus der Arbeitsmarkt- und Berufsforschung*, 7, 36–43.

Mulder, M., and van Lent, J. (1988) *Kantoorautomatisering. Een onderzoek voor Leerplanontwikkeling*. Lisse: Swets and Zeitlinger.

Mulder, M., Nijhof, W. J., and Remmers, J. L. M. (1987) *An Exploration of the Curriculumconference*. Paper presented for the AERA annual meeting, 23 April 1987, Washington.

Nijhof, W. J. (1983) *Over het ontwerpen van curricula* (oratie), (*Beyond designing curricula*) (inauguration). Enschede: Technische Hogeschool Twente.

Nijhof, W. J. (1985) Ontwikkelingen in het curriculumonderzoek. In R. Halkes and R. Wolbert (eds.), *Docent en Methode*. Lisse: Swets and Zeitlinger.

Nijhof, W. J. (1986) Van beroepsprofielen naar curriculum profielen: tussen aanpassing en innovatie. Paper presented at the Annual Meeting of the Dutch Association of Educational Research, Utrecht.

Nijhof, W. J., and Mulder, M. (eds.) (1986) *Basisvaardigheden in het Beroepsonderwijs*. (Generic Skills in Vocational Education). 's Gravenhage: Stichting voor Onderzoek van het Onderwijs.

Nijhof, W. J., Mulder, M., and Remmers, J. L. M. (1986) Basisvaardigheden beroepsonderwijs: Vooronderzoek en eindresultaten. In J. S. ten Brinke, J. Hooymayers and G. Kanselaar (eds.). *Vakdidactiek en Informatietechnologie in curriculumontwikkeling*. Bijdragen aan de Onderwijsresearch. Lisse: Swets and Zeitlinger, 153–171.

Nijhof, W. J., Remmers, J. L. M., and Mulder, M. (1986) Evaluatie van de leerplanconferentiemethode in het basisvaardighedenproject (Bavbo-project). In Nijhof, W. J. (ed.), *Van Beroepsprofielen naar Curriculumprofielen*. Een symposium over methoden en technieken en beschouwingen over de relatie tussen beroepskwalificaties en eindtermen. Enschede: Universiteit Twente, Faculteit der Toegepaste Onderwijskunde, 63–76.

Norton, R. E. (1985) *DACUM Handbook*. Columbus: The National Center for Research in Vocational Education, The Ohio State University.

Olbrich, G., and Pfeiffer, V. (1980) Darstellung und Anwendung eines Hierarchisierungssystem für Lernziele in der beruflichen Bildung. In *Berichte zur Beruflichen Bildung*, Vol. 25. Berlin: Bundesinstitut fur Berufsbildung.

Oliva, P. F. (1982) *Developing the Curriculum*. Boston/Toronto: Little, Brown and Company.

Peterson, N. G., and Bownas, O. A. (1982) Skill, task structure and performance acquisition. In M. D. Dunette and E. A. Fleishman (eds.), *Human Performance and Productivity: Human Capability Assessment*. Hillsdale, N.J.: Lawrence Erlbaum.

Robinson, F. G., Ross, J. A., and White, F. (1985) *Curriculum Development for Effective Instruction*. Ontario: OISE Press.

Romiszowski, A. J. (1981) *Designing Instructional Systems. Decision Making in Course Planning and Curriculum Design*. London/New York: Kogan Page/Nichols Publishing.

Smith, A. D. W. (1973) *Generic Skills*. Prince Albert, Saskatchewan: New Start.

Smith, A. D. W. (1974) *Generic Skills in the Reasoning and Interpersonal Domains*. Prince Albert, Saskatchewan: Training, Research and Development Station.

Spenner, K. J. (1985) The upgrading and downgrading of occupations: issues, evidence, and implications for education. *Review of Educational Research*, **55**(2), 125–54.

Stufflebeam, D. L., McCormick, C. H., Brinkerhoff, R. O., and Nelson, C. O. (1985) *Conducting Educational Needs Assessment*. Dordrecht: Kluwer Academic Publishers Group.

Teryek, C. J. (1979) An overview of job analysis. Methods, procedures and issues in vocational education. In Th. Abramson, C. K. Tittle and L. Cohen (eds.), *Handbook of Vocational Education Evaluation*. Beverly Hills London: Sage.

Van den Berg, E., and Nijhof, W. J. (1987) *Moduleren Technische Informatica in de MTS. Researchvoorstel voor de Stichting voor Onderzoek van het Onderwijs*. Enschede: Universiteit Twente Vakgroep Curriculumtechnologie.

7. Mimicking the Training Expert: A Basis for Automating Training Needs Analysis

Andrew Shepherd and C. J. Hinde

SUMMARY

Training needs analysis (TNA) relies upon the expertise of human analysts to supplement the formal task analysis methods of occupational psychology. Therefore, providing a computer-based approach to TNA entails mimicking the human expert. An approach to TNA, based on modelling organizations with task and context prototypes, is described.

INTRODUCTION

Training analysis and design has been a central issue in occupational psychology for many years. A major preoccupation has been the development of formal methods of task analysis to identify training needs leading to training design. These are reviewed by Patrick (1980). The main approach has been to break tasks down and categorize the resultant task elements according to psychological types from which training hypotheses can be inferred; for example Miller's information processing approach (for example 1967) or Gagne's conditions for learning taxonomy (for example 1970). An implicit aim of this work is to provide techniques enabling unambiguous training decisions to be made without reliance upon the skills of the analyst. People inexperienced in training analysis could thus make reliable practical training decisions by applying straightforward rules or procedures. Unfortunately, such techniques can never be applied so easily. Diagnosis of a training problem and the selection of training conditions are substantially influenced by *contextual* factors such as technology, safety, profitability, custom and practice and organizational culture. Hence, training analysis and design

Developing Skills with Information Technology
Edited by Lisanne Bainbridge and S. Antonio Ruiz Quintanilla
© 1989 John Wiley & Sons Ltd

invariably relies on the experience of the training analyst to interpret these contextual factors. Formal or semi-formal techniques, in the hands of experienced practitioners, are often very effective, but when appropriate discretion cannot be exercised, these techniques may be found wanting.

A large number of people in industry, commerce and the public services need to explore the tasks in their charge systematically in order to overcome problems and implement effective practices to optimize human performance. Unfortunately, too few of them are able or prepared to invest in the experience necessary for them to become effective task analysts. With the current interest in expert systems it is tempting to explore the potential for providing computer aiding for these training analysis procedures. One approach is to try to emulate the expert using formal task analysis methods. This is less promising than it may at first appear, because the formal methods themselves are found wanting with regard to dealing with the issue of task context, as discussed earlier. Examining how 'experts' involved in diagnosing human performance problems in organizations accommodate variations of task context within a formal approach is quite revealing, because it becomes clear that few such experts willingly use formal methods when they can get away with making judgements based upon their experience. We may, therefore, either persist in trying to sort out what experts actually do to try to make formal task analysis methods work or we may consider instead how training experts actually set about their task of training analysis and design.

This chapter will examine the feasibility of developing a computer-based training advisory system by reference to how training experts appear to set about the problem. At the outset it is important to state that the solution suggested is not claimed to be in any sense an emulation of the cognition of training experts. Instead, the strategies of human experts are examined to provide guidance on *what such a system should achieve*. It must be acknowledged, of course, that some notions of how experts think has prompted the structuring of the proposed system, but no means of validating this is apparent. Therefore, no claims will be made regarding the psychological validity of the knowledge structures suggested.

Rather than applying formal task analysis methods to problems with which they are familiar, training experts seem to deal with problems facing them on the basis of experience by matching a new situation to situations they have encountered in the past. Few real training problems are entirely novel; most situations can be constructed from the bits and pieces of other situations. Experts only resort to formal methods when they find no *prototypes* in their repertoire to help them deal with the situation they have now encountered. The chapter will first consider some of the features of training expertise by reporting the results of a series of discussions with training experts. Then it will describe the structure of a knowledge base that reflects the characteristics of these training experts.

DISCUSSIONS WITH TRAINING EXPERTS

In order more fully to understand the manner in which human training experts undertake their work, separate interviews were held with six experienced training consultants. The interviews, largely unstructured, included 'walking' interviewees through interventions they had recently carried out and freely discussing any issue that arose. The following observations were made.

The diagnostic processes of training needs analysis (TNA)

The first set of observations are concerned with the diagnostic processes that training analysts follow.

1. *Consultants pursue TNA from the basis of experience.* They operate informally, matching a new situation to situations previously encountered, rather than formally using established task analysis methods. This strategy leads to economy of effort and enables the experienced consultant to make rapid judgements with a minimum of inconvenience to a client.
2. *A major skill of human consultants is to recognize the limits of their expertise.*
3. *Different consultants use different strategies.* It was impossible for the consultants to express their strategies coherently, but three strategies emerged which can be characterized as follows.
   (a) TNA is carried out using a top-down approach starting at a general statement and then refining views as information is gained.
   (b) Analysis commences wherever the client chooses—the analyst progresses by exploring *task inputs* and *outputs* to track the source of a problem.
   (c) The consultant acts as a counsellor, helping the client to reach his or her own conclusions.
   It is likely that different strategies may be used on different occasions by the same consultant, depending on the manner in which the consultant perceives a client.
4. *Information gained is stored and used subsequently to refine later decisions.* Effective working memory is important for the client/informant relationship, since it will avoid irritating repetition.

System constraints on the diagnostic process

The second set of observations is concerned with constraints imposed by the structure and nature of organizations with regard to the inferences that may be drawn about causes from the symptoms presented. These constraints may be due to logic, economy or organizational culture.

1. *Organizations are complex systems—a problem developing in one area of the organization can affect several other parts of the organization by referring its symptoms to other departments.* For example, the cause of production problems may be deficiencies in accountancy or sales performance as much as production skills. This creates difficulties for the training analyst who must infer the cause of a problem from its presented symptoms.
2. *Not all problems presented as such are training problems.* Managers, often incorrectly, attribute problems to the skills of employees, where training and selection solutions are often uncontroversial, whereas acknowledging other weaknesses can be embarrassing.
3. *Training decisions must take account of the context of the task.* Context includes costs of error, variants in technology, codes of practice and cultural preferences.
4. *Training solutions must take account of the context of the task.* In this case, context includes the resources available for training and the culture in the organization which can influence whether or not a particular solution will be acceptable.

Sensitivity to the client or informant

The third set of observations are concerned with the manner in which the analyst collects information from human informants, with the emphasis on maintaining the informant's commitment and confidence.

1. *Users involvement in TNA is essential if the results are to be applied successfully.* Clients should be involved in the consultancy process for the results to be given much credence.
2. *Training should be explored within the context of a business analysis.* TNA should not be carried out for its own sake, but carried out as a means both to overcome performance problems and exploit business opportunities.
3. *Training analysts must be sensitive to the personal and social pressures on people providing them with information.* It is undiplomatic to question informants outside the scope of their competence or authority.
4. *Analysts must establish and maintain their credibility with the client.* Without this, the client will be reluctant to offer time for the analysis or attach importance to any findings.

A PROTOTYPE APPROACH TO TRAINING NEEDS ANALYSIS

In order to establish a basis for a computer-based training needs advisor reflecting the views of the experts we interviewed, a knowledge structure based on *task* and *context prototypes* was devised.

The manner in which prototyping may be used in *training needs analysis* is illustrated by the personal experience of one of the authors. The formal hierarchical task analysis of the accountancy task undertaken by Shepherd (described elsewhere in this volume) was justified because the analyst was unfamiliar with this sort of application. The analysis took several days to complete. On a subsequent occasion in another organization, a task with similar apparent characteristics was encountered by the analyst. Recognizing similar features, the analyst had no need for the formal methods in making sense of the problem, because the previously encountered accountancy situation had provided a task 'prototype' enabling attention to be focused very rapidly on the salient features of the new task. In a nut-shell, characterizing the experiences of training experts, which may have been acquired over several years, would provide the basis of a computer-based training needs advisor.

Context and task prototypes

A *task prototype* represents a common stage of carrying out a task or operation. Consultants familiar with a type of industry know through experience how things are done and that certain types of task follow set patterns, for example 'repetitive office work', 'data input tasks', 'batch process plant operation' each follows a generally similar pattern. In training analysis, the consultant must distinguish which subtasks contain the possible source of the presented problem.

Sometimes the consultant cannot know how a task is broken down into task prototypes because in different contexts the task must be treated differently. *Context prototypes* are commonly encountered in industrial or commercial contexts in which task prototypes may be represented in a similar fashion. For example, the consequences of poor 'materials handling' may be similar in different organizations, but training would differ depending on whether the materials handled were light/heavy, delicate/robust, safe/hazardous, etc. Thus each of these would be different *context prototypes*. The type of context must be distinguished before training needs can be suggested. The context hierarchy organizes the domain into classes and subclasses of different kinds of context prototype.

The task and context hierarchies interact. Certain task prototypes are only appropriate to certain context prototypes—obviously procedures for dealing with chemical fires, for example, will only be relevant in contexts where flammable substances are a hazard. Task prototypes are broken down into further task prototypes as long as the description remains consistent with what is known about a current context. When it is felt that the task prototype cannot be broken down further without refining the context, the context must be refined further—then the task breakdown can continue. The general structure of the knowledge base, then, is a series of task and context

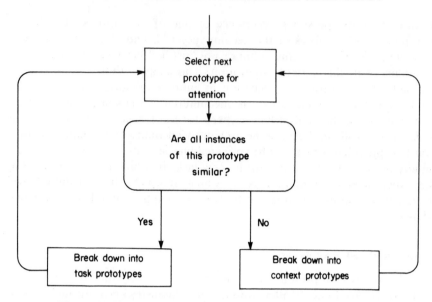

Figure 1. The interaction between task and context prototypes

redescriptions organizing the domain. The process of redescription is summarized in Figure 1.

This approach is illustrated in Figures 2 and 3 by reference to a small knowledge base we have developed for demonstration purposes. The general task prototype is represented as 'provide a service in accordance with resource constraints'. Most organizations fit this general description, from large multinationals to small voluntary services. This prototype is shown in Figure 2 and is broken down in terms of three further general *task prototypes*. The first two are broken down further into *subtask prototypes*. The task prototypes recorded so far are quite general. They are not intended to reflect any organizational structure, but all organizations implicitly carry out these functions.

'Provide services' cannot immediately be broken down into constituent subtask prototypes, because not all organizations can fit the same functional pattern. To break down 'provide services' it is necessary first to distinguish different context prototypes. There will be several of these. Four examples are shown in Figure 3. It is not necessary for context prototypes to be exhaustive at any level. An absence of a particular context prototype means that those contexts cannot be dealt with by the system until the deficiency is made good—just as a human consultant (should) withdraw from an unfamiliar context.

Each of these task or context prototypes is then treated as before, broken

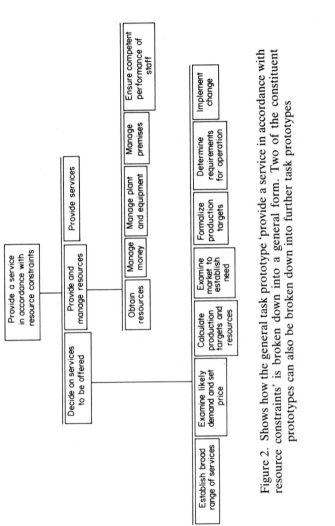

Figure 2. Shows how the general task prototype 'provide a service in accordance with resource constraints' is broken down into a general form. Two of the constituent prototypes can also be broken down into further task prototypes

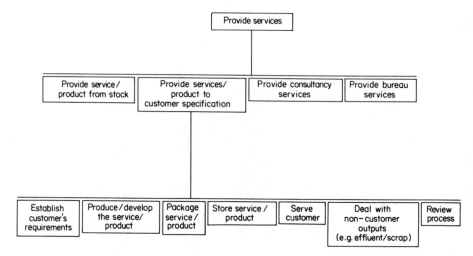

Figure 3. Shows how the task prototype 'provide services' is broken down in terms of a set of context prototypes. One of these, 'provide services/product to customer specification' is then broken down into a set of task prototypes

down into further task or context prototypes. Figure 3 shows how one of these, 'provide services/product to customer specification', is further broken down into seven task prototypes.

Some task prototypes require more context variants than others, for example 'produce/develop the service/product' will clearly depend upon the nature of the product and the technology available for producing it. Similarly, 'store the service/product' will depend upon the nature of the materials—hazards, sizes, shelf-life, turnover, numbers. Most of the contextual variants fall into the area of 'provide a service'. There are fewer variants in 'provide and manage resources' and very few in 'decide on service to be offered'. By mixing task and context prototypes in this fashion, a vast range of different organizations can be represented by relatively few prototypes.

Enabling systems

Carrying out any task successfully requires a combination of factors. *Human performance* must be satisfactory, of which training is but one contributing factor. *Equipment* to do the task must be suitable. Adequate *information* must be supplied and suitable *materials* must be provided. Each of these four elements may be treated as a prototype; the four elements together are called the enabling system for the task prototype in question. The output of any task is some combination of information and materials. A simple view of the

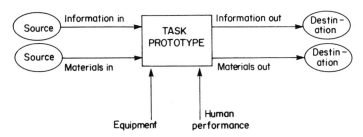

Figure 4. A simple representation of the enabling system

enabling system and its product is represented in Figure 4. Every task operates by virtue of its enabling system.

An organization works because the flows of materials and information between its various subtasks are successfully coordinated. The *information in* to a particular task is the *information out* from a task somewhere else in the organization. Similarly *materials in* map onto *materials out* from some source within the organization. The manner in which these features interact is illustrated in Figure 5. Figure 5 is not part of the real knowledge base we are developing in our research, but is an abstraction that has been specially constructed for this chapter to demonstrate the manner in which information and materials flow throughout the model. The actual knowledge base is far larger than this and the interactions more complex.

Not all tasks process materials, but they all process information of some kind. Some tasks receive information from a wide variety of sources; other tasks are relatively straightforward. Tasks in the area 'decide on services to be offered', for example are extremely complex, relying on information to be supplied from a wide variety of sources within the organization and, in turn, dispatching information to a variety of destinations. These tasks are usually regarded as *management* tasks. If 'formalize production targets', for example, is not carried out with appropriate information from, say, marketing, finance and production departments, then the decisions will be in error. In contrast, tasks in production areas are straightforward with regard to information and material flow. The linking of tasks as sources and destinations of information flows is a very complicated activity.

It is this complex flow of information and materials that accounts for the complex referral of symptoms that often occurs when analysing training needs or, indeed, any other feature of an organization. If someone makes a mistake in carrying out a task, either because of inadequate skill or inappropriate equipment, the consequences will be faulty information and materials output which will affect the performance of each task into which it flows until the error can be rectified. An inadequate flow of information or materials into a particular task may be compensated for by skilled performance or the

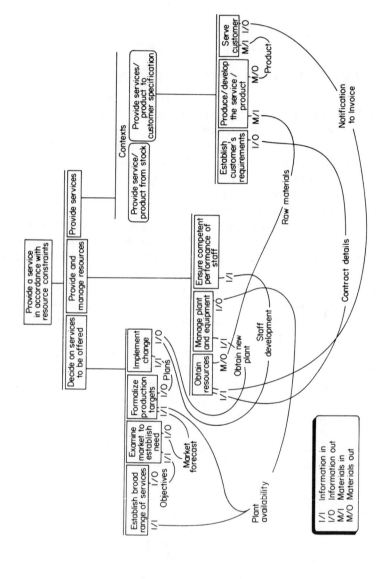

Figure 5. Sample structure showing typical interactions between task prototypes

expenditure of additional resources, or it may result in further inadequate performance of the task into which it has flowed, especially if the job-holders are unpractised in dealing with unfamiliar circumstances. This *seepage* of information and materials is a crucial feature in training needs analysis.

A closed system

Organizations must respond to their environments, for example to their customers, competitors, political climate, bank interest rates, relevant legislation, codes of practice, technological innovations, environmental pressure groups and the weather. In this sense, organizations are *open systems*. However, an open system would be impossible to model for the present purposes. For the present application, organizations are treated as *closed systems*. This is made possible by assuming that information and materials gathered from outside the organization are due to the capabilities of the relevant job-holder. In 'examine market to estabish need', for example gathering market intelligence from outside of the organization is the job of the relevant manager who may or may not be very skilled. Information from within the organization (I/I—information in) includes the organization's objectives. The product of the market analysis (I/O—information out) will be a market forecast.

Performance and identification syndromes

One more type of structure is required before the process of a training needs analysis can be mimicked. This is the *syndrome*. Attached to any task prototype is a *performance syndrome*, a set of statements describing features of acceptable and unacceptable performance. For example, attached to the task prototype 'obtain orders for standard product lines' is the syndrome containing the following set of characteristics:

— too few orders,
— lack of repeat orders,
— too few quotations requested.

If this pattern of features were supported by symptoms collected about an organization under scrutiny, then this prototype would warrant further attention.

Attached to any context prototype is an *identification syndrome*. For example, to identify a context 'provide services from stock', one needs to explore the following syndrome:

— no mass/bulk production facilities,
— technically qualified sales force,

— customer service or product designed from scratch each time,
— no long-term storage facilities for products.

Each of the input components of an enabling system, as in Figure 4, can be treated as an 'enabling prototype' with the same characteristics as task prototypes. Attached to any enabling prototype, therefore, is a *performance syndrome*. For example, problems with *equipment* within 'run packaging machine' would be indicated by:

— excessive downtime,
— high rejects due to faulty packaging,
— high bills for spare parts.

Problems with *human performance* would be indicated by:

— excessive downtime,
— high rejects due to faulty packaging,
— excessive time for resetting.

The various syndromes are clearly not mutually exclusive. It may well be that both of these enabling prototypes warrant further consideration.

Working memory

The need for effective working memory was noted in the observations of the human consultants. Within the proposed prototyping system working memory is obviously important to store answers to questions so that this information may be assumed later without continually requiring reiteration from the user. It must also be used to store those prototypes that warrant further attention but cannot be dealt with immediately.

A summary of knowledge structures

The knowledge necessary to carry out a TNA, using the proposed approach, consists of:

(a) a hierarchy of context and task prototypes;
(b) an enabling system for each task prototype which is not further described, with the sources and destinations of information and materials flows made explicit;
(c) a syndrome for each prototype, enabling acceptable performance to be distinguished from unacceptable performance.

This structure takes account of the features of training consultants listed above concerned with the diagnostic process (observation set 1 in the previous section) and the system constraints (observation set 2) imposed on the TNA. However, the analyst/consultant must also be sensitive to ensuring that the informant remains committed to the process and establishes confidence in the analyst (observation set 3). The human consultant deals with these issues by making judgements about the informant and tailoring questioning accordingly. The equivalent features of a computer-based system are the establishment of a *user model* and manipulation of the *dialogue* with the user.

Managing the dialogue

Several features of the dialogue with the user must be manipulated to maintain confidence and commitment. Four aspects of interfacing style to promote user commitment are noted.

Meeting the user's expectations

If a training analysis follows the processes outlined above, it may prove unnecessary to explore the services or products that the organization provides or how it provides this service. However, few clients would tolerate a human consultant if the basics of the business were not established early on. 'How can they understand our problems if they do not know what we make?' Therefore, questioning should start by establishing some basic company information in accordance with a user's expectation and storing it for possible later use, even if it subsequently proves to be unnecessary. *Data collection cannot simply be directed by the logical requirements of the knowledge base.*

Adapting to the user's competence

Another feature identified through discussion with consultants was the sensitivity that should be shown to the user. It is fruitless to persist with a line of questioning that the user is unable to cope with confidently. This is likely to jeopardize the long-tem relationship between analyst and informant. A manager familiar with marketing concepts may be less happy with engineering ideas and vice versa, and so a line of questioning focusing upon engineering concepts will not be worth while. The range of features in a syndrome to determine whether a prototype needs further examination is often substantial and related to a number of different aspects of the organization. If a user fails to answer certain types of question consistently, for example technical engineering questions, then these areas should be avoided and alternate questions should be selected, if possible from areas where greater competence has been demonstrated. Organizational problems are often so rich in the symptoms they present that they can be diagnosed adequately from a number of different perspectives—there is rarely a need to consider every item of information relevant to a syndrome. If, however, the diagnosis cannot be completed from a perspective that the user can deal with, then steps must be taken to seek this information from someone who is competent.

This feature can be exploited by considering the notion of *user prototypes*. Typical user prototypes might be 'engineer', 'marketeer', 'sales-person' and 'generalist'. As with other prototypes, each user prototype has a syndrome that helps identify the type of user currently being interviewed. Identification may be via eliciting user information directly, for example asking about qualifications and experience, or it may be indirect by making inferences from the questions the user is able or not able to answer during the normal dialogue, for example an inability to answer engineering questions makes it less worth while asking such questions. At the start of questioning the analyst has no knowledge of the user's competence. As questioning proceeds the analyst forms an impression of the kinds of questions it is reasonable to ask, and therefore selects alternative questions. If there are no questions left which the user is judged competent to answer, then the user must be asked to go away and find someone who can help. The interaction of user prototypes with the main diagnostic process is illustrated in Figure 6.

Transparency and collaboration

There is no logical reason why the knowledge base has to be revealed to the user. It can be used simply to guide the questioning and navigate the analysis. On the other hand, the user could be shown a list of competing tasks or competing contexts available at a particular time and be invited to choose where to go next rather than be directed according to the outcome of questioning. The user might be counselled in making this choice. One of the strategies listed above (observation 3c in the list of diagnostic processes) was a 'counselling' strategy, where the analyst reflected issues back to the client, enabling the client to determine the route of the analysis. This feature can be incorporated in the proposed system by making the knowledge base explicit, at least in parts. Thus, the user may on some occasions be asked direct questions regarding symptoms, with inferences drawn by the computer, while on other occasions the user is shown the prototypes available and invited to choose where to go. Users may be invited to choose their preferred mode of operation, they may be offered a variety of opportunities at different stages in the analysis or a style might be imposed in accordance with inferences drawn from the user prototype.

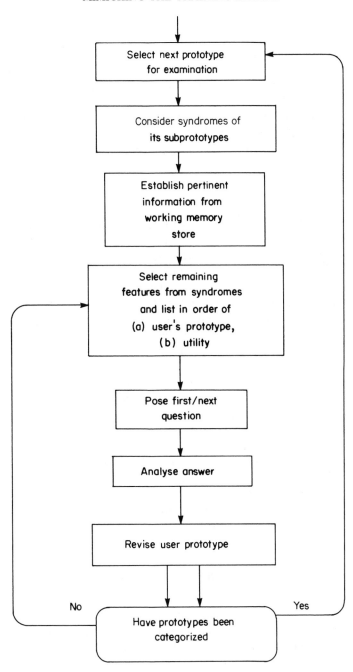

Figure 6. The flow of questioning to resolve task and context prototypes and update
the user prototype

Milestones

As a consultation progresses the user may require justification for interim conclusions reached. There may be psychological value in providing some respite from data collection as well as satisfying the user's curiosity. Simple 'back-tracking' of the progress of the analysis to date is usually only satisfactory to PROLOG programmers. Explanations in text-files, freely constructed by training experts, available to the user when required, seems the most likely approach to this problem at present.

The route of a diagnosis

The system described complies in most respects with the observations listed above concerning strategies and concerns of human analysts. Analysis can start with a general examination of the problem and move down the hierarchy in accordance with patterns of symptoms recorded, then moving across the bottom of the hierarchy in accordance with the information and materials flows. Alternatively, the analysis could start at any intermediate point that the client chooses, then trace symptoms down the hierarchy and across in accordance with information and materials flows.

When enabling systems are reached, examination of the syndromes of the constituent enabling prototypes will provide the first indication of the training needs that can be listed. If a *human performance* or *equipment* deficiency is identified, the information is stored as part of the subsequent TNA report— *human performance* deficiencies will contain training needs of operatives, *equipment deficiencies* will contain training needs of engineers (this view is somewhat oversimplified and will be extended shortly). If an *information* or *materials* flow is identified as a potential weakness, then the *task prototype* at its source is stored in the working store for further attention. If a faulty prototype is overlooked during earlier examination of its syndrome and has not been stored for further attention, the enabling system may prompt its further consideration via the information or material routes.

Validation of the model and refinement of the enabling systems

Validation requires field testing and implementation on a computer. Field testing has been done in one organiztion so far using a paper version of the model. The approach appeared sound but revealed inadequacies regarding the structure of the enabling systems presented in Figure 4.

The paper version of the approach was tried out using a senior manager in a computer software house. The study was primarily exploratory and unstructured and cannot be offered as a definitive piece of data collection. A more rigorous examination in this respect remains to be done. The study showed that the structure of the knowledge base was meaningful to the user and that the syndromes were a suitable means of distinguishing task prototypes needing further attention and identifying relevant contexts. The enabling systems also proved effective in refocusing attention on other parts of the organization. However, a problem emerged in attributing training needs to individuals within the organization. The system as presented fairly pin-pointed performance weaknesses, but it was impossible always to distinguish who in a department had a training need. It was not clear whether the training need rested with the person taking, say, a strategic decision or a clerk or operative responsible for supplying information or carrying out the decision reached by the manager. Indeed, deficiencies in the clerk or operative's performance may also be attributable to the manager responsible for providing the conditions for work. To this end a revision to the enabling system structure is proposed as illustrated in Figure 7.

In this structure, each task prototype for which an enabling system is provided has a series on *information encoding* or *materials treatment* tasks associated with it. As before, the sources and destinations of information and materials flows must be identified and named. In addition, a task that prepares the information or materials for operation within the task prototype must be carried out. For example, if sales figures are received via a telephone message, then the clerk receiving the message must record the data accurately and communicate this accurately to the person undertaking the sales forecast in the task prototype it feeds. This is an *encoding* task. Encoding tasks include filing of documents and dispatching electronic mail. Similarly, if materials are to be used in a task, they must be transported, received, labelled and stored temporarily in an appropriate fashion. These are materials *preparation* tasks. Similar examples may be offered to show how information and materials are dispatched when treatment has taken place within the task prototype. In this way, it becomes possible to distinguish between the performance of secretaries, clerks, managers, operatives and other personnel.

A further extension of the enabling systems is the development of the human performance prototype into the constituents—training/aiding, selection, human–system interface, environment, leadership (the list may be modified by human factors—specialists with different views to the authors). Thus, if the human performance prototype is identified by matching symptoms to syndromes, then further examination is necessary to distinguish between the contributing *human factors*. Only one of these represents a training need for the person who carries out the task. The remainder imply training needs for managers, engineers and management support staff responsible for designing the work.

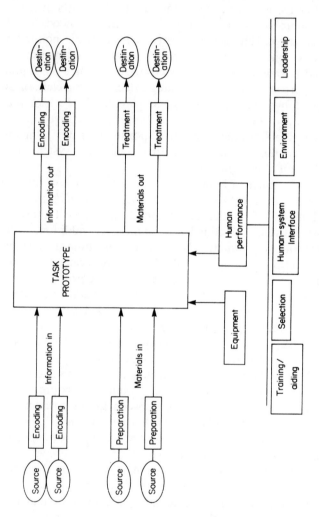

Figure 7. The extended enabling system

IMPLEMENTATION

Computer implementation so far has amounted to one version in PROLOG on a restricted prototype model. This has proven unsatisfactory in view of its slowness in execution, not enabling a satisfactory dialogue to be presented for trials with real users. The program exploits the major feature that all prototypes—tasks, context and enabling prototypes—can be represented with the same structure. However, the system must then do a number of rather complex things. It must incorporate *downward inheritance* of the *context properties* established at any stage; that is lower-level contexts are refinements of higher-level contexts—lower-level contexts logically inherit the identification syndromes of the higher-level contexts. Another inheritance feature is that higher-level tasks are accumulations of the performance syndromes of their lower counterparts. The system entails a *syndrome splitter* which looks for the most efficient way of deciding which prototypes need further attention and which do not. A feature of the syndrome splitter is that it should resolve its decisions, as far as possible, by hunting through the information so far collected in the consultation. Another major feature is the *seeper*, which traces the task prototypes at the sources of unacceptable information and material flows and puts them on the *backburner* for later consideration. The current system seems to do the right kind of thing but far too slowly for practical purposes. A proper implementation of this system, which can be used to validate the approach, therefore still awaits to be developed.

It is doubtful whether implementation of this full training needs analysis system can be via a commercial expert system shell. Using a commerical shell for training needs analysis may only be possible if the domain is restricted to a particular organizational function, say marketing or warehousing. With its domain restricted, a marketing problem is likely to yield a training solution in the marketing area and this may prove incorrect as the real problem may reside within a completely different function. Restricted approaches using commerical shells will be useful in that they will be easier to produce and provide utility in reasonably straightforward cases. However, it is doubtful whether they will ever attain the power necessary to cope with the real complexity of organizations and deal with more subtle organizational problems, where the manifested symptoms occur remote from their source.

In the light of a clearer understanding of the constituent processes of analysis and initial efforts at computer implementation, there are two main candidates for taking this work forward. One is to improve the existing PROLOG program; the other is to develop the system in an *object-oriented* programming environment. It remains to be seen whether either approach will realize a system of sufficient speed to satisfy a person who might wish to use the system.

A further computing requirement is a set of *input tools* enabling training experts constructing the prototype system to input prototypes, together with their syndromes, and link these to their related prototypes across the system. This has proven far from easy because the combinations that must be considered explode as the size of the model increases. On our first attempt at a computer implementation the model was small and reasonably easy to handle. At the same time, however, we developed a fuller knowledge base using an *ideas processor* which offered a convenient system for entering a hierarchical model. With this piece of software it was easy to enter new prototypes and their accompanying syndromes. The problem arose when enabling prototypes had to be linked across the model. A large high-resolution screen, with windowing to enable several parts of the model to be viewed simultaneously, would be required for this task. Additionally, some means of keeping a check on loose ends would be necessary. Developing a satisfactory input tool is a serious problem which has to be solved if a full prototype system is ever to be implemented and tested.

Extending the knowledge base

In addition to the structure of the knowledge base and implementation of the system by computer, it is also essential that the issue of the extension of the knowledge base is anticipated. Considerable effort may be devoted at the outset to establishing a large set of task and context prototypes, but contexts that have not been anticipated will be subsequently encountered. There must be a facility for recognizing when a required context prototype does not exist and enabling its input to the system. It is important that the syndrome splitter is not simply concerned with distinguishing between the alternative contexts presented, but seeks additional information to confirm that a syndrome is actually present. If no syndrome can be matched, then a further context must be defined and its constituent task, context and enabling prototypes must be analysed and recorded, along with their links to other task prototypes in the system.

The most likely way of implementing these extensions to the system is to employ human consultants to be available when the system is unable to match a syndrome. The job of the consultant will then be to analyse the problem in terms of task, context and enabling prototypes and update the system using the input tools.

COMPARISONS WITH HIERARCHICAL TASK ANALYSIS

The hierarchical nature of the prototype model prompts comparison with hierarchical task analysis (HTA) methods (for example Duncan, 1974; Shepherd, 1985). A similarity is that a task analyst almost certainly resorts to using task prototypes as hypotheses for redescription in HTA and that a proto-typing system may form the basis of an automated task analyser. It is also the case that, faced with a context which has not previously been encountered, the analyst developing the prototyping systems may well use HTA as a method of making sense of the unfamiliar situation. Having thus carried out the HTA, the analyst has a clearer understanding of the task leading to a more effective prototype being proposed for the training needs analysis system.

There are some important differences. The major difference is its purpose. The *prototyping system* provides a means for modelling *organizational* func-tions such that the consequences of any specific weakness in the system can be discerned through the flows of information and materials. HTA sets out to identify and relate the goals and subgoals that need to be undertaken by an operator to achieve a task, in order to identify sources of difficulty for the operator and hypotheses for overcoming these. The prototyping system, therefore, aims to identify the sources of observed problems in *organizations*, while the task analysis approach focuses upon the adequacy of performance of *individuals*.

HTA uses *plans* to control the selection and sequencing of subordinate operations. Plans are an important element of a task analysis because they relate to crucial conceptual aspects of performance. Moreover, they specify time dependencies. For example, subtasks may be carried out in sequence or in parallel—time dependencies are important to understand, because they qualify the nature of the skill the individual opertor must acquire. The prototyping system is somewhat different. Goals in an organization are rarely carried out in sequence, other than at the individual task level. Therefore, plans are often useless as units of control in describing the functioning of organizations. Instead, the enabling systems, and the manner in which they refer information and materials throughout the organization, enable the modelling of *parallel processes*, such as are found in real complex systems.

There is scope for reconciling these approaches and attention will be paid to this in further work.

CONCLUSIONS

It is suggested that training is based on the expert's utilization of experience with prototype situations, rather than the construction of novel solutions using formal methods of occupational psychology. This has provided the basis for development of a system for training needs analysis where a task is broken down into *task*, *context* and *enabling* prototypes and their accompanying syndromes which indicate which prototypes are pertinent to the present training needs analysis. By matching syndromes against symptoms observed in the real world, the system selects prototypes and thereby models the organization in a manner to assist the training needs analysis process. An important feature is the linking of task prototypes throughout the organization in accordance with flows of information and materials. These links, it is suggested, cause major difficulties in training needs analysis, because they cause symptoms of problems to be referred to remote regions of the organization and therefore confuse diagnosis. The structure that emerges appears to be a potentially effective basis for computer-based training needs analysis.

Careful consideration of the approaches adopted by human training experts was justified as a basis for informing the subsequent system design. Observations were made concerning the diagnostic processes that training analysts follow, constraints imposed by the structure and nature of organizations and the manner in which the analyst collects information from human informants. The various features entailed were embodied in the system developed, but there is no justification for assuming that the processes followed in the system emulate the processes of human behaviour.

The issues concerned with diagnostic strategy of training analysts and organizational constraints were catered for by the structure of the knowledge base. Issues concerned with how the analyst works with the client most effectively are catered for by sensitive design of the user–computer interface. In particular it is stressed that the dialogue style must seek to maintain the commitment and confidence of the user

Computer implementation so far has been too slow to enable serious user trials and the issue of the best method of computer development still pertains. It is difficult to imagine how readily available expert system techniques on their own would have coped with the problems set, particularly in view of the crucial fact that symptoms are referred throughout organizations in a complex manner.

The system proposed seems promising and worthy of further attention, but until a satisfactory computing environment can be devised, its true worth cannot be assessed.

ACKNOWLEDGEMENTS

We wish to acknowledge the support provided by the Manpower Services Commission in funding this work and the assistance provided by Synergy Logistics of Loughborough in providing facilities for enabling trials of the paper model of the system to be carried out.

REFERENCES

Duncan, K. D. (1974) Analytical techniques in training design. In E. Edwards and F. P. Lees (eds.), *The Human Operator and Process Control*. Taylor and Francis.

Gagne, R. M. (1970) *The Conditions of Learning*, 2nd ed. New York: Holt, Reinhart and Winston.

Miller, R. B. (1967) Task taxonomy: science or technology. *Ergonomics*, **10**, 167–76.

Patrick, J. (1980) Job analysis, training and transferability. In K. D. Duncan, M. M. Gruneberg and D. Wallis (eds.), *Changes in Working Life*. Chichester: John Wiley and Sons.

Shepherd, A. (1985) Hierarchical task analysis and training decisions. *Programmed Learning and Educational Technology*, **1985**, 22.

8. Cognitive Processes and Training Methods: A Summary

Lisanne Bainbridge

SUMMARY

This chapter reviews the training methods described in papers in this book. Task analysis methods, appropriate training experiences and the place of errors in training all depend on the cognitive processes to be trained, whether the task uses prespecified routines or involves problem-solving.

INTRODUCTION

As there is no specific section on training methods in this book, the aim of this chapter is to bring together the training methods mentioned throughout, within a framework of cognitive processes. This chapter will therefore indicate the main topics in training methods, but by no means gives complete coverage.

Information technology equipment, with its emphasis on flexibility of function, means that the focus of training is not on teaching standard prespecified working methods, but on helping the users to understand the device and to devise their own plan of action by choosing from a repertoire of possible methods. In this chapter we will distinguish between two categories of task situation:

1. Familiar task methods can be used, whether perceptual–motor or cognitive, so that training is mainly concerned with increasing the 'automaticity' of the behaviour.
2. It is necessary to devise a new working method, so training is concerned with developing and using the knowledge for doing this.

Developing Skills with Information Technology
Edited by Lisanne Bainbridge and S. Antonio Ruiz Quintanilla
© 1989 John Wiley & Sons Ltd

(For possible names for these two categories see Table 1 in the Introduction to Section 1 of this book.)

As we will see, the choice of training method frequently depends on which of these two general categories of cognitive process is involved. (We will not discuss cost-benefits, which also influence the best choice between methods.)

There are two main stages in devising a training programme: identifying the task to be done and choosing the methods by which it will be trained. The description of the task (the task analysis) needs to describe the knowledge, working methods and cognitive processes involved. Then developing a training method involves choices about the sequence of experiences used to optimize the trainee's mastery of the job content and about the equipment used to present and record these experiences.

There is a great mixture of techniques in developing training schemes, because they are for many different purposes, such as:

— describing the sequence of events in the task,
— guiding and developing new skills,
— supporting the learner in developing or revising new working methods,
— motivating continued learning, such as by progressively changing the task difficulty.

Equipment can be used for:

— presenting the training method,
— recording and analysing the trainee's behaviour.

Some aspects of training are involved in training decisions in many ways. For example, errors (most of the chapters in Sections 1 and 4 of this book discuss this) can be used:

1. As an indication of the cognitive processes in a task.
2. During training to:
   — guide the trainee doing control tasks,
   — indicate that the trainee needs to use a different strategy.
3. As the measured basis for adaptively changing workload throughout training.
4. As a performance assessment measure.

It is useful to keep these different potential functions in mind when discussing a method.

The rest of this chapter is in two main sections, on task analysis and on training methods.

THE TASK TO BE TRAINED

A 'task analysis' is a task description made as the basis for ergonomic intervention. There can be many different types of task goal and many different types of ergonomic intervention (such as interface design, simulator design, training, selection, human performance prediction, person–machine function allocation). Within training applications, the training programme may be intended to develop new skills, to maintain existing skills or for refresher training of skills which are not normally used. These many different purposes have led to many different methods for task analysis (see Patrick, 1980).

Task Analysis for training can have two main aspects:
A. identifying the task to be done.
B. describing the methods, processes and knowledge used in the task.

Identifying the task to be done

Leplat (Chapter 2 of this volume) discusses this, and points out that identifying the task to be trained, from what an existing expert does, raises the same problems as knowledge elicitation. Cognitive processes are not directly observable, and automated and integrated processes are intrinsically unobservable. With experience people develop new ways of doing a task, which do not necessarily have much in common with the original official task description. From this comes the frequently made suggestion that a person devising a training scheme should first learn the task themselves.

Describing methods, processes and knowledge

At its simplest, a task analysis describes:

— the task goals,
— the technical and organizational constraints on meeting the goals,
— the activity needed to meet the goals.

Task analysis methods for standardized tasks

In early task analysis methods, a task was described simply as a sequence of prescribed operations, which were expected to be always carried out. However, it has since been realized that it is important to teach trainees about the goal structure of the task. If someone does not know the reasons for an action or the conditions in which it is applicable, then there will be no transfer of learning: they will not be able to apply the method learned to somewhat different situations. Also, one working method cannot be optimum for all individuals. If people are aware of the task goals, they may be able to modify the task operations to take account of individual and environmental conditions, so increasing the likelihood of success and reducing stress.

Most methods of task analysis for training now make some type of hierarchical description of the way in which task goals are successively broken down into subgoals for meeting them, down to the level at which actual task operations are described (see reviews in Shepherd, 1985; Astley and Stammers, 1987; Sebillotte, 1988).

It is also increasingly being recognized that it is important to describe not only standard goal-working method relations but also several other dimensions of the task:

(a) the prerequisites/preconditions for carrying out each method (the required state of the environment and how to attain it,
(b) the knowledge needed to carry out the method,
(c) alternative methods of meeting the same goal,
(d) error routes,
(e) error recovery methods.

Task analysis for problem-solving tasks

Increased flexibility of behaviour, as needed in many IT tasks, has led to two additional emphases in task analysis:

1. Hierarchical task analysis methods need to be extended, so that subgoals are not tied uniquely to higher goals in a rigid tree structure, but instead the trainee learns the goal structure and how to plan for themselves using lower-level activities.
2. The task analysis needs to describe the knowledge used in understanding how the equipment works and what it does (see, for example, the review by Wilson, Barnard and MacLean, 1989).

We will look at these issues in more detail:

1. The goals of training. Shepherd (1985) discusses an adaptation of hierarchical task analysis, so that it is used to describe the knowledge base from which someone works in doing this type of task. The task analysis should not describe a rigid hierarchy of predetermined activity, but instead indicate:
   (a) the tools/methods available to someone for achieving given goals,
   (b) the conditions under which these methods can be used,
   (c) how they are organized together,

(d) the multidimensional criteria for assessing situations,
(e) typical/prototype events, and variations from them.

The emphasis is on the task demands and the context in which they are met, rather than on specific operations, so that with this information someone can choose their own plan of action.

In devising training schemes, we need to be aware not only of the goals in the task. Different methods of training also have different goals, in terms of what kinds of knowledge or experience they are intended to convey. Norros (Chapter 17 of this volume) points out that it is useful to make this clear to the trainees, so they can see the structure of their training programme, what they should focus on at each stage and how the parts of it fit together and build up into a final whole.

2. Types of knowledge. In problem-solving tasks, people need general knowledge about the equipment, environment and strategies available to them, from which they can think out new working methods. Bainbridge (Chapter 4 of this volume) distinguished between knowledge of how the equipment works and knowledge of one's own actions. Marshall and Baker (Chapter 11) and Norros (Chapter 17) give rather more practical detail.

In summary, training for problem-solving skills is concerned with conveying three general categories of knowledge/skill:

1. Subsidiary perceptual–motor skills such as:
    (a) identification (for example typical configurations on the interface and their meaning in terms of equipment state);
    (b) manual control;
    (c) procedures: what to do with the equipment, how to operate the interface and the help functions, or prespecified ways of reaching goals.
    These are trained by classic methods as above.
2. General knowledge of the equipment and environment:
    (a) the spatial location of parts; ·
    (b) the physical and functional structure of the equipment, how it works, and how its parts fit together and interact;
    (c) the constraints on its operations;
    (d) typical events;
    (e) probabilities of events.
3. Complex cognitive activities:
    (a) understanding the present state of the equipment and environment, that is interpreting the displays, and assessing the validity and usefulness of information;
    (b) thinking about the task, making predictions, plans and decisions;

(c) evaluating alternatives against multidimensional criteria, to select a method appropriate to all the circumstances;
(d) multitasking, thinking about several things at the same time, whether these are:
— alternative 'hypotheses' about the state of the equipment (for example during fault diagnosis),
— alternative plans of action on one part of the equipment,
— actions on different parts of the equipment.
(e) understanding the wider context of changes in technology, in the economy and in society, which justify the need and therefore motivation for changed approaches to working methods (Norros, Chapter 17).

The key features of doing each of these cognitive activities in a skilled way are the attention allocation strategy and access to appropriate knowledge structures that are involved.

TRAINING METHODS

We will discuss training methods in three sections, on:

— training procedures,
— maintaining motivation,
— the equipment used.

In each case, when classic methods are involved we will only mention them briefly.

The sequence of events for optimizing mastery of the task content

The best training sequence depends on the cognitive processes involved in the task. In perceptual–motor skills and familiar cognitive skills the emphasis is on increasing the extent to which the familiar task is done 'automatically', leading to guided perfection. In new method/problem-solving tasks the focus of training is on developing knowledge and developing people's ability to think for themselves, or guided exploration. In both cases, actually doing the task rather than listening to someone talking about doing it is essential in the development of the skill. In other ways, the relevant techniques are different and we will discuss them separately.

Skills in using familiar methods

Training for standard working methods uses classical techniques for developing new abilities and integrating task parts into a whole. These need large amounts of practice, and the effects of experience can continue for extended periods, as in the Crossman study quoted by Leplat (Chapter 2 of this volume). Both perceptual-motor skills and familiar cognitive skills are included here.

1. Perceptual–motor skills. For simplicity we can divide perceptual–motor skills into three categories:
   (a) Identification reactions. When there is a one-to-one relation between stimulus and name (for example the colour code on resistors) the association between the signal and its identification may be completely arbitrary. Programmed texts can be an effective way of conveying the multiple trials needed to learn these kinds of associations. Even in a sophisticated example, as in training for pattern-directed fault diagnosis (Shepherd *et al.*, 1977), the main methodological concerns are with developing simple equipment for presenting the alternatives and with ways of increasing the difficulty level of the task.
      There are also well-developed techniques for category training. However, note that there are two types of category: sets of items that have common features of appearance (for example cats) and sets of items that have common features of behaviour (for example dogs). The classic techniques apply to the former.
   (b) Acquisition movements, for example keyboard skills. Here again there are well-tried methods.
   (c) Execution of movements, for example operating a semi-automatic lathe (Taylor, 1978). These tasks are the primary focus of traditional training books, in which methods are particularly concerned with:
      — guiding the trainee to notice cues,
      — developing perceptual and control discriminations that the trainee was not previously able to make,
      — changing the performance monitoring used, particularly from visual to tactile/kinaesthetic sensing,
      — integrating task subunits into a whole.
2. Familiar cognitive skills. Again the focus of training methods is on developing standard methods of working, and the knowledge that is used in them. As in perceptual–motor skill, the training focus is on developing and integrating skills and on maintaining motivation.
   As we have seen (Section 1 of this volume), for a beginner there can be a considerable amount of problem-solving involved in learning to use a standard method. Much of the special focus in the design of training schemes for standard cognitive skills is to minimize this 'problem-solving' phase. Not only prior experience and training but also other aspects of ergonomic design (such as the interface, operating manuals, task allocation and support team availability) and incorrect mental models for or

attitudes to the new technology affect the difficulty of this stage. This leads to a wider perspective on the place of training in total systems design, which is discussed in the chapters in Section 3 of this volume. Eason (Chapter 12) gives a table of different ways in which the information and guidance that a learner needs can be supported.

3. 'Over-learned' skill. There is an irony in the development of 'automatic' behaviour, in that it can become too automatic and then the person releases behaviour without checking properly that it is appropriate to the environment. This is a 'slip' type of error (see Section 1 of this volume). Leplat (Chapter 2) suggests that it is necessary to train for, and frequently maintain, task variety. This should help to ensure that 'skills' do not become rigid through too much identical repetition, that people do check for environmental changes and that the knowledge base necessary to revise and extend cognitive skills is still available.

Problem-solving skills

Training for tasks in which people have to work out for themselves what to do requires a different approach. It is not only a matter of training people in working methods but also of developing their mental models of the equipment and the task, which they can use in choosing and devising their own working method. Most of the training methods described in this book are concerned with this sort of task, as it is particularly frequent in using IT-based equipment.

Such training involves helping people to actively use their own knowledge (rather than being passively taught) and to reflect on their own behaviour (metacognition) in order to improve it. This approach is not unique to IT equipment. The training methods involved have been found to be useful in any form of complex skill, such as 'craft' skills (in UK industry this means a skill requiring years of training), for example versatile machine tool operators (Taylor, 1978), or in training for emergency services management (Samurcay and Rogalski, 1988). Indeed, this approach has also been found to be more successful than traditional training methods in simpler 'semi-skilled' tasks (in UK industry this means skills that require weeks of training) such as sewing-machine operation (James, 1987). This links to the recurrent emphasis in this book on the learner as a problem-solver. The new approach to semi-skilled training involves training people in methods of making changes in performance by recognizing and resolving blockages to production (such as limits in machinery, raw materials, knowledge or skill level), rather than by simply instilling a 'new programme' of behaviour.

We will start by surveying the types of training experience that have been suggested. We will then mention the results of studies on cognitive difficulty, which have implications for training.

1. Learning experiences. As we have mentioned, at the most general level, people need training in knowledge and in how to use this knowledge. Eason (Chapter 12 of this volume) suggests that, when only a short training time is available, this should be used to convey a simple model of the system and to give people practice in learning to learn how to use the system.

The examples of large-scale tasks which are give in this book are nearly all concerned with operating complex dynamic processes which alter over time, so the operator has the extra problem of understanding and predicting not just a sequence of events but also of working within specific time constraints. Such processes are usually highly expensive, producing a product, and likely to be dangerous, so it is not possible to give people a full range of training experiences without using a simulator (as the chapters in Section 4 of this book discuss).

When training for these large-scale tasks, such as industrial process or flexible manufacturing system operation, one of the main issues is how the theoretical knowledge and its practical use should be integrated in the training experiences.

(a) Theoretical or practical training. If two main types of knowledge are used in problem-solving skills, about the equipment and environment, and about cognitive activities, then could they be trained separately? This raises problems of:
— how much background theory should be taught,
— whether training in theory or in practical methods is more useful for particular tasks,
— whether theory is best taught by practical experience or through off-the-job methods such as lectures.

There is much debate in the literature about whether theoretical or practical training is best. There is not space to discuss this here, but it is important to make one point. This is that it is almost always impossible to tell, from the descriptions given of experiments in this area, what is actually meant by 'theoretical' or 'practical' training. When one has access to the detailed reports on which journal articles are based one finds that 'theoretical' training can mean anything from lectures on nuclear physics, through well or badly written explanations of how the equipment works, which reason either from cause to effect or from effect to cause and may or may not be supplemented with demonstrations on actual equipment, to instructions about how to use the equipment which have been given in a lecture room rather than in front of the equipment. It is hardly surprising that combining the results from such experimental reports does not give a clear picture of the best teaching methods. Until investigators give fuller accounts of what they mean by theory and practice, instead of assuming that everyone uses the words with the same meaning, this situation will not improve, to the detriment of current training practice.

In order to give at least a background principle to consider in resolving this problem, it is useful to remember that discussions of cognitive skill (in Section 1 of this volume) are always concerned with 'knowledge about the equipment', not as an independent entity but as something that is organized in a way that is relevant to the task and that is linked to, and rapidly accessed by, the working methods that use it. These knowledge skills, of appropriate structures and access, only develop by using the knowledge in task contexts. There is no point in giving information about theory unless the trainee is helped to understand why it is useful to know it, and how it links to practical experience. People may need to be told the same things several times, in different contexts, before the information begins to fit together and make sense.

(b) Practical experiences. To develop cognitive skills, trainees must actually make the predictions and plans themselves, not work to answers provided by someone else. Both Marshall and Baker (Chapters 11 and 16 of this volume) and Norros (Chapter 17) (and see Tompsett, 1987) start their training with a relatively simple abstract introduction to the system and to its interface. They then go on to develop these concepts with various sorts of exercise, in which trainees use the conceptual knowledge ('models') of the equipment to do various tasks. These exercises work from demonstrations towards more practical experience and more concrete examples of real system complexities. Examples of relevant experiences are:

— 'what-if experiences: predicting the effects of various actions on, or events in, the equipment, with the opportunity to check the predictions on a simulator;

— given the current state of the system/equipment, as shown on the interface, working out what could have led to it (that is Marshall and Baker (in Chapter 11) explicitly train the process operators to reason both from cause to effect and from effect to cause, as mentioned by Bainbridge in Chapter 4);

— using the simulator to explore the effects of various events and actions, without being under particular task constraints. This should start with guided exploration, followed, when the trainees have more understanding of the equipment, with opportunities for free exploration;

— planning an operating sequence to achieve given effects, and testing it on a simulator. If a suitable simulator can be used it is possible to work in 'interrupted time', so that a trainee is guided through the task by the instructor and the simulator is stopped

after each phase for discussion. This gives the trainees time to work out what is happening and what to do, without being under the time pressures of the real task;
— experience with using the same strategy in different situations, and vice versa;
— experience with multidimensional assessment of situations;
— working in multitask responsibility, or inversely collaborative responsibility situations (for example diagnosing a process fault and returning the process to a safe state at the same time, or working as a member of a team);
— experience with assessing compromises when it is not possible to meet all the task criteria;
— experience with typical/prototype examples of categories of event or activity, to give reference points for reasoning. In fact, much of the training for complex tasks is in terms of examples of actual events, so is implicitly in this form. What is needed in addition is to think of these explicitly, not just as examples, but to check whether they give a coherent framework of opportunities for exploring the full range of thinking about the task;
— experience with events that do not fit the 'prototypes', to reduce 'perceptual set' and give experience in revising strategies.
Evidently, training for complex skills needs to be extensive, and usually too little time is given to it.

Discussion groups are useful, in association with these practical exercises. Discussion can be either before or after a practical session. Beforehand, people can work in a team to make predictions or suggest working methods. Afterwards, people who may have worked individually can come together to share what they have discovered about the equipment, to assess what more they could have done, to discuss the reasons for discrepancies between what they had planned to achieve and what they actually achieved, and to revise strategies to try next time. This can be done in more detail if the practical session has been recorded and can be replayed.

Norros (Chapter 17) suggests that, during these experiences operators use the simulator to discover the gaps in their knowledge and skills, and so to evaluate themselves. Her study, of a flexible manufacturing system, was particularly concerned with developing the use of an unknown new system. There were no established methods for meeting productivity goals. This is a higher order of training problem than developing the skills of operators in thinking out how to use a known system. Two related problems were raised, in the discussion at the workshop preceding this book, about this sort of exploratory and self-development learning. One was that while the gifted operators can 'boot-strap' their own knowledge and working methods in this way, we also need ways of increasing the skills of the less gifted. The other point was that the 'commissioning engineer' type of person, the person who is involved in getting a completely new system to work, may not have the same values as a 'production engineer'. The first may be interested in continuing to explore, perfect and learn more about the system, while the production person is more interested in pragmatic aspects of productivity and efficiency. Perhaps the optimum training for one is not best for the other. Certainly this is an area in which there is no shortage of topics for debate and research.

2. Cognitive task difficulty. An important aspect which needs to be developed further as a basis for effective training of complex cognitive skills is our understanding of what makes cognitive tasks difficult. We have very little knowledge of this or of what it implies that task analysis and training methods should focus on. Doerner (1987), in a brief review of his extensive studies of what causes difficulty in cognitive tasks, points out some interesting factors.

(a) People have difficulty with thinking about the development of events over time and with interactions, that is with networks of effects.

(b) If people are introduced to too high levels of task difficulty too quickly, this can lead to:
   — rapid changing between problems, which may be perceived as intractable, instead of concentrating on resolving any one,
   — solving problems that they know how to deal with and ignoring others,
   — low willingness to make decisions and accept responsibility.

(c) Under pressure people tend to:
   — not think critically about their working methods,
   — not think of the full range of alternatives,
   — not develop coherent overall goal-directed plans,
   — not notice that they are repeatedly trying the same method which does not work.

These are all aspects of cognitive behaviour which should improve with increasing cognitive skill. Without going into all the possible implications for training of this interesting work (due to being under pressure!), it has obvious implications for the types of experience that should be focused on in training schemes, and the importance of guiding people through training tasks of gradually increasing difficulty.

Maintaining the motivation of trainees

An important aspect of training is giving the trainees feedback about how well they are doing the task. This 'reinforcement' is an essential part of the learning process. A recurrent problem is how to present the sequence of learning experiences without the trainee becoming bored, depressed or frustrated by what they are managing to achieve.

We will briefly mention two aspects, progressive change in level of workload and the place of errors in training. (Initial motivation to take part in the training programme can be effected by prior attitudes to the technology; see Section 3 of this volume.)

Changes in workload

A central aspect of training new skills is to start at an easy level and progressively develop the skill to a level that was not previously possible. In classic training techniques this is done in a set way, with a standard sequence of progressive exercises followed by all trainees. Later the idea of 'adaptive' training was developed, in which the level of task difficulty is altered according to the level of performance of a particular trainee. IT equipment makes it easier to provide this sort of flexibility, as discussed by Ruiz Quintanilla (Chapter 18 of this volume). To do this it is necessary to measure the trainee's performance. Frese and Altmann (Chapter 3 of this volume) suggest using error rate as a measure of the workload experienced, so that the task difficulty is altered to maintain a constant error rate. Baker and Marshall (Chapter 16 of this volume) also mention that simulators make it possible to control the task stress level, and Leplat (Chapter 15 of this volume) points out that simulators can not only progressively alter the speed and/or accuracy of the task, or the number of different situations to be dealt with, but also the task complexity.

Use of errors in training

The use made of errors in a training programme is another area in which best practice depends on the cognitive processes being trained, that is whether these involve standard methods or problem-solving.
1. Learning to follow a prescribed method. An error indicates that the trainee is 'automating' the wrong behaviour. Therefore the aim of training for these skills is to minimize the number of errors made.
2. Problem-solving, developing working methods. In problem-solving tasks, an error is a clue that the wrong strategy has been used. Both Frese and Altmann (Chapter 3) and Norros (Chapter 17) consider errors as an opportunity for learning more about the task, and suggest that errors should be used explicitly for this in training. They both consider that trainees should work in an atmosphere in which errors are seen as an interesting opportunity rather than a mistake.

Frese and Altmann (Chapter 3) point out that an error is only a stress if it cannot be managed. Their discussion is focused on methods for explicitly helping trainees to make use of their errors. Error management in the development of the training scheme and training the learners in error management strategies, both give the trainees a feeling that they are in control, which is not stressful. There can be three stages in this error management process:

(a) The trainees should not have to deal with errors at first, as well as learning about all the other aspects of the task. Therefore, in the early stages of training, methods that minimize errors should be used. For example, category limits could be indicated by deliberately giving exemplars of non-category members, rather than by expecting trainees to learn the limits of applicability of their categories from their mistakes. The effect of errors can be minimized by using static simulation, in which the simulator is reset after each exercise, so that events in the next exercise do not depend on a successful response to the previous one (Leplat, Chapter 15). The aim of 'training wheels' is to avoid error states, as described by Ruiz Quintanilla (Chapter 18).

(b) Frese and Altmann (Chapter 3) also suggest that trainees should be taught about typical errors and their implications. As Shepherd (Chapter 9) points out, people think by analogy, relative to prototypes which are used as reference points in reasoning. 'Typical' errors give the trainees a starting point for understanding how to reason about errors.

(c) It is important to design the training, and training equipment, so that errors can be recovered from, and their implications for changes in strategy can be interpreted. The trainees need explicit training in making these error interpretations and recoveries. Frese and Altmann (Chapter 3) and Ruiz Quintanilla (Chapter 18) have some interesting comments on how to do this.

Equipment

In training programmes, special equipment is often used to convey and to record the training experiences. Information technology has allowed great developments in this area, and this is the focus of many recent books on training. The aim of this book has not been mainly in this direction, but in Section 4 there are many experienced comments on using simulation for both presenting and recording the training sessions. (Marshall and Baker (in Chapter 11 of this volume) also use simpler methods. They use programmed texts to present an initial understanding of the system, and slide-tape programmes to demonstrate the progress of events in a system, without the limitations of real-time.) Ruiz Quintanilla (Chapter 18) discusses the goals, limitations and problems of using computers as the basis of 'intelligent' training devices. For the purposes of this particular chapter, we have assumed that devices for presenting training experiences are possible and have concentrated on reviewing what these training experiences should be. We can, however, indicate one point, that the level of fidelity needed in training equipment is another factor which can depend on the cognitive processes being trained. To train skills in integrating all the task activities, a full-scope simulator is needed. To develop 'automatic' behaviour which transfers to the real situation, a high-fidelity simulator is needed. However, to convey a general understanding of the structure and function of a device and the method of using it, only a simulation with the same general properties is needed. This raises the problem of specifying what are general properties from a psychological point of view, which is raised by Leplat (Chapter 15).

CONCLUSION

Information technology allows the possibility of equipment that is flexible in function, so the users have to think for themselves, to understand the equipment and work out how to use it. This involves cognitive processes which are not developed by traditional training methods that concentrate on increasing the 'automatism' of behaviour. This means that the advent of information technology is stimulating a change of emphasis in all aspects of training: in task analysis, in the types of training experience given, in the way people are motivated to learn and to respond to errors, as well as in the equipment used to provide the training opportunities. This chapter has attempted to review these changes, particularly by referring to more extensive discussions of these points in other chapters in this book.

ACKNOWLEDGEMENT

The author would like to thank Antonio Ruiz Quintanilla for comments on an earlier version of this chapter.

REFERENCES

Astley, J. A., and Stammers, R. B. (1987) Adapting hierarchical task analysis for user–interface design. In J. R. Wilson, E. N. Corlett and I. Manenica (eds.), *New Methods in Applied Ergonomics*. London: Taylor and Francis, pp. 175–84.
Doerner, D. (1987) On the difficulties people have in dealing with complexity. In J. Rasmussen, K. Duncan and J. Leplat (ed.), *New Technology and Human Error*. Chichester: John Wiley and Sons, pp. 97–109.
James, R. (1987) Clothing industry training. Paper presented at the *Motor Skills*

Research Exchange Meeting on Training and Rehabilitation. Department of Psychology, University of Warwick, 7 March 1987.

Patrick, J. (1980) Job analysis, training and transferability: some theoretical and practical issues. In K. D. Duncan, M. M. Gruneberg and D. Wallis (eds.), *Changes in Working Life*. Chichester: John Wiley and Sons, pp. 55–70.

Samurcay, R., and Rogalski, J. (1988) Analysis of operator's cognitive activities in learning and using a method for decision making in public safety. In J. Patrick and K. D. Duncan (eds.), *Training, Human Decision Making and Control*. Amsterdam: Elsevier Science (North-Holland), pp. 133–52.

Sebillotte, S. (1988) Hierarchical planning as a method for task analysis: the example of office task analysis. *Behaviour and Information Technology*, **7**, 275–93.

Shepherd, A. (1985) Hierarchical task analysis and training decisions. *Programmed Learning and Educational Technology*, **22**, 162–76.

Shepherd, A., Marshall, E. C., Turner, A. and Duncan, K. D. (1977) Control panel diagnosis: a comparison of three training methods. *Ergonomics*, **20**, 347–61.

Taylor, R. G. (1978) The metal working machine tool operator. In W. T. Singleton (ed.), *The Analysis of Practical Skills*, Vol. 1. Lancaster: MTP Press, pp. 85–111.

Tompsett, P. A. (1987) An integrated initial training programme for a CEGB operations engineer. *Proceedings of the CSNI Specialist Meeting on Training of Nuclear Reactor Personel*, Orlando, Florida, 21–24 April 1987. NUREG/CP-0089.

Wilson, M. D., Barnard, P. J., and MacLean, A. (1989) Task analysis in human–computer interaction. In T. R. G. Green, J-M. Hoc, D. Murray and G. van der Veer (eds.), *Working with Computers: Theory Versus Outcome*. London: Academic Press.

9. Training Issues in Information Technology Tasks

Andrew Shepherd

SUMMARY

When developing training for an information technology task, attention often focuses on the IT aspects. A task analysis of an IT task is used to demonstrate that the non-IT aspects of tasks can create greater problems for the user. Task analysis should always treat the IT aspects of tasks in their proper context.

INTRODUCTION

Establishing effective arrangements for training tasks that involve information technology is necessary if new working methods are to be fully exploited. While it is tempting to assume that all training issues emerging from IT applications are novel, like the technology itself, it is better to treat information technology merely as an occupational context in which to apply training ideas, in the same manner as other industrial, commercial and social contexts. As such, *training needs* should be *analysed* as carefully as in other contexts and training options selected strictly according to merit. If certain task elements and skills emerge as novel and have never been encountered or seen as significant in any other context, then they are a legitimate focus for research into establishing useful guiding principles to develop training. The same, however, can be said for any context of application. To assume that IT applications will always reflect novelty in training requirements is wrong. Having made this general point, it is worth adding that as a context, IT offers some novel opportunities for *delivering* some of the training identified through training needs analysis. Furthermore, it is fair to say that IT places emphasis on certain training issues, by the manner in which it influences the *organization of work*.

Developing Skills with Information Technology
Edited by Lisanne Bainbridge and S. Antonio Ruiz Quintanilla

This chapter will consider training issues that emerge in IT tasks. It will consider two main aspects. First, it will consider training needs analysis and caution against the tendency to focus closely on the IT issues. Second, it will consider issues of delivering training in occupational contexts where IT is present.

TRAINING NEEDS ANALYSIS

There is always a temptation to focus directly upon that which appears novel and interesting in a task and overemphasize its importance. The identification of training needs in IT tasks is no exception. It is often assumed that it is the distinctive technological features of a situation that warrant special attention. Such focusing invariably results in poor training decisions. A major outcome from the extensive research in electronics maintenance training, for example, is that technicians' skills are founded not on knowledge of electronics but on strategies, procedures and experience (for example Dale, 1958; Rasmussen and Jensen, 1974). There is far more to most jobs than can be explained simply by reference to the main technology it uses. This will be illustrated in the context of IT by reference to a training needs analysis that was undertaken for the Post Office on a computer-based accountancy task.

The revenue recording task

The Post Office offers, on a contract basis, a wide range of services, including messenger services, bulk parcel services and business reply facilities. Customers are provided with docket books to indicate when and how much they use each of these services and voucher books in which to enter the payments they make for services used. Keeping track of the services used and the monies paid is a crucial task for which a computer-based revenue recording system has been developed. Operating this system is the subject of the present training needs analysis.

The working environment in which this work is carried out is a typical large office space. Computer terminals are prominent. Work at terminals is interspersed with telephone calls and reference to a paper-based filing system. Management was concerned that the job should be done properly, in view of the consequences of mislaying monies or making mistakes regarding overcharging customers. It saw the presence of so many terminals in the workplace as a new feature that would present major problems to their workforce and assumed that training needs would focus on the use of this computer system.

The training needs analysis

Following a general appraisal of the system, analysis of training needs was carried out using hierarchical task analysis (Duncan, 1974; Shepherd, 1985).

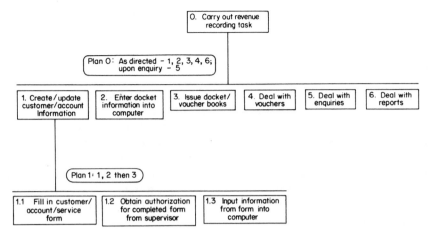

Figure 1. Part of the task analysis of the revenue recording task

This technique entails describing tasks in terms of a hierarchy of operations and plans—operations describing the various goal-directed activities undertaken; plans describing the conditions under which each operation is undertaken. It must be emphasized that, through this method, focus is made upon the actual task that the operator undertakes rather than the system he or she is controlling.

The main parts of this analysis are shown in Figure 1. Of these operations, it is only necessary to discuss the breakdown of operation 1 (that is 1.1, 1.2 and 1.3) and operation 5 to cover the critical features of the task. Operations 2, 3, 4 and 6 are each computer input tasks and are similar to operation 1.3.

Operation 1.1. Fill in customer/account/service form

The operator has to prepare a form for computer input from information sent from the postal sales department. The form will contain details of a new customer, a new account for an existing customer or a new service within an existing account. There will be mistakes in entering information into the computer (operation 1.3) if this is not done properly.

Operation 1.2. Obtain authorization for completed form from supervisor

Operators are required to seek confirmation from their supervisors that they have carried out operation 1.1 properly. In order to speed up the through-put of work, supervisors may be tempted to take short-cuts and allow operators to try to enter data from the incomplete memoranda sent to them from the postal sales department, without first completing the customer/account/service form. This is not a skills deficiency on the part of the operator but a failure to appreciate the likelihood and consequences of errors that might arise from incomplete data and may best be overcome by improved supervision.

Operation 1.3. Input information from form into computer

This task involves: (a) locating a required screen by making correct choices in the menu hierarchy; and (b) correctly following screen form-filling procedures. The same general procedures are required in operations 2, 3, 4 and 6. It was these tasks that gave the impression of extensive computer activity for which management assumed extensive computer-based training would be necessary. While there was a lot of computer work in total, specific procedures were carried out infrequently and intermittently. There was ample time for the operator to locate and use a suitable manual. This justified the development of a better manual.

Operation 5. Deal with enquiries

Enquiries are initiated by customers querying the invoices and statements sent to them. This proved to be a crucial task and accounted for much of the operator's use of the telephone and the paper-based filing system. Enquiries might be due to customers failing to understand the document sent to them, recognizing an apparent inconsistency in the document (which might be correct but appear wrong due to the anomalies of the accounting system) or recognizing a genuine error in the account, for example, a mis-keyed amount. The problem facing the operator was substantial, requiring patient listening to an irate customer's complaint followed by careful analysis of the problem and explanation to the customer, *all on the telephone*. Analysis of the problem entailed locating enquiry screens and making reference to documents filed away in filing cabinets. The diagnostic skills that operators required in these circumstances were substantial, as was their need to be able to direct the customer through paperwork, via the telephone, courteously and effectively. This activity represented probably the greatest training need of the entire task and it had little to do with IT.

Training recommendations

Through this training analysis, which is only described briefly above, the following general training recommendations were made.

On-job instruction

Many of the data entry routines can be taught satisfactorily on the job, especially with a suitable user manual. In addition, filing skills must be taught.

Computer-based training

CBT was recommended to teach important concepts of the system, for example the distinctions between the different types of account. It was also recommended to teach operators a model of the system to explain how information flows through the system and is stored. The trainee's understanding of the system would be measured by the extent to which simulated enquiries could be dealt with.

Customer service training

Operators must understand a customer's enquiry over the telephone and deal with it effectively and courteously. These are difficult skills to master, requiring diagnostic and communications training followed by simulated practice.

Supervisory training

Since both CBT and on-job training would be handled locally, there is a need to give first-line supervisors some training in how to make best use of these approaches.

Conclusions from the case study

One can obviously debate how representative is any IT task or whether the presented case is sufficiently sophisticated with regard to current developments in IT. This is not a 'state-of-the-art' situation, but it is a practical, professional, extensive and very useful application of computer technology in a commercial setting. It is one that is typical of many applications in industry and commerce. The major conclusion is that the IT context is incidental to the identification of training needs. Thus, social and cognitive skills emerge as the source of performance problems, along with those more clearly related to the technology. Dealing with any IT application, then, should entail an unbiased approach, which aims to identify problems according to the merits of the situation.

DELIVERING TRAINING

A feature of IT, probably unique, is that its technology is potentially useful in delivering training. For it to be used *effectively* it must be preceded by a task analysis such that it will address that which is pertinent to the task. For it to be used *economically* the analysis must be carried out in good time; what may have been cost-effective at the design stage may not be later. Moreover, earlier analysis will minimize training problems through the incorporation of more effective human factors in the basic design. If training needs can be anticipated early on and solutions sought in the operational technology itself, then what sort of training features should be incorporated? Before that question can be considered, the learning patterns of typical IT users should be examined.

Learning patterns for the IT user

Eason (1984) and Cuff (1980) have described the characteristics of typical users of IT systems, emphasizing the casual or intermittent use they make of facilities available to them. A number of these features are pertinent to their preferred pattern of learning and, hence, the types of training provision that should be offered to them. They apply equally to people using a purpose-built application, such as the revenue recording system described above, as to people using a piece of applications software, such as a word-processor, a spreadsheet or a computer-aided design package.

First, different users have *different operational needs* for the different functions available in the system. Over a period of time some functions will be used frequently, some rarely and others not at all. Moreover, the pattern of usage will vary between users, depending on the operational demands placed upon them—even the revenue recording task described is subject to these variations, because different geographical regions have different sorts of industrial and commerical concentrations resulting in different usage of the postal services provided. This means that training should be *adaptive* to the needs of different users. An initial period of concerted training to try to cover all skills, such as the 'short course' so often favoured by organizations, is unsuitable for these applications. Even if, with different patterns of usage of functions, such courses were economical to run, it is unlikely that a user will encounter a less-frequent operation in sufficient time following a training period to ensure that the correct response is remembered. Some form of 'point-of-need' training is essential, at least to train usage of the less-frequent functions.

Second, there are considerable *individual differences* between users regarding their capacity to learn new IT skills. People vary in their motivation, confidence, familiarity with similar products and procedures and the extent to which they are able to make use of teaching facilities offered.

A third general feature of intermittent users in their *production orientation*. Such people are rarely interested in learning a computer application for its own sake. They are ill-disposed to spend time learning when they could be 'doing'. It means they will favour 'point-of-need' learning so that they can seek or be prompted to seek training when they need it.

A fourth point is that users become satisfied with a small set of functions which enable them to meet their requirements even if they are inefficient in doing so. Most systems offer several ways to achieve specific goals. Most users become satisfied with a low level of efficiency if it means getting the job done and avoiding further learning (see Eason, Chapter 12 of this volume). This is often quite satisfactory for individual operators, but often less satisfactory for the organizations in which they are working, since time is lost—compare the efficiency of using a mail-merge program with copying out a list of addresses one by one. A solution is to monitor performance and invoke appropriate point-of-need training when it is required.

A final characteristic is that usually the tasks people are required to carry out in computer-based systems are idiosyncratic. There is no general body of knowledge or skill that can be taught separately from the task itself. The task must be *represented* in some fashion to inject any purpose into the training.

Training solutions in IT situations should be *flexible* to meet individual learning needs and *adaptive* to enable training to be matched to the current level of skill of the learner. To exploit both of these features, it is necessary to have the capability to monitor performance and adapt subsequent training to the individual learner's real needs. Moreover, training should be carried out in the context of an effective representation of the task, either through *simulation* or *training in the real situation*. More conventional approaches to training IT skills, such as short courses, are ill-suited to these purposes. Incorporating this range of features in a system at the design stage to support the training needs of the intermittent user implies development of an '*embedded*' *training system*.

Embedded training options

In an embedded training system, training facilities are installed within the system itself, available to the trainee as and when required. Applications would incorporate any useful ideas in computer-based learning, including appropriate areas of artificial intelligence. Much of the work to date in this general field has focused on teaching academic subject matter rather than supporting occupational tasks. One major area of interest has been in the investigation of natural language interfaces to improve explanations with a computer-based learning facility; another has been the development of 'student models' with which to regulate the progress of instruction. A variety of advances in this field are reviewed by Michalski, Carbonell and Mitchell (1983).

Becker (1987) outlines the facilities that would have to be provided in a comprehensive computer-based adaptive training system, such as would be found within an embedded trainer. These include facilities to monitor performance, update a record or model of the learner, adjust conditions for practice and provide extrinsic information to help the trainee learn. At present, such systems are still under development, but work is being done elsewhere on various aspects that could sensibly be incorporated. Carrol and Carrithers (1984), for example, describe the concept of 'training wheels' in which a special interface to a word-processor was built to lock certain functions away from the user until the user is ready to learn how to use them. It is precisely this sort of facility that one would wish to incorporate within an embedded trainer for a wide range of types of applications software.

CONCLUDING REMARKS

This chapter has focused upon a range of training issues concerned with IT contexts. Emphasis was placed on the need for caution when considering the training implications of an IT situation. IT contexts should be treated as any other occupational context. Training needs should be identified strictly in accordance with the conditions met in the situation; training solutions should be justified in terms of benefits. In the case described, the real training problems identified were not associated directly with the IT aspects of the task. Indeed, this should not be surprising. IT aspects should be reasonably well engineered and excessive training should not be necessary.

IT is unique as an occupational context since its technology is potentially invaluable in *delivering* training. If training needs can be identified at the appropriate stage in design, then a number of opportunities exist for embedding training within applications software to provide learning opportunities most suited to the typical 'intermittent' IT user.

Apart from the opportunities it provides for improving the delivery of training, there seems to be no real justification for treating IT as a particularly special occupational context. Admittedly, it embodies a number of features which emphasize some training problems rather than others. But so do other occupational contexts. By treating IT situations as nothing special, it is more likely that careful, critical, unbiased training needs analysis will be conducted. Such analysis should highlight training needs in accordance with the real characteristics of the situation under review, rather than encouraging unwarranted focus on the more glamourous aspects of the situation.

REFERENCES

Bainbridge, L. (1987) The ironies of automation. In J. Rasmussen, K. D. Duncan and J. Leplat (eds.), *New Technology and Human Error*. Chichester: John Wiley and Sons.

Becker, L. A. (1987) A framework for intelligent instructional systems: an artificial intelligence machine learning approach. *Programmed Learning and Educational Technology*, **24**, 128–36.

Carrol, J. M., and Carrithers, C. (1984) Training wheels in a user interface. *Comm. of the ACM*, **27**(8), 800–6.

Cuff, R. N. (1980) On casual users. *International Journal of Man–Machine Studies*, **12**, 163–187.

Dale, H. C. A. (1958) Fault-finding in electronics equipment. *Ergonomics*, **1**, 356–85.

Duncan, K. D. (1974) Analytical techniques in training design. In E. Edwards and F. P. Lees (eds.), *The Human Operator and Process Control*. Taylor and Francis.

Eason, K. D. (1984) The continuing support needs of end users. *Infortech 'State of the Art' Report on 'Information Centres'*. Pergammon Press.

Michalski, R. S., Carbonell, J. G., and Mitchell, T. M. (1983) *Machine Learning: an Artificial Intelligence Approach*. Palo Alto: Tioga Publishing Company.

Rusmussen, J., and Jensen, A. (1974) Mental procedures in real-life tasks. A case study of electronic trouble-shooting. *Ergonomics*, **17**, 293–307.

Shepherd, A. (1985). Hierarchical task analysis and training decisions. *Programmed Learning and Educational Technology*, **22**, 162–76.

Section 3

Training as Part of the Total Job Support System

Outline of Section

The chapters in this section raise an ever-widening range of issues. The last section pointed out that training for IT is concerned not solely with training for equipment-using skills but also with other skills which arise with changes in work. Chapters in this section will point out that training is not an independent solution to the problems of optimizing equipment usage; nor is it the only way of supporting the use of equipment. Training questions are not just related to the individual workplace. What affects peoples' attitudes to the new technology, and therefore the amount it will be used? How can we help people to understand and make decisions about what the new technology can do for their organization and to accept the organizational changes that will be involved? How can we train people to understand the impact of their industry on the national economy and to participate in decisions about these effects? How does the possession of new skills affect the status of people and their potential opportunities in society, and what do we want these to be? What changes can be expected in work-related values, like work centrality, motivating factors and work ethics and how do these interrelate with the requested new skills?

These questions are all interrelated. This is illustrated by the fact that the chapter by Shepherd (Chapter 10) was originally part of his chapter at the end of the previous section (Chapter 9), but has been separated to introduce this one. The chapters in this section are based on extensive field work experience, and are full of practical suggestions. We are concerned with a 'system' level of design. A design decision about any one point will have effects on many other aspects of the working situation, and there is no one sequential way of describing all these interdependencies. A short summary must be very inadequate in indicating the complexity of the points made.

TRAINING/INTERFACE DESIGN/ALLOCATION OF FUNCTION

As Shepherd (Chapter 10) points out, it is inefficient to consider the design of training schemes only after the equipment has been built. With any equipment, the better the interface, the less the need for training. Information technology not only alters the training needs and tools, it also alters the potential interfaces, and therefore this interface–training trade-off. In the area of automation of control decisions, as in the transport and process industries, the more carefully the allocation of functions between person and computer has been thought out, the less need there may be for special training to deal with low-frequency emergency events. Shepherd introduces these points, so it is only necessary here to point out some links between papers.

Interface design and training

A good interface can reduce the need for training. A poor interface design increases the need for training (as well as increasing the users' workload and liability to stress). Baker and Marshall point out in Chapter 16 of this volume that if the operator has to think in one way to use one device in a control room and in another way with another support facility provided by another manufacturer, then training so that the operator can integrate these sources of information poses difficulties. Frese and Altmann, in Chapter 3 of this volume, describe a study of learning to use word-processors, in which a word-processor with one type of interface is easier to learn than another. Eason (Chapter 12) discusses design for people who use IT equipment so rarely that they do not take training courses, by making the interface 'obvious' in meaning so that it supports 'learning by doing'. Marshall and Baker (Chapter 11) describe an interface to an industrial process which is intended to reduce the operators' difficulty in understanding what is happening in a highly complex process. On the other hand, although the operators may not need so much training in how to understand the process, they do need training in how to understand and use this complex interface, and this training is an essential part of any method by which such interfaces are assessed.

Allocation of function and training

Both Shepherd (Chapter 10) and Marshall and Baker (Chapter 11) point out a similar trade-off between training and allocation of function. The more successful the automation of a process, the fewer natural opportunities an operator will have of taking over operation of the process, and so the more extensive their training will need to be to ensure that they can deal with the unusual situations in which they are needed. There is some debate about the extent to which involving the operator in on-line decision-making will maintain the skills that are needed to deal with emergency situations. However, it is a point of logic rather than debate that the more that skills can be maintained by normal working the less they will require special training.

As Shepherd points out, the existence of these two trade-offs means that training cannot be considered in isolation but must be considered within the initial system design strategy. Information technology does not just increase the skills needed by the workforce; it also increases the range of skills needed by the ergonomist/training expert.

SUPPORT FOR THE DISCRETIONARY USER

Another interaction appears if we consider the wider aim of developing skills in using new technology, rather than simply of training. This is the interaction between the person's task and the level of training. Formal training is appropriate to the specialist user of IT equipment. However, what about support for learning to use the equipment by people who already have other professional skills, who are not interested in becoming computer experts, but whose work could be assisted by using some IT tools? Again we have the problem of skills in using equipment, and the link between task goals and the facilities available in the equipment.

Eason (Chapter 12) has an interesting and practical discussion of these issues. He suggests point-of-need support, by which help in using the system is provided while the person uses it. He gives a table of different ways of delivering information which can meet various learning needs. Both the interface and the system need to be 'obvious'. Designing the system so that it is based on a small number of general principles makes it more easy to understand, and identifying the task–facilities links for a particular individual is a crucial aspect of support. Otherwise, the more flexible the system, the less it may be used by people who have not got enough time to work out how to use it for their own purposes. This is ironical, as the main design aim in many pieces of IT equipment is to provide as much flexibility in facilities as possible. This aim in itself may be causing difficulties for non-specialist users.

ATTITUDES AND THE USE OF EQUIPMENT

People such as office workers and industrial process operators have to use IT-based equipment. Their attitudes to the equipment may affect how well they do their job, but they cannot do their work without it. The attitudes of people at professional and managerial levels have a more obvious impact. Professional people can decide whether or not to use the equipment; managers can decide what use to make of the equipment in their organization.

The cost–benefits of using the equipment

Eason (Chapter 12) has been involved in many interesting studies of what real users of IT equipment actually do, which may not be very close to the designers' dream world. He reports studies which have found that a wide range of available facilities are not used and that people frequently invent strategies using the facilities they do know, rather than exploring whether more appropriate methods are available. He has an interesting analysis of the high costs involved in learning to do something new, which will not be done frequently so do not encourage exploration. He draws practical conclusions from this about the design of systems that will be used.

Training to understand the uses and limits of the technology

Mercy (Chapter 13) and Olesen (Chapter 14) are concerned with training people to both understand the new technology and understand its potential impact on the functioning of the organization, so that they can participate in decisions about its use in organizational development. Nijhof and Mulder, in Chapter 6 of this volume, are also concerned with what needs to be included in technical education so that people can make an intelligent contribution to projects like this. Eason has also done many studies of this which are not reported here (for example Eason, 1982). Mercy is particularly concerned with managers. Olesen is concerned with a wider potential, with the extent to which computer models of an industry and its impact on the local economy can be used by non-computer specialists so that they can participate in decisions about its effects.

ORGANIZATIONAL REDESIGN

Attitudes also have a crucial influence on the success of training schemes that are part of introducing information technology into an organization.

One of the suggestions that Eason (Chapter 12) makes about supporting the intermittent user is to have a 'local expert' who people can talk to about their problems in using the system. He comments that this sort of social support structure tends to be informal and that the role of 'local expert' must be formally nominated. This of course would make a change in the organizational structure. In the discussion Frese, on the basis of a study similar to Eason's, said that only branches with a local expert used a new system successfully. Norros (Chapter 17 of this volume) pointed out that people who use only a few facilities use them within their previous mode of working; they do not redefine the whole task setting to consider how it might best be done given the new facilities.

So the important question arises about how to support this sort of organizational rethinking, and what are the problems. Mercy (Chapter 13) points out that involving the potential users in the design is both necessary and a useful form of training, but the problem is how to train them to understand the new technology and to rethink the structure of the organization. Mercy describes two case studies in which the same group of people discussed first the information structure of the organization and then the possibilities for improved working methods.

The first was successful, the second not, and the main difference seems to have been in attitudes, which links back to the previous topic. In the first study part, the team members developed a formal information structure for the organization, which is a necessary step for introducing computers. The people involved wanted to do this, because they had a common problem with communication difficulties in their normal work, so they were willing to learn a formalization language, which could describe the common properties of different sections of the organization, and to work on the problems of using it.

The second study part, intended to revise and integrate working methods, was not successful. In such a case, it is necessary to describe the organization's functions independently of the present internal divisions and then to redefine the divisions on the basis of natural groupings in the newly rationalized working methods. This the participants were not willing to do. Mercy suggests that this was because the participants were there as heads of their sections, and changing the working methods would involve changes in personal status and responsibility which they were not willing to consider.

Questions arise about how to encourage people to be willing and able to take part in this sort of 'organizational/working methods rethinking' exercise. (Norros in Chapter 17 of this volume is also concerned with ways of helping people to rethink their methods of working.) To ensure cooperative attitudes it seems to be necessary to discuss beforehand the need for organizational change and allay any associated fears. The people involved in the discussions should be there to represent a branch of expertise about the organization, rather than a particular function or status.

Although such people can describe the existing working methods, it is much more difficult to rethink them. Mercy suggests that using a formal language to describe the situation helps people to notice inconsistencies and incompleteness. He suggests that these languages need to describe the objectives, rather than particular working methods, as that gives too much detail and makes it difficult to handle complexity.

In discussion, Eason (Chapter 12) pointed out that it is necessary to give a physical demonstration of new ways of doing the work. A theoretical description of unfamiliar working methods does not break the 'perceptual set'. Actually seeing it being done is necessary.

WIDER SOCIETAL ISSUES

Olesen's chapter (Chapter 14) makes an important end to this group of chapters by reminding us of the much wider issues that are involved. His case study is concerned with the use of IT in a major industry in a country with such a small economic base that any decision about this industry affects the national economy. He is concerned that local people should participate in decisions about the design of the system, not just because the people are useful data banks of expertise, but because it is their right as members of a democratic local community.

This leads him to remind us of wider questions: Not just how, but for what and by whom is the IT to be used? As he rightly points out, all the other chapters in this book take a narrow 'cognitive' approach, considering training only as it contributes to a rapid increase in the knowledge and competence needed for a particular task. Such a perspective ignores emotional, cultural and political perspectives. Training does not just change technological effectiveness; it changes the person who does the task, their place in society and their potential opportunities. Should our approach be technology centred or community centred? Should people be trained to fit in with the needs of technology, or should the technology be designed to suit the needs of the community?

REFERENCE

Eason, K. (1982) The process of introducing information technology. *Behaviour and Information Technology*, **1**, 197–216.

10. Training Decisions at the Design Stage

Andrew Shepherd

SUMMARY

Training is not independent of other human factor issues in the operation or utilization of any system. Inconsistent interfaces, inoperable tasks, partial automation and developments in sophisticated interfaces can each influence or be influenced by the subsequent training of users.

INTRODUCTION

Most tasks are presented for training analysis after systems have been built. Managers rarely consider training much before the time when people need to be recruited and put to work. This has been a common problem in occupational settings which have not involved information technology as well as those that have. In non-IT situations, the reluctance to consider training early on is because it is to easy to put training decisions off until later. In IT situations, there is an additional factor in that acknowledging the need for training is somehow an indictment of the 'user-friendliness' of the computing system.

Considering training too late in the design cycle can be a serious mistake, since it limits opportunities to exploit the available information technology in the training solution, for example through computer-based training, embedded tutorials, advisory systems or providing a 'training mode' on expensive control equipment.

Equally important is the fact that by ignoring training needs, tasks may be developed that place an unreasonable burden on subsequent training. A result is that training is excessive, unduly expensive or incapable of delivering the standard of performance required.

We may view the effects of overlooking training considerations by considering their potential influence on other design decisions. We can see cases where training needs will be increased as a result of poor design.

Developing Skills with Information Technology
Edited by Lisanne Bainbridge and S. Antonio Ruiz Quintanilla

INCONSISTENT INTERFACES

Inconsistent features in human–computer dialogue can create serious problems which may add to the burden of training. A common example is if a data-base user becomes used to pressing the 'return' or 'enter' key following the input of data, this will become a habit. If activities are then encountered where this is not necessary, pressing the 'return' key may be interpreted by the computer as a null entry to the next computer screen. Recovery may be possible, but it will be inconvenient. If the user becomes used to a set of screens where pressing the 'return' key to enter data is not required, then he or she will become irritated if a return key is suddenly necessary, as the computer will not appear to accept the data. Maas (1983) draws attention to this problem, emphasizing how inconsistency may be expected as larger programs are built up from subsystems that have been designed independently by different people. Jorgensen et al. (1983), in the same volume, demonstrates that even individual designers cannot be relied upon for consistency in naming commands for computer users.

Inconsistent dialogue features in software mean that specific procedures have to be spelled out step by step to operators or system users. If users are expected to perform unaided rather than by reference to a user manual, they must learn by rote, which, under the circumstances, is unlikely to prove reliable.

Cases such as these reflect poor software and are all too frequent. It is usually possible to get people to operate these systems, but they spend a lot of time looking up procedures in bulky manuals or resort to guessing and make mistakes. Software is often produced without a full appreciation of precisely what the user is supposed to do. Early anticipation of training needs prompts the form of task analysis that will enable these potential problems to be uncovered. Failure to do this creates an unnecessary burden for training.

INOPERABLE DISPLAYS

Sometimes poorly conceived interfaces mean that people cannot be trained at all to any standard that would be regarded as satisfactory. Shepherd (1985) describes a case where training was required to help process plant operators, who were used to a conventional instrument display, deal with a new computer-based display on their plant. The plant, with which operators were familiar, comprised of three main areas, which interacted with one another in a complex manner. Because the operators were experienced with this plant, management assumed training would be minimal, merely involving familiarization with the new display. A task analysis, carried out to develop the training, indicated that a major operator skill was dealing with a range of perturbations that occurred from time to time, creating unbalance in the flows in the system. Operators had rapidly to examine information throughout the plant to decide what remedial action would compensate for these disturbances. In the original system, where all information was displayed on an array of conventional instruments, operators could scan their control panels to make their decisions. In the new display system, however, operators had to retrieve individual items of information via a menu system. The task analysis showed the sets of indicators from which information had to be sought to enable the different types of decision. As no thought had been given to the manner in which operators had to carry out this work, the information was arranged in a menu system according to the *geographical* location of the instrument sensors. The task analysis made it clear that, under this geographical organization, operators would be subject to an extreme memory load, as they had to move around the menu structure to locate specific items of information. Therefore, from the viewpoint of human decision-making, introduction of this computer-based system was a retrograde step. By redesigning the display to enable information related to specific types of decision to be collected and displayed on the same screen, the memory problem was abated, the task substantially simplified and the required training became straightforward. It was only through the process of considering training needs that this display problem was highlighted and a difficult or impossible training problem avoided. Had the task been analysed sooner, the solution would have been even more effective.

REDUCTION OF THE ROLE OF THE HUMAN OPERATOR

In a number of systems we see the trend towards the eventual elimination of the human operator, sometimes for altruistic reasons such as the removal of human beings from hazardous areas, sometimes for pure commercial reasons, such as the removal of the costs and consequences of human labour. Developments in IT make the opportunities for reduction of human control more available. New sensing devices reduce reliance on human senses and enable sensing of which humans are not capable. Robotics provides new opportunities for handling materials. Artificial intelligence techniques reduce the reliance upon human cognition. Not only are those systems where automation is already prominent becoming more automated, for example large continuous-process chemical plants, so too are systems where earlier technology has not enabled such developments, for example flexible manufacturing systems. Often the things humans find most easy are also most easy to automate. The things that are difficult to automate are often difficult to learn, so training solutions must be sought. In such systems, training needs become less numerous but more complex. Bainbridge (1987) describes the consequences of advanced automation for the human operation of complex systems. There are two main aspects that impinge upon training issues.

Human operation in situations of less than 100 per cent reliability

If near-complete automation is attempted yet system performance falls short of 100 per cent reliability, designers often rely on human operators for back-up, requiring them to perform effectively a potentially wide range of tasks with little or no practice. Moreover, the features that have improved the plant reliability often complicate the human operator's understanding of what is going on—simple control loops are replaced by complex control systems which obscure even the simplest of symptoms. The likelihood of error-free performance by the human operator under these circumstances is extremely low. The right kind of training is paramount. The operator must sometimes deal with situations never or rarely previously encountered. Hence, training must lead to performance that will *transfer* to novel situations, that will be retained over long periods and will hold up under stress. Routine practice is necessary for retention of these skills and training simulation will almost certainly feature in any training regime to meet these criteria. If these training implications are fully anticipated at a design stage, then they can be incorporated in that design, in the form of *embedded training*.

Partial automation

Developments in artificial intelligence make training considerations pertinent to the question of *allocation of function* between the human operator and a computerized system. Continuous processing systems usually entail control tasks, such as *monitoring, detection, pattern recognition, diagnosis* and *compensation* to be carried out. Information technology is increasingly employed to replace the human operator in some of these functions, with the result that system control is often by a mixture of human and artificial intelligence.

It is a real possibility that practice of one type of control task helps maintain the performance of another type of task. Under a less-automated operating regime, the operator's infrequently practised diagnostic skills *may* be partially maintained by more frequently practised system monitoring skills, for example. Indeed, early results by Kontogiannis (1988) indicate that subjects trained to start up and stabilize a simulated distillation column are able to demonstrate quite effective diagnostic skills which they have not been taught. Removal of the opportunity to carry out plant start-up on a routine basis, through the introduction of automation, may jeopardize acquisition and retention of diagnostic skill. The extent to which this is a real problem is uncertain. It is certainly an important topic for research, since the consequences of the problem could be serious. Most training research is not helpful in this respect, tending to examine training methods for different types of operation in isolation from one another, not considering the real possibility of transfer between them (Shepherd and Kontogiannis, 1987).

ELIMINATION OF TRAINING THROUGH 'IMPROVED' INTERFACES

Many software developers and many human factor specialists advising them seek to eliminate the need for training for applications software, such as word-processors, spreadsheets, etc. Their ultimate goal seems to be to develop systems that 'model' the user's intentions and dialogue style, without the need for the user to master any skills in controlling the actual interface. Users are expected to come to a system equipped with their expertise from whichever professional or recreational domain they belong to and express their ideas without any constraint imposed by difficulties with the interface.

Obvious examples of efforts to eliminate training through improved interfaces are those word-processors that use so-called 'WYSIWYG' ('what you see is what you get') interfaces, for example 'MacWrite' and Microsoft 'Word' on the Macintosh or Microsoft's 'Write', operating in their 'Windows' environment. The packages all employ the analogy of the normal page, using black text on a white screen and setting out the text as it would appear on the finished hard-copy document. The user is encouraged to adopt the written page analogy, but the analogy is often unhelpful. Entering carriage returns at the end of a line, as the new user is often tempted to do, especially with the page analogy presented, will severely limit the extent to which the document may be reformatted later. Further problems arise if the user tries to indent paragraphs using the space bar. The user may then assume that further text may be entered onto the blank area, as would be expected on a normal page. This cannot be done, however, if the machine is in the default 'insert text' mode—it simply pushes the existing text along the line until it 'wraps-around'. The more adventurous user will indent using a 'paragraph format' command. Now any attempt to enter text on a blank area outside of the paragraph's margins will be completely rebuffed, since the computer no longer recognizes these areas. While these WYSIWYG word-processors are often visually appealing and motivating for the new user, it is still essential to address the question of how the new user should be trained to use them if the full benefit of the word-processor is to be realized. Such training need not assume the proportions of a laboured and extended course; it may simply amount to providing a few key exercises to demonstrate some key points to the user. It is training none-the-less.

Training of some description nearly always features in introducing people to systems with which they are not familiar. A great deal is said about the benefits of 'natural' human–computer interfaces. Most people find it perfectly natural to undergo a phase of learning when encountering something new if they are to become competent, confident and come to trust the equipment they are dealing with. Denied such opportunity they may never become fully confident, even with a well-thought-out interface.

CONCLUDING REMARKS

Training is an integral phase of any design cycle in the development of systems that people are expected to use. However, it is naive simply to treat it as a final activity. The extent to which a task can be trained should be appraised at the design of the task itself. Knowing the extent of the likely training problems created by the human–computer interface, for example, should influence the interface design. However, training should not be seen as something necessarily to be avoided, or even minimized. Many tasks and many users need training as an integral part of preparation for competent operation. Often, a well-thought-out solution to training and operator support can avoid the need for expensive computing solutions and provide a context in which people are happier to work. If training needs can be sensibly assessed early on, training provision may be built into the software and hardware itself, often saving money and creating a much more satisfactory training solution.

REFERENCES

Bainbridge, L. (1987) The ironies of automation. In J. Rasmussen, K. D. Duncan and J. Leplat (eds.), *New Technology and Human Error*. Chichester: John Wiley and Sons.

Jorgensen, A. H., Barnard, P., Hammond, N., and Clark, I. (1983) In R. G. Green, S. J. Payne and G. C. van der Veer (eds.), *The Psychology of Computer Use*. Academic Press.

Kontogiannis (1988) Personal communication.

Maas, S. (1983) Why systems transparency? In R. G. Green, S. J. Payne and G. C. van der Veer (eds.), *The Psychology of Computer Use*. Academic Press.

Shepherd, A. (1985). Hierarchical task analysis and training decisions. *Programmed Learning and Education Technology*, **1985**, 22.

Shepherd, A., and Kontogiannis, T. (1987) Development of a specification for an automated instruction system for training process control skills. Paper presented to the *First European Meeting on Cognitive Science Approaches to Process Control*, Marcoussis, October 1987.

11. Training Operators to Use Advanced Display Systems for Process Control

Edward Marshall and Sue Baker

SUMMARY

Computer-based systems are bringing about substantial changes in the role of the operator in large-scale process plant. However, effective training must be provided if the operator is to be fluent in their use. This chapter describes training techniques for introducing operators to two novel display systems intended for nuclear plant control rooms.

INTRODUCTION

The increasing use of computers is bringing about substantial changes in the role of the operator in large-scale process plant. While sophisticated automation is relieving the operator of many repetitive and tedious tasks, computer-based display systems are making much more information available which should be exploited by the operator both for more efficient production and for safer management of faults and breakdowns.

In this chapter we will describe training techniques devised to introduce plant operators to two novel information display systems developed for nuclear power plant control rooms: the HALO alarm system and the critical function monitoring system (CFMS). Both these systems seek to render information more amenable to interpretation and are direct responses to identified problematic aspects of the operator's task. CFMS is already installed in a number of power plants, whereas HALO is currently implemented in the OECD Halden Project's full-scope nuclear plant simulator where it has undergone extensive trials. As a result of keen interest in these systems further development is continuing at Halden with a view to extended application in both the nuclear and off-shore industries.

Developing Skills with Information Technology
Edited by Lisanne Bainbridge and S. Antonio Ruiz Quintanilla
© 1989 John Wiley & Sons Ltd

Training operators to use these systems raises a number of issues. Effective training must be provided, particularly with systems of this type which will, by their very nature, be needed only occasionally, but yet require the operator to be fluent in their use. Three aspects must be considered: the concept underlying the system, the information display and the use of communication devices. We have been engaged in a number of evaluation exercises on these systems in which training was obviously an important prior condition. We have sought in our training to use a number of techniques to introduce operators to these new systems. Although the background for training was always a full-scope simulator, we have always emphasized the role of low-fidelity techniques and closely monitored self-instruction with liberal opportunities for 'hands-on' practice with the system.

In order to achieve mastery of a complex skill, opportunity must be available for systematic and frequent practice of the crucial elements of that skill. This represents an intractable paradox for the operators of complex processes which are for the most part controlled automatically. Indeed the declared function of the human operator is often expressed only in terms of carrying out rather infrequent actions or intervening in the event of a malfunction of the automatic systems. The role of the operator is further changing as advanced technology is increasingly implemented in the control room. Operators are progressively becoming more involved in systems management involving higher-level decision-making and the new computer-dependent information presentation techniques are intended to support this change.

Three basic strategies can be adopted by process design engineers in order to help overcome this problem—increased automation, enhancement of the man–machine interface and training. Increased automation, that is progressively taking the human out of the system, is certainly feasible. For example, in contemporary European nuclear plants, which are typically much more automated than those in the United States, the operator's task load is reduced by implementation of complex automatic systems—it is commonplace to use sequence controllers to execute a series of actions, such as opening and closing valves and starting and stopping pumps, etc., in order to implement a higher-order function. Currently the reliability of these devices is such that no one would realistically suggest running oil production platforms or nuclear power plants without operators present. Yet as more sophisticated automatic functions are included in the process it becomes correspondingly more difficult for the operator to monitor how and why particular automatic sequences are taking place. This may well make the operator's task particularly difficult when manual intervention is required to deal with malfunction of an automatic system.

Enhancing the man–machine interface is based on the assumption that improving the quality of information exchange between man and machine will bring about consequential benefits in operator performance. Whether or not innovation in the control room does bring about the benefits predicted by designers provides a major topic for research at the Halden Project.

The third approach is then to give better instruction and training to prepare operators for the unexpected and unusual events. In a separate chapter in this volume (Chapter 16) we have described how advanced technology has provided devices, in particular simulators, that can provide the opportunity for the operator to practise these difficult and rarely required tasks. In this chapter we will consider, within the context of a modern nuclear power plant, how the second approach, that of enhancing the man–machine interface, involves similar training issues.

NUCLEAR POWER PLANTS

The lack of reliance on computers is perhaps a surprising aspect when one considers the contemporary nuclear plant control room. Computers are only used for the display of information; they exert little or no control over the process. The microcomputer, ubiquitous in the office and business environment, is not evident in power plant control rooms. Where CRT screens are present, they usually present only monochrome information and the use of plain text lists is much more common than graphics. More contemporary computer features such as the mouse, touch-panel, screen windowing and advanced full-graphic displays have yet to be applied in the nuclear control console. The operator is still typically faced with a large array of conventional switches, buttons, dials and lights which may be combined with several CRTs. In an attempt to improve the operator's situation, particularly during a disturbance, new computer-based systems which use CRTs for display of information have been proposed for installation within the control room.

Computer-based alarm systems

A process disturbance, whether in a nuclear plant or not, can be expected to start with alarm signals. Alarms are usually single tiles which are illuminated when a particular parameter goes outside preset tolerance bounds. Design engineers assign alarms to any parameter that they feel should be noticed by the operator either on the grounds of economy or safety. This has resulted in a proliferation of alarms in the nuclear control room where there will be thousands of potential alarm messages. The problem is of course that in a serious plant disturbance hundreds of alarms can occur and the operator can overlook crucial messages embedded in this rush of information; indeed this was a specific problem implicated during the Three Mile Island (TMI) incident.

Where computer-based alarm systems are installed in nuclear plants, they are typically used to complement the hard-wired annunciator tile system—in that they provide a record of the sequence of alarms as they occur. This information is usually in the form of a text list of alarm messages, presented either on a line-printer or CRT. Other than giving a time sequence, such a system provides little additional help for the operator managing a plant disturbance—indeed the duplication of alarm signals may in itself be a source of confusion. We have argued that the computer should be exploited to structure and display alarm information systematically if it is to give valuable support to the operator during a process transient. In order to build an improved alarm system, a plain description of what the system should do is required. We have adopted the following three, ideally sequential, steps in disturbance management as forming basic requirements of any alarm system:

1. The operator should be alerted to any disturbance in the plant.
2. He or she should be guided to the disturbed plant area(s).
3. He or she should be aided in the location of disturbed parameters in the affected plant area(s).

The HALO (Handling Alarms using LOgic) system has been under development at Halden for a number of years and has been the subject of a series of evaluation studies. HALO uses logical expressions to generate a reduced number of alarms from the total array of process alarm signals and, in addition, it seeks to present these alarms in a clear and concise fashion. In order to achieve this it relies on extensive use of colour graphic presentation systems. The current version at present undergoing tests on our full-scope nuclear plant simulator uses a two-level hierarchy to represent data from about 2500 alarm signals. HALO alarms are formed on the basis of a combination of plant signals—in contrast to conventional systems where process alarms arise from the violation of a single parameter. This means that alarms can be related to plant mode, that is indications that may be unusual in one plant mode (for example shutdown) may be normal in another (for example power production). Further HALO permits automatic checking that all events that should follow a trip do take place—in which case an alarm is only required if any event does *not* occur. HALO also removes unnecessary alarms—for example if a parameter has reached an extreme limit (lo–lo or hi–hi) then less serious warnings (lo or hi) are redundant and can be removed from the alarm display.

Processed alarms are grouped in terms of main components or plant systems and also categorized on the basis of where relevant detailed information can be inspected. A dedicated, full-graphic display presents this information in the form of a detailed plant overview. The overview principally comprises a dynamic plant mimic where symbols corresponding to plant components are coloured according to alarm status. In addition text messages relating to crucial parameters and the location of detailed alarm information are included in the display. Colour is used extensively—light blue indicates a component that is operating normally, grey an inactive component, yellow is a second priority or warning alarm and red indicates a first priority (serious) alarm. Individual alarm signals are presented as dynamically embedded messages in the detailed plant mimic diagrams which the operator uses to effect control over the plant. In addition a text list of all current alarms in time sequence is available for the operator should it be required. For a detailed description of the HALO system see Øwre and Marshall (1986).

Safety parameter display systems

The safety parameter display system was another response to the TMI incident. It was concluded that a small subset of crucial plant signals should be extracted from the whole data array and presented on a dedicated panel in order to focus the operator's attention on the most important aspects of the process during a severe disturbance. A number of versions of this idea were developed in the United States and the critical function monitoring system (CFMS), produced by Combustion Engineering Inc., was probably the most elaborate. CFMS is based on the assumption that the safety status of a process can be expressed in terms of a small number of critical safety functions. CFMS is designed specifically to draw the operator's attention towards any threatened critical function which is defined as follows: 'A function that must be accomplished by means of a group of actions that prevent core melt or minimise radiation releases to the general public' (Corcoran *et al.*, 1980). The emphasis is on the maintenance of plant *functions* rather than on particular alarms or diagnosis at the component level, the philosophy being that the plant should first be brought to a safe state after which more specific diagnoses of underlying causes can be carried out. It should also be noticed that, since critical safety functions relate to the prevention of core melt or radiation release, a threat to a critical function constitutes a very serious plant condition requiring prompt and effective action. Thus, while it may be difficult for the operator to locate and diagnose the precise cause of a complex disturbance, the plant can nevertheless be kept in a safe condition so long as the critical functions can be maintained.

In the CFMS, computer algorithms use several hundred plant signals to express the status of each critical function. The status information is displayed by means of a three-level hierarchy of formats which use both colour and dynamic mimic diagrams. CFMS was subjected to a detailed evaluation study at the Loviisa nuclear plant in Finland where the system was fully implemented at the on-site training simulator. (For an account of this exercise see, for example, Marshall *et al.*, 1983.)

TRAINING FOR EVALUATION STUDIES

If a new piece of hardware is to be successfully exploited by operators in the control room, it is obvious that they must first be fully instructed in its use. Design of a training programme is, we would maintain, all too often neglected by the system designers. However, in evaluation studies of the type we have carried out in connection with both HALO and the CFMS, we have considered that prior training is essential and indeed we have emphasized the role of training in our experimental methodology. In general we have felt that the main principle underlying any instructional programme is that it should be both systematic and well structured, particularly as we have always had the problem of fitting training periods into tight schedules imposed on us by the limited availability of subjects. We also have to be sure that each trainee receives the same information and that they reach a similar level of competence before embarking on any experimental trials. In the case of the CFMS exercise this was particularly problematic because, in order that we could access a maximum number of operating crews, the experiment had to be carried out over a four month period. This meant that the training course had to be repeated with twelve different crews during this period. We were worried that instructors might become either more effective in their training as they became themselves more familiar with the material, or they might become bored and lose interest going over the same ground again and again. To ensure that training was robust, we maximized the use of programe texts and tape-slide presentation; in addition we used structured practice sessions and test problems with preestablished criteria for scores. For the HALO evaluation, which was carried out in our own laboratory at Halden, access to the team of fourteen subjects was much easier. As they could all be available at the same time there was no real difficulty in making sure that they all received similar pretrial experience with the system.

Broadly speaking there are three main areas to be addressed in preparing operators for the use of a new system:

1. They must know the theoretical principles underlying the system.
2. They must be familiar with the way information is presented and how the display may behave during the kind of process scenario for which it is designed.
3. They must have sufficient practice with the interface so that they can operate it fluently.

Theoretical basis

It is always a difficult question as to the correct amount of theory required in introducing a new system. Both systems considered here use elaborate software to produce the information though the underlying principles are fairly simple. Nevertheless, it is important that these basic concepts are understood. In the case of CFMS the operators should have a reasonable understanding of how the status of any critical function is generated, although we felt a detailed knowledge of all the steps in the algorithms was not required. For example, if the function 'core reactivity control' were threatened the operator should know which parameters were used to derive this conclusion.

In terms of actual training the theoretical basis of CFMS was given in the form of a series of short modules. Each module consisted of a tape-slide programme about five minutes long followed by a short test which used multiple choice items or questions requiring a short sentence response. After the test trainees were encouraged to discuss any problems with their instructor. A useful device employed in the tests was to include items from previous modules, so that trainees were continually reminded about earlier learned material. The topics covered in this way included a general introduction to the concept of critical functions and then a detailed guide to each of the seven functions included in the system.

With the HALO system we originally thought that such a detailed theoretical description of the system was unnecessary, and most of the training programme would be devoted to the way alarm information was displayed by the system. However, the trainees requested background information about how the system used logic to filter out unnecessary alarm information. Because of this interest, some time was spent describing the structure of the algorithms used to filter alarms, but no formal testing was carried out as we felt that this detailed knowledge would not affect operator performance.

Information display

We have adopted a number of strategies to give operators practice with new displays. Tape-slide provides a powerful technique for presenting and describing the use of symbols, colours and the layout of information. Again we have adopted the modular approach—each module consisting of a short tape-slide presentation followed by testing. Two types of problem are given during testing. First, trainees are asked to predict the condition of a display given certain plant or equipment status. At the simple level this could be: 'What colour and shape is a pump symbol is the pump is tripped?' At a more complex level the trainee is asked to predict how a display format will appear given a certain disturbed plant scenario. In the second type the problem is reversed—trainees are presented with a static snapshot of the display and are asked to report on the plant status. The complexity of these problems is related to the appropriate level of trainee competence. At later stages in training it is possible to present trainees with pertinent sequences of slides showing the development of a plant disturbance over time and the way it would be presented by the display system. These sequences provide a good lead into the next major topic—hands-on practice with the system.

Hands-on practice with the system

In the exercises described here hands-on practice was feasible because both systems were implemented on full-scope plant simulators. If this is not possible then the training options are more limited; nevertheless, it is possible to devise exercises to give useful prior experience. First, series of photographs of the display as described above can be used to represent stages in a plant disturbance, though deriving the state of the indicated parameters may be difficult without a simulator. Even so we have found that such slide sequences can provide a valuable supplement to simulator training because they allow faster and more flexible access to different process states.

In the HALO exercise, for a number of practical reasons, some training had to take place before the HALO system was completely implemented on the simulator. The alarm system was functional but the display system was not, which meant that alarms were signalled as simple text messages. In order to prepare operators for the system we used a modified version of the training technique proposed by Shepherd et al. (1977) and Marshall et al. (1981). Trainee operators were divided into two- or three-man teams and each team was asked to generate a list of typical plant disturbances. They then had to predict for each disturbance the alarm messages they would expect and a number of important plant indications, for example would the fault cause a trip and if so how long after onset of the fault? Each team completed this exercise and then described their faults to the other teams. The ensuing discussion sometimes resulted in revisions to the predicted process symptoms. The simulator was then run with each fault in turn and the observed alarms compared with the predicted ones. Further discussion between teams and instructors ensured in order to resolve any observed discrepancies. As a final exercise, the operators were presented with alarm lists from which they had to identify the plant fault in question.

Having achieved a good level of familiarity with the alarm system, operators were then permitted practice with the display system itself. In the case of this version of HALO the information displayed was compatible with the preexisting system so little practice was necessary. Even so, each team spent half a day learning to use the touch panel to access displays and exercising the system with a number of plant transients to see the way in which information changed as the fault progressed.

Because of the restricted time schedule there was relatively little opportunity for hands-on practice with the CFMS system. This was a problem especially because the CFMS displays were in many respects different from the operators' usual formats. Each crew had about half a day to practise with the system—learning how to address the various formats and familiarizing themselves with the way in which the displays corresponded to their preexisting instrumentation. They also practised the sequence of display accesses for a number of typical transients and they were allowed one full-scale trial with a dynamic plant scenario.

In both exercises subjects were enthusiastic about the training techniques used but complained that they had not had sufficient practice. They all felt more opportunity for practice would enhance their observed performance in the experimental trials. Nevertheless, we suspect that in training operators for real use of these devices they would not receive more prior training than this, and moreover in many cases it might not be feasible to implement the new system on a full-scope simulator.

Retention

A further important aspect of training is how to maintain crucial skills which are seldom, if ever, needed in the control room. Operators can maintain their ability to carry out frequently performed tasks through regular repetition. However, the more serious events such as handling severe disturbances are, fortunately, so rare that the majority of operators may only experience them during simulator training. The problem of maintaining rarely used skills is frequently compounded by the fact that, during an emergency, the operator may be faced, not only with an unfamiliar task but also with the necessity of using equipment or systems that are also unfamiliar. In this case the use of these two systems clearly provides a pertinent example. It is important therefore to obtain information on the retention of these infrequently used skills, both in terms of how quickly trainees forget what they have been taught, but also with regard to the type of forgetting that takes place. We have already observed in our laboratory that process knowledge tends to be retained fairly well from one experimental period to the next, but the use of the interface—touch keyboards, tracker ball, etc.—is forgotten relatively quickly. We are currently investigating techniques for providing systematic and regular practice in order to maintain an appropriate skill level in the use of infrequently required systems. Exploitation of computer-based training (CBT) seems to offer valuable possibilities in this area.

CONCLUSIONS

In conclusion, then, what can we recommend to plant design engineers contemplating the installation of advanced computer-based systems?

Experience from the HALO and CFMS studies demonstrated the value of implementing such systems on a simulator. Designers obtain a clearer view of the actual functioning of the interface. Instructors can identify potentially difficult user issues and trainees develop a realistic feel for the way in which the system presents information during a disturbance.

If the system is a standalone device only required in the event of a serious breakdown, then arrangements should be made to give operators regular, routine and systematic practice in its use. Although there is little directly applicable research data on retention, we are convinced that the annual retraining period typically in use in process plants is far too infrequent. We would propose frequent drills with such systems as well as including dynamic practice opportunities in conjunction with simulator training wherever possible. Inclusion of training and demonstration exercises as an integrated feature within the system could provide a basis for skill maintenance, particularly when it is not possible to implement it on a simulator.

With regard to the organization of training courses, our experience leads us to recommend that training should be carried out with small groups, preferably in their usual shift teams. We have found it valuable to train two teams at a time though numbers above six or seven do start to become unmanageable, particularly if the training requires access to a simulator.

Computer-based training techniques are now much more accessible and it is our intention to replace our existing tape-slide and written exercises with interactive CBT programmes. There are a number of ready-made systems now available, ranging widely in sophistication and price, which have many features valuable for this type of application.

Above all, we would recommend that training be seriously considered during the design and development phase, both to encourage acceptance and as a means of obtaining feedback on the usability of new systems.

REFERENCES

Corcoran, W. R., Finnicum, D. J., Hubbard, F. R., Musick, C. R., and Walzer, P. F. (1980) The operator's role and safety functions. AIF Workshop on *Licensing and Technical Issues—Post TMI*, Washington D.C., March 1980, C-E Publication TIS-6555A.

Marshall, E. C., Scanlon K. E., Shepherd, A., and Duncan, K. D. (1981) Panel diagnosis training for major hazard continuous process installations. *The Chemical Engineer*, **365**, 66–9.

Marshall, E. C., Makkonen, L., Kautto, A. M. T., and Rohde, K. (1983) An account of the methodology employed in the experimental validation of the critical function monitoring system. International Atomic Energy Agency Working Group on *Nuclear Power Plant Control and Instrumentation Specialist Meeting on Nuclear Power Plant Training Simulators*, Helsinki, Finland, September 1983.

Øwre, F., and Marshall, E. C. (1986) HALO—handling of alarms using logic: background, status and future plans. Paper presented at the ANS/ENS Topical meeting on *Advances in Human Factors in Nuclear Power Systems*, Knoxville, Tennessee, USA, April 1986.

Shepherd, A., Marshall, E. C., Turner, A., and Duncan, K. D. (1977) Control panel diagnosis; a comparison of three training methods. *Ergonomics*, **20**, 347–61.

12. Meeting the Information Technology Learning Needs of Professional Office Workers

Ken Eason

SUMMARY

The professional office worker is an intermittent, discretionary user whose learning needs cannot be met by conventional training before system use. Evidence is presented to show that existing methods of meeting learning needs are not successful and lead to the underutilization of computer facilities. A review of alternative methods emphasizes the provision of 'point of need' support for 'learning by doing'.

INFORMATION TECHNOLOGY AND THE PROFESSIONAL USER

Information technology is transforming the work of the office. For some time it has been changing the work of clerks, secretaries and other support staff. The computing industry has now set itself the target of having an equally dramatic effect on the lives of the principals—the managers and professionals of many types, for example accountants, solicitors, civil servants, engineers, administrators, etc., who work from an office base. The falling costs of computing and the emergence of personal computing means there are now many computer applications designed to serve the needs of this kind of office worker. The aim of this chapter is to discuss the problem this kind of user has in learning sufficient about information technology to be able to exploit the capabilities it offers. In the first part of the chapter we will examine some field evidence to assess the degree to which these users are learning about the technology and the way in which the learning is being facilitated. In the second part we will turn to some of the techniques that might be used in this environment.

Developing Skills with Information Technology
Edited by Lisanne Bainbridge and S. Antonio Ruiz Quintanilla
© 1989 John Wiley & Sons Ltd

THE UNDERUTILIZATION OF COMPUTER FACILITIES

Professional office workers have a number of characteristics that influence what they need to learn and the problems they have in learning it. They are only likely to be occasional users of computers because they have many duties to perform that do not involve computer interaction. They will have expert knowledge in their profession but may lack knowledge of information technology. They are therefore unlike the true 'naive user', for example a member of the public who understands neither the task nor the technology. They may have well-developed expectations about how tasks should be undertaken but know little about how they are undertaken with computers.

As a result of these characteristics, there is a pattern to the way these users respond to computer facilities. A survey of managers using computers (Eason, 1981) found, for example, that the systems were having very little effect upon the managers. In many cases they were designed to be used directly by the managers using an interactive terminal but in practice they were operated by an intermediary on behalf of the manager. Many of the systems offered a sophisticated array of facilities but only a few of them were used. In one example (Eason, 1988) we found, in a study of branch banking that, of 36 on-line facilities by which branch staff could obtain information about a customer's account, five accounted for 75 per cent of usage. Half of the facilities were rarely used although each facility was designed with common banking tasks in mind. In a similar study Hannigan and Kerswell (1986) report that ten facilities of up to 30 offered on digital PABX systems (private automated telephone exchanges) accounted for 73 per cent of the usage. Reporting a similar phenomenon in the United States, Smith (1984) notes that underutilization is particularly striking with respect to multifunctional workstations. There is a strong drive to provide this class of user with a wide array of services but it is not leading to widespread use. It is useful to classify the responses as *complete disuse*, returning to previous ways of working, *distant use*, where another person operates the system on behalf of the end user, and *partial use*, where only a few core facilities are used and the rest are forgotten.

One possible explanation for this phenomenon is that the systems offer little of value to the user and the user is being rational and reducing usage to that which is relevant. It is undoubtedly true that the practice of throwing functionality at users leads to much that is of no interest, but in the studies reported above investigations always revealed a lot of potential in the systems the users were not exploiting. In the bank case, for example, investigation showed that users were often faced with the tasks for which the unused facilities were specifically designed. Under these circumstances they found various, often inventive ways, of 'getting by' using the facilities they did know. Unfortunately these strategies were often inefficient, misleading and led to mistakes. Without assuming that everybody will use every facility, it is necessary to seek ways of enlarging users' knowledge of these systems so they can make their own decisions about exploiting the tools at their disposal.

In order to understand why this phenomenon occurs we need to look more closely at the circumstances under which these people work and the nature of their motivation to use these systems. Managers and professionals have varied work and only occasionally need to use the computer tools available. They are also largely autonomous with respect to how and when they will engage in their tasks, which means they have choice about the degree to which they use available equipment. It is useful to consider the user as making a series of 'cost–benefit' judgements about system use. In these judgements the 'benefit' is the value of employing the system (or a specific facility) as compared with any known alternative. The 'cost' may be, in part, financial, but includes the time it takes, the effort required, the risk of failure, etc. The central concept is that the user will operate a 'least effort' principle (Zipf, 1965) and will select the alternative that gives benefit for minimum effort. While there is an absence of extensive research on the cost–benefit judgements of intermittent users, there is evidence to support the following conclusions:

1. *Limited training.* The fact of intermittent use means that on a 'cost–benefit' basis it is rarely worth the user undergoing comprehensive training before using a system. As a result the intermittent user rarely begins system use with an organized understanding of what it contains, what benefits it can provide and how to use it.
2. *Initial exploration.* In the first stages of usage there is a 'honeymoon' period in which the user is prepared to devote time to trial and error and getting to know the system. A number of researchers (for example Englebart, 1982; Gambino, Johnson and Wilson, 1983) have noted that this phase quickly comes to an end with professional office workers and is replaced by a phase in which task performance dominates the user's thinking. In this phase 'costs' become much more critical.
3. *The domination of known facilities.* When a user is primarily concerned with task completion there is a tendency to favour known ways of achieving task goals rather than explore unknown alternatives. Exploration of unknowns involves extra effort with no guarantee of success, which puts up the 'costs' side of the equation.
4. *Implicit judgements.* It would be wrong to infer that users spend their time making conscious selection decisions. A better description is that in many circumstances there is habitual execution of familiar procedures until they do not work, in which case there may a forced exploration of alternatives.
5. *Unknown benefits.* The minimizing of effort and time 'costs' appears to be that dominant factor but there is a consequence on the 'benefit' side of the

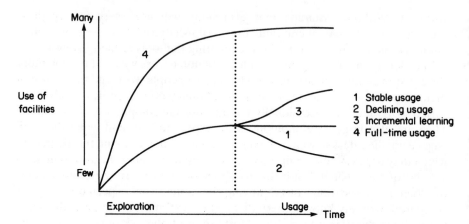

Figure 1. The learning curve of full-time and intermittent users. (*Reproduced from K. D. Eason, 1988, Information Technology and Organisational Change, by kind permission of Taylor and Francis, London*)

equation. Since there is no formal training and limited exploration of capability there is a tendency for users not to appreciate the benefits they could get from the system.

The effect of these factors on the knowledge state of the user is depicted in Figure 1. The most frequent progression in user knowledge is that identified as (1). Although this is described as a learning curve it might be more correct to call it a non-learning curve. The user tends to learn some features of the system to an operational level in the early exploratory phase and this becomes the core knowledge for the stable phase of usage that follows. Alternatively, with (2) there may be a decline as some of the facilities initially learned may in practice prove to be of little value. Another alternative (3) is seen under some circumstances where knowledge continues to increase during the period of operational usage. There appear to be three conditions under which this occurs:

1. The enthusiast. Although it may not be central to the work tasks, there are nearly always a few managers or professionals who become excited by the technology and who spend much more time on it than their colleagues (sometimes to the annoyance of their colleagues who want them to get on with the 'real work instead of playing').
2. Spare resources. In a study of regional banking, Maskery (1987) found that some offices detailed people who were temporarily spare resources, for example management trainees, to learn about the system and support others in its use. This process formally took the pressure off the 'cost–

benefit' assessments and allowed exploration to continue for a longer period.

3. Enhancement of benefits. Under some conditions users found they had tasks that meant that exploring unknown facilities was worth while because there was no existing way of achieving required benefits. One specific way in which this could happen was when superiors or colleagues adopted practices that required the user to make use of a particular facility. An example might be when the rest of the work group is using electronic mail for communications and you become isolated if you do not use this facility.

Although these situations can work to continue the learning process after the normal exploration period the dominant patterns of behaviour appear to be (1) and (2) in Figure 1. For comparative purposes Figure 1 also includes the ideal learning situation (4) where the potential user can be given a full training course before operational usage which will develop both a comprehensive knowledge base and the range of operational skills necessary to fully exploit the system. When people are to become full-time dedicated users of a system, for example in process control, operator or clerical roles, it may be possible to proceed on this basis. Much of the training literature is predicated on the belief that this is desirable and possible. Unfortunately intermittent and discretionary users can rarely be treated in this way. Even if it is possible to get them to full training courses the chances are that, because they only make intermittent use of facilities, they will forget most of the operational detail before they have cause to use a facility. It is necessary therefore for us to look for other ways of promoting learning in these users under the conditions in which they work. Unless effective ways of promoting learning can be found we can look forward to increasingly sophisticated products being implemented only to gather dust or to be used in simplistic ways. In some ways it is reminiscent of the man who carried the red flag in front of early motor cars to stop them going too fast.

CURRENT TECHNIQUES FOR PROMOTING LEARNING

Before turning to ways we might promote learning we should look at the ways currently in use when these products are delivered to users.

Familiarization sessions

Although full training is rarely possible short sessions of perhaps an hour's duration are often acceptable to discretionary users and are used by trainers to convey the rudiments of the system. These sessions usually involve a demonstration of the range of facilities on offer, concentrating on the ones that will be used most frequently, perhaps with some limited 'hands-on' opportunity. I have myself been through three such training sessions recently, to learn about a personal computer, a sophisticated photocopier and an automated telephone system. In each case, through no fault of the trainers, I am left with a hazy idea of the range of facilities, operational knowledge of one or two things I have used subsequently and a deteriorating memory of how to do anything else.

Manuals

All new products come with some kind of documentation which in theory enables the user to make use of any of the facilities. Many of them are badly designed and offer users very few cues as to where they will find the single pieces of information they need in order to proceed. Even if a manual is well designed, with indexes using the task need terms from which users start their searches, manuals are often underutilized. The practice of most users, intent on achieving their task purpose, seems to be, as one user described it, 'to blast my way through the problem' by a trial-and-error procedure and to use the manual only as a last resort. In our user studies we have found a remarkably low level of search behaviour among intermittent users, seemingly because they are usually working under an immediate task deadline. For example, in the branch banking study many users justified their lack of use of the manual by saying that 'when you have a customer standing at the counter waiting for you, there is no time to look in a manual'.

'On-line help'

Most systems now include some kind of on-line support for users, for example help buttons that give more information about current options, informative error messages when the user is behaving inappropriately, 'pull down' menus which, at any time, will list the facilities available and demonstration routines and examples to show how facilities could be used. Undoubtedly these facilities could provide a rich and easily accessible learning environment for users but they are often the Cinderella of the system design process, left until last, neglected and starved of resources. As a result when they do exist they are often not very good. The response of a group of secretaries when asked if they used the help facilities on a computer-based administrative system was that they had now stopped using them because 'you need help facilities to understand the help facilities'.

'Hotline' support

Intermittent users often find themselves in a similar position to the average motorist; they have very little technical knowledge to fall back upon if they run into difficulties. They need the equivalent of roadside rescue services. This is often provided in the form of a telephone 'hotline'—a permanently manned service whereby any user can discuss problems with a technical expert. These services are often provided within an organization by in-house technical specialists or are offered by suppliers as part of their support services. In theory these services should provide a very flexible form of support but in many of our surveys the answer to our question 'To whom do you turn for help?' is not the official support staff but a member of the user's immediate work group. We have christened this person the 'local expert' (Damodaran, 1986). It is usually a person who is an enthusiast about the system or who has been given the time and responsibility to learn about it. As a result the local experts have the advantage over their colleagues of being knowledgeable, accessible and they know the task environment. The only danger is that their knowledge may not be very reliable and they could lead their colleagues into bad habits and false beliefs. Another problem is that often these people do not have an official responsibility to support their colleagues and they and their superiors might consider it a nuisance that impedes the performance of assigned tasks.

TOWARDS AN ENRICHED LEARNING ENVIRONMENT

From the earlier field evidence the current forms of support for intermittent users are not sufficient to promote the kind of learning that will enable users to exploit the potential of the tools at their disposal. The main problem is that we cannot rely on effort being provided for learning purposes except for a short initial period. Thereafter learning has to be a secondary activity associated with completing the task; 'learning by doing' is the order of the day. As a result 'point of need support', providing the specific knowledge needed to answer a particular need at the time of the need, becomes the main priority, and reducing the effort needed to locate this information is a crucial corollary. If we can achieve these objectives knowledge can grow in an evolutionary manner as tasks occur for which features of the system may be beneficial.

It will be apparent from the earlier discussion that there are a number of different kinds of learning necessary if a user is to exploit a system, from learning what benefits it can bring to which key to press. We can now look at each kind of learning and ask how it can be supported given the requirement of 'learning by doing'. Figure 2 presents a matrix in which a range of ways of delivering learning is evaluated against the different kinds of learning required.

The types of learning that are required range from those that are specifically related to the technology to those that are about the application of the technology to the user's tasks. A common mistake is to believe that all the training needs are about the technology when in fact the link between the

	Learning needs					
	System centred ←———————————————————→ Application centred					
Delivery modes	IT basics	System model	Command learning	Skills	Task-system match	Application build
General education	√√					
Familiar-ization	√√	√√	√		√	
Main interfaces		√√	√√	√√	√	√
On-line help		√√	√			
Manuals and prompts		√√		√		
Expert support						√√
Local experts			√		√√	√

Figure 2. Learning needs and modes of promoting learning (*Reproduced from K. D. Eason, 1988*, Information Technology and Organisational Change, *by kind permission of Taylor and Francis, London*)

system's capability and the user's tasks is often the blind spot preventing effective use.

In order to use the information technology the user will have to have some basic idea of the nature of the technology, concepts of inputting information, holding it in a temporary or permanent store, being able to manipulate it electronically and output it in various forms. There is very little need for the average user to understand the technical basis of these operations or to be able to program. Early texts which purported to be guides for managers went far too far in this direction, even to the extent of teaching the manager binary arithmetic, and this simply created another hurdle the user had to jump before beginning to use the technology. The analogy with the car owner is again useful; as the industry matured it realized the car owner did not have to be a mechanic and the driving tuition concentrated on driving skills and road craft.

If the user has the basic idea of the technology, the next stage is to convey the specifics of a particular system. The obvious things to teach are what and how: what it can do and how you get it to do it. Most training concentrates on the command structures, for example the command words, menu items, etc., which are needed to operate the system and the physical skills necessary to evoke them, for example keyboard skills. Early attempts to train managers and professionals were particularly concerned about their lack of keyboard skills but, as we shall see later, this may not be as big an obstacle as it appears.

If command knowledge and operating skills are acquired in a piecemeal fashion as is likely with intermittent use, there is a danger that the user will not obtain a coherent or accurate view of the total system. Each facility of the system will be learnt separately by a rote procedure, details will be forgotten from one occasion to the next and there will be no generalizable knowledge that can be applied to unknown facilities in the system. It would be much easier for the user to learn the system if it operated consistently on a small number of general principles which could be easily grasped by the non-technical user. The user could then operate from known principles when trying a new facility or return to a facility not used for some time. The learning procedure should therefore attempt to convey a system model—some general principles which will help in understanding and operating the system.

The above forms of learning may teach the user about a system but it is of no value until it can be related to work tasks and benefits can be clearly perceived. Another learning need therefore is to look outwards from the system at the work tasks and to seek task needs which system provisions can beneficially serve. It is likely that no two managerial or professional users will have quite the same profile of task needs and therefore this kind of learning need tends to be unique to the individual. If a beneficial use of a system is identified it may just be a case of applying the relevant commands and completing the task, for example operating the code on the telephone so that it monitors a busy line until it is free. However, there are many other beneficial facilities which require a lot of preparatory work. Maskery (1987), for example, notes that, of a range of facilities on a personal computer, users had to spend a lot of time learning how to build a useful application with the spreadsheet and data-base packages. Applications that have to be built locally involve quite a lot of learning and operating effort before there is any benefit, a major problem for the busy executive. Packages are increasingly offered that are flexible and adaptive so that users can tailor them to their own specific requirements. However, if this requires an unacceptable amount of learning effort it is not likely to be a successful strategy.

There are other forms of learning that might be considered which relate to the consequences of computer use for relations with colleagues, organizational implications, etc., but it is sufficient for our present purposes to stay close to the technology and examine the different ways in which we can best meet this array of learning requirements.

Figure 2 identifies seven main ways in which we can try to deliver the required learning and indicates the major kinds of learning each could service together with some secondary roles it might play. We can examine these possibilities in four groups:

Preuse learning

The users are intermittent and discretionary so we will assume comprehensive training is not a viable option. We rely therefore on general education about information technology and short familiarization sessions that can be held before implementation. There is an oft-quoted belief that the problems we have at the moment will only apply to this generation of managers and professionals because with children becoming familiar with the technology at school and at home, they will be well prepared when they enter employment. While this must be true to some extent it is important not to expect too much. Children and people who use other systems may usefully learn the underlying principles of the technology, develop realistic views of what it can and cannot do and appreciate that they are able to cope with it. All these lessons are important. Many new users make extreme and unrealistic assumptions about the technology and are very nervous about their ability to cope with it. If they come to a new system with realistic expectations and confidence about their own ability they have made a good start. On the negative side, however, such is the lack of standardization in the information technology industry and such is the rate of change that almost nothing of the specific learning associated with any earlier system they have mastered can be transferred to the new system. Indeed there are many cases of negative transfer, where, for example, the RETURN key on the previous system is the DELETE key on the new one. It will be necessary to rely on specific rather than general education to cope with these forms of learning.

The familiarization sessions before implementation, although short, can be extremely valuable. They run into difficulties if trainers treat them as a limited time period into which to cram all that they would put into a full training session. The result of this can be very confused users. It may be that these sessions should not attempt too much operational detail. Instead there are two areas in which they can usefully contribute. If the users have not developed a general familiarization with the technology and are wary of it, they may need an opportunity to explore and 'play' with it outside formal sessions. A useful strategy is to make available equipment (which may run other applications than the ones it is planned to implement) and allow people individual access to these in an entirely risk-free environment, that is with no monitoring, performance assessment or group pressure.

The other kind of familiarization relates to the specific system to be implemented. This is an ideal opportunity, and may be the only one, to give users a coherent overview of the system: what facilities it contains, what value they may have in the user's task world and, above all, a simple model of the system, that is the general rules by which it operates. Ideally these need to be presented in their general form and demonstrated on specific facilities. Given that users will subsequently have to learn most of the system while working it is also useful to convey general principles about how best to learn about the system, for example the use of search strategies, the use of on-line help facilities, the structure of manuals, etc. The aim has to be to set people up for learning and not to assume this is the only learning session.

Main interface features of the system

If users are not going to engage in extensive learning or exploration before attempting serious use of a system, the main interfaces of the system, the means by which the user accomplishes tasks, must support the user directly. There are two ways this can be accomplished. The interface can be made self-explanatory so that it carries all the learning that is necessary or it can be designed to minimize the necessary learning. The former case means, for example, that all options open to the user should be explained on each screen along with the actions required of the user. In practice this means the system structures the interaction for the user. This is usually welcomed by beginners but becomes tiresome and limiting once some experience has been gained. Some systems as a result have adaptable interfaces offering the same facilities via a structured, self-explanatory procedure for the beginner and a fast flexible command-driven procedure for the experienced user. In the latter case the user has to know the commands in order to use the system; in the former this is unnecessary. In the ideal system the beginner screens not only get the job done but teach the commands so that, after some experience, you can move onto the command-based dialogues.

A more radical approach is to try to minimize the learning necessary by changing the nature of the interface. One way of doing this is to create the system so that it obeys a simple set of rules at all times, so that when users have acquired this model of the system, they have complete control over the system. A linked idea is to base the system model upon a set of rules or stereotypes which already exists in the user's environment. An example is the 'untidy desktop' model where the interface treats documents in the same way as a user might treat documents on his desk, for example forming piles, taking some from in-trays, putting others in out-trays, others in the waste bin, etc. The principle behind these approaches is to render the operation of the system natural or transparent so that the user can concentrate upon the task in hand and not upon the mechanics of operating the system.

Considerable progress has been made in this direction in recent years and the development of WIMP interfaces are based on Windows, Icons, Mouse and Pull-down menus. Windows allow the user to have a lot of small items on the screen which can be made large by a single action as though you were pulling them towards you and into your field of view. Icons are pictorial representations of actions that can be taken and objects that can be manipulated. They replace the verbal commands that previously the user had to learn. If they are correctly chosen the user should be able to guess their function from their content. It is the equivalent of replacing a road sign saying ROAD WORKS with a diagram of a man digging. The mouse is a device the user can move around on the desk top which controls the location of a cursor on the screen. It enables the user to point and select screen items without having to operate a keyboard and is one way—speech input being another— in which reliance on keyboard skills is being reduced. Pull-down menus are a way into help facilities which require only the selection of one part of the screen to bring them into view. Together these methods offer what is widely recognized as a much more natural way of operating a system than the verbal commands and keyboard entry methods, that have been the norm. Other interface design principles are also being used to provide a natural 'user-friendly' interface. An example is WYSIWYG (What You See Is What You Get) which ensures compatibility between what you see on the screen and what actions ensue or what appears on the printer.

If they are successful, interface designers who follow these principles will succeed in rendering much of the operational knowledge currently necessary to use a system obsolescent. In Figure 2, therefore, the main interface is described as the principle route by which a system model is acquired, commands are learned and the necessary skills developed. This is because the self-explanatory mode will support learning and the natural interface relies on existing knowledge and skills which makes new learning unnecessary .

Formalized point of need support

In this category we can include the on-line help provided within the system (help facilities, informative error messages, demonstration routines, back-up menus, etc.) and the manuals and other forms of documentation provided with the system. These facilities are likely to be useful to intermittent users when they want to remind themselves of commands or are having difficulty. It will be interesting to see whether advances in interfaces can reduce the necessity for these support features.

Human support

The other main kind of learning the users need is to find ways of beneficially harnessing system potential to the specific tasks they wish to undertake. Since the task needs are, at a detailed level, going to be defined locally, perhaps at the time of using the system, it is difficult to see how formal pre-prepared learning support can be a complete solution. The system and the documenta- tion can explain themselves but they cannot explain the user's own task world or relate the two. In practice users seem to rely on other human beings, the technical support staff and the local experts, for this kind of support because they are able to explain their problem or need and ask the other person to relate it to the way the system operates. One of the main reasons for underutilization at the moment is that no one has responsibility for helping users establish useful task–tool connections, that is what is worth using for what purposes, with the result that many users limit themselves to the few obviously useful connections. The person who can most easily help at this level is the local expert who understands the person's work and has sufficient knowledge of the technical system to be able to link the two. Unfortunately this role is often unofficial and, until it is formally recognized, it is unlikely to give users this kind of support. An alternative is to use the technical support staff, but they are often distant and not very knowledgeable about the user's tasks. One possibility is to devolve the support structure so that each group of users has easy access to their own technical support officer. Another important role for the technical support staff is to help the user build an application when a suitable opportunity is found. Many users having found something worth doing then lose their momentum when they find it is going to take a lot of time and effort to get it established

CONCLUSIONS

There are no simple solutions to the provision of the learning needs of the professional staff of the office. Their needs are such that most of the conventional ways of providing training and support are not possible or adequate. As such they represent an interesting challenge. Matching methods to learning needs suggests that no one way of meeting these needs is going to be effective but that different methods may serve different needs. In the analysis we have effectively identified three ways forward: to use the pre-use opportunities as ways of creating basic awareness, confidence and a strategic basis for self-help; to use the design of the interface to reduce the amount of learning the user has to do in order to operate the system so that learning can be concentrated on exploiting the facilities of the system for the tasks that have to be undertaken; and finally to use the human support resources to help users identify and create suitable applications.

By developing these sources of support for users we may be able to encourage users to exploit the exciting capability of modern information technology. There is, however, one more obstacle to discuss. At present none of the routes to learning that we have examined are in the hands of training staff or people who necessarily have any specialist knowledge of user training. The fact that these users are not susceptible to going on lengthy training courses to learn about these forms of technical support for their work means that it is usually not the training department that meets these needs. Often the trainer in familiarization sessions is a technical expert who may not see the user's difficulties. It is often a virtuoso display of expertise by the 'trainer' that leaves the user breathless with admiration but none the wiser. The design of interfaces and of support documentation is usually the responsibility of technical experts and they may have little formal understanding of user psychology. Finally, support staff are usually technical in origin; local experts, while they have the advantage of being local and non-technical, usually become local experts because of their interest in technology rather than in their fellow users. It is necessary but insufficient to identify the routes to the facilitation of user learning. It is also necessary to build up the knowledge and skills of those who man the routes.

REFERENCES

Damodaran, L. (1986) User support. In N. Bjørn-Andersen, K. D. Eason and D. Roby (eds.), *Managing Computer Impact*. Norwood: Ablex.

Eason, K. D. (1981) A task–tool analysis of manager–computer interaction. In B. Shackel (ed.), *Man–Computer Interaction*. Alphen aan den Rijn. The Netherlands: Sijthoff and Noordhoff.

Eason, K. D. (1989) Patterns of usage of a flexible information system. In S. D. P. Harker and K. D. Eason (eds.), *The Application of Information Technology*. London: Taylor and Francis.

Englebart, D. C. (1982) Integrated, evolutionary, office automation systems. In R. Landau, J. H. Bair and J. H. Siegman (eds.), *Emerging Office Systems*. Norwood: Ablex, pp. 297–308.

Gambino T. J., Johnson, T. W., and Wilson, D. D. (1983) Micro-computing learning curve. *Computer World*, 30 May 1983, pp. 35–42.

Hannigan, S., and Kerswell, B. (1986) Towards user friendly terminals. In *Proceeding of the ISSLS 86 Conference*, Tokyo, Japan.

Maskery, H. S. (1987) *An Investigation into the Usage and Learning of Discretionary Computer Users*. Doctoral thesis, University of Technology, Loughborough, Leics., England.

Smith, J. (1984) Beyond user friendly—towards the assimilation of multifunctional workstation capabilities. *Behaviour and Information Technology*, 3(2), 205–20.

Zipf, G. F. (1965) *Human Behaviour and the Principle of Least Effort*, 2nd ed. New York: Hafner.

13. Development of Partners' Capacity for Action in the Integrated Design of Information Systems

J. L. Mercy

SUMMARY

Literature about the introduction of computerized management techniques stresses the importance of user participation. However, there are some major obstacles to this participation: the members' lack of technical expertise, the complexity of work situations, the different aims and interests. Solutions to some of these difficulties are mentioned in the chapter, using two case studies. Self-training of participants in formalization languages can be useful, but some participation problems, due to organizational changes and divergent interests, cannot be solved in this way.

INTRODUCTION

Integration

As far as training is concerned, the introduction of new office technologies in various organizations often underlines a twofold phenomenon:

1. There is a classical separation between design tasks and performance ones. The designers and decision-makers have been trained in computerization and project management, whereas the users receive training centred on their own work and its processes.
2. The users' training often takes place when the system is integrated into services, when most of the decisions have been made. Sometimes this training looks like a promotional campaign for the new task support tools.

Developing Skills with Information Technology
Edited by Lisanne Bainbridge and S. Antonio Ruiz Quintanilla
© 1989 John Wiley & Sons Ltd

However, another tendency is growing (for example Mélèse, 1979; Tardieu, Nanci and Pascot, 1979; ACTIF, 1980; Rolland, 1986), which aims to integrate the introduction of new office techniques at the levels of:

— the partners in the introduction process, through a reduction of the distance, and maybe the distinction, between the designers and the users;
— the process in itself, where the different technical, organizational, social and ergonomic components are taken into account at each stage;
— the tasks themselves, which are reanalysed and rethought according to their objectives and the surrounding tasks.

Such approaches are more expensive; it takes a longer time to do the analysis and design, they involve a larger number of people in the organization and the partners have to make use of unusual knowledge, which may have consequences as far as their training is concerned.

Participation

If we consider computerization as a decision-making process (with Algera, Koopman and Vijlbrief, 1986), however, the above tendency should, it seems, be strengthened. Algera demonstrates, in fifteen situations, that user participation in the decision-making process is an essential condition for the subsequent efficient functioning of the computer system, given some conditions:

1. The project is limited.
2. It is important to bring the users' knowledge to the fore.
3. It is not necessary to get uniform applications.
4. There is consensus on the project's aims.

There are various mechanisms through which user participation improves the efficiency of the project. Generally, we can group them as follows:

1. Sociopsychological causes. Participation favours dialogue, the broadening of points of view and the acceptance of change.
2. Functional causes. The information held by the users may be necessary and they are sometimes the only guarantee of the project's functionality during the design stages.

As far as this latter point is concerned, we know (Leplat and Pailhous, 1973, 1977; and Leplat, Chapter 5 of this volume) that an important distinction may be made between the prescribed task (the objective to be reached and some of the rules necessary to attain it) and the real activity (the behaviour). In the field of work analysis, and of running administrative organizations, the distinction can be considered as a continuum:

1. Relative to the prescribed tasks, a study of actual activity reveals the objectives that are reached and those that are partly or not reached at all.
2. The analysis of the activity will show the inertia, inconsistency and dysfunction, but also the control, the necessary information, the communications and the variability, that are present in the daily functioning of the organization.

As far as information is concerned, there is a relevant question: Which aspect (the task or the activity) should be taken into account in the design process? Basically we can say that:

1. This choice is neither dichotomous nor exclusive; the analysis is twofold.
2. The computerization objectives, the real situation and the size of the project are deciding elements. Should a limited number of procedures which already function be automated? The actual activity is then a good basis for analysis. Or should an important, complex, dysfunctioning sector be automated? It will then probably be useful to redefine the tasks and to consider what is going to change in the activity.
3. The two focuses of approach each have their interest and limits. The process of computerization must consider at the same time the functional objectives of the work and its concrete possibilities for achievement, to modify them if necessary.

It appears that the users' knowledge of the actual ways of performing the work is, in many circumstances, an important element of the design during computerization. The remaining problem is to know how to understand this knowledge. In comparison with the classical approach, which entrusts the analyst of a computer project with the inventory and organization of the information necessary for design, this chapter, illustrated by a case study, presents a participative process of design, as well as demonstrating the process of acquiring new knowledge or broadening of previous knowledge that can take place.

Although participative design of computer applications is full of possibilities, it also comes up against some grave problems that can lead to failure, to a false consensus or to a refusal to participate:

1. The complexity of the work situations and of the information. This could lead to oversimplifications or to accepting the status quo, because of a lack of methods for approaching the problems.

2. Lack of users' technical expertise (computer skills, abilities in the field to be computerized, skills in project management, etc.).
3. Clash of interests between the different partners in the design process.
4. The fact that the conception of new computer applications often provokes organizational changes. When these changes are feared or refused, they bring about a paralysis of teamwork.
4. The difficulty of organizing the design process. Who intervenes and when? According to what criteria? How are decisions made?

We will try here, in particular, to clarify the problems of the partners' ability and the complexity of the situations.

Participants' ability

The partners' abilities in analysing and acting on the system are various. With reference to training, it is important to know how to develop those abilities in order to enable everyone to take part in the process of design.

To provide capacities for action involves (for ACTIF 1980):

(a) making partners aware of computer science, and in particular identifying the degrees of freedom of the techniques;
(b) making partners aware of the impact of the new techniques:
    — to develop a general approach to work situations,
    — to support ability to diagnose and forecast work situations,
    — to help in the design and evaluation of computer systems.

Certain concepts will be used in the following case study, and they will be defined now (see Figure 1).

The systematic approach to organizations that was developed by Mélèse (1983) suggests a relevant distinction between 'data' and 'meaning'. The datum is a signal that reaches a unit of the organization. It does not mean anything as such, and can even be nothing but noise. It will become meaningful if it produces an effect on the receiver's behaviour. Since this deals with people at work, the process of giving meaning is complex. It depends on the activity in which the receiver is involved, on the one hand, and on his or her abilities to perceive and recognize information, on the representation of its history, on the ability to reorganize it, on wishes and expectations, and on the representation of the transmitter, on the other hand.

Therefore, according to Mélèse, the enrichment of meanings which the partners give to the data within an organization, the increasing complexity of meanings, has a positive effect on the running of the organization when the 'semantic networks' given to the data by the different partners are more

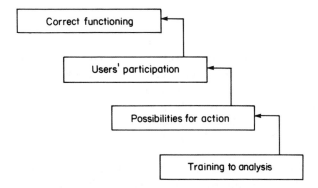

Figure 1. Synthesis of the reasoning that guides from the functioning to the training. To ensure a good functioning, it seems to be useful to have the participation of the end users. This participation can not be effective without improvement of the user's possibilities for action, because of their usual lack of technical expertise. This improvement may, in certain cases, be acquired by training or self-training in the analysis of work situations

similar, when the languages of the different organization units become more understandable to the other units.

Lawrence and Lorsch (1967) developed a pattern for analysing organizational phenomena in terms of 'differentiation–integration'. They defined differentiation as the 'state of segmentation of the organisational system into subsystems, each tending to develop special attributes in relation to the requirements posed by its relevant external environment. Differentiation, as used here, includes the behavioural attributes of members of the organisational system'. Integration is 'the process of achieving unity of effort among the various subsystems in the accomplishment of the organisation's task'. Observing the behaviour of different companies, they noticed that complex production processes, requiring adaptation to a changing environment, have both great differentiation and great integration.

CASE STUDY

The setting of the study

Two situations have been observed in detail in an organization that is restructuring and wants to acquire more effective methods of administration. This organization also finds it difficult to integrate its different subsystems. There are partitions between the subsystems, which bring about dysfunctions in communication and in work consistency. In order to avoid these difficulties, various solutions have been developed. Among these, we have first some thinking about improvement of work procedures and second the greater automation of the information system.

These two approaches to the problem have been analysed more deeply: in both cases, we had work groups consisting of executives (five and eight) and the person in charge of computing, and two psychologists who intervened within the context of a broader contract for work readjustment and personnel redistribution. All the executives who participated in the first group belonged to the second group as well. Not counting the person in charge of computing, two of them were second-generation users.

In the first situation, a general conceptual 'information model' of the information used by the organization had to be designed, in order to define the content of a computerized data base. In the second situation, the participants were asked to reorganize and to improve the office work procedures, with a staff that had been reduced by spontaneous leaving.

Therefore we have observed two situations that had common characteristics and also differences. In both cases, we have a work group consisting of the same people. Over half the people are responsible for studying the problems of internal organizational functioning. In the first situation, the participants were asked to describe and design an information organization. In the second one, the main task was to implement an organizational change through description/design of the present work procedures and of the planned ones. Since these two activities took place successively, it is possible to make the assumption that there was continuation, from one situation to the other, of a thinking method devised in the first situation and of the knowledge that had therefore developed.

Situation 1

The conceptual information model of an organization is an important stage in the computerization process. The information, which the organization needs to act, must be identified, recorded and represented, independently from the storage medium being used (computer, paper, etc.). The subsequent stages of functional analysis, or carrying out and introducing the system, will be conceived and planned on the basis of the data model. The coherence and integration of various subsequent applications are based on the quality of this conceptual model.

In fact, the stake in information mastery for an organization becomes such that this conceptual model goes beyond the strict frame of computer science and becomes a representation the organization can give of its functioning, at least as far as stability in the administration of basic data is higher than the stability of work procedures or computer processing.

Different phenomena have been observed during this study, which took place over four months, two days per week.

First, we noticed a certain amount of mobilization among the participants in the data-base project, in so far as their daily work was often hindered by the lack of reliable, complete or up-to-date data. The expectations for the data base that was supposed to solve these problems were extensive. The group accepted very quickly the need to represent the knowledge produced, by using a formalization language (see below). At the beginning, this language was settled with the computer personnel, in order to make it common to everybody. In practice, every sector was reviewed: the information used in each was identified and organized. When there was no particular problem the data were simply clarified and recorded, but when the information concerned another sector, or when the participants considered that it was not satisfactory for functioning, it was left pending, on a list that was destined for more global and integrated processing. For example, the need to represent the division of the organization into sectors and subsectors appeared very early, as it was needed in order to represent the means at the disposal of each structural unit. The different departments had their own divisions, necessary to their own needs. In the book-keeping service, for example, each internal account is appointed to an administrator who is responsible for it. In the personnel service, each agent is responsible to a section head, and so on. The concepts are not equivalent and prevent cross-checking of the structure. Consequently, the problem was shelved and solved at the end of the work, after detecting all the relationships and characteristics this concept had in each sector. Moreover, in order to get a more reliable description of the realities and needs, and since the participants did not know all the sectors in detail, exterior members of the group were called on frequently: this made it possible to complete and refine the model.

Very quickly the point of origin, that is computerization, was outrun by more general thinking on the mastery of information and on the knowledge in the organization. The objective, that is the description of the conceptual data model, was reached by the end of the study. The most tangible result, in the form that is described below, is the representation in Figure 2. The results of this work can be analysed into three aspects.

Mutual enrichment of the significations

Before the work, each participant had a more or less complete representation of the information used in the sector and a more fragmented view of the other sectors. This work gave rise to relevant exchanges on the useful data and the relationships between them. The piece of information 'balance of account', for example, is provided by the book-keeping service, which makes use of it. However, it is also used by the personnel service and others. Each participant could thus reconstruct the procedures of information handling and its multiple meanings according to the specific objectives of each service. The same piece

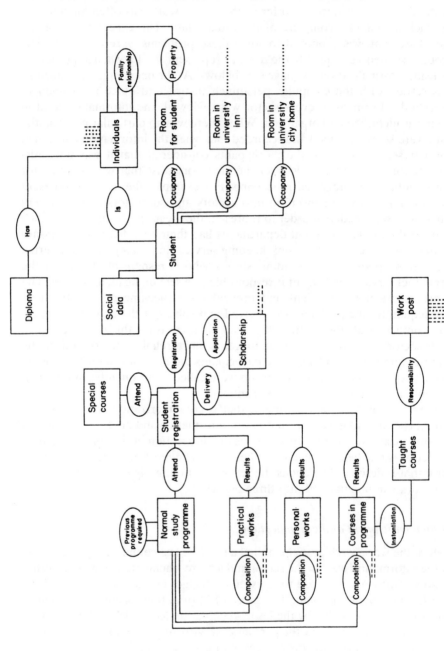

Figure 2. Part of the synthesis of the conceptual data model. The abstraction level is the second given in Figure 3. The entities shown represent one of the six fields designed as the 'academic field'.

of information 'balance of account' can in certain circumstances mean 'insufficient resources: expenses must be cut down, by dismissing some personnel for example' for one service, and for another one can mean 'balance that must be spent with the utmost urgency, otherwise it goes back to the public revenue department: dismissals must be put off'. With this example, we see the possibilities that arise from comparing the information and the meanings of the information among the partners, that is better organizational understanding and better integration of actions.

Working out a common representation

While making this inventory, various differences in meaning, redundancies in the information, gaps, etc., appeared, as well as useful and unsuspected possibilities. From these observations, a revised representation was built up, which rearranges the information. What we have here is a redefinition, at a high level of abstraction, of the organization's tasks and also of the structure of a model that is common to the different partners and accepted by them.

Learning

During this work there were different types of learning:

— technical learning of computer principles for data administration;
— learning of the formalization languages that are necessary for the representation of the data model;
— collective organizational learning.

To sum up, interesting dynamics were triggered off in this first situation and resulted in the completion of the task and in the participative working-out of a representation for the functioning of the organization.

Situation 2

The reorganization of work and office procedures was a stage towards the improvement of administration efficiency, which aimed at making the later introduction of computer techniques easier.

After the experiment in the first situation, one supposed that a similar process would take place (mutual enrichment, global and integrated view, etc.). One expected some kind of transfer of the mechanisms and knowledge that were developed previously. In order to understand those mechanisms better we recorded the first meetings of the second group, which met once per week over four months.

The work procedure that was proposed consisted of a first stage of describing what existed, then deciding on the necessary changes and adjustments, and finally achieving them.

With the same type of description as for the first situation, we could observe that the project was not accepted by all the participants, in so far as some of them expected certain changes while others seemed to be apprehensive of them.

The description of the procedures used in each sector (they were originally rather precise) have not been represented in a particular language, in spite of the existence and presentation of such tools which were more complex than the previous ones.

In practice, the dynamics of the group functioning was not very productive. Topics that had already been discussed and left unsolved often reappeared periodically. There was an exchange of ideas or a discussion of certain topics rather than an explanation of the problems, which often remained unclarified. The members of the group did not call on external people to provide an explanation for those problems. Gradually the partners tended to restrict the field of their thinking to the external aspects of the work organization—the organization chart and the limits between the different services—and gave each head of service the autonomy to improve the procedures in practice.

The initial objective was therefore only partially reached: the work procedures have not been analysed nor the general level of the organization redefined. The organizational change that should have resulted from the initial objectives seems to have been considerably reduced.

Evaluation criteria

The choice of objective evaluation criteria for comparing the two situations is not easy. We can, however, compare some elements in the first situation (S1) point by point with some in the second situation (S2).

1. *Setting*. The same firm, the same work technique (group), the same organizational concern.
2. *Members*. The seven participants in the first situation were present in the second one as well, with three additional people. However, in S1 the members represent the different sectors and in S2 they stand as persons in charge of these sectors.
3. *Aim*. In both cases, the aim is linked with computerization. In S1, a conceptual data model must be described and designed. In S2, work procedures must be reorganized and improved; the description is only a means that should result in organizational change.
4. *Task*. In S1, the task is primarily cognitive. In S2, it is a question of changing some aspects of the organization.

5. *Results*. In S1, the objective was reached. In S2 only the organization chart and the delimits between the services were discussed. No general adjustment took place.
6. The *languages* for representing the knowledge can be considered as revealing the will for progress. Such a language was learned quickly in S1 but not in S2.
7. The *appeal* to external members can also be interpreted as a will to clarify the complexity of the situations and to understand them better. This occurred in S1 but not in S2.
8. *Research domain*. In S1, the domain considered stretched to the very functioning of the organization. In S2, while this objective was becoming concrete, the field was reduced to some outer aspects of the organization.

Comparison between the two situations

In order to understand the differences between the two situations, two main hypotheses have been proposed.

The first one deals with the fact that a formalization language, for knowledge and group progress, was found in the first situation. The second one deals with the differences in the objectives and strategic stakes of the participants.

Formalization languages

Hoc (1985) describes a twofold mechanism in individual planning tasks (including designing):

(a) a schematization that, at different hierarchically organized abstraction levels and in different languages, underlies the significant elements of the problem;
(b) anticipation, which can be temporal (the estimated subsequent state determines the planning now in progress) or details that allow the activity to develop at different abstraction levels.

Indeed, details are relevant in the planning activity:

1. When they are too precise, it is too expensive to discuss them again.
2. When they are too vague, they do not allow an estimation of the solution.

This framework for analysis, which was worked out by Hoc for the case of an individual subject who had mainly cognitive activity, can account for some of the situations described here.

1. Fields

2. Entities-relations

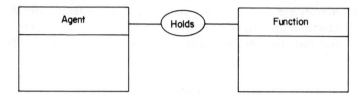

3. Entities-contents

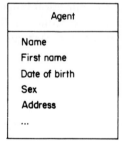

4. Data format

Name	24C	
First name	24C	
Date of birth	DD/MM/YY	
Sex	1 C	chart 1 man
		2 woman
Address	50 C	

Figure 3. Different levels of abstraction allowed by the formalization used in the first situation

In the first situation, in which a conceptual model for information had to be designed, a representation model was introduced, which makes different levels of schematization and abstraction possible. This language is technically fairly simple and is commonly used for that kind of task. It is based on the principles for relational administration of computerized data. It allows reasoning with the terms shown in Figure 3.

In this situation, we can observe skips between different levels of abstraction. For instance, the entity 'agent' (level 2) has been reviewed, because another entity (temporal anticipation) seemed to have identical data (level 3, anticipation of details). A new formalization (level 2) was introduced, in which common data are gathered in a single entity (see Figure 4).

No description language was introduced in the second situation, although such languages promoted taking complexity and interactions between the

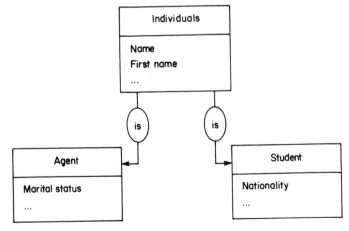

Figure 4. Evolution of a formalization in the first situation

different levels into account. A local microchange (at the level of details) can have important consequences on another sector, situated either above or below, and even on the general structure of a procedure or a service.

In the second situation, there were no available languages to describe these phenomena, so the complexity remained complete. Only part of it has been analysed.

The procedure for 'contracts administration' within the organization is an interesting example to illustrate the feasibility and usefulness of such a process. Although it has not been represented by the group, we can explain it at a general level as in Figure 5.

Four main stages can be observed, each of which includes different operations. The stage 'beginning of the contract' (Figure 6) developed in rather the same way in both the personnel and book-keeping services:

— Either the contract and the demand for the service arrive more or less simultaneously, in which case the services will analyse the contract in order to find the information that will enable them to go on;
— or, and this is much more frequent, the demand for the service comes alone, requiring an active search for a contract before it can be analysed.

Then, in both cases and if certain legal statutory conditions are fulfilled, the personnel service hires the required staff and the book-keeping service will open and credit the necessary accounts.

An analysis of the process shows that important delays and harmful misunderstandings occur at this stage. Indeed, the preliminary search and

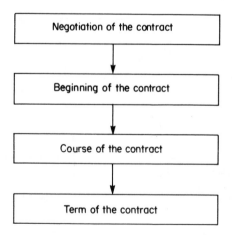

Figure 5. Procedure of contract administration at level 1

At the staff service

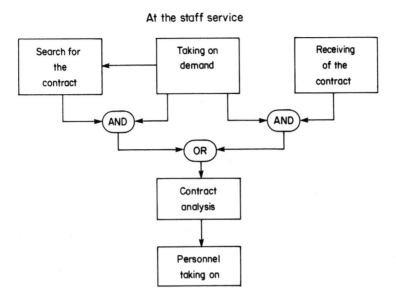

In the Book-keeping service

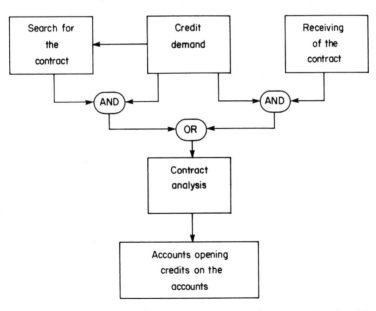

Figure 6. Partial view of the stage 'beginning of the contract' at level 2

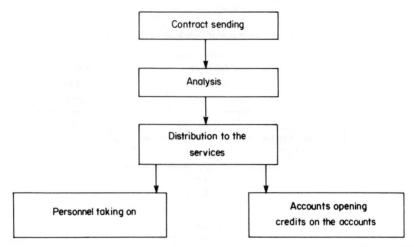

Figure 7. Partial view of the adjusted stage 'beginning of the contract' at level 2

analysis can take a considerable time, and they are redundant in both sectors, with little coordination between them.

In order to rough out real solutions to these problems, dropping to a more substantial level of details may be necessary, but in this present context, the possibility of making a preliminary analysis of the contract, which is common to both sectors, can be mentioned. It would then give Figure 7. At this level, no internal division is mentioned. We do not know yet who will do what.

Differences in objectives and interests

This interpretation in terms of representation languages is not the only one. A strategy-type analysis also makes the process clear.

In the first case a collective effort at conceptualization, without any individual stake, had to be made. The group had a common objective. In the second one, in so far as the process aimed at organizational change, the participants' personal stakes were relevant (individual limits of operation, restricted areas, etc.). The interests were more individual than collective, which may have blocked the discussions and the descriptions. These two explanations, however, the one in cognitive and the other in psychosocial terms, are not mutually exclusive. They certainly interact; no common language was developed, in order to ensure individual autonomy, and no common language was allowed to go beyond the clashes of interest.

TRAINING IN THE LANGUAGES

The first, cognitive type, interpretation provides some possibilities for intervention. Such observations support a certain kind of solution to the problems of introducing new information techniques. Indeed, each problem of computerization is individual; the objectives, the means available and the working situations are different. A solution in stages adapted to one situation cannot be applied generally because of local particularities. Some design methods tend to define strict procedural guidance for the activities (ordered in terms of stages and sequences). Though some stages and checkpoints seem to be relevant, we can ask whether declarative guidance (ordered in terms of objectives) would not be more effective. Once the objectives are made clear, the introduction of various rich languages, that are within the reach of the different partners, favours solution mechanisms that are adapted to the situation by considering more of the complexity and the whole of the work situation.

Objectives and languages could be emphasized more, as far as participative design is concerned, than procedures and links between stages.

If these observations turn out to be generally applicable, as far as training for the capacity to analyse and act on the system is concerned, the implications are clear. It is important to teach description languages for the different aspects of the work situation (these languages can be organized into a hierarchy), which allow the readjustment and redesign of work.

Usually, when they deal with computing, these languages have two main aspects:[1]

— a static side, mastery of the data;
— a dynamic side, data processing.

The complexity of work situations cannot be reduced to what the computer needs for running. The importance of the information system that is not automated remains, and can probably be described with languages akin to the previous ones.

These descriptions/conceptions can be analysed by the partners on different dimensions:

1. The functionality of the described or designed system. Is the functioning related to the objectives of the organization, to its resources and its environment, on the one hand, or to the concrete situations faced by the users, on the other hand?
2. The planned division of the activities into services, workplaces, etc.
   (a) What are its degrees of integration/differentiation? Which posts are specialized? Which posts are multipurpose? How are the integration problems solved?

---

[1]Help software for the design of information systems is available on the market. Its contribution could be interesting, as the administration of the description/design process can be heavy. However, besides the fact that it is not easy for a group to use it, it does not seem at present to favour the schematization required by the process. Details must be provided from the very beginning.

(b) Where is the complexity? Who makes the real decisions? On the basis of which information? Which posts only convey information?
(c) What is the richness of the described tasks, the responsibility for problems, or for division of the tasks?
(d) What is the work load at each workplace?
(e) What are the areas of autonomy?

How can one promote learning of these languages? The answer to this question is probably linked to the partners' level and to the complexity of the languages. The observations show that, to some extent, self-training can be suggested.

The second situation underlines the interest of self-training the participants during the process. We can think, indeed, as has already been mentioned, that the cognitive and strategic aspects of the second situation interact to slow down the language learning and to prevent access to the details in each service that are necessary for the description/designing of the system. Each participant was in charge of a service. Sometimes they had different interests and these divergences were rarely expressed. A kind of consensus prevailed about the level of detail that had to be considered in order to preserve individual autonomy. This level of detail was, however, not sufficient for estimating new solutions. We can wonder, in this case, whether imposing a language, in a more interventionist process of training and exercises, which would have somehow forced the participants to reveal and to consider details and languages, might not at least have allowed them to point out those divergences that remained latent in the process, and maybe to solve them.

CONCLUSIONS

This chapter aimed at mentioning solutions to some of the problems faced during computerization of office tasks. It has been said that new approaches need the participation of the users, in certain circumstances where knowledge of their own activity is relevant to design. However, this participation comes up against some problems, in particular the complexity of work situations and information, as well as the lack of technical knowledge.

The case study suggests that these two problems could be solved by training or self-training the participants in using some formalization languages. These languages are characterized by the fact that they are shared by the different partners and they make possible certain cognitive activities, such as schematization and anticipation. They represent knowledge, and help the work to progress.

When used in a real situation this technique gave, in one case, interesting results which went broadly beyond the strict computer context to lead to a reconception of the organization and a mutual improvement of organizational knowledge and information. In the second case, this process does not seem to have occurred. Other obstacles remained: the need for an organizational change and for a period of disequilibrium in the organization during which respective positions can change, and the partners' divergence of stakes.

REFERENCES

ACTIF (1980) *Informatisation et Vie au Travail*. Paris: Les Editions d'Organisation.
Algera, J. A., Koopman, P. L., and Vijlbrief, H. (1986) Management strategies adaptating organizations to new technologies. In *21st International Congress of Applied Psychology*, Jerusalem, Israel, 13–18 July 1986.
Hoc, J. M. (1985) Aides logicielles à la résolution de problème et assistance aux activités de planification. In R. Patesson (ed.), *L'Homme et l'Écran. Aspects de l'Ergonomie de l'Informatique*. Editions de l'Université de Bruxelles.
Lawrence, P. R., and Lorsch, J. W. (1967) Differenciation and integration in complex organisations. *Administrative Science Quarterly*, **12**, 1–47.
Leplat, J., and Pailhous, J. (1973) L'activité intellectuelle dans le travail sur instrument. *Bulletin de Psychologie*, **XXVI**, 673–80.
Leplat, J., and Pailhous, J. (1977) La description de la tâche: statut et rôle dans la résolution de problèmes. *Bulletin de Psychologie*, **XXXI**, 149–56.
Mélèse, J. (1979) *Approches Systémiques des Organisations: vers l'entreprise à Complexité Humaine*. Paris: Editions Hommes et Techniques.
Mélèse, J. (1982) *L'Analyse Modulaire des Systèmes de Gestion*. Paris: Editions Hommes et Techniques.
Rolland C. (1986) Introduction à la conception des systèmes d'information et panorama des méthodes disponibles. *Génie Logiciel*, **4**, 6–11.
Tardieu, H., Rochfeld, A., and Coletti, R. (1984) *La Méthode MERISE, Principes et Outils*. Paris: Les Editions d'Organisation.

BIBLIOGRAPHY

Bouch Y. S. (1986) Media: de l'informatique à l'ingénierie des systèmes d'information. *Génie Logiciel*, **4**, 53–7.
Bronlet, R., De Keyser, V., and Mercy, J. L. (1986) The mastery of information within organisations: a case study. IFIP task group 6.3, subgroup workshop on software ergonomics and system adaptivity, Bonn, September 1986.
Codd, E. F. (1970) A relational model of data for large shared data banks. *CACM*, **13**(6).
Groupe, A. T. T. (1986) L'administration et le gestion à l'Université. Internal report, University of Liège.
Koopman, P. L. (1980) *Besluitvorming in Organisaties*. Assen: Van Gorcum.
Lacrampe, S. (1974) *Système d'Information et Structure des Organisations*. Suresnes: Editions Hommes et Techniques.
Mercy, J. L., Bronlet, R., and De Keyser, V. (1986) Organisational analysis of administrative operations and a computerisation project. *21st Internationnal Congress of Applied Psychology*, Jerusalem, Israel, 13–18 July 1986.
Peaucelle, J. L. (1981) Les Systèmes d'Information—La Représentation. Paris: PUF.
RACINES (1982) *Schéma Directeur de l'Informatique*. Paris: La documentation Française.
Tardieu, H. Nanci, D., and Pascot, D. (1979) *Conception d'un Système d'Information, Construction de la Base de Données*. Paris: Les Editions d'Organisation.

14. Information and Control: Qualifying for Information Technology and Industrial Democracy

Henning Salling Olesen

SUMMARY

The example presents a contrast to the often too narrow definition of qualification requirements in connection with information technology and to a qualification strategy that freezes or aggravates the existing division of labour and that does not exploit the potential of information technology to democratize work.

The chapter describes the development of a computer model for analysing, managing and planning in the fishing industry in Greenland. Apart from coordinating information, the aim is to supplement existing information technology for registering production and for elementary management with a tool that *partly* can link internal data with external conditions of production that have to do with economy and resources *and partly* make possible a broader qualification and involvement of workers in the use of information technology for analysis and planning. The implementation of the model is linked to the qualification of the personnel and organizational devleopment.

INTRODUCTION

It has been quite a surprising experience to become familiar with the research being carried on within the fields of industrial psychology and theory of information about the need for training staff to work with information technology. It is unfortunately a fact that even the most fundamental changes in society are analysed and evaluated by professionals who are not very good at exchanging ideas and making use of each others' knowledge. It is perhaps the case that such changes give rise to very strong feelings and attitudes which get in the way of such an exchange of ideas.

Developing Skills with Information Technology
Edited by Lisanne Bainbridge and S. Antonio Ruiz Quintanilla
© 1989 John Wiley & Sons Ltd

As an outsider with a research background in pedagogy and the sociology of education, I must start with the observation that pedogogical research and the formalized educational system do not take into account a number of practical pedagogical problems of great importance consequent with information technology, and naturally they are therefore tackled less appropriately than they could be if the commonsense experience that exists within our area were to be used. Second the question of the need for qualification training, when defined from the point of view of information technology and industrial psychology, is asked quite differently from the way I, as an education researcher, would ask it. In my opinion the question is too narrow and the result is that some crucial social questions as to *how*, for *what*, and by *whom* information technology is to be used are not considered at all. However, as often occurs in this kind of connection, the question is answered in practice.

I cannot avoid drawing attention to this professional point of view and I should like to return to some observations regarding these questions of principle later.

First, I should briefly like to present some experiences from a project that provides a positive example of how the use of information technology can be connected with the broad qualification of employees in an industrial concern. The project is an offshoot of some research into conditions for industrial development in Greenland which has been carried out by members of NORS (the Centre for North Atlantic Regional Studies) at Roskilde University Centre in recent years.[1]

The model developed here (the NORS model) is briefly described in the Appendix.

THE BACKGROUND

For the most part the Greenlandic fishing industry has been run at a loss and only some small parts of the most profitable shrimp production have shown a profit. As the fishing industry has a central position in the economy of the country as the most important export sector, and as the only export sector that to a large extent is based on Greenlandic labour, the income from this industry has had a key position in industrial development in Greenland since the country obtained Home Rule.

An ambitious programme of investment has been started and the aim is to bring the Greenlandic fishing industry, which is largely in public hands, up to world technological standards. This is to a high degree a matter of informa-

---

[1]The work has been done mainly by J. Brinch, P. Friis and R. O. Rasmussen and has resulted in a computerized data base and a model of calculation described in *Grønlandsprojektets model til resourcemæssig og økonomisk planlagning* (The Greenland Project's model for planning of resources and economy), RUC, 1985. The model has since been given the name, the NORS model, after the research centre.

tion technology, from communication and calculation equipment on the trawlers to the use of electronic weighing machines and process control in the factories.

Great efforts are being made to improve the use of existing and future investments. Systematic attempts are being made to improve registration, analysis, planning and the organization of the work. The processing of information will therefore become a key factor in achieving effectiveness; this is also the case when it comes to the connection of information processing with other factors such as the organization of work and the daily well-being of the workforce and their interest in production.

It has been the aim of the publicly owned section of the fishing industry that they should gradually increase local control and participation.

The key position of this sector in the national economy and the dependence of this economy on the vagaries of nature makes it necessary to have a much closer association between internal planning in the industry and national economic planning, the labour market and natural resources. It is therefore desirable to develop information tools that do not merely illustrate operationally technical and economic aspects of the running of the production, but also make it easier to illustrate consequences and preconditions in relation to existing parameters, for example the labour force, fishing and the buying of fish, related national economic effects, etc.

It is therefore necessary to develop information tools that are suited to being used decentrally and by users with little technical or economic, not to mention computer, skills. There is naturally a need to put them to use and to train the staff who are going to work with them.

THE AIM OF DEVELOPING THE MODEL

The work of developing a computer model has had this use in View. The model has many aims:

— to illustrate the knowledge about fishery and the fishing industry and the connection with other areas of society that the rest of the project's analysis pointed to, and which cannot be ignored by industrial planning and development in Greenland (including information about supplies of resources, products, use of technology, technical limitations on electricity and water supply and the like, and information about the actual production over a number of years);

— to develop tools for planning in the form of a data base and a computer model that can be used operationally in order to simulate these complex connections both in central public planning (the Home Rule Government), local public planning (the local authorities) and in the dispositions of the individual enterprises, whether publicly or privately owned;

— to test the possibilities of using computer science for making large amounts of information and complex issues manageable for 'laymen' with no specialist skills, so that the tools also can be used to further the democratization or participatory development of planning, political decisions and the individual places of work.

PREVIOUS USE OF INFORMATION TECHNOLOGY IN THE FISHING INDUSTRY

The need for reliable information about both technical and economic aspects of the daily running of the plants is absolutely necessary both to ensure the better exploitation of existing plant and production capacity and of future investment in advanced technology.

In the production itself electronic weighing scales are used which can be connected to a microcomputer. In the simplest version the weights are sent from the scales to the computer where the information is stored for an hourly report or daily report or whatever is required.

A very advanced version is when the scales are a part of a packing belt for the retail packing of shrimps. Apart from functioning as a controlling and regulating device, for example for controlling automatic packing machines, the computer also functions as a gatherer of data about weights for the production of price tags and for production reports.

The version of the POL weighing system described here is mostly concerned with the technical level of the production process and primarily takes care of supervisory functions.

Many plants have also bought a Faroese data program, COMDATA, which works out a series of management parameters on the basis of these weights and which will also be able to be used both for overall analysis and for carrying out a number of administrative functions (paying for raw materials, controlling the stores, calculation and payment of wages and salaries). The Home Rule Government's production company, KTU, is constructing a large, central data system which will include administrative, budgetary and statistical functions.

In contrast to the NORS model, the COMDATA program is designed for daily operational control, but does not contain connections with more complex external parameters and is not suited to carrying out the functions of simulating and of formulating problems. The basis of the COMDATA program is the weighing of the raw materials and the product throughout the whole production process. These records may be used for several purposes:

1. Effectiveness at each stage in the process is calculated quantitatively and qualitatively (utilzation of raw materials).

2. Calculations of quantity of production with a view to stocktaking, dimensioning and manning.
3. Calculating the basis for settling with the suppliers of raw materials.
4. Computerized accounts for paying piece workers.
5. Collecting data pertaining to the accounts.

COMDATA is primarily a control system for ensuring the appropriate use of resources. On the economic level the functions of the system are of a more technical/administrative nature.

Today in practice it is mainly used in direct production supervision on the management level. Through the automatic weighing the production flow, utilization percentage, etc., are registered at each phase in the processing. On this basis, combined with a few economic parameters, a managerial economic calculation of production can be made per day, per shift, etc., noted as internal gross profit. Management is given an overview of operational costs constantly and very quickly; it is possible to localize shortages and problems as a point of departure for closer diagnosis; and finally it is possible to use these records for analysis in connection with more long-term improvements of effectiveness, including investment decisions, etc.

In practice this production registration system has been introduced either by establishing a staff function in connection with the management or when one of the works managers has made a special effort to become acquainted with the tools in order to be able to use them.

This has not been done without problems; the understanding of its use among management and other staff is limited, and as using the program also requires a certain amount of manual data input, problems of competence or division of labour have arisen, for example between the production and the administrative personnel.

THE IMMEDIATE QUALIFICATION NEEDS OF THE FIRM

The degree to which the firms are in need of staff with further training is naturally dependent on how the information systems are integrated into the organization.

There are at least three categories of short-term need:

1. The very basic qualification of some administratively or technically trained personnel to plan and introduce data-based information systems, often on the basis of practical experience with already existing information systems.
2. A relatively thorough qualification, on the user level, of all personnel who are going to use the information systems and their output, that is the managers of the various plants and the personnel who are in charge of planning and operations centrally and decentrally.

3. An introduction to the meaning and possibilities of use of information systems for all personnel, or at least for all foremen, administrative and planning staff and staff representatives (shop stewards etc.).

A more ambitious aim from the point of view of industrial organization and democratization would be to have the qualification named in point 3 to approach point 2, that is a user qualification on a level where the user is able to use and evaluate information systems.

As a minimum these needs must be met in relation to systems already existing or planned. On the longer view, even in terms of a more limited aim, it is quite crucial to make the qualifications mentioned under points 1 and 2 independent of the information systems and machines actually being used, in order to enable the fishing industry to use and evaluate other possible tools, both standard software and machinery. The historical binding to one machine and the COMDATA software should not be repeated.

In reality the NORS model takes over where the other systems let go, that is as a tool for coordinating data and evaluating the possible alternatives, primarily alternatives as to choice of raw materials and form of processing, in relation to their economic and political consequences.

A SOCIETAL EVALUATION OF NEEDS

Increasing the influence of workers on production is an independent aim of Greenlandic industrial development policy. This is closely tied to a broader idea about local autonomy and decentralized structures, and it is also tied to a demand made against the enterprises not to operate only on the basis of criteria of managerial economics but also to take matters of national economics, resources and employment into account. Today this takes place mainly via the central management of catch quotas, dividing up buying, investments and plans for production.

The aim in the development of the NORS model has been to find a tool that was suited to uniting decentralized, democratic planning and decision-making, and this broad foundation of planning.

The content of the data base of the model and the rest of the structure of the program is described in the Appendix.

Thus the NORS model, much more so than the previous systems, is aimed at planning on a socioeconomic level. Where the first-mentioned systems deal with the best possible organization of the production actually in progress, the NORS model deals with evaluating this production in relation to alternatives, both with regard to the organization of work in progress and with regard to alternative items of production and methods of production.

The model has now been put at the disposition of Greenlandic firms, partly in its published form and partly in the form of offers to train staff. In the course of the next year we hope to have the opportunity to carry out more extensive development work, where the development of information technology and the development of organizations and in-service staff training are all part of the same context. The firm we primarily have worked together with, Godthåb Fiskeindustri, is already in the middle of a thorough organizational development project, which unites efforts at effectiveness with in-service training and establishing a permanent staff with greater responsibility.

THE BASIC DILEMMA IN CONNECTION WITH INFORMATION TECHNOLOGY

The radical change brought about by information technology on human beings and their surroundings is, on the one hand, a further development of technology that was known earlier, that is the societal organization of experience and knowledge and its incorporation into a machine. On the other hand, it radically changes one of the main conditions in industrial technologies: the division of labour between brain and brawn as a means of increasing production and as a basis of social control.

The tendency towards a moralism that is powerless or frightened of technology has had a great influence on the relation of pedagogics and eductional research to the introduction of information technology, and has also had a great influence on public discussion, for example in the trade union movement.

On the other hand, a great deal of technological and administrative access to information technology, both in the public sector and in private concerns, has borne the mark of a criterion of technological effectiveness, which in practice leads to an uncritical acceptance of the demands made by the new technology and the possibilities (in reality often only too limited) that it presents.

The qualification problem is no exception. *In practice* the problem is treated as a question of enabling people to *serve/use* the new technology. On the research level this expresses itself in two problems that I can only briefly mention here.

In the first place there is an economically determined *strengthening of the qualification hierarchy* between groups of personnel with key functions and groups of personnel who are appendixes to information systems like in the good old Taylorite factory. It is worth while to train specialists and technicians to use the tools of information technology and to be able to see the limitations of these tools and their interaction with those aspects of problem-solving and sequence of events that have not (yet) been incorporated into the machine system (hardware and software). Other special groups of users like, for example, control-room operators with key functions may receive similar treatment. However, for the larger groups of personnel it will primarily be a case of training them to carry out the routines and operations defined by the machine system.

If there are to be alternatives to all of this that are economically realizable, it cannot just be a case of education or training ('overeducating' or increased general education). Integrated with this, concepts of industrial organization and management and a new division of labour must be developed, which exploit the *new* productive powers of information technology better, thereby making an equalization of the qualification hierarchy economically possible.

The other recurrent problem, that sometimes keeps pace with the first but sometimes cuts across it, is the tendency towards a *cognitive* frame of analysis both in the qualification analysis and in solving the pedagogical problems.

If the new technology and the problems of eduction connected with it are dealt with on a largely cognitive basis, which is what is happening in practice, this is in fact to regard this new technology on its *immediate material* level and to try to train people who can work with the new technology on this level. To a certain extent this is of course necessary, but in practice, as a research base, it becomes strongly reductionist in its understanding of how people learn and act. Also, all the emotional, cultural and political aspects of the relation between the machine system and the workforce as an organized whole is only residually present in the conceptual framework.

This is, of course, not the intention, but for an educational researcher it is difficult not to see a repetition of the history of different theories of learning such as they have emerged in periods where an attempt was made to ensure a rapid increase of knowledge and competence. These sides of pedagogy and educational thinking were suppressed and only very slowly was it possible to reintegrate them.

If the reader has difficulty in seeing the connection between the most advanced technological systems—for example atomic energy stations and chemical plants—and what at the moment is an underproductive fishing industry in a cold corner of the world, or if the problems connected with training the operators in such a firm seem banal in content and pedagogical substance, then read this as a contrast, a projection of a number of problems that seem to be extremely important in the reception of information technology by the industrial countries of Europe. On the other hand they do, of course, represent the question as to whether information technologies give new opportunities to develop high technology in peripheral economies and societies, such as those in the North Atlantic area.

APPENDIX

A short description of the NORS model for the consistency analysis of economy and resources for the fish industry in Greenland.

The aim of the model

The local level

In the village plant or the industrial plant of the town the model is a management tool that can provide the production committee and the rest of the management with the possibility of judging the operational economic or staffing consequences of suggested changes, whether they have to do with processing alternative raw materials or other products or changing the way the raw materials are treated. Thus the model can provide an answer to a number of strategically important questions when decisions have to be made locally.

The regional level

On this level the model is an instrument that can be used to say something about the economic and labour results of, for example, controlling the supply of raw materials to the individual production plants in the municipality or the region.

The strategic questions that the model can help to answer could be, for example, where investments should be placed, if an equal use of the work-force is required, or what new investments in certain types of production material mean.

What would be the consequences for the industrial economy and employment in the individual town or village in Southern Greenland if part of a future line fishing was reserved for certain villages, all villages or a town?

The central level

Here the model can be a help in getting a quick overview of what is being produced, where and with what economic result. This overview of the state of things at any given moment will also help the central sales organizations to know which finished products and how many of them, and in which qualities, they can try to sell.

In the following the model, its foundation and use will be briefly presented.

The structure of the model

The model consists of two main parts, balance and calculation, and of a number of smaller units that are more service oriented. The individual parts are freely chosen from a main menu, and when the model is started up, a data base is automatically read in which means that the model can be used without having first to load data into it.

The balance section

This consists mainly of an extensive data base that has to do with the structure of production, the structure of resources and technology in the southern Greenland fishing industry. The data base is built up around both a technical and an economic side. This means that at the same time as the economic consequences of any given increase of production are being evaluated, the consequences and limitations as far as the technical aspect of resources is concerned can also be checked.

Therefore the data base contains a complete survey of the existing production structure with details about which processing possibilities, machines, etc., the individual firms have, and what capacity with regard to electricity supply, water supply, etc., the individual businesses and towns/villages have at their disposal. In addition, the data base contains the actual production data and data about the accounts for the single production unit for the previous three years, and a survey of the total resources purchased and the general conditions of production such as the average wage and the price of electricity, water, oil, etc.

The users can choose to use the existing data for their work or they can establish a set of data that suits a specific need, perhaps by revising the existing set of data. Likewise the data base can constantly be kept up to date by the user as new information comes in, just as it can be supplied with supplementary information centrally, for example via the telephone modem, diskette, etc. Thus it is possible to link information from several different users and to keep both the figures for the individual business and the figures that have to do with towns, villages, local authorities, regions and the higher levels of planning up to date.

The calculation part

Seen from the side of the user, this is the heart of the model. Here the user is confronted with a number of problems of distribution that either need a decision to be made or demand a solution that is an average of the previous year's figures. Thus the user has the possibility of altering things that must be evaluated, while other less interesting problems can be taken care of by the model.

Month for month the user must make decisions as to how the available resources are to be used, and the model can present information that will support the decision-making process.

For the individual factories, information is given as to the gross profit of the individual products, how great a proportion of the capacity is being used and how many can be employed depending on which choices are made.

When the monthly result has been calculated the user can freely change the dimensions chosen until the desired—or at any rate the best possible—result has been achieved. The user then proceeds to the next month.

At the end of the year a summing up of the year's results is given. Likewise the investments made are added up and an evaluation is given of the yield of these investments. The user can also see the consequences for employment and the budget which the distribution of any given resource has for the different factories. If the user is interested, the model provides the possibility for evaluating how the resources can be used to give the most jobs possible, the best economic result, etc. In this way the consequences of, for example, reserving certain quotas for villages, special towns, etc., can be evaluated.

On a higher level a number of the general conditions of production can furthermore be experimented with, making it possible to evaluate the consequences of, for example, intervening in relation to the rates for water, electricity, etc., or the consequences of fixing wages and prices.

The model also includes a number of more service-oriented items, for example a part that makes it possible to write out the desired elements from the data base and a part that can file and call up the suggestions for solutions found by the user.

The use of the model

The model is constructed for use on a microcomputer or a PC. This means that it could be used anywhere there was a need for information and possibilities of evaluation within the sectors that the model touches on.

The model is completely menu-controlled: All information given to it is written in partly on the basis of certain possibilities of choice and partly as answers to a series of questions put from the model. This means that everyone can use it. It does not require any knowledge of data processing and computers.

The model contains all the necessary information. The data base contains all the information about production equipment, technology, products, expected buying and selling prices, running costs, etc. This means that knowledge of technology and economics is not a precondition for being able to use the model.

The model provides a number of advanced tools for making evaluations as to budget and resources. This means that the model can also be used to advantage by users with special knowledge.

It can be used on all levels—by the individual enterprise, the village and the town, the local authority and the region and all the way up to the highest levels of planning. All levels are defined in the model, and in its calculation section the possibility is provided for evaluating the information on the different levels, just as it is possible to evaluate the consequences that the decisions made on one level will have on another level.

Thus the NORS model is a tool that will be able to be used in future production and regional planning in Greenland.

Section 4

Training Tools

Outline of Section

The title of this book *Developing Skills with Information Technology* points at the twofold implication of new technologies (NT) for employees' qualifications. While the earlier parts of the book have concentrated on changed qualification needs and requirements, the following section focuses on NT training tools and their possible modes of application in the training process.

With the growing complexity of systems in industry, simulation has become an alternative to training and practice on the job, and not only where safety reasons forbid active participation of learners. This might have led to the belief that a good simulator should reflect its reference system as adequately as possible. Used for training purposes, the fidelity of a simulator is not mainly a question of physical accuracy , as Leplat (Chapter 15) points out. For the psychologist the reference system is not, in the first place, the technical system but the tasks that have to be fulfilled by the operator of this system. The psychological fidelity, as Baker and Marshall (Chapter 16) call it, is crucial because to transfer skills from training to the workplace means, as Leplat puts it, to relate the activities in the simulation situation to the work activities in the reference situation.

Following this argument, even a simulator which is physically quite different to the reference system can have its value in training certain skills, if these skills are needed in the work environment. Using simulation in training is not a sensible thing in itself. As is pointed out by the following contributions, a consideration of learning goals and principles is needed in training complex tasks. This will have implications for the design and use of simulators in training, depending on the skills to be learned.

This stresses the importance of work analysis techniques. Leplat explains what simulation can contribute to the understanding of the work tasks and how this knowledge again can be used to design improved simulations. Norros (Chapter 17) applies this way of using simulation for research to the single training situation, when she encourages trainees during the training process to use the simulator to experiment. To give the learners the possibility to develop, test the value of and revise their cognitive models for understanding the dynamics of the system, she sees the need to distinguish between the working situation and the learning phase.

This is also true for Baker and Marshall, who show how simulators can be used for assessment purposes. Here, in contrast, the quality of the performance measurement is dependent on the realistic environment over and above the physical accuracy, which needs a strong commitment from all parties involved.

The importance of integrating the simulator tools will in the training process become even more apparent in the effort to computerize training units in intelligent tutorial systems (Ruiz Quintanilla in Chapter 18). In addition to the simulators usable as learning environments, what is needed for training is: an expert knowledge about the domain to be taught, diagnostic competence to identify misconceptions on the side of the trainee, tutorial competence to find out what and how to present next, and communication competence to explain things in a way understandable for the learner. Trying to implement parts of complex tutoring problems for up-to-now restricted knowledge domains can be seen as both stimulating research and giving us hints towards better understanding of learning and tutoring as processes between humans. Even if there might be technical boundaries for realizing ITS systems, the results have their value in improving the competence and expertise of human trainers.

15. Simulation and Simulators in Training: Some Comments

Jacques Leplat

SUMMARY

This chapter focuses on the operator's activity and the relation between activity in the real situation and in the simulator. The steps in a simulator study are described and also the relevant principles of learning. Good training requires task analysis. A simulator may be used during task analysis, and the best use of a simulator should be chosen relative to task analysis.

INTRODUCTION

Implementation of the simulation method is now facilitated by the progress of computerization, and its place in training actions is growing. In particular the use of simulators in the transport and nuclear industries contributes to the increasing interest of this method. Simulation can be considered from different points of view: here the psychological point of view will be adopted, which places the operator's activity at the centre of study. From the training perspective, it is a matter of determining how much the activity practised on the simulator contributes to the success of the activity in the reference situation. It must also be noted that simulation constitutes a tool for activity analysis, and can help to give better knowledge of psychological training mechanisms.

This chapter aims to give, in a practical manner, the elements of a frame of reference for simulation studies, and it approaches some problems related to the design and use of the simulation situation.

According to the *Encyclopedia Universalis*, 'simulation is experimentation on a model . . . . it consists of realising an artificial production (model) of the phenomena one will study . . .'. In training, simulation is the exercise of the subject on a model of the conditions in which this subject will perform an

Developing Skills with Information Technology
Edited by Lisanne Bainbridge and S. Antonio Ruiz Quintanilla
© 1989 John Wiley & Sons Ltd

activity. In this case, the phenomenon to study is the process of learning, in order to understand and improve it. The word 'model' indicates that only part of the features of the situation studied is retained. This part must be relevant to the goal of the simulation, contribute to explaining the mechanisms of the activity at their different stages, and at the same time participate in the shaping of this activity. One finds this same idea in Stammers' definition of simulation (1983): 'Any situation that departs from the real world task demands and exerts some control over the learning progress of the trainee can be termed a simulation' (p. 229).

The simulator can be considered as a model of the simulated technical system. For the psychologist, the relation between this model and the simulated system is defined with reference to the operator's activity. Therefore, the training simulator is a good model of the technical system if it permits the trainee to acquire more quickly a mastery of this technical system for the task that has to be achieved.

One can also find a simulator that simulates the technological system badly, because its characteristics give rise to activity having few relations with that produced in the situation studied.

These definitions and comments will be expanded in the following sections.

THE PSYCHOLOGICAL POINT OF VIEW ON SIMULATION

In this section we will develop the requirements to be taken into account in simulation, from the focus of the subject's activity and training.

Simulation situation

To examine clearly the psychological problems raised by simulation, it is necessary to define some important terms, the meaning of which varies according to the author. In a wide sense, a *task* is a goal to achieve in particular conditions. This notion is decomposed here by distinguishing, for the convenience of this presentation, between:

— the goal of the task,
— the technical conditions or controlled systems,
— the physical and organizational conditions,
— the operator.

We will call the interaction 'operator × task' the *situation*. The reference situation is the situation to be simulated.

From a psychological point of view, the emphasis is on activity, and the central problem of simulation is to know the relation between the activity

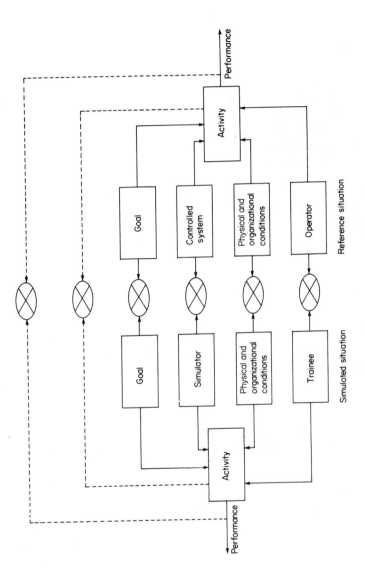

Figure 1. Variables to take into account in simulation

involved in the reference situation and the activity involved in the simulation situation.

Figure 1 schematizes the essential groups of variables to be taken into account in the study of simulation. They are related to those indicated by different authors involved with this problem (Hollnagel and Rasmussen, 1981; Stammers, 1983; etc.)

1. The goal. Two situations can be distinguished by the goal assigned to the subjects. The goal is often identified as the task. What problems are given to the subject to solve in the simulation situation? What is their relation with those of the reference situation?
2. The controlled system. This consists of the simulator in the simulation situation. Relations between the technical conditions in the reference system and in the simulator should be characterized from the point of view of the operator's activity, that is by comparing the features taken into account to accomplish the task.
3. The physical and organizational conditions. These characterize the physical ambiance in its different aspects, and the organizational constraints (prescribed rules for execution, temporal constraints, hierarchical role, etc.).
4. The operator. The operator is here essentially characterized by the personal features intervening in task execution: professional experience, familiarity with the technical system, motivation, etc.
5. The activity. This has internal and external aspects. The external aspect is obtained from the observable behaviour: spontaneous (usual behaviour) and provoked (verbalization). The internal aspect, which regulates the external one, is induced from it by an observer.

A situation is a simulation of another one to the extent that the activity it produces is related to the activity produced in the other one. 'Relation' can be understood in various ways. The activity in the simulation situation can be a part or component of the reference activity. Example: diagnosing the state of the reference system, from a slide representing the interface of this reference system, produces an activity that is a component of the activity that takes place at the moment the real task begins.

Relations can be expressed as a positive transfer between the reference and simulation situations. This can also occur when the physical appearance of the two situations is different (Pailhous, 1970).

The general processes in a simulation study

Figure 2 represents the different steps of the general process of simulation. Two main phases can be distinguished in this process. One, of bottom-up type, starts from the data and extracts a model. The other, of top-down type, consists of implementing the model and experimenting with it, especially by training the operator on it. Here is a brief comment on the different steps of this simulation process.

The starting point, which must never be forgotten, is the work situation itself for which the operators must be trained. The goal of the simulation,

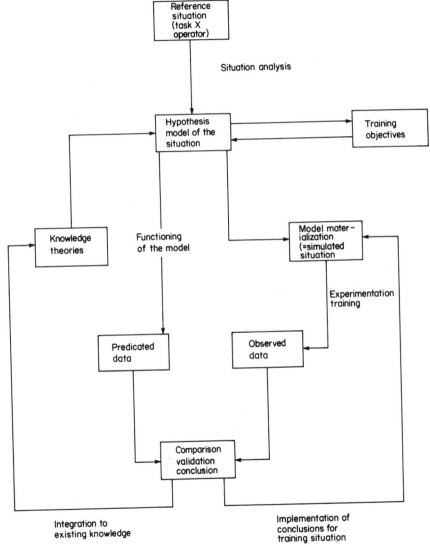

Figure 2. Schéma of a psychological simulation process

finalized by training, is to improve the operators' competence and to bring them to meet the task demands with greater efficiency. This work situation is called the reference situation in order to stress that it is the one against which the conclusions of the simulation study must be compared: it is in this reference situation that their ultimate validity must be tested. At the beginning of the simulation process, the analyst has at his or her disposal knowledge acquired in cognitive psychology, and also in work psychology and psychopedagogy, especially the knowledge acquired by the use of simulators —which unfortunately still contains gaps.

A preliminary step, essential to every simulation study, is a work analysis which tries to identify the work difficulties for the expert operator and also for the trainees. The knowledge of these difficulties brings indispensable elements to the evaluation of the interest of the simulation, and it contributes, with the existing knowledge, to defining the goals and modalities of this simulation. At this stage, by considering the training objectives, the analyst refines his work analysis to constitute a model of the reference situation or of a part of it.

This model is then implemented as a simulator and a simulated situation. This implementation raises technical and economic problems, as well as psychological problems, and the chosen solution is frequently a compromise between various sorts of demands. This implemented model can support more process hypotheses about the types of tasks and the operators who have to execute them. With these hypotheses, predictions can be made that are tested against the data gathered during the simulation sessions. These data are oriented to the training, the experimentation, or a mixture of the two. If the data validation is positive, it can lead to modifications of the training or of the work situation. The conclusions enrich the corpus of knowledge and theories, and they can do it all the more because the simulation exercises have been better designed in relation to existing knowledge and theories.

The schema presented for this process is not operational, but it helps to show the place of simulation, and it contributes to the structure of this paper. It is possible to distinguish two main phases in it: an elaboration phase, which leads to the simulation design, and an exploitation phase, in which the simulator is used for training or research. In numerous studies, the simulator is designed by engineers after little preliminary work analysis and without precise knowledge of the real activities of the operator in the work situation. In this case, the psychologist must use a tool, in the design of which he or she has not participated, and which can present in consequence some important gaps. These gaps must be identified in relation to the intended simulator use and the tasks proposed for the operator. The study of transfer between the activity in simulated—and reference—situations is then particularly useful in evaluating the simulator as a training tool.

Role of principles of learning: knowledge of results

The role of a simulation in training can be defined in relation to knowledge about learning. It is actually possible to understand the simulation as the implementation of this knowledge in terms of didactic goals. The simulation contributes to activity training (shaping?) and can usefully lean on principles coming from research on skill acquisition. Some of these principles are common to, though sometimes with different names, different learning theories (Galperine, 1966; Gagne, 1970; Anderson, 1981). It is not our intention to give an inventory of them here, but to underline the important role of one of them, namely the 'knowledge of results' principle. According to this principle, one learns thanks to the knowledge one obtains from the results of one's own activity. This knowledge of results has a double function, informational and motivational. It has an information function, as the knowledge of results informs the operator about his or her own activity and the consequences of it for the environment in relation to the intended goal. It has a motivation function insofar as it brings satisfaction if successful and annoyance if it fails: the operator is thus encouraged to accept or reject the corresponding activity. Knowledge of results is, at the same time, knowledge about the adequacy of the activity for the goal and evaluation of the activity in comparison with more general motives. Knowledge of results is very related to the concept of feedback and plays a particularly important role in behaviour regulation models. It is also intimately related to the concept of error, as it is not only knowledge of results in itself but in comparison with the goal. Knowledge of results is in fact knowledge of deviation from the goal, that is of errors.

Simulators, which do not have productivity constraints, allow systematic exploitation of the principle of knowledge of results. They make it possible to introduce knowledge of results not only at the end of an action, that is the results of global performance, but also during the course of an action, at a level of practical performance. This possibility can sometimes be exploited for action shaping. In this case, every deviation from the method that is considered to be the best and to be acquired is noted as an error. Simon (1979) has emphasized this interest of errors in relation to the canonical course of action: 'The method the subject actually used, not necessarily the same as the one in which he was instructed, could be determined with reasonable certitude by examining the kinds of errors he made . . . . Hence the errors committed by a subject were characteristic of the method he was using.' What he says for a particular task, simulations can obtain for more complex tasks, and can thus be an efficient tool for this shaping of action.

Studies on training also show that it is possible to facilitate the learning of complex tasks by decomposing them into units that have significance for action, and training the operators on these units or elementary tasks.

Simulators can permit this progessive introduction of complexity, and so they can permit the design of adaptive learning (Kelley, 1969; Pask, 1976). The principle of this type of learning is to make the operator work at a constant level of difficulty. When too many errors are made the difficulty is lowered. When few errors or none are made, the difficulty is raised. The level of difficulty can be determined in different ways depending on the situation: speed, permitted delay of execution, type of task, etc. Pask (1976) has determined the programme of progress for a coding task, and he has shown that too slow or too fast transition to greater difficulty gives bad results, and optimal ones are obtained when the solutions were in the intermediate zone.

This brief overview shows how principles from the psychology of learning can inspire the simulation method. It shows that this can be usefully done only with careful analysis of the reference situation, which precisely determines the goals and task demands and the skills to be acquired. It is on this basis that the principles of learning can be incorporated in the simulation. However, if the simulator, to be well designed, needs an activity analysis of the reference situation, it also constitutes an analysis tool for this activity and a means of testing hypotheses about the mechanisms regulating this activity.

DESIGN OF TRAINING SIMULATIONS

Simulation for training must be designed within a training programme. Now, as Baker and Marshall (1989) rightly remark, 'while a great deal of time and effort is expended on simulator related hardware and software, it can nevertheless be argued that disproportionately little attention is given to the development of the training courses on which such simulators will be used'.

The place of the simulator within a training programme can be varied. It may intervene in initial training, in the treatment of exceptional cases, in evaluation. Studies of simulation training are often inadequate in relation to the design of the situation, and concentrate more on the implementation of the existing situation. In particular, little is said about the simulator design. This design of the training situation is essential for the success of the simulation as a training tool; it rests on good knowledge of the reference situation and of the technical and organizational conditions imposed by the designer.

Preliminary activity analysis

The simulation is based on a model of the situation, and this model must be elaborated before every intervention. For the psychologist, this model is focused on the operators' activity: it seeks to define the personnel, technical and organizational determinants of this activity. The methods of work analysis are well known (Singleton, 1978; Fleishman and Quaintance, 1984; Leplat and Cuny, 1984; Karnas, 1987) and only some of its main features will be evoked here. This analysis can be increasingly enriched by the methods elaborated in knowledge elicitation. These methods aim to characterize the expert's skill, in order to design a system able to substitute for or to help him or her. One can suggest that a device which aims to train the expert can be strengthened by the same methods of analysis. As Kuipers (1986) notes: 'an expert system is often a shallow model of its application' (p. 289) and 'the symbolic manipulation of qualitative description also appears to be a plausible model of human expertise' (p. 289). The perspectives on 'qualitative simulation' developed by this author, as well as the work on qualitative causal reasoning, can give a formal framework to simulation studies.

Classic work analysis methods aim first to define the prescribed task, that is the goal to be obtained and the conditions imposed on execution. However, this step constitutes only a first facet of the analysis because, on the basis of this preliminary knowledge, the determination of the real task remains, that is the task that corresponds to the activity really implemented by the operator to respond to the prescribed task. Indeed, the conditions to take into account, the prescribed task, are not always those that are really taken into account.

When the task to be simulated already exists, the analysis will rest on it. When it does not yet exist, and when the design of the simulation takes place at the same time as the design of the reference situation, then the real task must be anticipated from knowledge acquired on a similar task, and from more general psychological knowledge. Thus a supplementary difficulty is introduced, similar to that met in the ergonomic design of new systems.

As the elaboration of a simulation often requires considerable expense it is essential to justify its usefulness and size. The justification of training-oriented simulation is stronger when training is long and execution errors can have serious consequences. The work situation analysis, when it is possible, consequently applies especially to identifying the critical moments in the work and to diagnosing their source.

A better knowledge of error sources and of error production processes gives, at one and the same time, a solid basis for the simulation design and for the definition of the tasks that will be presented to the trainee during training. The error study constitutes a very useful guide to orienting the work analysis and to hierarchizing the problems to be solved. The activity analysis is in a kind of dialectical relation with the error study, as far as each of them contributes to the deepening of the other.

Activity study in a work situation includes the gathering of observable data during normal activity, and also the study of provoked activities, which can be grafted onto this activity to disclose the underlying cognitive mechanisms. Verbalization is a typical example of these provoked activities (Leplat and Hoc, 1981; Ericsson and Simon, 1984).

Hollnagel and Rasmussen (1981) define the steps which go from data gathering to the description of competence: performance fragments (raw data), actual performance (intermediate data format), formal performance (analysed event data), prototypical performance (conceptual description), competence (competence description).

Methodology for the study of human errors was reactivated by investigations of human reliability (Leplat, 1985; Rasmussen, Duncan and Leplat, 1987). Several aspects of them can be noted:

— constitution and exploitation of a corpus of errors,
— statistical studies of these errors using descriptive variables,
— models of error analysis,
— clinical analyses to trace back to specific error causes,
— experimental studies on the detection and recovery of error by the operator.

The results obtained by all these methods will guide the choice of simulation features, because several solutions are then offered. Some characteristics of these solutions will now be described.

Characteristics of the simulation

A simulation is always a simplification of reality: it retains only some features that are judged especially important to the objective, which here is efficient training. This idea is expressed well by Schuffel (1984). For this author 'the concept of psychological fidelity is more ill-defined. It is usually taken to refer to the extent to which the simulator produces behaviour that is the same as that required in the real situation, perfect psychological fidelity would be found in a simulator that yielded a hundred percent transfer of learning to the real situation' (p. 234). The difficulty of evaluating transfer is also noted.

Several types of simulation exist: the choice between them depends not only on psychological considerations but also on technical and economic conditions. The degrees of freedom in the design are numerous and the best solution from the psychological point of view is rarely the best one when other criteria are taken into account. What is important for the psychologist is to evaluate the gain and loss of efficiency in training with the chosen solution.

It is common to distinguish two extreme types of simulation validity (or fidelity, this term often being considered as a synonym of the former one): 'face validity' based on the appearance and 'functional validity' in which the simulator reacts 'in the way the real equipment does' (Stammers, 1983). For

Schuffel (1984): 'On simulators, the image representing the ship's surroundings necessarily has to be simplified. The extent to which simplification is allowable depends on the information which the mariner extracts from the surroundings to perform the ship control task' (p. 151).

We will now examine some general characteristics of simulation from the psychological point of view.

High- and low-fidelity simulation

Two extreme types of simulation are often contrasted: the high-fidelity (or full-scope) simulation and the low-fidelity (or partial) simulation. A report by Sheridan and Hennessy (1984) correctly defines the characteristics of these two types of simulation.

High-fidelity simulations bring 'the opportunity to simulate rarely occurring faults and conditions in a realistic world configuration, and the feasibility of very systematic and complete data collection, measurement and processing'. They are also 'an excellent means for teaching skill-based and rule-based behaviour' (p. 32). However, this type of simulation offers some potential disadvantages. It requires extensive training, which is often 'unrealistic in terms of cost and time', but it can be used as a tool for 'refresher training'. 'While high-fidelity simulation may have all the external appearance of an operational system, an important concern is whether the operator will react to simulated events in the same manner as he would to actual events' (p. 33).

Low-fidelity simulation partially reproduces the reference situation. It is concerned only with those characteristics of the reference situation that are judged crucial for the activity concerned. In these conditions the behaviour can be easier to observe and to interpret. In consequence, 'experiments conducted at this level of simulation are likely to produce insights into the manner in which the human supervisor brings up an internal representation or mental model of the task to be performed, the system to be controlled and the disturbance to be expected' (p. 34).

However, it is never certain that the observed activity in this condition is the same as in the reference system: 'low-fidelity simulation can miss critical aspects of the subject–environment interaction'. However, if the task has been well structured, one can note with Schneider (1985) that 'in many situations there is substantial transfer of component training' (p. 288). There is much evidence to indicate that effective training can be obtained through the utilization of devices with limited fidelity (Rolfe and Waag, 1982).

Moreover, Sheridan and Hennessy (1984) remark that in the future the difference between low- and high-fidelity simulators will decrease, due to increased automation, which gives more technical possibilities and reduces the number of display and control devices.

Static versus dynamic simulation

In static simulation the presentation of the state of the system does not depend on the subject's responses. The presentation can be fixed or changing, but in the latter case, the change is predicted independently from the subject's responses. Therefore, it is possible to present slides representing a control panel to train an operator in diagnosis. A static simulation of air-traffic control consists of defining a control situation and requiring the subject to respond to each entry of a new aircraft. This simulation is easy to implement: it often allows training to cope with basic operations at low cost.

In dynamic simulation the state of the system presented at any moment also depends on the subject's response at previous moments. For example, in air-traffic control (Leplat and Bisseret, 1965) a decision made at one moment will change the state of the control field and thus the system state at the following moment. If an operator instructs a plane to change flight level, the traffic situation for his following decisions changes. Many examples of this type can be found in the simulation of ship control (Lazet and Schuffel, 1978; Schuffel, 1984). The realism of this simulation is higher, but it makes comparison between operators more difficult since the system states to be exploited vary according to the operator's responses, which are not necessarily the same. It is sometimes possible to reduce this drawback in the following way: the operator gives a response, then the experimenter gives the standard response. Thus, one avoids any divergence of the system states and the appearance of increasingly different situations. It is also sometimes possible to discretize the presentation of a continuous process by giving the state of the system to the operator only at fixed intervals (Hoc, 1987).

The static-dynamic dimension can be applied equally to high and or low fidelity simulation. Particularly typical examples of partial dynamic simulation are described for big ship control by Gerhardt (1984).

Technical system simulation and environment simulation

It is sometimes useful to distinguish two aspects in the simulation. The first concerns the simulator we think of more spontaneously when we talk about simulation. The second concerns the conditions in which the simulator, or the technical system in the reference situation, functions. The simulation can be the only environment in the case where a driver trains on a track or on a previously defined itinerary. The two types of simulation can also be combined, for example Gerhardt (1984) defines the environment problems which will be presented to the trainees in an 'anticollision' task simulated on a microcomputer.

Simulation of the environment sometimes defines the simulator inputs or the type of perturbation to be introduced in the simulator function.

Adaptation of the simulator

The operator who learns with a simulator modifies activity during this learning. Therefore, at successive moments, it is not the same type of action that is implemented and it is not the same simulation characteristics that will be relevant. This underlines the interest of flexible simulation, which is adaptable to the subject's skill level. Partial simulations make it easier to control the acquisition of basic skills, and so planning the acquisition of general skill. As Baker and Marshall (1989) note, 'simulators provide the instructor with the ability to control the sequence of events and to regulate the difficulty or speed of the training'.

CONCLUSION

In order to define the role of simulation and simulators in training, it rapidly becomes apparent that we must study the expert activity that constitutes the objective of training, and also the activities corresponding to the different stages of training during which this expert activity is elaborated. For this large research field, only a brief overview has been given. In this chapter, we have attempted to clarify some important problems which are the many questions to which the simulation user has to respond. To conclude we will recall some of the essential points, which also indicate the direction of future research on simulation and simulators.

1. Simulators are tools at the service of simulation. Simulation takes on its meaning and function in training only if defined in relation to training goals and means, and trainee features. Considering simulation objectives, criteria of validation are of primary importance. From this aspect, the simulation is a tool at the service of work design. It permits the testing of new or modified situations at the same time as it gives the possibility of training the operators to respond to the demands of these situations.
2. In its training-centred use, simulation is the source of an apparent paradox: it is necessary to know the operator's activity and acquisition processes to design a valuable simulation but, at the same time, it is often necessary to have recourse to simulation to obtain this knowledge. In fact, we have here a dialectic process which enriches itself at each step: the quality of the simulation enriches the knowledge, and reciprocally. By an analogous process, knowledge of activity and knowledge of error are mutually enriched.
3. General psychological knowledge relative to the mechanisms regulating activity and learning intervene in the former process. Several models exist for these mechanisms. We emphasized some of them, which seem especially adapted to training design, without ignoring the other ones, which are

relevant according to the type of task. The models bring a frame for the analysis and at the same time a set of knowledge to help in the elaboration of specific simulation situations.

The simulation situation has to be thought of not only as a set of elements but as a set of rules of use, based on a model of learning relevant to the specific activity to be learned.

4. The simulator, as a technical system, has specific properties, which can be implemented in different ways according to the proposed types of task and the execution conditions. In simulator training, declarative and procedural aspects of knowledge are intimately mixed. A rational task (Resnick, 1976) can be defined for simple tasks, but for complex tasks, such as those often met in workplaces, the procedures are difficult to specify. It is necessary in these cases to have recourse to heuristic rules. Simulation can also contribute to their acquisition: indeed, simulations permit one to vary systematically the nature and conditions of the tasks. Hopefully, future technical improvements will help the design of adaptive simulators capable of fitting the simulation conditions to the trainees' competence. The programming of these different uses of simulation will always require a deep knowledge of the acquisition process for the previously determined skills.

ACKNOWLEDGEMENT

The author would like to thank Dr Leena Norros for many interesting and useful discussions during the preparation of this chapter.

REFERENCES

Anderson, J. A. (1981) *Cognitive Skills and Their Acquisition*. Hillsdale, N.J.: Lawrence Erlbaum.

Baker, S., and Marshall, E. (1989) Full scope simulators for training and performance evaluation of process operators. Paper 16, this volume.

Ericsson, K. A., and Simon, H. A. (1984) *Verbal Reports as Data*. Cambridge, Mass., the MIT Press.

Fleishman, E. A., and Quaintance, M. K. (1984) *Taxonomies of Human Performance: the Description of Human Tasks*. New York: Academic Press.

Gagne, R. M. (1970) *The Conditions of Learning*. London: Holt, Rinehart and Winston, 406 pp.

Galperine, P. (1966) Essai sur la formation par étapes des actions et des concepts. In *Recherches Psychologiques en U.R.S.S.* Moscow: Editions du Progrès.

Gerhard, D. (1984) Utilité de l'ordinateur pour la formation professionnelle: rapport des expérimentations de simulation en psychologie du travail. Roneod document, OPEFORM, Malakoff, 9 pp.

Hoc, J. M. (1987) Mise en oeuvre des connaissances de conducteurs d'un processus à long délais de référence: le haut fourneau. Analyse d'une simulation en marche dégradée. Internal report, Department of Psychology, University of Paris VIII.

Hollnagel, E., and Rasmussen, J. (1981) Simulator training analysis. Report M. 2301, Riso National Laboratory.

Karnas, G. (1987) L'analyse du travail. In C. Levy Leboyer and J. C. Spérandio (eds), *Traité de Psychologie du Travail*. Paris: PUF, pp. 609–26.

Kelley, C. R. (1969) What is adaptive training? *Human Factors*, **11**(6), 547–56.

Kuipers, B. J. (1986) Qualitative simulation. *Artificial Intelligence*, **29**(3), 289–338.

Lazet, A., and Schuffel H. (1978) Dynamic simulation: a tool in research on human behavior in navigation. *Navigation*, **31**(1), 133–40.

Leplat, J. (1985) *Erreur Humaine, Fiabilité Humaine dans le Travail*. Paris: A. Colin.

Leplat, J., and Bisseret, A. (1965) Analyse des processus de traitement de l'information chez le contrôleur de la navigation aérienne. *Bulletin de CERP*, **XIV**(1–2), 51–67.

Leplat, J., and Cuny, X. (1984) *Introduction à la Psychologie du Travail*, 2nd ed. Paris: PUF, 305 pp.

Leplat, J., and Hoc, J. M. (1981) Subsequent verbalization in the study of cognitive process. *Ergonomics*, **24**, 743–55.

Pailhous, J. (1970) *Le Représentation de l'Espace Urbain*. Paris: PUF.

Pask, G. (1976) *Conversation, Cognition and Learning*, New York: Elsevier.

Rasmussen, J., Duncan, K., and Leplat, J. (eds.) (1987) *New Technology and Human Error*. Chichester: John Wiley & Sons.

Resnick, L. B. (1976) Task analysis in instructional design: some cases from mathematics. In D. Klahr (ed.), *Cognition and Instruction*. Hillsdale, N.J.: Lawrence Erlbaum.

Rolfe, J. M., and Waag W. L. (1982) Flight simulators as flight devices: some continuing psychological problems. Communication to the XXth Congress of IAAP, Edinburgh. Roneo, 10 pp.

Schneider, W. (1985) Training high performance skills: fallacies and guidelines. *Human Factors*, **27**(3), 285–300.

Schuffel, H. (1984) The interaction of rate movement presentation with ship's controllability. Conference on *Maritime Simulation*.

Sheridan, T. B., and Hennessy R. T. (eds.) (1984) *Research and Modeling of Supervisory Control Behaviour*. National Academy Press.

Simon, H. A. (1979) What the knower knows: alternative strategies for problem-solving tasks. In F. Klix (ed.), *Human and Artificial Intelligence*, Amsterdam: North Holland, pp 89–100.

Singleton, W. T. (1978) *The Analysis of Practical Skills* London: MTP Press.

Stammers, R. B. (1983) Simulators for taining in T. O. Kvalseth (ed.), *Ergonomics of Work Station Design*. London: Butterworths, pp. 229–42.

16. Simulators for Training and the Evaluation of Operator Performance

Susan Baker and Edward Marshall

SUMMARY

The introduction of new technology into the control room has been matched in many cases by a change in the conduct of training, notably in the use of full-scope simulators, which are increasingly regarded as essential, though still expensive, tools in the training repertoire. The use of such simulators is particularly advocated in industries where the nature of the process renders it difficult, if not positively hazardous, for the trainee to obtain the necessary practice 'on the job'. This report, however, makes a distinction between the use of simulators for practice and assessment and argues that the major advantage of simulators in the training sphere is that they provide a very real environment which can be used for the systematic assessment of operator performance. A variety of potential methods for the observation and assessment of operator performance is discussed, drawing on experience from both the NORS simulator at the Halden Project and work in the off-shore oil industry. Data are presented from a recent study of operators under simulator training and the attitude of these operators towards simulators is also discussed. The report concludes that the distinction between practice and assessment is a valid one, but points out that the major benefits from simulator usage can only be obtained if there is a strong commitment from all those involved in building up the reality of the simulator environment—management, instructors and trainees alike.

INTRODUCTION

The introduction of new technology into the control room has been matched in many cases by a change in the conduct of training, notably in the use of full-scope simulators, which are increasingly regarded as essential, though still

Developing Skills with Information Technology
Edited by Lisanne Bainbridge and S. Antonio Ruiz Quintanilla
© 1989 John Wiley & Sons Ltd

expensive, tools in the training repertoire. The use of such simulators is particularly advocated in industries where the nature of the process renders it difficult, if not positively hazardous, for the trainee to obtain the necessary practice 'on the job'. Aviation and the nuclear power industry are cases in point.

Some reasons for training simulators

There are a number of, by now, relatively familiar arguments for the value of simulators in training. A number of these arguments are listed below:

1. Training in the real situation may prove hazardous.
2. Failures in the real situation may be rare.
3. It may be too expensive to use real equipment for training purposes.
4. Simulation allows trainees to practise a variety of coping strategies.
5. Simulation allows the trainer more control over the training process.
6. Simulation training can more easily allow for the use of training aids.
7. Simulation allows trainees to practise infrequent but crucial operations.
8. Simulation allows the trainer some control over the stressfulness of the training process.

However, these arguments, while valid in themselves, are not peculiar to simulator training; they are arguments for off-the-job training in general. However, there are other arguments supporting the value of simulator training which are based principally on the assumed value of the reality of the simulator-provided task environment. Rolfe has proposed (Rolfe and Caro, 1982) that these arguments can be summarized as follows:

> I am liked—I am real—I am used
> Therefore I must be good for you

We will suggest in this report that a major advantage of simulators in the training of process operating skills is that they provide a very real environment in which to *assess* performance. We will argue that the degree of reality necessary for effective training may not be the same as that required for assessing subsequent performance. In many instances of learning a skill or facet of process operation, the task will, of necessity, have to be broken down into smaller constituent elements, particularly in the early phases. At this stage of learning, the trainee may well benefit from a simplification of the task which might well be achieved effectively without the use of full-scale simulation. It is at a later stage when the various task elements are combined at a higher skill level that the simulator really comes into its own.

Simulator fidelity

When considering the degree of reality or fidelity required for training and assessment purposes it should be borne in mind that fidelity is not a unidimensional concept (Rolfe and Caro, 1982). A number of features can contribute to the overall realism of the training environment and, in terms of the plant operator, we may consider three main dimensions of fidelity, though there are others:

1. Physical fidelity. How accurately the simulator represents the control room in terms of size, layout, arrangement of instruments, etc.
2. Operational fidelity. How well the simulator mimics the process itself, with regard to process operation under a variety of conditions.
3. Psychological fidelity. In what respects the simulation duplicates psychological features of real operation, including task complexity, perceptual skills, decision-making and stress.

These three types of fidelity can be manipulated throughout the training process to suit various instructional goals. For example, in the early stages of learning about operation, the physical fidelity of the training environment may not be of paramount importance, nor would it be advisable to include complex or stressful tasks. However, in the more advanced stages of training, and especially for assessment purposes, we can assume that a greater level of fidelity in all three dimensions will provoke more realism in the observed performance of trainee operators.

With regard to simulator usage, we would thus argue that a fairly fundamental and useful distinction can be made between the training or instruction process, that is the acquisition of information and skills and practising these, and assessment, which we shall define as the *systematic* evaluation of trainee performance. Moreover, this distinction is germane to any consideration of the value of incorporated fidelity in training simulators. This distinction will be enlarged upon below with a number of suggestions as to how such systematic assessment can be carried out in a simulator, together with a consideration of some of the problems involved.

ASPECTS OF ASSESSMENT

While it may not be altogether a good idea for operators automatically to equate the simulator with assesment, if they become used to being evaluated during simulator exercises this is likely to render the task of the trainer much easier. We have, in the past, suggested that training courses contain an element of continuous assessment (Baker and Marshall, 1985). This has the double advantage of familiarizing operators with the assessment process and also of allowing the trainer to monitor progress as the course continues.

Rehearsal or practice is naturally an important part of learning a skill, particularly if practice can take place in the realistic setting of the simulator. However, practice, in itself, does not allow the trainer to assess either the progress made by the trainees or the efficacy of the training programme in conveying the necessary information. With appropriate data on the strengths and weaknesses of the trainees' performance, the instructor is able to provide both feedback and remedial training where necessary.

Assessment of performance in the laboratory

From the point of view of the Halden Project, there are two main aspects to the work on evaluation in simulators: evaluations undertaken as part of the experimental programme in the NORS simulator and evaluations of operator performance in industrial training simulators.

In effect, a sizeable proportion of the work of the human factors group in connection with the NORS simulator is concerned with the evaluation of operator performance. Even when systems are under test, they are evaluated in the context of their effect on the performance of the operators using them.

The NORS simulator

The NORS research simulator situated in Halden is a full-scale simulated pressurized water reactor (PWR) and, while not being a replica of a specific power plant, is nevertheless representative of a typical power reactor of this type (see Stokke and Petersen, 1983). The NORS experimental control room is 'futuristic' in that information presentation is by means of CRT displays while process control is effected using touch keyboards and tracker balls. In addition, a limited section of the process has also been 'conventionally' instrumented to allow for experimental comparisons (Baker, Holmstrøm and Marshall, 1985, Baker et al., 1986). Regarding operator observation, the simulator is equipped with video and audio recording facilities together with an experimenter observation gallery that allows a complete view of the experimental control room.

In terms of the recording of performance data, there is automatic logging of such items as information requested by the operator; which CRTs are used to present this information; and operator actions in relation to the process such as opening or closing of valves and stopping or starting of pumps. In addition, there are data on plant status in terms of selected process parameters, alarms activated and so on. Coupled with this, experimental data gathering normally involves subjective data collected through subject interviews, debriefing sessions and questionnaire responses. The facilities therefore allow for the gathering of a variety of data types.

Performance assessment in the NORS simulator

As can be seen from the above, there is no lack of facilities for the observation of operator performance in its many aspects. However, the situation is not so simple when it comes to the *assessment* of this performance. A typical instrument for the assessment of effective operator performance might be an ideal path of the particular operational sequence that is being tested.

Performance is then assessed by ticking off the various elements of the appropriate course of behaviour as each is, or is not, performed. This approach has been used fairly successfully for experimentation in the NORS simulator (for example Baker *et al.*, 1985; and Reiersen, Marshall and Baker, 1987). A number of problems present themselves, however, in assessing operating performance, particularly with repect to an appropriate division of a task into its constituent elements. In assessing performance on a fault-finding task, for example, behaviour is typically subdivided, representing various stages in the process of detecting a problem, diagnosing its root cause and perhaps carrying out, or at least suggesting, appropriate remedial actions. While this represents a usable schema for scoring purposes, it is obviously inadequate as an accurate description of human behaviour, since it must, of necessity, take a rather structured and compartmentalized view of behaviour. The type of checklist utilized in NORS experimentation is, in fact, an amended and somewhat simplified version of that developed by Rasmussen and his associates in Denmark, which also sought to categorize, on-line, the type of errors made by operators during simulator training sessions (for example Hollnagel, 1981, 1982; Hollnagel and Rasmussen, 1981).

Performance baselines

In order to undertake a systematic assessment of training effectiveness over time, throughout the duration of a particular training course, for example, it is necessary to establish a baseline level of performance. Under experimental conditions, this is usually achieved by providing all trainees or experimental subjects with identical training and then testing against some predetermined criterion of performance. If performance falls short of this level, remedial or additional instruction or practice is provided until the desired criterion is reached. While it may be possible to achieve this goal under laboratory conditions, it has to be recognized that such a strict level of control is seldom, if ever, possible in the real world. Industrial trainees often approach a particular training course with differing levels of knowledge or expertise and it may not be possible, or indeed economically viable, to bring all such trainees up to the desired level before the course begins. Nevertheless, it should be possible for the trainer to carry out some kind of test which would allow an evaluation of the competence level of the trainees before the course begins. This information can then serve as a baseline from which to evaluate subsequent progress and performance. It also allows the trainer to estimate individual training needs.

Retention of skill

Regular assessment of trainees not only allows the trainer to monitor how much they have learned but it also provides a useful means of checking the extent of forgetting. In other words, it provides a measure of retention between training courses. This is important, not only for assessing how much the trainee has forgotten but also to illustrate the *type* of forgetting that is likely to occur.

Though we have not, as yet, conducted any systematic studies of retention in connection with the training of our experimental subjects at the Halden Project, we have observed differences in the type of forgetting that takes place from one training session to the next. Observation of trainees on return visits to the simulator after a number of months (typically there is a gap of approximately three months between major experimental sessions) have shown that, while trainees retain a reasonably sound working knowledge of the process, they display a distinct tendency to forget the mechanics of dealing with the interface. They may need time to familiarize themselves with the use of the tracker ball, for example, or be uncertain as to the use of the touch-sensitive function keyboard. This degradation over time was unanticipated, since we had rather assumed that retention problems would be focused on the process itself and the maintenance of process knowledge.

This observed tendency of forgetting with regard to the interface may be considered as not being too serious in the industrial context, since operators seldom experience long periods away from the control room. This naturally militates against forgetting and encourages retention of process knowledge and the various aspects of process operation. In the nuclear industry, this would almost certainly be the case since, with the exception of the holiday period, operators will normally be working, more or less, continuously at the job. The same is, however, not true of the oil industry, where a period on the platform is typically followed by two, and sometimes as many as four, weeks on-shore. In this case it is probably necessary to take steps specifically to bridge this 'familiarity gap', for example by staggering shift teams to allow a period of overlap among control room personnel.

Performance measures for assessment

As mentioned above, attempts at assessing operator performance frequently involve imposing a rather artificial structure on behaviour. With this in mind, it is perhaps worth while to look at each of the measures that can be adopted in turn, to consider the appropriateness of these measures and the criteria by which performance may reasonably be judged.

Accuracy

In any assessment of performance it is reasonable to consider the accuracy of that performance. For purposes of assessment, accuracy can be subdivided into what we shall term overall or 'end-product' accuracy and procedural accuracy. Both of these will be considered in turn.

1. 'End-product' accuracy. By end-product accuracy we refer to the overall success of the performance. In other words, was the behaviour correct? Was the desired aim achieved? Was the plant brought to a steady state? This is not too difficult to assess; the trainer or experimenter will know beforehand the nature of the problem and the correct solution. It should then be a relatively straightforward decision as to the accuracy of the performance. This does not, of course, take account of the methods used to achieve these aims. This is considered in more detail under the heading of procedural accuracy discussed below.
2. Procedural accuracy. This can be more difficult to assess and score. In many problem-solving tasks, particularly one as complex as transient handling in nuclear power plants, there can be more than one way of achieving a satisfactory solution. The problem arises in attempting to rate one solution as better or more effective than another. The overall goal of bringing a plant to a safe condition, for example, can be accomplished by shutting down the plant, or perhaps more elegantly, and more economically, by stabilizing the plant without shutting down and with less loss of production. The solution judged to be the best will depend on a number of factors such as the potential hazard involved in the respective methods, the nature of the plant disturbance and, in the real world case, by the overall operational philosophy at the plant in question. In any event, judgement of the elegance of a solution is best conducted by individuals with a substantial depth of plant and process knowledge.

Time

The time taken to perform an action or the speed with which a diagnosis is made has the advantage of providing a numerical score, which is useful for experimental purposes, particularly when statistical analyses are to be performed. However, a significant difference in time in a statistical sense may have no 'significance' in operational terms, when other factors may be more important. Nevertheless, the time an operator takes to perform a particular operation or function would seem to be a reasonable measure to consider in the overall assessment process.

Depending on the scenario that is being used for assessment purposes, the relevant weightings attached to each segment of performance can vary. An instructor may, for example, be interested to know that an operator can diagnose a problem correctly but less interested, within limits, in the length of time that is taken to do it. On another occasion the instructor may be particularly concerned about the trainee's ability to perform remedial actions.

The successful functioning of such an assessment scheme depends on the instructor having a clear picture beforehand of the type of performance that is expected at the various stages and, ideally, some estimate of the possible time scale for each section of the operation. However, because of the variability possible in the normal operation of process plant and in the handling of process disturbances, it may be difficult to follow exactly the ideal solution established beforehand. The instructor has to be prepared for this eventuality and, accordingly, make allowances in the assessment of the performance in question. Nevertheless, experience from the use of such an assessment scheme in the NORS simulator has indicated its usefulness as a feasible assessment tool.

TRAINING FOR TRANSIENT MANAGEMENT

One of the most persuasive arguments for simulator-based training is their potential application for training operators to cope with rare and unscheduled events which cannot be systematically practised on the job. Yet the operator's skill in being able to cope with these incidents both promptly and skillfully probably represents the chief reason for including the human in the control system. In order to achieve mastery of such a complex, high-level skill opportunity must be given for systematic and frequent practice of the crucial elements of that skill. The instructor thus faces a very real paradox—how to maintain a high level of performance in a complex cognitive skill that is rarely (hopefully—never) required.

In Table 1 we have listed some of the more crucial elements of the task of coping with a complex, automatically controlled process during an unexpected event such as equipment failure. The first four elements can be seen as being roughly sequential in time. Once the disturbance is detected then it must be identified. The operator should be able to identify failures that have been either predicted by design engineers or experienced previously. The operator should also have some skill in diagnosing situations not previously experi-

Table 1: The task elements

1. Detection of disturbances
2. Recognition of expected events
3. Diagnosis of unpredicted events
4. Implementation of unusual procedures
. . . .
5. Working under stress

enced. Once a particular fault or disturbance is identified then the operator will implement the appropriate remedial procedure. It should be remembered, of course, that carrying out these actions will itself be an unfamiliar activity. It is therefore unlikely that the operator will be subjected to conditions liable to provoke stress.

Clearly a plant simulator can be used to help the operator learn how to detect disturbances, but there can be problems. For example, it is possible with most simulators to run a number of fault scenarios within a short time, and this is a tempting technique for practising detection skills. However, a disadvantage that we have observed is that the trainee starts to expect the onset of a fault and therefore pays more attention to the plant alarm indications than would be the case on a normal shift. This may be an advantage during training, but during assessment the instructor will probably be more interested in seeing how well the trainee can cope under more realistic conditions. The question of what constitutes 'realism' in the simulator is one to which we shall return later.

Overall, three phases in training are proposed:

1. Basic instruction, in which the essential task elements are described and trainees practise the principal components using, in the main, static simulation techniques such as tape/slide presentations, paper and pencil exercises coupled with appropriate simulator demonstrations. Performance can of course be assessed at this stage and a satisfactory level should be required before they move on to the second phase.
2. Dynamic simulator practice, in which trainees practise detection in the simulator but with considerable help and guidance from the instructor, who can, during this phase, exploit all the 'helpful' facilities provided by the simulator.
3. Realistic performance assessment, in which trainees are expected to behave as though in a real plant environment and throughout the session their performance is closely assessed.

Detection of disturbances has been chosen as a particular example because it is obviously the first skill required in transient management. What we would emphasize, however, is that all these three phases of simulator instruction can be generally applied in the training of the other necessary task elements we have already listed.

PROBLEMS WITH TRAINING SIMULATORS

Facilities for performance assessment

In terms of the facilities available for the assessment of operator or trainee performance, such as automatic logging of operator actions together with audio and video recording of speech and other interactions, the NORS simulator has a number of advantages not always found in simulators used specifically for training purposes. Under these circumstances, other methods have to be found of gathering data for assessment purposes. One of the major problems is to devise a technique for gathering appropriate data on both operator performance and interaction 'on-line' without the aid of video or audio recording. In addition, care has to be taken to ensure that relevant information is not lost since there is no opportunity for recovering it as there is when automatic methods of data recording are employed.

Evaluation of individual and crew performance

Generally speaking, operators will almost always be working as part of a team in the performance of their normal tasks. For purposes of evaluation, however, it is probably worth while to make the distinction between the evaluation of individual operators and the assessment of the team as a whole.

Individual assessment

It is, of course, possible to evaluate the performance of individual operators while they are working as part of a team, and we shall return to this aspect later. Nevertheless, for a close evaluation of operator progress throughout a training course individual observation and assessment on particular tasks probably provides the most accurate information on progress. This is particularly the case in the early stages of training or when new information has been introduced. It is probably less relevant on retraining courses when actual operating teams may be undergoing retraining together. Using the simulator for the assessment of individual performance is time consuming, but with a properly constructed training course, other operators can be working off-line on other aspects of the training. Individual assessment sessions need not be as long as those required for a thorough evaluation of team functioning.

Crew assessment

In addition to the basic evaluation of the knowledge of individual team members, crew assessment naturally involves assessing the functioning of the team as a whole, both in terms of the effectiveness of the team in operating the process and with regard to interactions among team members in terms of the degree of cooperation and task sharing, for example.

As far as is practicable we would suggest running the team evaluation section of a training course as a normal shift. When the team arrives, they would, for example, be provided with handover information from the previous 'shift', which might include details of perturbations to be taken into account during their session.

The role of the supervisor

In terms of the running of the shift team, the supervisor plays a fundamental role. As a starting point in the gathering of data on personnel interaction, therefore, we would suggest a closer look at the role of the supervisor in the control room. Again, a prerequisite for assessing the supervisor is the setting up of some overall criteria related to the supervisor's position in terms of what is required of the supervisor and what is regarded as 'good' performance. The execution of authority is subject to a great deal of variation in personal style and the supervisor's role is no exception.

The role of the supervisor can be evaluated under a number of basic headings related to the degree of involvement in the day-to-day performance of the control room personnel—whether the superivisor adopts a purely managerial/authoritative function or behaves as one of the crew with little or no directing role. Discussion with industry would suggest that ideally the supervisor should be 'involved' in the control room but without losing the ability to delegate and without taking over the function of the operators.

The more specific requirements placed on the functioning of the control room personnel will, of course, depend largely on the demands and characteristics of the process in question. To this end, some kind of analysis of the tasks of the various personnel should ideally be performed before an assessment scheme is drawn up (for example Duncan, 1974). Such a task analysis also provides an ideal starting point for the establishment of training goals, since it provides the instructor with information on what the trainee needs to know to perform subsequent tasks.

Task scenario

One of the major problems in evaluating crew or individual performance on process transients is to provide a realistic setting in which the transients can be introduced. The problem with giving trainees a transient in a steadily running process is that frequently they may be concentrating too closely on the information displays so that any disturbance is spotted unusually quickly. This is not only unrealistic but can give a rather distorted view of how good operators are at detecting faults (Baker and Marshall, 1987a). Therefore, for the crew assessment particularly, it might be useful to have the crews in the simulator for relatively long periods. Crews could then be observed under more realistic conditions than the shorter sessions more appropriate to individual testing.

When it comes to an evaluation of operator interaction during team work, the availability of video/audio recording is an obvious advantage since this allows close scrutiny of both operator movements and verbal communication during the session. Closer analysis of these data can, of course, take place after the training session is completed when the instructor or experimenter is at liberty to study the tapes in more detail. An additional advantage of video recording is that the tapes can later be replayed and viewed together with the operators in order that they can observe and analyse their own performance and also provide explanations for behaviour which the instructor may have found difficult to comprehend or score. The availability of audio and video recording also makes it easier to investigate errors in operation which may be attributable to failure in communication among operators. The results of such communication breakdown are not always easy to detect simply by means of scrutinizing the sequence of operations.

The scope for assessment is limited and more difficult without recording facilities of this type since other ways have to be found to collect data on-line. The performance aspect is perhaps less difficult to cope with than attempting to analyse operator interaction without some means of recording that interaction on film. In this case, the instructor is faced with using other means such as checklists on which to record interactions like the giving and receiving of instructions, and which operators show leadership tendencies and which are more inclined to adopt a more passive role with regard to initiating activities in the control room. This kind of pencil-and-paper data recording also makes demands in terms of the number of staff who must be available to complete the records. Obviously with automatic recording of operator actions and video/audio recording of operator interactions, the number of staff necessary to conduct assessment is reduced by comparison with other potentially more labour-intensive methods. It is, nevertheless, possible to construct methods for this on-line assessment of operators (for example Hollnagel, 1981; Norros and Sammatti, 1986; Baker and Marshall, 1987b), but the success of these techniques will depend on having a clear picture beforehand of the type of behaviour that is of interest together with some means of codifying the data-gathering so that the instructor is not involved in lengthy note-taking during the session or too dependent on memory for completing the notes after the session has ended.

TRAINING FOR NEW TECHNOLOGY

As we mentioned previously, for experimental or assessment purposes, an attempt is frequently made to subdivide operating behaviour into discrete sections. This division is often reflected in the structure of operator support systems. There are, for example, systems for the early detection of faults, systems for diagnostic help and systems designed to assist the operator in taking appropriate steps to alleviate or prevent a crisis. This is not to suggest that such systems have no value, but rather to make the point that the presence of these systems poses questions regarding the way in which training should be carried out. Focusing, as such systems do, on different phases of the process, means that operators have to be trained to integrate the functions of the various support systems for optimal performance of their task. The increasingly remote nature of process control, not only in terms of the physical remoteness exemplified by centralized control rooms but also the remoteness which is potentially a function of more abstract representations of the process, means that operators no longer have to be taught simply to run the process, they also have to be taught to run the devices which run the process. The picture may be further complicated if the support systems represent different philosophies with regard to information manipulation and presentation. Put simply, problems can be envisaged if the operator is expected to think in one way for one device and another way for a different device in the same control room.

System integration

In many process industries, control rooms are generally in a state of flux in terms of instrumentation. Newly established industries or new plant for existing industries have the advantage of being able to construct a control room 'from scratch' with, it is to be hoped, an integrated process control and information presentation system. This option is, however, not available in the majority of cases when the only alternative is retro-fitting existing control rooms with updated equipment. Such a change may take many forms having differing implications. It may, for example, involve the installation of a new plant computer which may speed things but not fundamentally alter the operator's task or it may consist of the introduction of new operator support systems.

While the simulator may provide an appropriate environment for the evaluation of such systems and also for training operators to use them, frequently little attention is paid to the integration of such systems into existing control rooms. From the operational point of view, new systems cannot simply be grafted on to the existing configuration without serious consideration of how the systems will be used and what implications the backfit will have for the operator. We have previously made the point (Baker and Marshall, 1987a) that, for a number of reasons, systems are frequently not tested under the conditions in which they will be used after installation. In fact, during both the testing of systems and the training of operators measures are taken more from considerations of expediency than validity. Although operators may be trained to use a system, they are not necessarily trained to use it in conjunction with the existing control room equipment: nor are the implications of introducing new systems always fully considered.

While new technological developments in the control room may not involve a fundamental change in training philosophy, although the tools may change, the way in which some new systems conceptualize and represent the process may make new demands on the operator's thinking. The difficulty for the instructor may well be to teach operators to utilize a variety of different systems which represent the process in subtly or not so subtly different ways. There is perhaps a danger that systems are often developed and equipment designed more because the appropriate technology is available than because of any need for such a device. Training for particular operator functions such as fault diagnosis may be carried out with little regard for its implications for the performance of other aspects of the operator's task. In much the same way, development and testing of systems may be carried out *in vacuo* without due regard for the way such systems will be used or integrated into the process control milieu.

Focus on abnormal situations

Much of the impetus for exploiting new technology in the control room stems from the desire to improve operational safety, particularly with regard to the handling of process disturbances. This is, in itself, a worthy enough aim, but it does mean, in practice, that the majority of the effort tends to be focused on abnormal situations without due regard for maintaining a perspective on the total operating environment. In this regard, it is worth noticing that while instructors may wish to concentrate on disturbance handling, operators themselves may prefer to spend more time on the rehearsal of so-called 'normal' operations, or situations which they, themselves, have experienced and would like to repeat in the simulator.

Acceptance of new technology

Generally speaking, acceptance of technological innovation in the control room is relatively high. Operators responses to what may be termed a computerized environment are on the whole positive. This positive attitude is also evident with regard to new operator support systems. A common element of many evaluative studies of such systems, however, is that operators often show a preference for new systems, even when the use of such systems yields no demonstrable improvement in performance (Baker and Marshall, 1987a).

Nevertheless, despite this somewhat positive attitude, operator responses indicate that if computerization of process control is to be extended, full advantage should be taken of the capabilities of computerization to provide the operator with more 'processed' information than would normally be the case in the more 'conventionally' instrumented type of control room. Computers have the capability not merely of replicating existing information displays but of combining and processing information from a number of sources, and displaying this in novel ways, often to serve a specific purpose.

Subjective realism

A great deal has been written on the question of simulator fidelity and whether or not the simulator should completely resemble the plant that it is designed to simulate. Questionnaire responses which we have obtained from operators indicate that, while they may be satisfied with the layout of the simulator with regard to the equipment included and while the process model may behave more or less as they would expect, what tends to be lacking in the simulator are a number of additional features, which may be extraneous to the process as such, but which nevertheless can have a profound influence on the operator's task. This may include additional equipment for other tasks, distractions due to visits from other staff not directly related to the control room, and noise or vibration from the process itself. A recent review of simulation in training (Rediffusion Simulation Ltd, 1986) echoes this point: 'It is surprising how simulators . . . can lose their "street credibility" for the sake of some seemingly minor characteristic. Probably this characteristic is a function of the experience of the trainee.'

All this takes no account of other features that are potentially even more difficult to simulate, such as the possibility of stress involved in certain phases of the process. If (and it is a big IF) the decision is taken to opt for maximum realism in the simulator, this cannot be confined to considerations purely of the control room architecture or even of the simulator model. The striving for realism has to encompass the whole field of simulator usage including the attitude of instructors and other training staff.

Much can be done to create a realistic atmosphere in the simulator over and above the physical accuracy of the simulation as a representation of a real plant or process. A relatively simple but effective step could be the exclusion from the simulator of all those not directly concerned with its operation. In addition, while the evidence suggests that operators are not unduly worried about being observed during training, it is obvious that something can probably be gained in terms of realism if facilities exist for observing operators from an observation gallery outside the control room rather than in the room itself. Figure 1 shows responses from operators who have recently undergone simulator training for the off-shore oil industry (Baker and Marshall, 1987c). As can be seen, responses tended towards the positive end of the scale, though there was some spread of opinion regarding the realism of the simulator in question. Subsequent discussion with operators indicated that while the simulator model and control room were adequate representations, there were a number of additional tasks which the operating staff were expected to perform off-shore that were not simulated.

Since our work with this particular group of operators specifically involved observation and the development of an assessment scheme, it was natural to ask operators for their feelings on being observed in the simulator (see Figure 2). As can be seen from the figure, although some operators expressed concern about being observed during training, on the whole less anxiety was reported after the operators had actually experienced being observed. This finding, together with experience from the NORS simulator indicates quite strongly that operators quickly adapt to observation provided that appropriate care is taken in limiting the number of observers and in maintaining the confidentiality of the results, audio and video recordings, etc.

In addition to specific questions relating to the training, operators were also asked to indicate whether they enjoyed simulator training. Figure 3 shows clearly that all the operators, with the exception of one, strongly agreed that they enjoyed training in the simulator. It should perhaps be noted that the single operator who reported not enjoying simulator training before the session is not the individual missing from the second part of the diagram. In other words, the individual who initially expressed a negative attitude to simulator training changed his mind quite clearly after experience with the simulator. The fact that operators like simulators and enjoy simulator training is, of course, insufficient justification for their use in training; nor is it proof of their effectiveness as training devices (Rolfe and Caro, 1982). Nevertheless, it can probably only help the instructor if the trainees have a positive attitude towards training in the simulator.

It is frequently assumed or expected that reality in the training environment will, in turn, generate realistic behaviour by the trainees. In other words, the simulator, by virtue of its fidelity, will engender trust and cooperation on the part of the trainees so that they feel confident to 'act' realistically. Thus, it may be argued, the training situation should, ideally, be similar to the real task and trainees should be assessed in situations as close to the real task as possible. However, as we have said, the creation of task reality necessitates more than just an accurate plant model and a replica control room. During assessment trainees should expect to treat the simulator as though it were real; they should be given a typical activity to carry out and they should accept that all actions are to be recorded and scored. Neither trainees nor instructors should be allowed to treat the simulator casually.

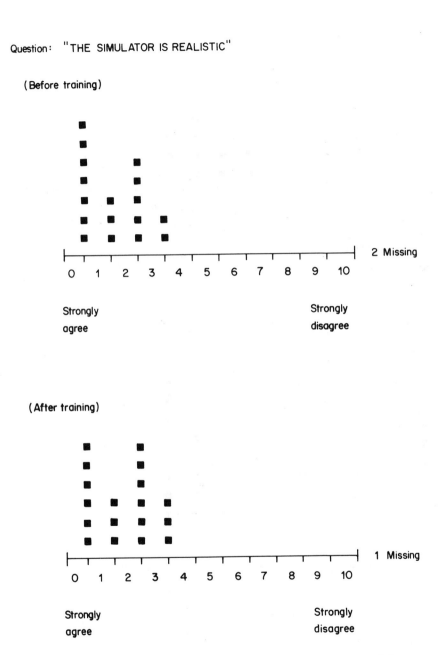

Figure 1. Questionnaire responses before and after simulator training

Question: " I AM ANXIOUS ABOUT BEING OBSERVED"

(Before training)

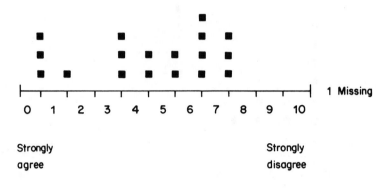

(After training)

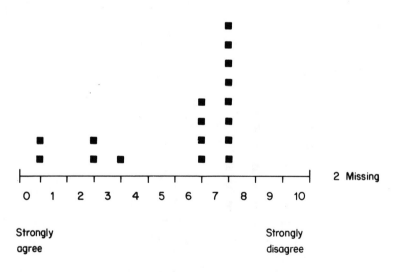

Figure 2. Questionnaire responses before and after simulator training

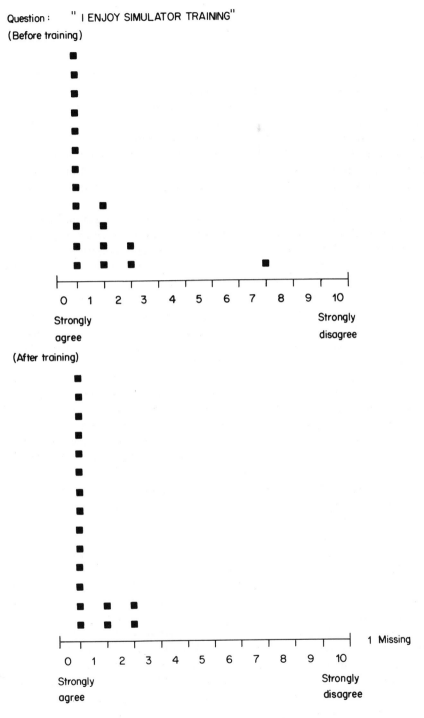

Figure 3. Questionnaire responses before and after simulator training

SIMULATION AND STRESS RESISTANCE

It was mentioned at the outset that one of the prime arguments given for using simulators in training is that they allow the instructor a degree of control over the stressfulness of the training environment. There is also a strong suggestion in the literature that training in the simulator should provide resistance to the effects of stress if and when a similar situation arises in the real world (for example Cooper, 1986). While this contention might be supported by common sense, it remains, for the most part, nothing more than a suggestion, since evidence for the building of stress resistance through practice is not easy to find.

Common sense would, however, indicate that rehearsing situations such as emergency drills, disturbance handling and problem-solving procedures should provide the individuals concerned with some resistance to the stress of these events when they actually come up against them in reality. This common-sense assertion forms the basis of much of the motivation for simulator usage. The problem for simulation remains, however, that it is just those features of a situation that create the stress, that are often the most difficult to replicate in the simulator. Although a trainee may be concerned about his or her performance during simulator training and experience a degree of stress as a result, generally speaking, simulator training is conducted in a relatively stress-free environment. The operator who is quite capable of performing adequately in the simulator may find the demands very different when an attempt is made to perform the same tasks in a genuinely frightening or dangerous situation. It has already been noted that simulators, however adequate as representations of the process, often lack a number of situational elements such as noise or vibration which can cause problems on the job. Paradoxically, by providing simulator training to prepare operators for dealing with difficult situations we may be lulling them into a false sense of security with regard to their ability to cope with these situations should they arise in actuality.

There is no easy solution to the problem of providing these more extreme types of potentially stress-inducing situations in the laboratory or process simulator. Again, the aviation industry has tackled this point by constructing the so-called 'evacuation trainers'—simulators specifically designed to mimic the type of situation likely to be met by cabin crews, for example, in the event of an engine fire and a smoke-filled cabin. We understand that some airline companies have decided against using such simulations for training on the grounds that the degree of realism provided is likely to prove too stressful for the crews, inducing a high level of anxiety about encountering a similar situation rather than confidence in their ability to cope. The problem of creating too stressful an environment is not one that the process industries have yet had to face.

CONCLUSIONS

Throughout it has been argued that the use of simulators in training can be regarded as having a number of basic elements: the acquisition of information or new skills, the rehearsal of these skills and the subsequent assessment of the operator's performance of what has been learned. In particular a distinction was made between practice and assessment. It was argued that, while a good deal of training can be carried out using relatively low levels of simulation, particularly in the early stages of training, a situation where the full-scope simulator really comes into it own is in providing a realistic environment for the systematic assessment of operator performance and the evaluation of the efficacy of training programmes. Stammers (1979), for example, has made the point that, '. . . It is likely that the simulator is the only place where performance can be effectively and comprehensively measured at present.' Systematic assessment does, however, require the provision of adequate facilities for the observation and recording of operator performance. Unfortunately, not all simulators are ideally equipped for performance assessment and other methods have to be found to evaluate performance. A number of these possible methods were described.

In addition to the demands made on equipment, conducting systematic performance assessment also places demands on management, training staff and trainees, in terms of the conduct of the simulator sessions and the effort that must be made to create a realistic atmosphere in the simulator. Such realism goes beyond considerations of the physical resemblance of the simulator to the plant, or even of the simulator model to the process, and encompasses the whole manner in which the simulator is treated by users.

ACKNOWLEDGEMENT

The authors would like to express their gratitude to the staff of the Statoil Training Centre, Bergen, Norway, and to the operators who took part in the training and evaluation sessions mentioned in this chapter.

REFERENCES

Baker, S., Holmstrøm, C., and Marshall, E. (1985) *Conventional Instrumentation in the Advanced Control Room—Experiment 1: A Comparison of Operator Performance Using Three Display Modes.* OECD Halden Reactor Project, HWR-152, Halden, Norway.

Baker, S., and Marshall, E. (1985) *An Operator Training Programme for Experiments using the NORS Simulator.* OECD Halden Reactor Project, HWR-137, Halden, Norway.

Baker, S., and Marshall, E. (1987a) Evaluating the man–machine interface—the search for data. In J. Patrick and K. Duncan (eds.), *Human Decision Making and Control*. North-Holland.

Baker, S., and Marshall, E. (1987b) Full scope simulators for training and performance evaluation of process operators. Paper presented at Workshop on *New Technologies and Work*, Bad Homburg, 9–11 April 1987.

Baker, S., and Marshall, E. (1987c) *Report on Gullfaks, A Simulator Course 111—Discussion and Comments*. OECD Halden Reactor Project, Halden, Norway.

Baker, S., Hollnagel, E., Marshall, E., and Øwre, F. (1985) *An Experimental Comparison of Three Computer-based Alarm Systems: Design, Procedure and Execution*. OECD Halden Reactor Project, HWR-134, Halden, Norway.

Baker, S., Holmstrøm, C., Marshall, E., and Reiersen, C. (1986) *Conventional Instrumentation in the Advanced Control Room—Experiments 2 and 3: Further Comparisons of Operator Performance When Using Differing Display and Control Modes*. OECD Halden Reactor Project, HWR-178, Halden, Norway.

Cooper, C. L. (1986) Job stress: recent research and the emerging role of the clinical occupational psychologist. *Bulletin of the British Psychological Society*, **39**, 325–31.

Duncan, K. D. (1974) Analytical techniques in training design. In E. Edwards and F. P. Lees (eds.), *The Human Operator in Process Control*. London: Taylor and Francis.

Hollnagel, E. (1981) Simulator training analysis: directions for using the decision analysis scheme. Internal report NKA/LIT-3 (81) 107, p. 15.

Hollnagel, E. (1982) Report from the IEOP pilot study of training simulator analysis methods. Internal report NKA/LIT-3.2 (82) 114.

Hollnagel, E., and Rasmussen, J. (1981) Simulator training analysis. A proposal for combined trainee debriefiing and performance data collection in training simulators. Internal report NKA/KRU-P2 (81) 38, p. 56.

Norros, L., and Sammatti, P. (1986) Nuclear power plant errors during simulator training. Research Report 446, VTT, Finland.

Rediffusion Simulation Ltd (1986) *Simulation in Training—A Guide for Trainers and Managers*. Training Technology Section, Manpower Services Commission.

Reiersen, C. S., Marshall, E. C., and Baker, S. M. (1987) *A Comparison of Operator Performance When Using Either an Advanced Computer-based Alarm System or a Conventional Annunciator Panel*. OECD Halden Reactor Project, HPR-331, Halden, Norway.

Rolfe, J. M., and Caro, P. W. (1982) Determining the effectiveness of flight simulators: some basic issues and practical developments. *Applied Ergonomics*, **13**, 243–50.

Stammers, R. B. (1979) Simulation in training for nuclear power plant operators. Report 12, Ergonområd Ab, Sweden.

Stokke, E., and Petersen, F. (1983) *NORS, the Full Scope Research Simulator*. OECD Halden Reactor Project, HPR 301, Halden, Norway.

17. Simulation in Industrial Work Training

Leena Norros

SUMMARY

Simulation is interpreted as a specific form of activity within the complete learning process, a model of which is presented in this chapter. This model is used for analysing the results of a nuclear power plant simulator experiment from the point of view of operator training. The ideas of the complete learning process are further used in developing a new training concept. This is demonstrated in the light of the results from a case study concerning the implementation of a flexible manufacturing system.

REASONS FOR SIMULATION TRAINING IN INDUSTRIAL WORK

Simulation has typically been used to aid learning in vehicle control or in control of complex industrial processes, for example nuclear power production. In these work activities simulation training is motivated by the importance of some of the tasks for the safety and availability of production, or because of the stressful nature of the context in which they are performed (Stammers, 1983). In other cases, for example practising production and organizational decision-making with the help of different games, training simulation has been used for enhancing the quality of the complex working activities without an immediate connection with safety problems. It can be assumed that, as the result of implementing new technology, those characteristics of the above working processes that make the use of simulation training necessary are increasing in all working processes. What are these characteristics and why would they demand the use of simulation in training?

In some recent studies on automation work, it has been argued that the functioning of complex technological processes necessarily requires the development of a new way of working by the operators of such processes. The

Developing Skills with Information Technology
Edited by Lisanne Bainbridge and S. Antonio Ruiz Quintanilla
© 1989 John Wiley & Sons Ltd

essence of the new way of working is claimed to be the ability and need for comprehensive mastery of the process and the operative decision-making based on it (Hirschhorn, 1984, Kern and Schuman, 1984; PAQ, 1987). For the purpose of conceiving the essence of the changes in present working processes, a typological comparison between the traditional way of working in industrial processes and the emerging new way of working was created (Toikka, 1986; Norros, Toikka and Hyötyläinen, 1988a). One of the results of this comparison indicates that, in the traditional way of working, thinking and learning focus on single tasks and machines. These cognitive processes could be characterized as empirical, being based on immediate sensory data and having predominantly a tacit nature. In this way of working, the expertise is mainly acquired through personal experience and practice, and the corresponding training paradigm is 'on-the-job' training.

In contrast to the above, in the new system way of working, the object of activity is the whole production process. Work could be characterized as theoretical, being necessarily based on models of the system and production and using explicitly formulated concepts of the process. In these circumstances learning has to be based on conscious and systematic acquisition and use of these models, and would eventually require creation of a new theoretically oriented training process.

Modern cognitive psychology offers means for developing such advanced training. Under the demands of fulfilling the needs of postwar industrial development a major change appeared in psychological science: 'Develop a sufficiently complex technology and there is no alternative but to create cognitive principles in order to understand how people can manage it' (Bruner, 1983, p. 62; see also Gardner, 1985). The discovery of cognitive principles of activity meant a revolution in psychological research. Its effects on practical working processes were in general, however, slow and the cognitive approach is still today only partially applied in the domain of learning and training in work. The use of simulation in industrial work training is a sign of adapting to the new demands of work, and an important step towards cognitively more articulated training.

THE COMPLETE LEARNING PROCESS AND THE ROLE OF SIMULATION

Basically, simulation is experimental problem-solving, with the help of a model that crystallizes the essential features of the problem. Thus, in simulation, conceptual models are extracted and applied explicitly as tools for creating new knowledge, that is as tools for research. The claim in this chapter is that, when used in training, simulation should have the same nature, that is it should be a process in which conscious cognitive models of the object are used for studying the dynamics of the object. During this process further models of the object can be derived for better mastery of the object. This would require a structured learning process in which simulation is integrated to serve its special function.

The theoretical positions of Galperin (1969, 1979) and Dawydow (1977, 1982) give a starting point for the above sketched role of simulation in training. Dawydow (1977, 1982) points out that the structure of the learning process is basically identical with that of a real research activity. The difference between the two are more quantitative than qualitative. What distinguishes between the two activities is the fact that in learning the search, which in research is often very long, for the essential features of the object is shortened. In a learning process this search is reproduced as a particularly structured process which is carried out through a set of tasks to be solved by the learner.

In analysing the structure of learning activity, an important starting point is that it is a separate activity which can and must be distinguished from work. In learning it is necessary to create reflective and experimental attitudes and corresponding actions towards the object. Modelling and, perhaps, also simulation as a special way of experimenting are considered as central actions within learning activity. Later the learning process is again integrated into the working activity. The complete learning process is assumed to comprise the following phases (Dawydow, 1977; Engeström et al., 1984):

1. Problem definition. Learning is initiated through identifying the problems and needs for development, in practical working situations. This phase is not only significant for defining the training needs but also for motivating people to learn.
2. Orientation. During this phase the problems are worked up to first approximations of the solutions of the problems. This is carried out with the help of modelling, which results in forming the conceptualized objects of learning. This can be called the orientation basis for learning. Special tasks must be designed for creating the modelling activity, for example when the trainees in flexible manufacturing are supposed to be able to take over the new production they ought to conceive the difference between the old and the new production. Thus, they can be asked to construct a functional model of the production control and use it to conceptualize the differences between them, that is the change.
3. Model utilization. During this phase the external models are internalized by using them for explaining the phenomena of the studied system. Basically this means experimenting on the object by using the models, that is simulation. During this process the attributes of the models are clarified and new knowledge is tested against old. As in the previous phase, different kinds of tasks can be created to use the models, for example we

can let the flexible manufacturing trainees create optimal production strategies by using functional and layout models of the system.

A special type of task is particularly important for simulation activity. It is the predictive tasks that could be called what-if experiments (Kay, 1985). The idea in such tasks is to postulate a situation, make a prediction and test the outcome with the model. As Kay notes, there are no limitations other than the imagination of the user to creating situations through which the dynamic characteristics of the system can be learned. One could perhaps consider these tasks as prototype simulation actions.

As a result of this learning phase the trainees should internalize the models used externally during orientation as a new cognitive model of the object.

4. Solving real problems. In the next phase the new cognitive model will be externalized by applying it to real problems of work. This would be directed to systematic analysis, require actions and tasks of the problems and generation of possible solutions.
5. Evaluation of the knowledge to be learned.
6. Control of one's own learning process.

The two latter aspects can be seen as further circles of the primary process of creating new knowledge of the system. Through these the results are critically examined and corrected. An advantage of forming the models for learning in the orientation phase is that they can be used as the criterium and tool for evaluative and control functions during the learning process.

This concept of the complete learning process has two implications for the design of learning processes in industry:

1. The role of simulation training in the qualification process. Seen from an overall point of view, the model defines the role of simulation training in an extended qualification process. The continuous interplay between training and practical work is thus important. The structure of this inter-play should be defined in a training process model aiming at continuous development of work and the system.
2. The structure of simulation training. The above concept of the complete learning process can, second, be used more specifically to aid in designing the structure and didactic principles of simulation training. An important prerequisite should be that simulation training is considered as a learning activity instead of a quasi working activity. Further, one could demand that the ideal simulation process (in Leplat, Chapter 15 of this volume), which appears in its full form in research, should be reproduced in a shortened form in every simulation training. This would constitute the above described structure for training.

In the next section we examine the use of simulation in industrial work training from the latter point of view. Thus the following questions should be raised in the course of the analysis:

1. What is the nature of the models used in training?
2. What is the trainee's role in defining the models used in simulation training?
3. Do the tasks carried out during simulator practice show signs of experimenting with systematic and controlled simulation actions?
4. Are the results of the simulator exercises defined in any way and are there plans for applying the results in normal work?

The result of the learning activity depends on the nature of the models used in training. Models that are simple descriptions of the desired operations are of less use than those that result from an analysis of the significant task components. These could further be derived through a profound analysis in which the essential structure and dynamics of the studied object are discovered.

According to the study of Engeström (1984), the models used in teaching are typically algorithms or rules. As a consequence the students' learning activities become restricted and the acquired knowledge can only provide answers to questions of 'how' to do something but leave untouched the questions of 'what' and 'why'. Larkin et al. (1980) came to the same conclusion regarding teaching and learning university physics. Paradoxically, the normal goal of teaching procedures seems to prevent the students from knowing how to manage a novel problem situation because they are unable to derive new procedures. The models used in training are, futhermore, normally given in ready form and applied as such. The trainees themselves are not performing modelling activities.

There is not much direct evidence of industrial simulator training in which trainees were asked either explicitly to create the orientation bases or to work systematically in an experimental manner. The most extensive simulator training programmes are found in nuclear power plants and range from 6 to 8 weeks. They comprise approximately 50 per cent practical exercises and 50 of theoretical training, including preparation and evaluation of the exercises (Qualification of Nuclear Power Plant Operations Personnel, 1984; Pfeffer and Kraut, 1985; Experience with Simulator Training for Emergency Conditions, 1986). These data would suggest that there was enough time devoted to theoretically oriented modelling and simulation actions. However, no details of the didactic methods are given. On the contrary, it has been noted that there is little transfer of information between psychological knowledge and training practice (Experience with Simulator Training for Emergency Conditions, 1986). This indicates that the principles of the learning process are not yet effectively realized in this most advanced industrial simulation training.

If modelling and experimenting actions are untypical in simulation training, as could be suspected, the training would tend to become reduced to a mere imitation of the real-life situation. As pointed out, for example, by Brehmer (1980) and Fischoff (1986), this is not a sufficient condition for effective learning. On the other hand, when operators can, through simulated situations, experience some of the problems that can only be anticipated in real work, some spontaneous learning effect certainly appears. This would help in coping with one of the ironies of automation—how to learn from situations that practically never occur (Bainbridge 1983). Still we think that better learning effects could be achieved if the learning processes were consciously planned and didactically well designed.

EVALUATION OF A SIMULATOR EXPERIMENT AS A TRAINING PROCESS

As a part of a larger study on defining the developmental needs of nuclear power plant operator work, a simulator study was carried out at the Loviisa power plant in Finland (Norros and Sammatti, 1986). Through using the method of error analysis the aim was to define the critical demands and problems of operators' work.

As well as this research aim, the simulation also served as the operators' yearly simulator training. The method used in classifying operators' errors was originally developed as a tool for ordinary simulator training, and thus questions of training were an integral part of the general research aims (Hollnagel and Rasmussen, 1981). In the following we make an attempt to analyse the simulation exercises from the point of view of fulfilling the structural requirements of a complete learning process.

All of the twelve crews of the plant performed a series of two experiments in which the task was to handle two serious plant disturbances.

1. What is the nature of the models used in training? In this experimental simulation training the problems studied and the psychological models for training were formulated better than normally. The criteria for selecting the simulated disturbances were made explicit. Furthermore, the events were carefully modelled. These models comprised, first, the procedural flow charts defining the ideal path of handling the disturbance. These kinds of model are often, but not always, prepared for simulator training and they define what the trainees are expected to do during the session. In this case there was also a model that conceptualized the crucial difficulties in the work. This model was a classification of the possible errors in performance which were defined according to deficient cognitive processes and to the error cause.

   A performance model that is based on a procedure or an ideal performance sequence is very strictly algorithmic. It describes how to act in a given situation. The model specifying the possible difficulties in the activity was a more developed one, in the sense of giving a system description of the decision-making and causal explanations for their occurrence.

2. What is the trainees' role in defining the orientation basis? Even though the psychological models for simulation were well defined they did not serve as an orientation basis for the operators. The operators were unaware of the context of the training sessions. They were simply asked to act on the simulator as they would in normal work. In such a task the operators do not explicitly know what they should learn, that is they lack the possibility of forming an orienting model, an orientation basis, for learning.

   In this case the above procedure was motivated by the need to evaluate the operators' existing knowledge and performance. However, this kind of definition of the simulation exercise is typical in the yearly refresher courses performed in the simulator. Thus, it can be said that the trainees' problem definition and modelling are normally rather minimal during these exercises.

3. What are the signs of experimental simulation activity? Due to the aim of evaluating performance during a disturbance, the conditions were designed to be as real as possible. As was said above, this was the reason for not working towards an explicit orientation basis, and it also explains why experimental tasks were not planned for the session. We did not find any indications of spontaneous testing or experimenting during the session itself.

   Because of the aim to analyse the deficiencies in the activity, the usually rather unstructured evaluation of simulator performance was in this case carried out with the help of the error classification model. Through this instrument, the operators were actively involved in a systematic evaluation of their own knowledge and performance. Critical features of the diagnostic and planning tasks were formulated, and basic physical phenomena of the process were handled in explaining the operations and actions.

4. What definition of the simulation results is given and how are they applied in work? In this case the success of the performance and the results of the postexperiment discussions were more profound and better documented than normally, and these results were analysed and reported by the researchers. The results of the error analysis show that there were problems in actualizing the existing models and performance schemes, and in some cases their adequacy could be questioned. These problems became more evident in the more difficult disturbance, in which case the procedural way of handling the situation appeared to be inadequate. On the basis of the results it was possible to define hypotheses about the causes of the difficulties and some preliminary ideas for overcoming them. In short, there seemed to be a need for developing more advanced conceptual and

strategic means for more cooperative operator activities (see Norros and Sammatti, 1986).

An interview was carried out with the crews of two months after the last experiments, in which the operators' opinions of the usefulness of such experimental sessions were asked. Over half of the operators evaluated the significance of such studies as not very high or expressed ambivalence about their value. This result was somewhat surprising when considering the positive attitudes and good results the operators could reach during the experimental session and discussions. The reduction in interest might be due to the fact that the results of the experimental training were not commonly discussed and the researchers' generalizations of the problems not collectively evaluated. Thus, transformation of the results into daily practice could not take place.

In summary, the simulator study demonstrated the potential of using explicit models for enhancing the operators' comprehension of the object process and their own activity. In the above study a first phase, in which the problems of work were conceptualized, could be achieved but conscious use of these models as a basis for orientation to learning was not yet carried out. Further studies are currently in progress in order to achieve this goal and to find means of transforming the models into work practice.

IN SEARCH OF A NEW CONCEPT IN INDUSTRIAL TRAINING

The idea of the complete learning process was said to have at least two kinds of implication for designing industrial training. In the above section the more specific aspect of designing the didactic structure of simulation training was brought up. In this section the view is changed and the role of modelling and simulation within the comprehensive qualification process is discussed. Thus, some basic principles of a new training concept are demonstrated, on the basis of a case study concerning the implementation of a flexible manufacturing system (FMS) (see, further, Norros, Toikka and Hyötyläinen, 1988a, 1988b; Toikka, Norros and Hyötyläinen, 1988).

The starting point in the study was the analysis of the training requirements for work in new technology. As pointed out in the first section there are fundamental changes in the character of work. One generalization of the nature of these changes is that mastery of production requires mutual interaction between design and operation. The necessity of the design–operation integration has been shown by Rosenberg (1982). According to him, the functional properties and economics of complex production systems can never be fully anticipated in design. Knowledge concerning optimal functioning and, consequently, the optimal design of the system is more or less a result of 'learning by using', by which the users have much to give to the planners. According to the above, new practices need to be created for the traditionally 'top-down' controlled design and for the 'botton-up' learning of operative practices. Particular means are needed in order to develop both activities. An experimental qualification process has been suggested to serve this function (Norros, Toikka and Hyötyläinen, 1988a; Toikka, Norros and Hyötyläinen, 1988). This process was designed to consist of three functionally different but mutually interactive phases.

Solving production problems

Problems and disturbances in production define the real user demands of the production. As the users adopt different individual and collective ways to face these challenges they simultaneously create different strategies for their own learning at work. We have separated four basic options in reacting to a disturbance as a developmental opportunity (Norros, Toikka and Hyötyläinen, 1988a). These options differ in their potential for leading to enhanced activity.

1. Withdrawal. The user does not intervene in the problem but, instead, according to his or her own choice or due to the division of labour, leaves it to others.
2. Disturbance as a 'normal' problem. The user intervenes but considers the disturbance as a deviation from the normal towards which he or she tries to return. Repeated disturbances are handled in a routine way.
3. Disturbance as a symptom. The user considers the disturbance as a sign of functional problems in the system. After recovery the problem is retained in memory and questions the goals and conditions of the task, seeking solutions to it individually, and mostly within the given division of labour.
4. Disturbance as a conscious developmental demand. The functional problems brought to light through the disturbance are considered consciously and explicitly as the object of activity.

The last option includes the true learning and developmental potentials which, however, are not realizable without specific means.

In our case study the bottom-up learning process was studied through an intensive follow-up of the implementation process. During this period particular interest was paid to the problem and the disturbance situation and the users' responses to them. The users' inventive role during the design could be shown and the determinants of the differences within the user responses could be analysed tentatively. (The analysis and the study are still unfinished at the time of writing this paper; Norros, Toikka and Hyötyläinen, 1988a, 1988b).

Experimental system training

A particular form of experimental training, called system training, was meant to be the conscious method in trying to intervene in the spontaneous bottom-up development. In our case study, the assumption was that this training should contribute both to developing user qualifications and to FMS design (Norros, Toikka and Hyötyläinen, 1988b).

We came to the conclusion that adequate mastery of the system requires not only control over the normal operation but also includes disturbance handling and continuous optimization of the system. In order to form such qualifications in training, a three-level model hierarchy becomes necessary:

1. The first level consists of performance models, that is algorithms for different operative situations. It is essential that the models are consciously formed. Thus it is possible to create and change procedures flexibly according to the needs of different situations.
2. In order to achieve the above goal the second-level models become necessary. These are the system models. These characterize the system elements and their interactions (for example material flows and manufacturing phases, control systems). With the help of these, typically graphical, models it was possible to study the functional principles of the system. The simulation, carried out with the help of system models, was a major tool in producing performance models.
3. Because system models corresponding to the users' needs did not exist, and because it was our aim to teach the users to create the models they require in operation, a third level of models became necessary. Thus, the training was started with 'constructing' the FMS through following the historical development of manufacturing. This developmental history can be divided into particular phases which are materialized in the FMS itself as its system levels (machine, NC, FMS). Through analysing the essential changes in the economy, technology and social organization of work during the different phases it was possible to explain the elements of FMS and the complex interactions between them.

In their previous tasks the users were not used to conceptualize their working. Thus, learning was organized according to the following didactic principles:

1. The collective production of the models. To form a genuine learning activity, the models are not given as ready-made results but the trainees create them in group work and collective discussions, on the basis of the preparatory work of the researchers and other experts.
2. The functional and logical connection between the models. The models are

produced by ascending from simple and abstract to concrete and complex models. Models produced earlier are used as tools for creating new ones.
3. The practicability of the models. The models have to be externalized as tools for real problem-solving.

System training was initiated before implementation, and nine one-day training sessions were carried out. The research data collected during the training sessions include the training programmes, complete protocols of the group work and discussions, and the results of the modelling tasks. A detailed analysis of the data is in preparation.

Preliminary results show that the FMS users were able to fulfil the demands of the modelling activities. During the sessions the users were able to acquire the models and use them in further model construction. Thus the models served, first, as instruments during learning. As the users could also complete and correct models that were prepared by the researchers the models were, second, used as instruments for creating new knowledge.

Third, modelling functioned also as a means for joint planning. The results of the last training session demonstrate this most clearly. This session was aimed at teaching the users the functions of the central control system in controlling gear production. After producing the models that served as instruments, the users were asked to solve a simulation task to find optimal operating strategies for a typical production situation with three simultaneous batches.

After working on the simulation task the three user groups presented their solutions for optimal operation. It became evident that different groups weighted optimality criteria differently or did not always consider all the criteria. When discussing these questions it was found that the strategy that appeared optimal (maximizing system load, minimizing transportation of pallets, minimizing settings) caused a system disturbance, due to a particular specification in the central control concerning the handling of empty pallets in the system.

It was found that in an earlier phase of design the question was considered as a technical detail and that the system engineer did not see the significance of that detail for system functionality. To discover this problem required the joint tool, the simulation and the cooperative work and discussions between the designers and users. As a result two possible solutions were also suggested.

Experimental development activities

It is anticipated that the models function also as the means for normal operative work. As the study is still unfinished there are no results, as yet, regarding this goal. Special developmental activities are going to be prepared for guiding this model-controlled operation. It is expected that systematic diagnostic activities and strategies of production optimization could be produced in this way. Preparations have been made for the use of computer-based simulations in studying the problems of production optimization.

On the basis of the experiences gained so far in the FMS case study, the proposed experimental training model seems promising in producing the new qualifications demanded by the working processes of new technology.

CONCLUSION

The above two examples, the simulator experiment in a NPP and the FMS implementation study, demonstrate that simulation in training should, perhaps, not be considered only as a specific training technique but rather an essential form of learning activity which is closely integrated with the fundamental modelling activities during taining.

Our examples indicate that the role of simulation in training is not only restricted to learning something already existing and given but, instead, simulation can also serve as a collective means of creating new knowledge for enhancing the design and operation of the system. The models and experimental forms of activity that have been acquired in simulation exercises can, in further phases of the learning, be utilized for the formation of developmental activities in practical work.

REFERENCES

Bainbridge, L. (1983) Ironies of automation. *Automatica*, **19**, 775–9.

Brehmer, B. (1980) In one word: not from experience. *Acta Psychologica*, **45**, 223–41.

Bruner, J. (1983) *In Search of Mind. Essays in Autobiography*. New York: Harper & Row.

Dawydow, V. V. (1977) *Arten der Verallgemeinerung im Unterricht*. Berlin: Volk and Wissen.

Dawydow, V. V. (1982) Inhalt und Struktur der Lerntätigkeit bei Schulern. Berlin: Volk and Wissen, pp. 14–27.

Engeström, Y. (1984) *Orientation in Instruction* (in Finnish). Helsinki: Vasltion painatuskeskus.

Engeström, Y., Hakkareinen, P., and Hedegaard, M. (1984) On the methodological basis of research in teaching and training. In Hedegaard, M., Hakkareinen, P., and Engeström, Y. (eds.), *Learning and teaching on a scientific basis*. Aarbus Universitet, Psykologisk Institut.

Experience with Simulator Training for Emergency Conditions (1986) IAEA Expert Meeting, Vienna, 15–19 September 1986.

Fischoff, B. (1986) Decision making in complex systems. In E. Hollnagel *et al.* (eds.), *Intelligent Decision Support in Process Environments*, NATO ASI Series F, Vol. 21. Heidelberg: Springer Verlag, pp. 61–86.

Galperin, P. J. (1969) Stages in the development of mental acts. In M. Cole and J. Malzman (eds.), *Handbook of Contemporary Soviet Psychology*. New York: Basic Books, pp. 249–73.

Galperin, P. J. (1979) *Introduction to Psychology* (in Finnish). Helsinki: Kansankulttuuri.

Gardner, H. (1985) *The Minds New Science*. New York: Basic Books.

Hirschhorn, L. (1984) *Beyond Mechanization: Work and Technology in Postindustrial Age*. Cambridge, Mass.: MIT Press.

Hollnagel, E., and Rasmussen, J. (1981) Simulator training analysis. Internal report. Nordisk kontaktorganet för atomenergifrågor, NKA/KRU-P2 (81)38, Risö National Laboratory.

Kay, J. M. (1985) The use of modelling and simulation techniques in the design of manufacturing systems. In V. Bignel *et al.* (eds.), *Manufacturing Systems: Context, Applications and Techniques*. Padstow: Basil Blackwell, pp. 242–53.

Kern, H., and Schuman, M. (1984) *Das Ende der Arbeitsteilung?* Munich: C. H. Beck.

Larkin, J., McDermott, J., Simon, D. P., and Simon, H. A. (1980) Expert and novice performance in solving psychics problems. *Science*, **208**, 20 June 1980, 1335–42.

Norros, L., and Sammatti, P. (1986) Nuclear power plant operator errors during simulator training. Research Reports 446, Technical Research Centre of Finland, Espoo.

Norros, L., Toikka, K., and Hyötyläinen, R. (1988a) Constitution of the new way of work in flexible manufacturing (in Finnish). In *Information Technology and Work*, Final report. Helsinki: Työsuojelurahasto.

Norros, L., Toikka, K., and Hyötyläinen, R. (1988b) FMS design from the point of view of implementation—results of a case study. *IFAC Man–Machine Conference* Oulu, 14–16 June 1988.

Pfeffer, W., and Kraut, A. (1985) *Qualification, Training, Licensing and Retraining of Operating Shift Personnel in Nuclear Power Plants*, Brussels:. EUR 10118 EN Commission of European Communities.

Projektgruppe Automation und Qualifikation (PAQ) (1987) *Widersprüche der Automationsarbeit*. West Berlin, Argument Verlag.

Qualification of Nuclear Power Plant Operation Personnel (1984) *A Guidebook*, Technical Report Series 242. Vienna: IAEA.

Rosenberg, N. (1982) *Inside the Black Box: Technology and Economics*. Cambridge: Cambridge University Press.

Stammers, R. B. (1983) Simulators for training. In T. O. Kvålseth (ed.), *Ergonomics of Workstation design*. London: Butterwoths, pp. 229–42.

Toikka, K. (1986) Development of work in FMS—case study of new man-power strategy. In P. Brödner (ed.), *Skill-based Automated Manufacturing*. IFAC Workshop, Karlsruhe, FRG, 3–5 September 1986, pp. 7–12.

Toikka, K., Norros, L., and Hyötyläinen, R. (1988) Studying developing work—methodological questions (in Finnish). In *Information Technology and Work*, Final report. Helsinki: Työsuojelurahasto.

18. Intelligent Tutorial Systems (ITS) in Training

S. Antonio Ruiz Quintanilla

ABSTRACT

The impact of new technologies on training issues is twofold. First, it results in skill demands that emphasize the importance of cognitive skills as discussed in this book. Second, new technologies can be used as training tools themselves. The following chapter reviews the technology from the point of view of their usefulness in training. Main research streams and recent developments or prototypes are discussed.

INTRODUCTION

That new skill demands emerge as a consequence of introducing new technologies seems undisputed. Changes of the technostructure at the workplace ask for a new division of labor, a restructuring of jobs and organizational changes such as establishing a different qualification structure in line with the different set of skills required, which has consequences for the applied 'staff appraisal scheme' and 'staff development scheme'. Effects might well be that traditional skills become obsolete, as drastically demonstrated in the printing professions. Similar trends can be observed for industrial workers due to the introduction of numerically controlled machines and robots, in process industries and lately in office settings, due to the growing complexity and integration of the computer systems used.

The introduction of computer systems is accompanied by a shift from execution tasks towards monitoring and control tasks. Therefore, implementing new technologies does not imply obsolescence of human qualifications and skills, but it stresses different skills. Cognitive skills, especially higher-level ones like problem-solving or reasoning become more and more important compared to traditional manual skills or routinized decisions (see Chapters by Bainbridge or Leplat in this book).

The demand for cognitive skills softens the frontiers between education and training. The main goal of training is enabling persons to fulfill the tasks of a certain job, using their performance as the criterion, while education aims at

Developing Skills with Information Technology
Edited by Lisanne Bainbridge and S. Antonio Ruiz Quintanilla

providing conceptual principles to facilitate further learning and especially training (Harmon and King, 1985, p. 237). The contributions in this book demonstrate that training skills in the context of new technologies means helping people learn to develop effective heuristics for problem-solving rather than to learn routinized action sequences.

Many job descriptions still do not adequately define the cognitive skills and broader system knowledge needed to fulfil the task at issue. In these cases training cannot just concentrate on the tasks mentioned in the job description but has to be broader; in helping the novice to understand the system (Frese, 1987, p. 135) 'drill and practice' becomes less important.

Applying the traditional techniques of training on the job in organizations with high-level automated systems is unlikely to be successful for at least two reasons. First, mistakes in these systems are very costly and dangerous. This prevents the novice from gaining experience using, for example, trial-and-error strategies. Second, the complexity and missing transparency of these systems does not facilitate learning. Since much of the process is hidden, due to the complexity of the system, the novice needs a learning environment with clear guidelines to be able to develop the required knowledge and skills.

One approach to realizing this guidance is known as 'training wheels'. Interfaces are modified for training purposes in such a way that troublesome error states are unreachable. Side tracks, known to confuse novices by leading to error states of the system, are blocked and the beginner is informed that the function required is not available on the learning system. Experiments show (Carroll and Carrithers, 1984a, 1984b) that learning and comprehending the complete system is faster. While the shorter learning time is mainly due to the time saved for error recovery, the results speak also for the advantage of training wheels in learning and understanding basic functions. This is due to the reduced complexity allowing an easier orientation in the limited system.

Still, training wheels offer only a limited possibility for mastering systems with a greater complexity than, for instance, a text editor or other business software. It is less obvious how one might reduce the complexity of operating, say, a propulsion engine system. Simulations would seem to offer opportunities for learning to control the complexity of tasks, as discussed in the contributions from Leplat, Baker and Marshall and Norros in this volume (Chapters 15 to 17). They share the view that simulators can be valuable tools in training if they are well integrated in the learning process. In short, the availability of a simulator for training does not mean that there is no need to define the training goals and didactics of the training process, such as the most preferred order to present the learning tasks to the student or which additional instructions ease learning.

Trying to implement parts of these pedagogical hints for an effective use of a simulator on a computer was the approach taken by a research group that designed STEAMER. STEAMER is an intelligent simulator for the purposes of training Navy personnel in propulsion engineering (Williams, Hollan and

Stevens, 1981; Hollan, 1984). Besides being one of the greatest training problems in the Navy the topic of propulsion engineering was chosen because it is a good example of a complex training problem.

Starting with a high-fidelity simulator which was used to train personnel in propulsion engineering the designers of STEAMER added an intelligent tutor to the simulator. This tutor explains the performance of the system (simulation), identifies and corrects students' misconceptions and guides the student in his or her interaction with the simulator. The simulator runs on a transportable lap-top computer and is able to model the components of the steam plant with the help of graphics and animation.

STEAMER purports to help the students to become experts as quickly and efficiently as possible. To accomplish this goal the students should develop conceptual knowledge and build up a device model rather than learn a collection of procedures and single facts. This mental model of how the system works is developed by experts through their years of experience and used to mentally simulate operations of the system. The main difference to the mathematical model which underlies the system design is that it simulates qualitative aspects of the system rather than mathematical ones. Experts do not memorize single operations but rather they develop hypotheses and knowledge about where to look for the confirmation of their hypotheses.

STEAMER can be seen as a step in the direction towards adaptive simulators (Leplat, Chapter 15 of this volume) or tutorial systems.

STEPS TOWARDS THE DEVELOPMENT OF INTELLIGENT TUTORIAL SYSTEMS

What is an intelligent tutorial system? As the name suggests the idea behind the ITS is to provide the learner with a personal tutor(ial system), which enables him or her to learn according to his or her prior knowledge, individual abilities and preferences and adapted to his or her motivational state, needs and learning rate. This is to be achieved with the help of appropriate individual instructions. To achieve characteristics similar to that of the human tutor (mainly flexibility) seems to be possible with machines, due to developments in hard- and software. This allows adaptation of instructions to the learner at a finer level than could be done with media such as books, film or video—the 'forefathers' of ITS. Classical material like books, film or video allowed the choice of appropriate subject matter based on a prior evaluation of the learner and in line with precise learning goals. Computer-managed instruction (CMI) systems and computer-assisted interactive instruction (CAII) systems went one step further.

The aim of *computer-managed instruction (CMI) systems* was to help teachers and trainers with the recording of behavioural process data and analysing it to provide a diagnosis of the state of the learning process. The products delivered by the system were the results of the diagnosis and sometimes included advice about which subject matter should be presented next.

CMI systems assist the trainer in his or her instructional and administrative task during the instructional process and thus are used in conjunction with other instructional material or systems (for example tutorial lessons, field exercises, individual studies, instructional groups, meetings with the training staff). While for the early systems there was no direct interaction between the learner and the system, nowadays CMI systems (for example PLATO learning management from control data; Lyman, 1981) are used by the student directly. On registering at the system, the students receive their printed copy of the first lessons and additional information about available resources, goals of the unit and estimated time needed for completion. During the learning process the student can ask for feedback concerning progress (learning tests), can request additional help or material, or ask for a meeting with the training staff. At the end the student will receive a report from the system describing the competencies that have been acquired.

The main restriction remains the limited flexibility of the CMI systems in response to individual learning demands.

The *computer-assisted interactive instruction (CAII) systems* developed by Crowder (1959) and Skinner (1954, 1968) were further steps in the direction of ITSs. In the beginning this form of individualized learning was mainly influenced by behaviouristic thinking. The learning process was understood as shaping and chaining the respondent's behaviour with the help of adequate stimulus material and reinforcement strategies. To avoid errors on the side of the student, the material was preselected in such a way that correct answers had a high probability. When an error was made, the last stimulus was repeated. The lack of flexibility of this approach in adapting to individual learning states led to the idea of branching programs. Here incorrect responses were used to identify the student's misconceptions and then to branch the program sequence to try to overcome these errors, for example by presenting further information. However, these programs had the disadvantage that branching options were chosen according to stereotyped responses and not in accordance with a model of the learner, reflecting individual difficulties and learning styles. Thus all eventual branches had to be foreseen in advance; reactions of the learner needed to be anticipated in the design phase. Additional restrictions were posed by the limited capabilities of computers at that time (Crowder 1959; Atkinson 1976). In spite of these limitations, it was demonstrated that a computer can be utilized in an active way in a learning process. To some extent learning became independent from the human teacher. Most of the so-called tutorial diskettes on the market are still built along this philosophy and, as such, they are mainly helpful in enabling practice and consolidating knowledge which is already understood.

What is the state of the art today? In principle it is now possible to realize a dynamic adaptation of the system, parallel to the learning process in each moment in time. 'The computer tutor takes a longitudinal, rather than a cross sectional, perspective, focusing on the fluctuating cognitive needs of a single learner over time, rather than on stable interindividual differences' (Ohlsson, 1985, p. 2). In order to fit the changing needs of the individual learner it is desirable to adapt at each moment of the learning process both the content of the subject matter presented and the form of the presentation.

To consider how this can be achieved, we shall now discuss issues of general tutor construction and their accompanying difficulties.

INTELLIGENT TUTORIAL SYSTEMS

To ease understanding we will limit ourselves here to one of the central approaches in ICAI research, which tries to simulate the tutoring behaviour of a human expert. Another approach, the 'adaptive learning simulator' manipulates conditions for practice (for example see Leplat in Chapter 15). The advantage of the latter is that it can take on functions that a human tutor cannot carry out. Following the approch of simulating a human tutor, an ITS needs four different modules:

1. It has to be an expert in the topic to be taught (the expert module).
2. It needs to have information about the learners and their process-dependent knowledge state (the learner module).
3. There has to be a unit that develops adaptive learning strategies and directs the interaction process (the tutor module).
4. Finally, a unit is needed that is responsible for elaborating the learner system dialogue in a way that comes close to natural language (the communication module).

The expert module[1]

The contents of an expert component are facts, conceptual knowledge, strategic knowledge and rule knowledge concerning the topic to be taught. In addition, there are procedures for the activation of specific knowledge domains. The main purpose of the expert module is to help the ITS generate problems for the learning process and to diagnose the answers of the learner. The diagnosis is needed for evaluation of the knowledge state of the learner during the process.

There are two different approaches to structuring expert modules. The *'black box' representation* (cognitively opaque; Dede, 1985) does not try to build a model of the human knowledge system. The problem-solving mech-

---

[1]It is not possible within the scope of this contribution to give more than a short overview about research on expert systems. The interested reader should refer to Harmon and King, 1985; Garg-Janardan *et al.*, 1987)

anisms of the system are different from human problem-solving procedures (for example SOPHIE-I; Brown, Burton and Bell, 1975). The knowledge system is used only to evaluate the answer of the student and to help in deducing the system's responses.

The *articulate expert* (glass-box model; Goldstein and Papert, 1977) is an attempt to let the system simulate the human problem-solving process. Because the solution path of the system is analogous to the human one, the system can help the learner by making single problem-solving steps transparent. To simulate human problem-solving, the system needs to have procedures for knowledge acquisition, reasoning, planning and problem-solving and to generate and test hypotheses.

There are different ways to present knowledge in a system. Most common are sematic and procedural nets, scheme-based scripts, production systems, analogue representation techniques and problem-solving grammars or graphs. Often systems use a multiple approach.

Due to the process character of learning, the expert module has to adapt its inner structure continuously to the knowledge state of the learner. Depending on its actual state, the information to be delivered is modified. In the beginning the system starts with simple or non-complex information and becomes more differentiated and complex in later learning periods. One needs a model of the learning process dependent upon changes of human knowledge. This requirement represents a large task for cognitive and learning psychology. This model determines the optimal expert representation at each point in time, through the adequate student module, and allows futher planning of the learning process. Developing and adapting the learner module continuously with actual learning process data about the knowledge, understanding and skill level of the learner quickly leads to a level of combinatorial explosion. It is impossible to take account of all possible alternatives for the explantion of certain behaviour sequences. Thus the diagnostic modelling is always incomplete and restricted.

Finally, since the expert module represents a type of expert system, it shares the common problem of finding a good method for knowledge acquisition. Instruments currently in use such as observation techniques, mental protocols, task analysis all have disadvantages. They only deliver incomplete knowledge. One reason for this fact is that complex knowledge does not have to be completely conscious, which makes access to knowledge bases a difficult problem (Leplat, 1986).

The learner module

The learner module represents changes in the knowledge, abilities and skills of the learner during all stages of the learning process. Its main function is to decide about the actual optimal (adaptive) process of learning, For this, the learner module needs as much information relevant to learning as possible. Relevant information includes, for example, the individual learning strategy and information-processing style. An evaluation of the action regulation of the learner is useful. (How do they plan, analyse and control the dialogue? Are they modifying the interaction?) This kind of dialogue data helps in the development of hypotheses about the actual state of knowledge and skills. it also recognizes deficits and identifies suboptimal problem-solving behaviour by the learner.

The system must be able to compare the strategy chosen by the learner with the strategies stored in the system's knowledge base.

The quality of the learner module depends on the quality of the methods used for identifying relevant system knowledge. Here, again, we find the same problems that were discussed under the section on the development of expert systems.

Two approaches for realizing a learner module can be distinguished: the subset model (overlay) and the derivation model (differential).

The subset model defines the knowledge of the learner as a subset of the knowledge stored in the expert module. In consequence, the learner is expected to reach the knowledge level that equals that in the system.

The derivation model allows substantial differences between the knowledge of the user and the system. It takes into account that equivalent solutions might be achieved in different ways. The advantage of this conceptualization is that systematic errors by the learner are recognized and can be included in the learner module as erroneous knowledge.

Barr and Feigenbaum (1982) categorized the information sources available to analyse knowledge of the learner. They identified four categories:

— implicit evidence (derived from the problem-solving behaviour),
— explicit evidence (derived through active questioning of the learner),
— historical information (derived through analysis of the learning history and self-evaluation of the learner),
— structural information (assumptions about the competence of the learner derived from the mastered task difficulty).

Studies of these categories indicate that analysing the knowledge structure can be reduced mainly to attributing the cause of the errors. The system has to determine the prerequisites for tasks solved incorrectly. Because of the difference between performance and competence, due to individual variabilities (capacity, attention, emotional and motivational state), and because some learner answers might be ambiguous for the system, there is always a lot of 'noise' in the learner module. Knowing this, hypotheses derived from the module have to be tested for their validity with the help of later information from the learning process.

To develop an ITS one needs information about who will be the user later. As with other software products, three groups can be identified. First the design can be based on a 'typical user' or a diversity of different users. Second, the designer focuses the specification of the ITS on observations of a defined set of users. Third, these systems may vary in the extent to which specific user criteria is taken into account. For example, in some systems the user model may only hold for a specific task and a short time period. In other systems emerging expertise may be assumed across a wider domain or set of tasks or situations. Up to now, most ITSs fall into the second group.

The tutorial module

The function of the tutorial module is to control the teaching–learning process between the system and the learner. To do this, the system has to:

— choose learning strategies that depend on the situation,
— control and lead the learning process,
— decide when to take a certain route or branch from the programmed possibilities,
— motivate the learner, for example by presenting tasks with an adequate difficulty, and avoid aversive failure experiences,
— ensure that additional information and help is always available when needed.

In the absence of an instruction–psychological theory, which can be applied easily (Glaser, 1978), recent approaches try to identify systematic bugs in the learning process and confront the learner with them to initiate problem-solving behaviour. The confrontation with one's own mistakes and the task of debugging assisted by information and help from the system aims at helping the learner to learn from failures and overcome them (see also Frese and Altmann in Chapter 3 of this volume for a discussion of the possibility of learning from one's own errors).

As indicated, the tutorial module determines the preferred pedagogical strategy and the pedagogic–didactic principles to be used. Some systems are oriented towards the 'Socratic dialogue' approach, while others try to establish a 'non-directive interaction' or coaching situation.

The Socratic dialogue tries to fulfil the criteria of a well-structued inter-action, it presents the learning information in a systematic way and gives help if mistakes occur. Active questioning is used to stimulate the learner's initiative. The learning process can be controlled by the learner within the limits of the system design and aims.

The non-directive interaction approach can be characterized by the absence of well-structured learning units and predetermined interaction sequences. The knowledge to be learned is presented in a kind of play-milieu. The learner has to discover the milieu itself ('discovery learning'; Neber, 1975). The learning process is fully controlled by the learner and the intrinsic motivation is increased through the play character of the interaction. This system encourages the learn, discover, play behaviour of the learner with intermediate information and coaching. This means the 'system coach' has to be able to discover (recognize) the plans and knowledge state of the learner from the interaction data. It needs knowledge about the success of the learner's discovery behaviour.

The communication module

The communication module has to be concerned with a natural language surface of the system's interaction with the learner. Daily communication has to be assisted by non-verbal techniques like menus, windows, mouse and graphic tableau.

To decode the natural language inputs of the learner, the system needs a broad domain of independent knowledge (common sense), a generalized interpretation scheme to interpret content according to the intentions of the learner, and syntactic and pragmatic routines to analyse difficult or incomplete language constructions. Currently, systems seem not to reach criterion goals. Most systems restrict the analysis to key words (for example SOPHIE) to deduce the content, because of time and capacity limitations. Recent technological developments, such as rising storage capacities and process speed, offer the potential development of more complex systems. However, a new quality of systems can be derived only with new approaches. Artificial intelligence and linguistic researchers are working on the development of new and better ways of knowledge organization. They try to build a capability for automatic knowledge enrichment (learnability) into the system.

Finally, all of the popular criteria in software ergonomics are relevant to the communication module of ITS. The system should be transparent, controllable by the user, reliable (have a high tolerance to errors), acceptable, self-explantory, especially in the beginning phase (easy to learn), and should have a knowledge- and context-dependent help system.

In conclusion, this theoretical overview demonstrates the complexity of the task of designing a flexible and adaptive computer-based intelligent tutorial system. Because of the many open research problems to be solved and the different paradigms favoured by research groups, usable systems can be considered as prototypes, giving an idea of applications in the near future.

REFERENCES

Atkinson, R. C. (1976) Adaptive instructional systems: some attempts to optimize the learning process. In D. Klahr (ed.), *Cognition and Instruction*. Hillsdale, N.J.: Lawrence Erlbaum.

Barr, A., and Feigenbaum, E. A. (1982) Application-oriented AI research: education. In A. Barr and E. A. Feigenbaum (eds), *The Handbook of Artificial Intelligence*. Stanford, Calif.: Harris Technical Press, pp. 225–94.

Brown, J. S., Burton, R. R., and Bell, A. G. (1975) SOPHIE: a step towards a reactive learning environment. *International Journal of Man–Machine Studies*, **7**, 675–96.

Carroll, J. M., and Carrithers, C. (1984a) Blocking learner error states in a training-wheels system. *Human Factors*, **1984**, 377–89.

Carroll, J. M., and Carrithers, C. (1984b) Training wheels in a user interface. *Communications of the ACM*, **27**, 800–6.

Crowder, N. A. (1959) Automatic tutoring means of intrinsic programming. In E. Galanter (ed.), *Automatic Teaching: the State of the Art*. New York: Wiley.

Dede, C. (1985) Intelligent computer assisted instruction: Review and synthesis of research (unpublished manuscript). Houston, Tex.: University of Houston.

Frese, M. (1987) Human–computer interaction in the office. *International Review of Industrial and Organizational Psychology*, **1987**, 117–65.

Garg-Janardan, C., Eberts, R. E., Zimolong, B., Nof, S. Y., and Salvendy, G. (1987) Expert systems. In Gavriel Salvendy (ed.), *Handbook of Human Factors*. New York: Wiley, pp 1130–76.

Glaser, R. (ed.) (1978) *Advances in Instructional Psychology*, Vol. 1. Hillsdale, N.J.: Lawrence Erlbaum.

Goldstein, I. P., and Papert, S. (1977) Artificial intelligence, language, and the study of knowledge. *Cognitive Science*, **1**, 1–21.

Harmon, P., and King, D. (1985) *Expert Systems. Artificial Intelligence in Business*. New York: Wiley.

Hollan, J. (1984) Intelligent object-based graphical interfaces. In G. Salvendy (ed.), *Human Computer Interaction*. Amsterdam: North-Holland, pp. 293–6.

Leplat, J. (1986) The elicitation of expert knowledge. In E. Hollnagel, G. Mancini and D. D. Woods (eds), *Intelligent Decision Support in Process Environments*. Berlin: Springer, pp. 107–22.

Lyman, E. R. (1981) *PLATO highlights*. Urbana, Ill.: Computer-Based Education Research Laboratory, University of Illinois.

Neber, H. (1975) *Entdeckendes Lernen*. Weinheim: Beltz.

Ohlsson, S. (1985) *Some Principles of Intelligent Tutoring*. Pittsburgh, Pa.: Learning Research and Development Center, University of Pittsburgh.

Skinner, B. F. (1954) The science of learning and the art of teaching. *Harvard Education Review*, **24**, 86–97.

Skinner, B. F. (1968) *The Technology of Teaching*. New York: Appleton-Century Crofts.

Williams, M., Hollan, J., and Stevens, A. (1981) An overview of STEAMER: an advanced computer assisted instruction system for propulsion engineering. *Behavior Research Methods and Instrumentation*, **13**, 85–90.

Index